ERSKINE CALDWELL, MARGARET BOURKE-WHITE, AND THE POPULAR FRONT

ERSKINE CALDWELL, MARGARET BOURKE-WHITE, AND THE POPULAR FRONT

PHOTOJOURNALISM IN RUSSIA

Jay E. Caldwell

The University of Georgia Press ★ Athens

Athens, Georgia 30602
www.ugapress.org

Designed by Erin Kirk New
Set in 10 on 14 Warnock Pro
Printed and bound by Thomson-Shore
The paper in this book meets the guidelines for permanence and durability of the Committee on Production Guidelines for Book Longevity of the Council on Library Resources.

Most University of Georgia Press titles are available from popular e-book vendors.

Printed in the United States of America
20 19 18 17 16 C 5 4 3 2 1

Library of Congress Cataloging-in-Publication Data

Names: Caldwell, Jay, author.
Title: Erskine Caldwell, Margaret Bourke-White, and the popular front : photojournalism in Russia / Jay E. Caldwell.
Description: Athens : The University of Georgia Press, [2016] | Includes bibliographical references and index.
Identifiers: LCCN 2016016096 | ISBN 9780820350226 (hard bound : alk. paper)
Subjects: LCSH: Caldwell, Erskine, 1903–1987—Travel—Russia (Federation) | Bourke-White, Margaret, 1904–1971—Travel—Russia (Federation) | Novelists, American—20th century—Biography. | Photojournalists—United States—Biography. | World War, 1939–1945—Journalism, Military—United States. | World War, 1939–1945—Journalism, Military—Russia (Federation) | Photojournalism—Russia (Federation)—History—20th century.
Classification: LCC PS3505.A322 Z533 2016 | DDC 813/.52—dc23
LC record available at https://lccn.loc.gov/2016016096

For Makena Jae, KaiLani-Jay Erskine, and Ty James

who came along at the perfect intervals to rejuvenate my moments of flagging inspiration

CONTENTS

ILLUSTRATIONS

PREFACE

This book is about the journalism of two unlikely Americans in Moscow during the summer of 1941, during the first months of Operation Barbarossa, Adolf Hitler's surprise blitzkrieg against his former ally, the Soviet Union. It is about Erskine Caldwell, just then riding the cresting notoriety from his two jaw-dropping novels about the American South, *Tobacco Road* and *God's Little Acre.* And it is about Margaret Bourke-White, his wife, just then riding the international fame from her *Life* magazine exploits as one of the most well-known and most well-remunerated photographers in the United States.

Veterans already of three volumes of paradigm-altering photo-text books—*You Have Seen Their Faces* (1937), *North of the Danube* (1939), and *Say, is this the U.S.A.* (1941)—Caldwell and Bourke-White had contrived to find themselves in Moscow in May 1941, on the hunch that big news might be in the offing. They were right. There was but a handful of credentialed Western journalists in the country when they arrived. During that summer of 1941, Russian battlefield losses were staggering, Kremlin control of information and the press was blanketing, and newsgathering and reporting were exceedingly fraught enterprises, yet both Russia and the West had a vested interest in portraying the Soviet response to the Hitlerites, as the Soviets referred to them, as steadfast, patriotic, and sanguine.

Caldwell and Bourke-White were able to exploit their connections, and their fame, to gain unprecedented access to Russian news sources. Though they insisted they were apolitical, their agenda—like that of the Roosevelt administration and like that of the Kremlin itself—was to make the USSR appear as a wholly worthy ally of the West against the Nazi world menace. Through daily newspaper articles and radio broadcasts, through photo-essays in *Life*, through a series of books written upon their return to the United States, they were successful. The legacy of their contributions to the war effort was somewhat eclipsed by the turn of events in the Pacific after the December bombing of Pearl Harbor, but during those first few months of Barbarossa, they were instrumental in sending out to the West what news they could glean (and get past the enshrouding Soviet censorship) from behind the Soviet western front.

This is their story of the summer of 1941. It is based on the letters, telegrams, and diaries Caldwell and Bourke-White wrote, their published material, and the memoirs and writings of other members of the Western press based in Moscow that summer. It begins, as all such stories must, at the beginning.

This is a work of scholarship. But in the service of full disclosure, I cannot let it pass unsaid that Erskine Caldwell is my father. He and Margaret Bourke-White were divorced long before I was conceived. Sadly, I never discussed with my father his career, his literature, nor his experiences in the Soviet Union during World War II. Instead, my father encouraged me to navigate my own childhood and adolescence and later to embark upon an ongoing and now nearly half-century career as a physician.

The genesis for this work, its "Rosebud," was a black Nazi helmet with a bullet hole through its temple that, for my entire life, sat alongside an olive drab Red Army helmet on one of the low bookcases in my father's study, which housed a collection of his own books along with a panoply of awards and memorabilia (see figure 1.). This book is the result of my sleuthing into that helmet's origin and significance. How it came from a tattered September 1941 battlefield in Belarus to pass into my awed young hands is the cord that binds this document.

I doubt that this work can be entirely free from personal bias, but I have endeavored, with the assistance of my scholarly mentors, to keep such bias to a minimum. I have tried to limit my conclusions to what can be drawn only from the evidence I uncovered in archival material, the literary works themselves, and other published sources. I have eschewed drawing suppositions from personal interviews with family members. If I have been unsuccessful in any area, the responsibility is entirely mine own.

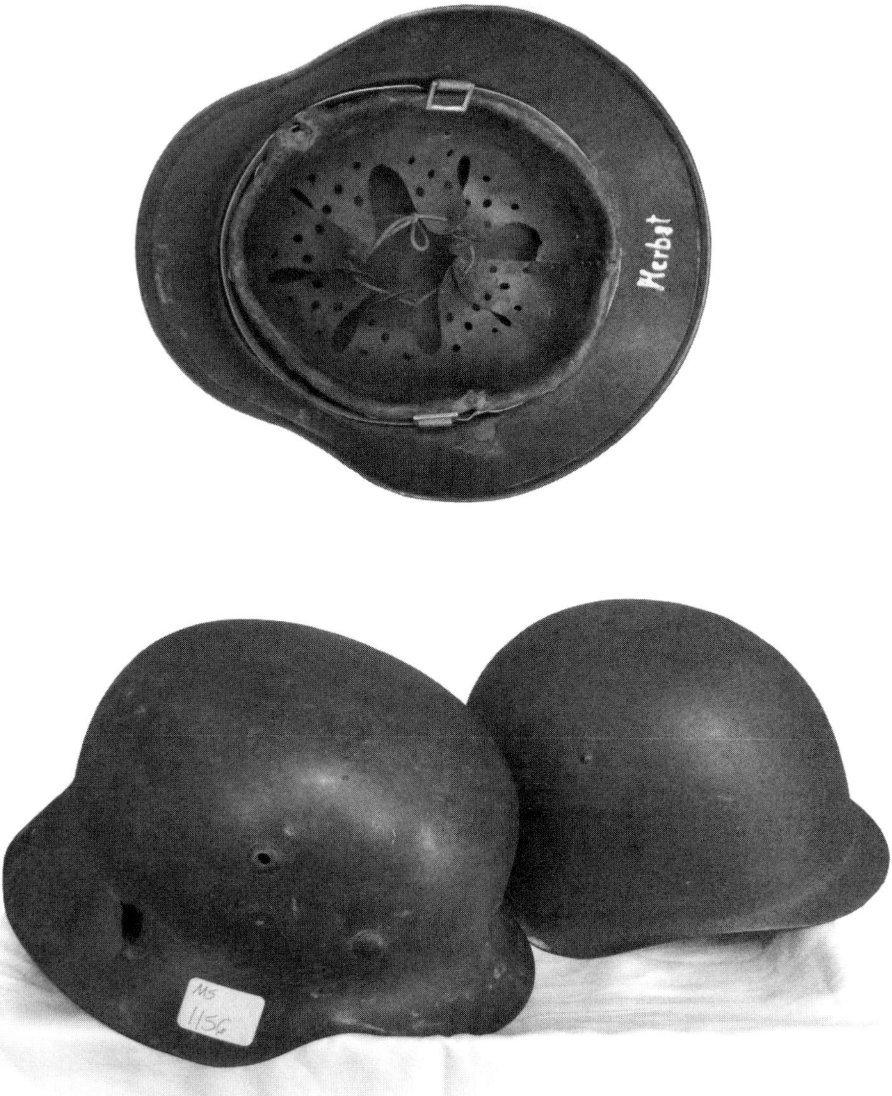

FIGURE 1. Nazi and Red Army helmets from the battlefield at Yelnya

ACKNOWLEDGMENTS

This book originated as a doctoral dissertation for the Department of English at the University of Arizona in 2014. Professors Jennifer Jenkins, Daniel Cooper Alarcón, Charlie Scruggs, and my dissertation director, Jerrold Hogle, all contributed to its coming to fruition. I am especially indebted to my fifth committee member, "Rob" McDonald (from VMI), who strongly encouraged me to revise the dissertation into book form. David Christenson of the Department of Classics has been instrumental in shaping this work from its outset into its preliminary and final forms, and he has offered friendly if spirited and challenging criticism along the way. Only he and I know how much he contributed to this work.

I twice visited the Special Collections Research Center at the Syracuse University Library, where extensive collections of Bourke-White and Caldwell material from 1936 to 1942 are maintained and superbly archived. There I am indebted to Nicolette A. Dobrowolski, reference librarian and head of public services, who proved to be both kind and patient. I also twice visited the Rauner Special Collections Library at Dartmouth College, where a vast collection of Caldwell-related material has been gathered. Jay Satterfield, the special collections librarian there, proved particularly knowledgeable and accommodating. Chuck Barber, the manuscript librarian at the Hargrett Rare Book and Manuscript Library at the University of Georgia, was especially kind in directing me to several unexpected troves of Caldwell family letters as well as retrieving, if only briefly, the "Herbst" helmet that had been the spark for this entire investigation. Several other archives yielded smaller amounts of useful material. Emily Walhout, a reference assistant in the Houghton Reading Room at the Harvard University Library, tracked down several letters from Caldwell to Alfred Morang that helped me piece together the dénouement of Caldwell's Russian venture.

I also wish to thank those not already mentioned who have taken the time to read and comment on portions of this work, including my mother, June C.

Martin (who married my father in December 1942 following his *Mission to Moscow* stint in Hollywood), Tim Rawson (Alaska Pacific University), David H. Culbert (LSU), and Boris Shoshitaishvili, a former classics graduate student at the University of Arizona, now in the Comparative Literature PhD program at Stanford.

One of the most serendipitous contacts I had was Gary Johnson in the Newspaper and Current Periodical Room of the Library of Congress. Not only was he able to locate, retrieve, scan, and electronically forward to me articles from vintage newspapers and magazines, but he also turned out to be an Erskine Caldwell enthusiast. On his own time he scouted out material of which I had been previously unaware. It is unexpected surprises like this that reinvigorate a researcher spending interminable hours at a computer keyboard.

I also was able to contact and communicate with several scholars in the fields of Soviet culture, military history, biography, and photography: Michael David-Fox (Russian cultural history expert, now at Georgetown University), Vicki Goldberg (Bourke-White's biographer, now in New Hampshire), Jason Hill (scholar of *PM* newspaper, now at École Normale Supérieure, Paris), Harvey Klevar (Caldwell's biographer, now at Luther College), Robert McDonald (VMI), Dan Miller (Caldwell's biographer, now head of Wheeler School, Providence, R.I.), Sheila Webb (cultural historian, now at Western Washington University), and Erika Wolf (scholar of Soviet photography, now at University of Otago in New Zealand). I even tracked down Herman Wouk, who had mined the Caldwell and Bourke-White books for his own World War II novels. He was gracious enough to respond to a query from me and to offer his own encouragement.

I also appreciate the contributions made by my two families. The Raven Society, since 1995 a reading group in Anchorage, Alaska, has been a valuable sounding board for my thoughts as this work evolved. In 2011 I selected *All-Out on the Road to Smolensk* for us to read and discuss; to gain their goodwill I supplied each member with a first-edition copy of the book. Shawn (Lord HaM) Delaney and Charles (8) Lindemuth, the founders of the Raven Society, have been particularly helpful, and Charles supplied the maps for this book. But all have offered suggestions, books, and other readings directly or indirectly relevant to this undertaking: Jim (Ras Jym) Case, Paul (Moriarty) Dworian, Jamie (Shaolin Master) Kenworthy, Louis (The Lou) Mass, John (McTeeth) Murray, Doug (Dougie) North, Tim (History) Rawson, Jim (Bimba) Reeves, Mark (Markrates) Faller, and Lewis (Gear Boy) Schnaper.

And then my own family. My mother volunteered her recollections of my father during the years immediately following his Russian campaign and read and critiqued portions of early drafts. My stepmother and stepbrother, Virginia Caldwell Hibbs and Drew Fletcher, helped steer me toward the current location of "Herbst." My wife's half brother, Geoffrey Breyley, dug up valuable details of the commercial operations of the Pan American clippers in the early 1940s. My two children, Twila and Maile, maintained a bemused detachment, not quite comprehending why their father would undertake such a daunting task when there seemed so much else he could be doing.

Walter Biggins of the University of Georgia Press provided patient and helpful encouragement while I worked through the often-tedious but ultimately fulfilling process of revising my original dissertation into publishable book form. I am forever grateful. Jon Davies, also of the University of Georgia Press, was my editor during the final year of this book's birth. His assistance with the myriad details of academic publication (such as obtaining photo reproduction permissions) was invaluable.

To my great surprise and delight, Daniel Simon, editor in chief of *World Literature Today*, copyedited my "final" manuscript with remarkable insight, streamlining it into a shape I had not thought possible.

Finally, and perhaps most importantly, I owe the world to my patient, forbearing, and loving wife, Diana, who has lived with this project for quite a few years and has often allowed our times together to be postponed in order to allow me the opportunity to complete it. She even graciously permitted me to read the entire manuscript aloud to her during its preparation, offering cogent comments and contributions as we went along.

ERSKINE CALDWELL, MARGARET BOURKE-WHITE, AND THE POPULAR FRONT

PROLOGUE

North of the Danube ★ A First Waltz with Russia

In the Moscow summer of 1941, Erskine Caldwell and Margaret Bourke-White experienced the menacing ruthlessness of Nazism firsthand, but their introductory brush with it had been three years earlier. In 1938, under the aegis of *Life* magazine, they had traveled to Czechoslovakia and Hungary via France and Spain to "get the feeling of the people of those two countries, to get their personalities, how they live, their racial characteristics, and where they work," as they told a reporter for the *International Herald Tribune* on their arrival in Paris that April.[1]

At the time, *Life*, founded in 1936 with a Bourke-White photo on its first cover, was attempting to raise its profile in the field of international news. Both Bourke-White and her biographer Vicki Goldberg assert that *Life* sent her to Europe to cover the Spanish Civil War and the embattled nations of Czechoslovakia and Hungary.[2] Bourke-White was already a veteran European traveler, thrice having visited the Soviet Union earlier in the decade. But in 1938 her traveling companion had never been out of North America.

Caldwell recollects the inspiration for the trip differently. In his autobiography, he writes that it was his idea to go to Europe. Bourke-White "was so pleased with our first collaboration [*You Have Seen Their Faces*] that she was hoping we could do another book together."[3] Together the two pored over maps, he recalls, and selected their itinerary after considering the ever-changing political climate. He even was able to get Viking, his publisher at the time, to partially cover his expenses.

It must not have been with an especially sanguine outlook that Caldwell and Bourke-White embarked from New York on the SS *Normandie* on March 31, 1938, a day so foggy that the liner was forced to drop anchor in Gravesend Bay, off Staten Island, until the following morning. As became the standard in their foreign travels, they went first class whenever it was available, and on the *Normandie* their suites adjoined. The Broadway adaptation of Caldwell's novel about a rapscallion southern preacher, *Journeyman*, into which the two had sunk a joint investment of five thousand dollars, had opened on January 29, but forty-one dismal performances later it closed on March 10.[4] At the same time, Caldwell was embroiled in an uncontested but unpleasant divorce from Helen, his wife of thirteen years with whom he had three children. He had retained Bourke-White's own personal attorney, Julius Weiss, to negotiate a settlement. On April 18, Easter Monday, while he and Bourke-White were traveling in Czechoslovakia, Caldwell received a telegram that back in Maine a divorce decree had been issued.[5]

This first overseas trip together was successful and doubtless added to Caldwell's credentials as not just a writer of fiction but a reputable international journalist. In addition to Bourke-White's striking photographic essays on Czechoslovakia and Hungary for *Life*, done in collaboration with *Life* staff photographer John Phillips (1914–96)[6]—*Life* published a dramatic seventeen-page photo-essay on Czechoslovakia in its May 30 issue and on September 12, two weeks after their return, another twelve pages on Hungary—their expedition resulted in their second book-length photojournalism collaboration, *North of the Danube*. Priced at three dollars, it was published in February 1939, the same month in which they officially became Mr. and Mrs. Erskine Caldwell in Silver City, Nevada. Though reviewers thought well of the book at the time and it remains in good standing with critics to the present day, both Caldwell and Bourke-White thought it had shortcomings.

Caldwell knew he was more at home with people with whom he could communicate directly and whose culture he shared and understood, as was the case when he was traveling in and writing about the rural South. In a letter to his parents written just after Christmas 1938, he expressed his concern that *North of the Danube* would not be as satisfying as *You Have Seen Their Faces* had been two years earlier: "I am not sure it is as good as the other book," he wrote. "For one reason, we spent six months there [in central Europe], while I feel as though I spent a lifetime in the South."[7]

Bourke-White was especially unhappy with the book because she believed she had not been able to get close to her subjects. She wrote, "My pictures lacked the depth I wanted to give them." She blamed this on Caldwell's periodic and unpredictable dark and icy mood swings: "Many times, it seemed to me I was bringing only half of myself to the subjects I wanted to understand and photograph. My first thoughts had to go toward Erskine and his moods, and my fondest hopes were that the hidden glaciers would not come to the surface in the middle of an important series of pictures."[8]

The episode that she recalled most clearly in her autobiography, written nearly a quarter century later, involved a trip taken with the press officer of the Czechoslovak government and his wife to a border town near Hungary. It devolved into what Bourke-White called one of Caldwell's "great freeze-ups."[9] Perhaps tellingly, she dates this episode fairly specifically, calling it their "Easter trip." Biographer Harvey Klevar has hypothesized that Caldwell's ill mood might well have been related to the recent news of his now-official divorce, especially since the accepted grounds for the decree had been "cruel and abusive treatment."[10]

Nonetheless, the timing for this trip was impeccable. The Nazi Wehrmacht set the stage by crossing into Austria on March 12, 1938. The Austrian *Anschluss*, or political annexation, followed quickly and was "confirmed" by a phony plebiscite a month later on April 10. The sinister quality of this German bellicosity had clear ramifications for Czechoslovakia, a hybrid nation that had been stitched together following World War I. Its union was so tenuous that, whenever it is mentioned in *North of the Danube*, it is hyphenated "Czecho-Slovakia." Caldwell subtly reflects the ominous nature of the time in his prose, though Bourke-White rarely follows suit in her photographs. In compiling *You Have Seen Their Faces*, they had spent many weeks studying the available photographs—and even took a second shorter trip through the South to fill in gaps in their project—to ensure a perfect mesh between text and pictures, but in *North of the Danube*, such an effect was not achieved because the two portions were assembled independently of each other and in greater haste.

Despite one unsettling major printing error—an unknown quantity of text is missing between the last line of page 75 and the first line of page 76—*North of the Danube* is handsome.[11] Eight pages of Bourke-White's inimitable black-and-white photographs follow each of Caldwell's sections, pictures that correlate with, but are rarely illustrative of, Caldwell's adjoining prose. Both the front and rear endpapers bear a detailed map of "Czecho-Slovakia" in 1939 with "ceded lands shown by Shaded Areas" at a scale of forty miles to the inch. Unfortunately, many of the cities and regions mentioned in Caldwell's text and in Bourke-White's captions do not appear on the map.

Bourke-White's seventy-nine photographs are typically stark and carefully staged but are curiously similar in style, point of view, *mise-en-scène*, and subject matter to those published in *You Have Seen Their Faces*; only the costumes and backgrounds have changed. They lack the social passion of *Faces*, though there are the aggrandizing salt-of-the-earth portraits in which she shoots a farmer, worker, or peasant from below as he or she contemplates the world beyond his or her implements. There are majestic landscapes with towering clouds, peopled only for scale. There are bustling, architecturally detailed cityscapes, again peopled for scale, but these citizens are also evidence of urban vitality. There are carefully posed "candid" photos of tidy people at work, in school, at play, and at home, and fine portraits representing the social strata of life north of the Danube, a society far older and more developed than the rural Depression-era American South of *Faces*. There is even one of Bourke-White's signature studies of industry: a massive piece of equipment, tended by a lone Bohemian metalworker in Plzeň, carefully lighted to accentuate the product being extruded, "Forging Skoda Cannon" (see figure 2).[12] All these photographs demonstrate Bourke-White's gift for composition, lighting, contrast, and context but seem oddly estranged from their human subjects.

Caldwell's gaze is that of an outsider, of an American on his first trip abroad with mixed motives, as several Czechoslovaks are quick to point out (a grandmother in one home they visit for an afternoon packs and leaves because she fears they are American spies—or so Caldwell tells the story).[13] Though his prose is at times lyrical, his view is necessarily superficial. Wherever Caldwell and Bourke-White traveled—whether from east to west, as he claims in his autobiographies, or in the opposite direction, as biographers state and the text itself suggests—a guide/interpreter would have been necessary, especially outside urban areas. Caldwell claims that in Bohemia and Moravia they communicated with their subjects using hand signals, some rudimentary German, and English, though they also had the help of Caldwell's Prague literary agent, the daily newspaper's editor, and the Czech translator of *God's Little Acre*. But the rural eastern part of the country presented major hurdles. The language problems limited their understanding of such a polyglot land and frequently led them into a kind of shock and disdain. At other times, however, this distancing effect provided them insight into the effects and causes of poverty and nationalist classism as well as a premonition of the hovering Nazi menace.

In *North of the Danube*, they record their first stop as Užhorod in eastern Ruthenia, where in the late spring they visit a street market "filled with peasants, housewives, herdsmen, cows, horses, carts, sheep, goats, merchants, and traders," as well as "beggars [sitting] on their haunches, holding out trembling hands and crying out at fitful intervals to attract attention" (*ND* 9). Before they leave, they watch as two men in tweed suits, accompanied by a Ruthenian interpreter, try to entice two local farmers into emigrating to Canada. Despite their clearly desperate poverty, the farmers decline the offer. Bourke-White captures a rainy-day street scene hauntingly reminiscent of Gustave Caillebotte's *Paris Street; Rainy Day* (1877), except for the class of people on the street (figure 3).

From there Caldwell and Bourke-White find themselves hapless, helpless visitors in Uzok (Uzhok), where their driver hands out loaves of bread to the starving and desperate residents. It is a rural tableau of famine, ignorance,

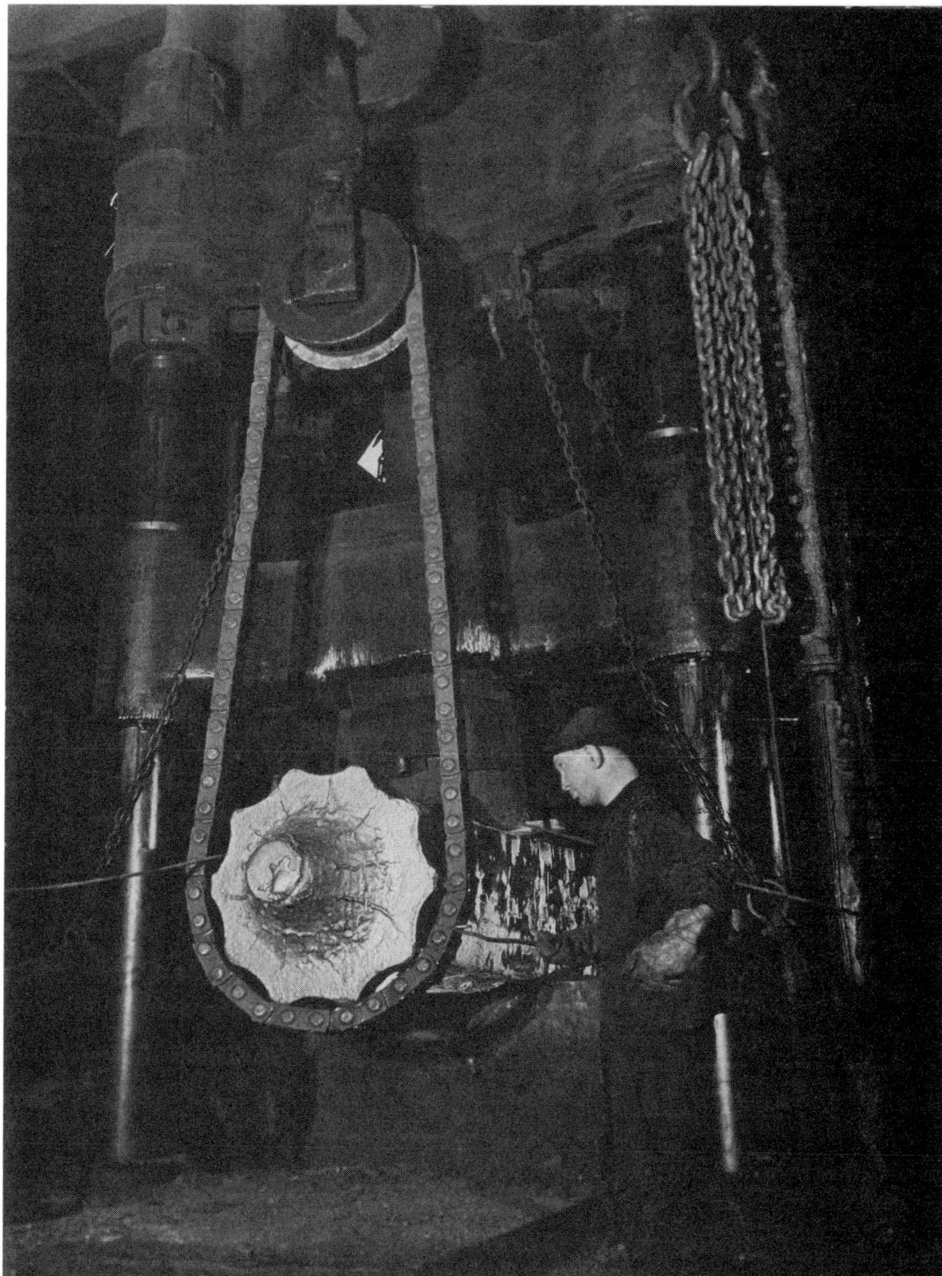

FIGURE 2. Original caption: "Forging Skoda Cannon, Plzeň, Bohemia" (From *North of the Danube*; photo © Estate of Margaret Bourke-White/Licensed by VAGA, New York, N.Y.; courtesy of Syracuse University Libraries)

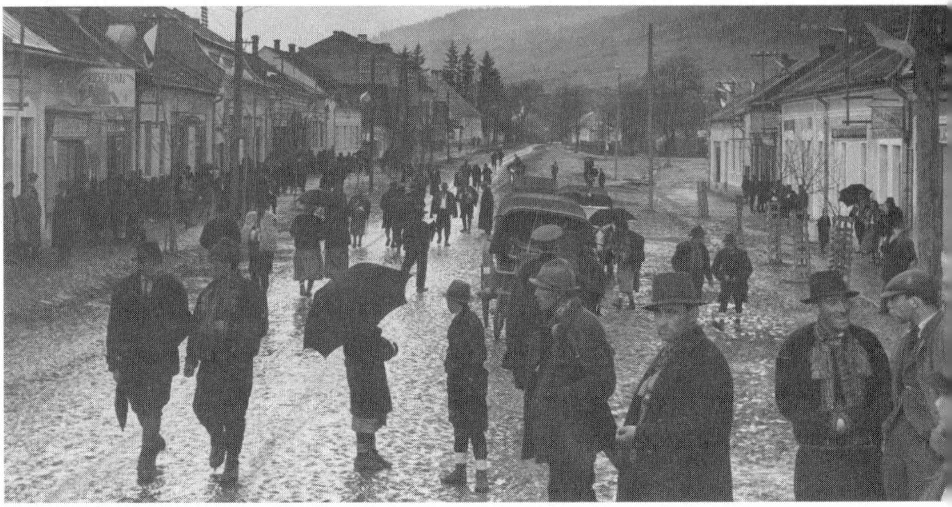

FIGURE 3. A painterly rainy-day scene (From *North of the Danube*; photo © Estate of Margaret Bourke-White/Licensed by VAGA, New York, N.Y.; courtesy of Syracuse University Libraries)

and disease that recalls the Lester family of backcountry Georgia about whom Caldwell had written six years earlier in *Tobacco Road*, except that the villain here is not a banker but a Hungarian prince. This sequence from "Bread in Uzok" is evocative of the rural poverty and helplessness of *Tobacco Road:*

> "Why haven't you had bread in all this time?" she was asked.
>
> "The Prince who comes from Hungary does not want anybody on his land any more, because he said human beings scare away the wild boars he keeps there to hunt."
>
> "Are all his peasants as hungry as you are?"
>
> "There are five or six or seven hundred who are hungry. The Prince is angry because he thinks the State is going to take his land from him and give it to us. He said he would never give us work and food again as long as this is a part of Czecho-Slovakia."
>
> "There are fields behind these houses. You have a right to use them to keep from starving. You could raise grain there, couldn't you?"
>
> "There is no wheat in my house to sow the fields," she said. "Seven years ago when we were hungry we ate the wheat. There are oats, a little, but oats won't make bread. I grind the oats and cook it with water, and that is all. It is not bread. It is only oats."
>
> The woman bent her head as if in prayer and caressed the chunk of black bread with trembling fingers. Turning, she passed through the crowd that made way for her and shuffled slowly towards her house. (*ND* 28–29)

Bourke-White memorializes Uzok with a pair of domestic interior studies, two of the several photographs reminiscent of those she had taken for *You Have Seen Their Faces* (see figure 4). In one, a woman and three children are busy at household chores while, sharing the space to their left, stand two emaciated cattle, their heads just outside the right frame of the photo, an effect that accentuates their washboard-like ribs (*ND* 34).

After leaving the Carpatho-Ukraine in the far eastern portion of the nation, they board the Košice–Žilina Express headed south out of the Tatras Mountains in Slovakia, again helpless observers as a belligerent Nazi couple verbally abuses an Austrian couple—"not markedly Jewish in appearance"—over the rights to space in the overhead luggage rack. "'You Jewish swine!' the German *frau* yelled at her. 'You'll be taught your place!'" (*ND* 47). Bourke-White captures this same Nazi swagger even in the children, as is evident in a photo from a Moravian classroom (see figure 5). Although it is not indicated in the text of *North of the Danube*, the Caldwells made more than one sally through Czechoslovakia, trips that Caldwell then sutured together into a single account. Evidence for this is a letter he mailed in July 1938 from Barcelona to his parents back in Georgia, a handwritten one that also provides insight into his sociopolitical sentiments regarding Fascist aggression at the time, ones fully congruent with those of the left-leaning international Popular Front:

> Dear Mother & Father:
>
> Just a note to say I'm safe and sound here, even after a trip to the Euro front and a few Munich air bombings. I don't see how a people like this one can ever be defeated—unless it is by the outside world. It is a shame the way England, France, and America allow other nations to blockade it. Otherwise, there would never be any question about who would eventually win. In the end the [Spanish] Republic is going to win, regardless of anything else.
>
> We expect to be in Czechoslovakia by the end of this week.
>
> Love, Erskine[14]

By the time summer comes they report they are drinking bottle after bottle of local wine with the Slovak owners of a vineyard and a paprika and beet farm. Caldwell admits, "We understood little that was said. He and his wife were Czechs, and they spoke neither English, French, nor German. We leaned forward and listened closely while he spoke slowly and distinctly to enable us to hear each sound. Every once in a while we grasped the meaning of a Czech word, and then waited hopelessly for others that we might understand. Only in that way were we able to follow what was being said" (*ND* 59). Two lines later, though, he has no trouble "quoting" the owner extensively. But a couple of pages further on he writes, "There were long pieces of conversation that

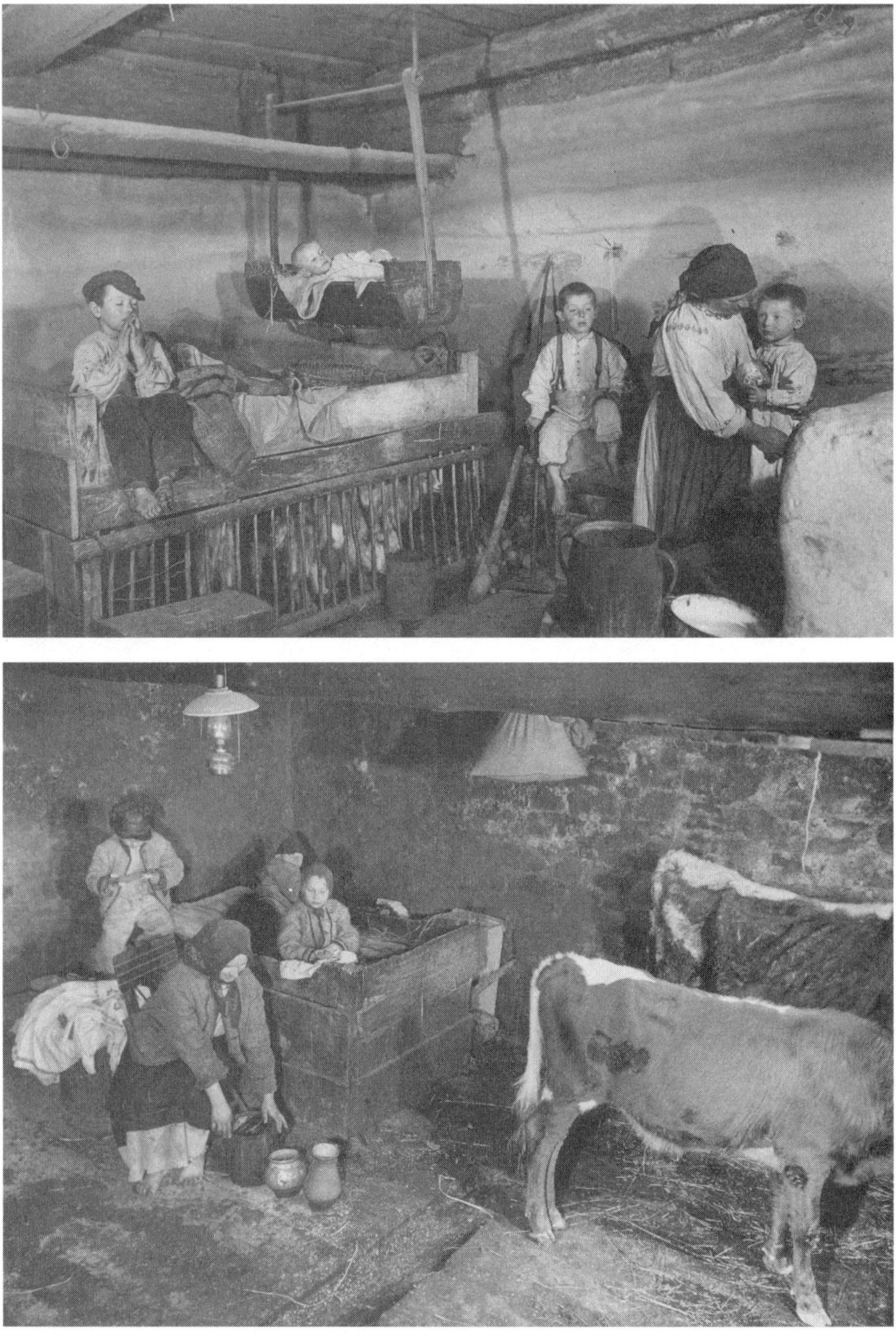

FIGURE 4. Original caption: "Home, Užok, Carpathian Ruthenia" (From *North of the Danube*; photo © Estate of Margaret Bourke-White/Licensed by VAGA, New York, N.Y.; courtesy of Syracuse University Libraries)

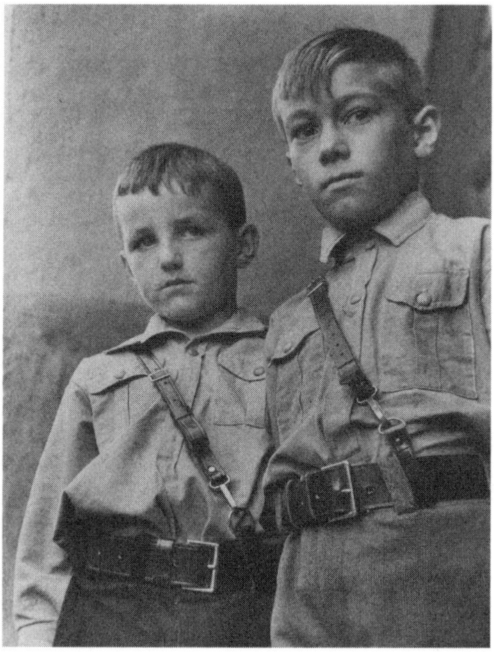

FIGURE 5. Original caption: "Nazi Stormtroopers' Training Class, Mesto Javornik (ceded to Germany), Moravia" (From *North of the Danube*; photo © Estate of Margaret Bourke-White/Licensed by VAGA, New York, N.Y.; courtesy of Syracuse University Libraries)

we could not make head or tail of. We sat and wondered which was easier to understand, a flood of Czech words from him or a jumble of English, French, and German from us" (*ND* 61). Caldwell, however, does take note of the farm's Hungarian Simon Legree: "While we stood there, one of the overseers used his stick on the finger-knuckles of one of the women who had fallen several steps behind the line [of other workers]. While she was striving to catch up with the others, he cursed and abused her for her slowness" (*ND* 58).

Caldwell recognizes this Eden is a sham. As the afternoon dwindles, the workers are finally discharged home, but as they pass by the owner's wine party they are forced to sing. Caldwell expresses his sympathy: "Their faces were tired and haggard, and they were relieved when they no longer had to perform a task they had been taught to do. They looked much happier when they passed out of sight into their village, where they would not have to sing for the landlord and his guests, and where the overseers could not threaten them with words and hit their knuckles with sticks until the next morning" (*ND* 62). These are Slovak peasant workers, and the landlord makes their and his hopeless political situation clear: "Perhaps we should go back to Bohemia and live or die like good Czechs. The Hungarians want my land here, even though it really belongs to the Slovaks. If the Hungarians take it, the Slovaks will become their serfs instead of mine. The Slovaks are the losers. And while all of us wait to find out who is master and who is serf, the German God Almighty is coming as the master of us all" (*ND* 64).

In the Moravian city of Brno, Caldwell observes "unhurried and friendly" German and Austrian refugees in the marketplace, but one young Jew, whose wife has been "taken away," tells them: "If I could get to America, . . . I would feel safe. Here it is safe for the present, but tomorrow it may not be. I feel as though I am being trapped, that from all sides I'm being surrounded. I do not know which way to go" (*ND* 75). Later, an eighteen-year-old whose parents have been taken to a concentration camp approaches them. All he wants is to get to America where his aunt lives, but he has lost her letter and so does not know even the city where she lives.

During a cross-country walk in western Moravia, the Americans encounter a proud "free" Czech landowner who "spoke to us as though we had known each other all our lives. He was rugged and brown like the wheat itself" (*ND* 89). They find peasants gleaning the recently harvested wheat fields, rustics who, Caldwell writes, have mixed feelings about Americans coming to their country to observe them. Just before they leave, one sympathizer rhapsodizes, "We have so many enemies that we cannot always live without help from our friends. It will be a good thing to have a great country like America helping us, because someday our enemies will try to take our country from us" (*ND* 94).

Autumn finds them in Moravia where Caldwell seems, at first, fixated on writing about the dogs and dogcarts of the town of České Budějovice, but in doing so he creates an extended metaphor for the pervasive poverty and hardship in the region. Rarely do Bourke-White's photos match up with Caldwell's prose, but in this section she includes a picture of the very Saint Bernard that Caldwell has been watching. Finally, in Praha (Prague), the central city of the western canton of Bohemia, they visit a Sudeten German public affairs office and are given a tour of the city by a "slight-built, blond-haired," Oxford-educated Nazi official who demonstrates to the Caldwells the inferiority of Czech architecture and its "so-called" culture.[15] "The stupid Czechs will succeed in contaminating us if we are not strong." They ask repeatedly to see the newspaper the office produces since they too are journalists. Exasperated, the public affairs representative admits, "Surely you must know by now that our newspaper is purely a convenience," but he then thanks them "for this opportunity to talk to you about our movement" and sends them off in a taxicab—but not before breathing "'Heil!' into our faces."[16]

As evidence for the seriousness with which Caldwell undertook the composition of *North of the Danube*, each of the eight chapters concludes with a quotation expressing the delicacy of Czechoslovakia's political status, the last being from Karel Čapek (1890–1938), the Czech political and science fiction writer, author of the 1920 play, *R.U.R.*, in which he famously coined the word "robot": "The most terrible struggle in our recent history is being played out. It is not only a struggle for our land, it is a struggle for our soul. . . . A thousand years of tradition suffice for a nation to learn once and for always these two things: to defend its existence, and with all its heart and all its strength to stand on the side of peace and liberty" (*ND* 128).

Čapek died of natural causes, as it happened, on Christmas Day 1938, soon after the Nazi annexation of Czechoslovakia. Knowing this, the postscript to "The Dogs of Ceske Budejovice" is even more ominous:

> Czecho-Slovakia is a tumor which is poisoning the whole European organism. If the situation were allowed to go on, it would infect international relations until they broke down in final collapse. This condition has lasted for twenty years—no one can calculate what it has cost the peoples of Europe in that time. It is a tumor which has got to be ended once and for all and ended now.
> —Adolf Hitler, 1938 (*ND* 112)

Reading *Danube* induces a brooding sense of despair regarding events of the day. Whether Caldwell felt this way during his and Bourke-White's spring and summer visit, while the March 11 Nazi takeover of Austria, the so-called *Anschluss*, would still have been fresh in their minds, is unknown. But by October, when he was back home working on the book, the sense of a Western "betrayal" of Czechoslovakia following the Munich Pact of September 30—permitting Hitler's unopposed annexation of German-speaking areas of Czechoslovakia—would have been manifest.

However, a sense of photographic inadequacy lingered for Bourke-White. She wrote in her autobiography: "Later, when *North of the Danube* came out in book form, I believed that it added little to the understanding of this interesting country facing a crisis. Certainly nothing of the loving thoroughness went into *North of the Danube* that went into *You Have Seen Their Faces*."[17] Caldwell, however, must not have been quite so displeased, because in 1939 five of his eight *Danube* vignettes appeared, minimally altered, in magazines as standalone pieces. In the 1959 anthology *When You Think of Me*, he included two of those and one additional vignette.[18]

Danube's reception was for the most part positive. The left-wing press appreciated it for its sociopolitical perspective. In *The New Masses*, Bertram Gale wrote that *Danube* "emphasizes as effectively as any political treatise the enormity of the crime at Munich. For while these pictures and observations of Czechoslovakia were made before the robber's pact in September, they make us visualize more distinctly than ever what Munich really meant in human terms." For Gale, "It is also true that Caldwell is most at home in the treatment of people whom he can immediately see and touch rather than in the study of men in the mass."[19]

In *The New Republic,* Maurice Hindus, who had written the introduction to Bourke-White's first book, *Eyes on Russia* (1931), called *North of the Danube* "one of the most extraordinary travel books I've ever read." He heartily compliments the couple's "record[ing] only those scenes and experiences which have inner meaning." He recognizes that while Caldwell is unable to fully appreciate the "magnificent . . . eloquence" of the peasants' language, "he never fails to perceive the inner meaning of their words or their lives." Hindus, then one of the nation's foremost slavophiles, is particularly attuned to the political milieu and pressures that brought this trip and the book about. Not surprisingly, he is especially pleased with Bourke-White's contributions: "Miss Bourke-White has caught all the drama and pathos of an aspect of the Munich agreement and its aftermath which no journalist has as yet bothered to record."[20]

In *The Saturday Review,* Henry C. Wolfe saw *Danube* as a valuable memorial for the tiny Czech Republic, once "a bulwark of enlightened government in Central Europe." In 1937 Wolfe had warned in a piece for *The Atlantic* that it was only a matter of time before Hitler set his sights on the Czech Republic, Romania, and ultimately the Soviet Union, with its beckoning space and its oil reserves.[21] Two years later in the *Review,* Wolfe concluded that although both his and Caldwell's "sentences have proved politically prophetic, Mr. Caldwell does not emphasize politics. He is interested in the people, their customs, their thoughts, their attitude toward life and death and the threatened loss of liberty."[22]

Margaret Marshall of *The Nation,* not always a Caldwell supporter, was positive about *North of the Danube,* which she appreciated from a sociopolitical point of view: "It is an illuminating and touching footnote to the Nazi conquest, so timely as to be painful," but she also found its prose worthy of praise: "It consists of eight vivid close-ups, written with the direct clarity of Mr. Caldwell's best vein, of the peoples and countrysides of the Czechoslovakia that was, until March 14."[23]

More recent scholarship has been kind to *Danube* as well. Sylvia Cook, in a thorough study of Caldwell's nonfiction, concludes that it is "in some ways the most interesting of their three collaborations [with Bourke-White], since the camera provides . . . a coequal study to the text, not merely an illustration of it . . . or a tangent to it." She argues that Bourke-White's photos of urban life, industry, and architecture serve as a counterpoise to Caldwell's "rather agrarian and personal bias." She also notes that the book is highly political, a tone accentuated by the quotations appended to each chapter.[24]

For Cook, though, the most glaring of the book's weaknesses is the inevitable one created by the insurmountable language and culture barriers:

> Caldwell's distance from its people may be measured in the relative dearth of humor in it, for if the comic/grotesque mode that dominates so much of Caldwell's writing is not to appear brutal, it depends on considerable intimacy with the lives of his people. In *North of the Danube* Caldwell wisely restricts the humor to situations where he himself, as the ignorant outsider, or the more prosperous and successful people, rather than the poor, bear the brunt of it.[25]

On the other hand, this distancing created a book in which there is little sense of an invasion of privacy. Except for the rare domestic study, like the one of the Uzok home, Bourke-White's photos maintain their distance. Subjects are cleaned up, dressed up, and placed in poses and contexts of dignified self-mastery rather than abject degradation.

Scott MacDonald, in a commissioned pedagogical essay for a 1979 special issue of *Pembroke Magazine* on the value and methods for teaching Erskine Caldwell at the college level, lauds Caldwell and *Danube*. "*North of the Danube*," he writes, "is not only the best of Caldwell's travel books and, in terms of *his* contribution, his most successful collaboration with Bourke-White, it is one of the high points of his career." Its special quality, he avers, is "Caldwell's ability to communicate his deep respect and admiration for a nation most of us know little about, while revealing the ever-growing, seemingly-inescapable threat to the Czechoslovakian republic posed by the Nazi Party." He concludes that several of the essays "number among the best short pieces Caldwell has ever written. With *For Whom the Bell Tolls*, *North of the Danube* may be America's most powerful anti-fascist literary work."[26]

Both of Caldwell's biographers, Harvey Klevar and Dan Miller, as well as Vicki Goldberg, Bourke-White's, agree that while the book itself was well received, well reviewed, and, despite its high price, well merchandized, much of the attention the authors received during their travels was of a more personal nature because they were celebrities. The press covered both their departure for and return from Europe, but especially their return on the *Aquitania* on August 30. Most of the questions then were about their love life and their marital plans, plans she denied, and plans he hoped for. The lede for the *World-Telegram*'s coverage went right to the point. The pair "arrived today in separate staterooms on the same alleyway and same deck on the *Aquitania* and denied that they are man and wife": "'No, no, no,' said Miss Bourke-White, 'we are certainly not married. I don't even want to be married. I want to be single, and that's all there is to it.'"[27]

This paparazzi-like adulation by the press was to be a fact of their lives for the next several years and would hound them even in Russia later, although there they were able to parlay their individual and joint statuses into financial success, privileged accommodations and perquisites, and, most importantly, access, especially for Bourke-White's camera.

Although Caldwell's writings during much of the 1930s had been well received in socialist circles, he was personally apolitical. His concerns were social and monetarist, not politically doctrinal. This first trip to Europe opened his eyes to the potentially dangerous parochialism of America's officially isolationist stance. Although the people of central Europe were not being impacted by devastating socioeconomic pressures similar to those affecting the rural denizens of the American South, they were clearly at an even greater risk because of the implications of the racial policies being promulgated by the German Reich. It must also have been obvious to him, as it was to intellectuals such as Wolfe, the *Atlantic* writer, that the Reich's interests extended beyond central Europe, and even to the Soviet Union with its vast land, agricultural, and mineral resources. In fact, only a year later in 1939, Caldwell and Bourke-White began planning for a fall-winter trip into the Soviet Union through China and Siberia on the Trans-Siberian Express and went so far as to contact the Chinese embassy for introductions. But their next collaboration, in which they traveled the United States analyzing its post-Depression, prewar recovery, resulting in *Say, is this the U.S.A.*, shelved these plans until 1941.

In sum, *North of the Danube* represents for Caldwell and Bourke-White their first foray into international politics. For Caldwell, this was a new approach to storytelling, one in which he was at an arm's distance from the people themselves, not just because of the language barrier but for cultural reasons as well, but he was still sympathetic to their plight. For Bourke-White, it was the first real taste of the emotional difficulties she would face in attempting to share careers with a husband. But at this point, neither had to wrestle with the dread specter of the political censorship they would later face. They were free to gather what information and impressions they could, to the extent that their energy and enthusiasm held up. Once they arrived in the Soviet Union in 1941, they would have to cope with a host of added pressures.

CHAPTER 1

Context ★ Caldwell and Bourke-White

When Adolf Hitler turned on his erstwhile Russian ally and sent the Wehrmacht across the eastern border of Poland into the Soviet Union early on the morning of June 22, 1941, the world was cast into a momentous and unexpected crisis. If Operation Barbarossa, as the German High Command labeled this lightning attack, were to be successful, Moscow would be in Nazi hands before summer's end, and the geopolitical map of Europe would be even more drastically redrawn than it already had been in the prior year or so.

Only a few Western news correspondents were credentialed to the USSR when the Germans opened this new front, among whom were the novelist Erskine Caldwell and his wife, photographer Margaret Bourke-White. They had arrived in Moscow in May after an arduous journey across the mainland of Asia. Whether the original idea for this fortuitous expedition was truly their own or that of Wilson Hicks, Bourke-White's photo editor at *Life*, is debatable; what is *not* debatable is that, once war erupted, they were in an opportune position for the journalistic scoop of a lifetime.

Caldwell and Bourke-White occupied a singular status in the literary world of 1941. Though neither was a true ideologue,[1] they both were readily identifiable representatives of the international left-leaning, anti-Fascist Popular Front that included Hollywood writers, American folk singers, and authors like Ernest Hemingway and John Steinbeck. Yet their commercial successes over the preceding decade, both individually and jointly, had made them wealthy celebrities. Caldwell, in particular, had found publishing success and popular fame in the Soviet Union, though he often joked that he had to travel there to spend his money. A southerner by birth and inclination, Caldwell had taken on the issue of poverty in the rural South in his early short stories and novels, *Tobacco Road* (1932), *God's Little Acre* (1933), *Journeyman* (1935), and *Trouble in July* (1940), which had laid bare the tattered social, economic, and racial fabric of the Deep South. By 1941 Bourke-White, the lead photographer for *Life* magazine since its inception in 1936, had an international reputation and in the United States was arguably the most well-known photographer of the period. Having been an inventive and resourceful freelancer prior to her full-time affiliation with *Life*, her work had brought her commercial and critical success. By 1936 Bourke-White's interests had shifted from modernist representations of architecture and industry to humanist studies of the proletariat. At about the same time Caldwell was seeking to document his allegations about the appalling socioeconomic conditions throughout the South. The intersection of these needs and interests resulted in their collaboration on *You Have Seen Their Faces*, an oversized book published in 1937 that combined photography and text and established a much-imitated pictorial style of social realism.

By mid-1941 they had collaborated on two more photo-text books—*North of the Danube* (1939) and *Say, is this the U.S.A.* (1941)—and had become quiet but active supporters of a variety of social concerns backed by the Popular Front, an international movement with its roots in the Communist International (Comintern). In the United States the Popular Front had evolved into a semirespectable anti-Fascist, pro-labor, antiracist lobby incorporating both left-wing and centrist constituencies, which had gained particular purchase with artists, intellectuals, and progressive politicians. On the other hand, conservative isolationists saw the Popular Front principally as a conduit for communism and accused President Roosevelt of being just that, a Communist.[2]

Neither Caldwell nor Bourke-White was without detractors: Caldwell for his willingness to flout the boundaries of sexual explicitness and the "norms of decency" in his writing, and Bourke-White for her willingness to advance her career by employing her feminine charms and exhibiting a personal flamboyance. As concerns about a new turn in the war mounted in 1940, they had achieved remarkable personal success by exploiting the popular press while remaining true to their core social beliefs, which aligned well with those of contemporary left-leaning intellectuals and politicians and with those of the Popular Front.

For some time, the Roosevelt administration had been lobbying Congress and the American people to become more actively involved in what until then had been a mostly European war. In the spring of 1941 Congress had passed legislation to provide American allies material, logistic, and economic support for their resistance to continental fascism, but it remained adamant that no direct military support would be authorized. Even so, even this partial shift by American industry to a war footing further bolstered the U.S. economy, which had finally begun to dig itself out of the savage doldrums of the Depression. At the same time, the administration's endorsement of the Soviet cause was

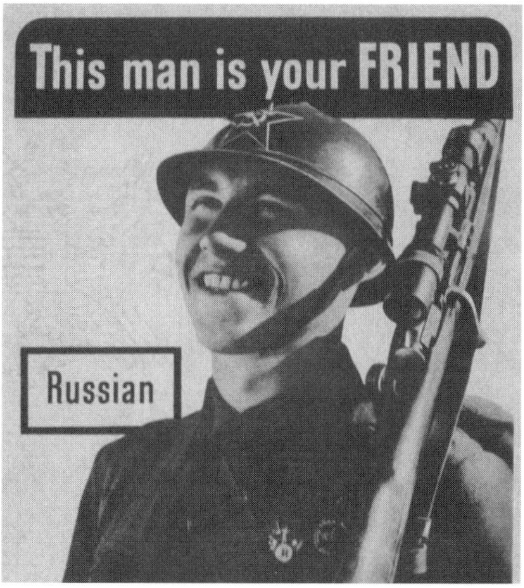

FIGURE 6. Pro-Soviet U.S. Department of Defense poster (National Archives, photo number 44-PA-2097C)

more measured. In January 1941 Roosevelt lifted the "moral embargo" that had been levied against the USSR in late 1939 following its invasion of Finland, and in March he ensured that the wording of the Lend-Lease Bill did not *exclude* Russia from receiving aid. Still, the isolationists held sway in Congress so that beyond these indications of support, Roosevelt deferred further action until such time as a clear German act forced his hand, which occurred on June 22, 1941.[3]

After the onset of the Nazis' Operation Barbarossa, the American Left, which had vigorously taken up the cause of socialism during the Depression, became a vocal advocate for a Russian alliance. One of the hurdles to cooperation with Russia was a deeply held distrust of the Soviet Union in the West, especially its ruling Communist Party. Despite widespread Western anxiety about the evil specters of communism, the Communist Party, and the Comintern, fears about the known perils of Axis fascism and its potential for world domination were even more substantial. Polls in the summer of 1941 documented that Americans remained wary of the Soviet Union and that support for the Soviet cause was low, even when the alternative was Nazism.[4] Yet internationalists were able to mobilize a variety of resources in support of their cause, none more important than the influence of the Fourth Estate and of leftist intellectuals, groups that included both Caldwell and Bourke-White.

Bourke-White and Caldwell had arrived in the Soviet capital in early May 1941 with the idea that they would tour the country as guests of the government and the Soviet Writers' Union in order to construct a photo-text collaboration along the lines of their previous ones. But with the advent of Barbarossa they were suddenly caught up in an entirely different scenario. They found themselves at the center of a journalist's fantasy, a "scoop" of cataclysmic proportions. It would take weeks, and even months in some cases, for other Western correspondents to navigate official channels and to locate safe transportation into the Soviet Union. In the meantime Caldwell and Bourke-White, along with just a few other members of the Western press corps, were in the enviable position of foreign correspondents. By the end of the summer an additional dozen representatives of the press had taken up residence in Moscow, but in June the West looked to these few on-site correspondents to provide details of the titanic struggle on the "eastern" front.

Ironically, extensive Kremlin control of the Soviet news media and censorship of foreign correspondents' texts placed the journalists in the unenviable position of having little hard information to relay to the West. Caldwell's and Bourke-White's prior alignment with the Popular Front's iteration of literary social realism—through which they had become adept at addressing both socioeconomic and consumer issues in America—meshed well with their new undertaking: (re)presenting the Soviet government, the Russian people, and the war itself to the West in order to welcome the Soviet Union into the Western anti-Fascist coalition.

Caldwell's approach, in both his Moscow writing and his radio broadcasts, was to portray the Russians as hardworking citizens, family people, and patriots, qualities with which Americans could readily identify and of which they would approve. He was never a "hard" reporter, giving just the facts—the when, where, who, how, and why of events. He was a storyteller par excellence, and his Russian reporting reflects this style. Admittedly, the newspaper pieces he filed from Moscow could best and most charitably be described as features writing. In some cases, when Bourke-White and Caldwell were at the same location at the same time, Bourke-White's memoir and photography do not fully corroborate Caldwell's published reporting. But in all his stories and articles, the subtext of Russians as next-door neighbors comes through strongly.

On the other hand, when he finally got to the front near Smolensk in September and experienced a nearly direct-hit bombing attack in Vyazma, then sat in on the Red Army's subsequent debriefing of the captured pilots, and finally visited the torn-up battlefield at Yelnya, he shifted into a realist style of newspaper journalism, though not without some romanticizing flourishes. His description of the remnants of a battlefield paints an honest and vivid portrait for readers who would never experience one firsthand. Separating Caldwell's artifice and story from "fact" can be problematic, as was evident as early as 1935 in his travel book *Some American People*, in which he mixed fanciful impressions with on-the-spot reporting; rarely does he write purely journalistic nonfiction, and his work is rarely free of embellishment.

Though Caldwell was first and foremost a writer and Bourke-White a photographer, during the first heady weeks of the war their impact on American public opinion transcended their primary spheres of competence. For most of the summer, Caldwell broadcast live once or twice daily by shortwave to the CBS radio network in New York City. Bourke-White also briefly took a turn at the microphone, but her *Life* editors quickly put a stop to her moonlighting after just a few broadcasts. They insisted she focus on the photography she was acclaimed for and for which they were paying her. In New York, the couple's live reports, along with those of other correspondents worldwide, were incorporated into *The World Today*, CBS's signature international news roundup. Broadcast nightly at 6:45 Eastern Time six days a week, it reached almost all CBS affiliates nationwide.[5] Though his voice did not ring with the regal baritone of Edward R. Murrow or Robert Trout, and atmospheric interference often made his transatlantic broadcasts difficult to understand clearly, Caldwell was the only American transmitting from within the USSR. His pro-Soviet sentiments came through and were clearly in line with the solidly anti-isolationist stance of CBS, which at the time had the second-largest radio audience in the country.[6]

Bourke-White's representation of the Soviet Union reveals considerations other than those in Caldwell's texts. Photography's meaning derives from its deployment of symbolic reality. Furthermore, from its earliest years, photography has had to shoulder the opposing burdens of reality/authenticity versus art. The photographic artist has the leeway to add, subtract, or reorient reality, not necessarily by artifice, but through subjective choices made about the inclusion or exclusion of elements of reality and their (re)arrangement. Bourke-White was a virtuoso in this art, meticulously honing the skills she had learned from the masters of modernist photography in the 1920s.

From its earliest period Bourke-White's black-and-white photography, almost all of which was static and frequently architectural, stressed tonal contrasts, repetition of forms, grandiosity, compositional integrity, and an appreciation of the machine aesthetic. Such images of objects often mirrored prevailing social, economic, and political concerns. In Russia, huge industrial facilities like the Magnitogorsk Dam on the Volga River typified Stalin's vision of his nation's arrival in an industrialized twentieth-century world through successful central-government planning. In the United States, automobiles, toasters, and other tangible merchandise emblematized the growth of a recovering

American economy through the promotion of free-market consumer capitalism. Admittedly, dams, cars, and kitchenware all seem devoid of human pathos. Initially, Bourke-White incorporated human elements only for scale. But as she grew fascinated by the role human labor played within the industrial and agricultural systems she was photographing, she increasingly integrated people as the focus of her art and became more adept and confident in her portrayal of human subjects.[7] By the time she and Caldwell teamed up both professionally and romantically in the mid-1930s, she was fully committed to addressing a variety of social issues using the photographic virtuosity that had made her the United States' most well-known and visible photographer. In the 1920s and 1930s an accepted role for documentary photography had been to illustrate social inequity and thus press for social change and economic fairness.[8] Bourke-White's style of realism in the arts would become the tacit official coin of the Popular Front.

Caldwell came to this Russian project with enthusiasm. He had begun his literary career working on small newspapers in the South writing book reviews, then enriching his storytelling craft in the genre of regional, especially southern, short stories. An impassioned series of novels about the agrarian failures of the American South soon followed. In particular, *Tobacco Road* and *God's Little Acre* addressed sharecropping, a form of indenture that fostered pervasive poverty, malnutrition, and lack of education. *Journeyman* implicated organized religion in the moral bankruptcy of the South, while *Trouble in July* graphically addressed lynching. When Caldwell and Bourke-White left for Russia in March 1941, he was a wealthy celebrity—particularly as a result of Jack Kirkland's successful dramatization of *Tobacco Road* for a record-setting run on Broadway—though one with a taint of disrepute, due in part to the banning of several of his novels in certain quarters of the nation for indecency.

Between 1936 and 1940 Caldwell and Bourke-White worked together on several books of social activism and commentary. In the innovative *You Have Seen Their Faces*, they undertook the task of authenticating the deplorable status of the American agricultural South, which Caldwell had been writing about so passionately in his novels and short stories. By emphasizing the victims, the "faces" of the title, Caldwell and Bourke-White humanized the social issues, then offered firm suggestions for the kinds of governmental actions needed to rectify them. In *Say, is this the U.S.A.* (1941), they captured the spirit of the nation as it began to emerge from the Depression. By combining text with photography in a highly successful commercial format, they popularized an entirely new way of presenting the genre of social realism. Although works such as *Faces* later passed through a period of critical disaffection, at the time they were as successful in achieving their social purpose as their authors, their publishers, and the authors' backers had hoped they would be (see appendix).

Photography, too, has a language, but the difference between writing and photography is that the latter carries the burden of a much higher expectation that it convey and present facts and truth. A single photograph, as the old saw runs, is worth a thousand words, but therein lies the danger of photography: its presumptive authority is too readily manipulable, and this malleability can be difficult to detect because of photography's association—even more than prose fiction's—with transparent realism. Even the reputable photographic section of what was to become the Farm Security Administration, established in 1935 by the Roosevelt administration to document the social conditions it was designing relief programs to combat (for which Bourke-White never worked), was not beyond accusations of the manipulation of images. The "real" in a photograph is problematic.

Soon after June 22, 1941, American news media avidly sought to employ Caldwell and Bourke-White to describe to their anxious readers and listeners the *reality* of the Soviet Union. Like many of the correspondents that summer, the couple arrived with their own preconceptions, motives, and agendas, all of which were incorporated implicitly, and at times explicitly, into their reports. Tactically marshaling the powerful forces of representation in the service of persuasion as they had in the past, they set about their task of selling to a doubting and hesitant American public a détente with communism and acceptance of a Soviet alliance. All of which is to say, they endorsed the goals of the Popular Front.

Although the Federal Bureau of Investigation placed both Caldwell and Bourke-White on its watch list as probable Communists to be corralled and detained in case of war, neither ever was a member of the Communist Party,[9] though they were clearly left-leaning.[10] Evidence for this includes not just the themes and messages of their art but also the causes they supported financially and/or materially and the organizations to which they belonged or which they supported.[11]

While Caldwell and Bourke-White *were* ideal emissaries for one of the most important items on the Left's political agenda—rallying support for a U.S.-USSR alliance to combat what at the time seemed to be the inexorable escalation of Nazi military adventurism, notwithstanding the 1939 Ribbentrop-Molotov Pact by which Germany and the Soviet Union had pledged mutual nonaggression—some aspects of their trip reflect that a purely leftist agenda was not why they traveled there in 1941. In the beginning it was an adventure, especially for Caldwell.

CHAPTER 2

Connecticut to Moscow ★ Spring 1941

That Caldwell's and Bourke-White's two-month expedition from Connecticut to Moscow *was* an adventure is evident from the form of the book Caldwell later wrote about it: *All-Out on the Road to Smolensk*, a kind of quasi-nonfiction novel. On the other hand, Margaret Bourke-White's account of the same adventure, *Shooting the Russian War*, is a more conventional reminiscence of their not always quotidian activities.

Although they traveled as celebrities and were accordingly furnished celebrity publicity and preferment, it is clear from interviews Caldwell gave along the way that he had more than self-promotion and relaxation in mind. This was, presciently, a politically motivated trip, but one devised with careful attention to its possibilities for pure adventure. While President Roosevelt remained both deeply suspicious of yet sympathetic to Soviet intentions in early 1941 and carefully avoided the political quagmire of promoting a Russian aid package,[1] this *was* on the agenda of the left-wing Popular Front in the United Sates, a movement whose social ideals were entirely in harmony with Caldwell's and Bourke-White's. Once their work in Moscow had wrapped up, Caldwell would return to Connecticut to draft a book that is far from reportorial. Bourke-White's *Shooting the Russian War*, on the other hand, is a meticulous accounting of their summer's undertakings, the people with whom they worked, the places they—but especially she—visited, and, to some extent, the social swirl.

The Adventure Begins

In *All-Out on the Road to Smolensk* (1942), Caldwell begins: "For several years I had a growing desire to visit the Soviet Union, but it was not until the first week in 1941 that I finally decided that the time had come for me to go. My reason for going then was that I wished to reach Moscow before the Germans began their attack on the Russians. I believed this would take place before the year was over."[2] This opening is telling for parsing Caldwell's attitude toward his and Bourke-White's project. Notable are the six occurrences of first-person singular pronouns. There is no indication here that the decision was, in the least, shared with his wife, or even involved her; in fact, Caldwell claims full credit for the project and even elevates his premonition that Germany would invade the Soviet Union to near fact. There is little suggestion that this was to be a mutual undertaking. He intends it to be a very personal one. Throughout *Smolensk,* the dominant personal pronoun is "I." Bourke-White is nearly whitewashed out of the text, though occasionally Caldwell refers to "my wife," and even more rarely provides her first name. He foregrounds the contemporary political situation in the Soviet Union as the reason for the trip, stressing his intuition. It is in this opening that we first sense there must be a difference between the first-person narrator Caldwell and the author, Erskine Caldwell, erstwhile journalist.

Shooting the Russian War opens on a completely different footing. Bourke-White's recollections begin with a gush of enthusiasm characteristic of the entire book: "I suppose it was those Irish ancestors of mine, deep-sea sailors all of them, whose sons in each succeeding generation ran away to sea when anyone tried to dry-dock them at home, who are responsible for my passionate love of seeing the world. . . . In view of this ancestral roaming tendency, it was a lucky thing, I think, to marry a man who knows how to read maps."[3] Clearly, Caldwell's and Bourke-White's posttrip recollections have very different perspectives (and purposes), though as histories they are roughly parallel. Bourke-White's is a glossy, gossipy report, an expanded diary, an entertainment, and is fully illustrated with eighty-nine black-and-white photographs on smooth paper;[4] Caldwell's is a man's adventure of pure text, printed on standard coarse-stock paper, requiring the reader to form his or her own mental images based on Caldwell's words and style. Bourke-White's text's attention to detail and its photographs make hers a longer book, whereas Caldwell's narrative posture makes his more succinct.

But what can be gleaned about the actual origins of this trip? In *Call It Experience,* a literary autobiography written eight to nine years after the event, Caldwell recalls more accurately and modestly, "While we were completing *Say! Is This the U.S.A.?* [*sic*], Margaret said she would like to collaborate on a fourth book of photographs-and-text and this time go to Russia for the material." He adds, "the prospect of taking such a trip appealed to me."[5] Many years later, on December 1, 1982, Vicki Goldberg interviewed Caldwell for the biography she was researching on Bourke-White, and they touched on this very point: "At the Russian embassy in Washington one day, Margaret 'casually mentioned that we would like to go to the Soviet Union,' Erskine Caldwell says, 'just casual conversation, but the way it happened was that someone in the embassy said, "Well, if you want to go you'd better hurry up and get there before war starts.""[6]

Five years after that interview, when Caldwell was writing his own second autobiography, *With All My Might*, which was published just months before his death in 1987, he seems to recall much more, especially his and Bourke-White's conversation "one evening after dinner" during which she brings up the notion of "collaborat[ing] on a fourth volume of text-and-photographs." He continues, "When I did not respond immediately to Kit's [his pet name for Bourke-White] comment, I could see that she was twisting her fingers nervously and glancing at me hopefully in the silence."[7] Several biographers have commented on the ever-present stress in the Caldwell–Bourke-White marriage, strain that eventually doomed it, and in just this single sentence, written nearly a half-century after their divorce, one can still sense the edginess of their power struggles.[8]

In any case, Bourke-White makes her argument. Caldwell retells it with all the skill of a gifted novelist, though his once-perfect ear for dialogue has turned tin:

> "But how could you work on another book so soon—and work for the magazine [*Life*], too?" I asked presently.
>
> "Oh, I can do both," she said at once, her expression bright with delight. "I've already talked about it with the editors. All of them are very enthusiastic."
>
> "That's very kind of them," I said, "but you can see that I'm not jumping with joy."
>
> "That's because you don't know what I have in mind—where I'd like for us to go."
>
> "Where for us to go?"
>
> "The U.S.S.R."
>
> "Russia?"
>
> "Yes, Russia."
>
> "Why?"
>
> "Because it's the thing for us to do, that's why," she said at once. "It will be an exciting experience for you and me—for both of us. We'll be together all the time—just like it was when we went to Mexico together [summer 1940]. And you'll like the Russians. They can be so friendly when they want to be. Almost without exception, everybody was so helpful and kind when I went there the first time [1930 for *Fortune*]. And something's going to happen there soon. That will be exciting—"

Caldwell seems to demur, briefly, but soon their negotiation grinds to its conclusion:

> "War is going to happen there, Kit. That's what will happen. You know that. The Germans—Adolph Hitler—"
>
> "Of course!" she exclaimed excitedly. "That's it exactly. Now, don't you want to go, Skinny? Please say you do!"[9]

He doesn't offer us his final response.

Not surprisingly, Bourke-White's remembrances about the genesis of their trip take a more domestic tack. In *Shooting the Russian War*, she makes a tactful observation: "When two persons who have deep professional interests marry, there are two ways of pursuing those interests: together or separately. In our family we do both" (4). She continues, almost blissfully, about their harmony:

> Sometimes both of us feel that the time has come to work together, in the same country, he with a typewriter and I with lens, and then we do something that we both greatly enjoy. We make a trip together and work together.
>
> Russia was one of those countries which we elected to do together, and we had a joint and urgent conviction that we should get there soon, to record in words and pictures what we expected to be the coming tide of the war. We kept our plans somewhat secret, for we do not like to talk about things until we are sure we are going to accomplish them. (4)

In fact, the trip may not have been either of their ideas. Wilson Hicks, *Life* magazine's photo editor, had sent Bourke-White out on previous wartime photo shoots, and now *he* seemed to be the one with the premonition about what the Russian future held. He had "an extraordinary hunch," she writes in her 1963 autobiography. "He [Hicks] felt I could make some valuable comparisons between Russia of ten years ago and contemporary Russia," she recalls, then adds, "Erskine had always been eager to go because his books were read widely in the Soviet Union."[10] But in *Shooting the Russian War* she claimed the top of the mountain: Hicks, she said, "shared our conviction that Russia was the coming key country in the march of the war" (5). Although her conclusion embraces a certain amount of hindsight, Bourke-White makes clear their trip had had serious political overtones. By "march of the war" she implies support for the then-liberal cause of America's uniting with the USSR in an anti-Fascist partnership, a central element in the Popular Front's credo.

The Trip That Never Happened

Whatever the actual sequence of events, they had been planning this sort of trek for some time, though not with the same political overtones present in 1940–41.[11] In July 1939 Bourke-White had written a long letter to Constantine Oumansky, the Soviet ambassador to the United States, laying out a fanciful road and rail itinerary she had in mind through China, Mongolia, and Siberia to Moscow that fall and winter. Already on her mind was the money her husband had on account in the USSR: "Mr. Caldwell has been notified that he has rubles deposited to his account in Moscow [from the sale of his books there]. Will it be possible to have part of these, sufficient for two railroad tickets and traveling expenses, transferred to a border or near border point which we will have to decide upon later as our plans are more advanced."[12]

At the same time, Caldwell had written his Moscow counterpart, Timofei Rokotov, the deputy editor of *International Literature*, who earlier in the year had advised him, "If you come to Moscow, please bear in mind that there is money here at your disposal."[13] Caldwell explained to Rokotov their planned itinerary and their need for cash:

> By a good combination of circumstances I may be crossing the Trans-Siberian railroad into the Soviet Union during the early part of 1940. I am planning to go to China the middle of September, staying through the winter, then meeting the Trans-Siberian railroad at some convenient point and crossing the country to Moscow.
>
> There is one thing with which you can probably help me. You've written me that there are rubles deposited to my account in Moscow, although I don't believe you have ever sent me any records indicating just how much there is. Will it be possible to have part of these, sufficient for two first-class railroad tickets and traveling, [*sic*] expenses, transferred to a border or near border point which I will have to decide upon later as my plans are more advanced?
>
> My wife, Margaret Bourke-White, who will be traveling with me, has already taken this matter up with Mr. Koukin in the Soviet Consulate here and has written to Mr. Oumansky in Moscow. I thought perhaps if you were working on it too, arrangements might at least be started before we leave for China in the fall.[14]

In August, Caldwell's agent, Maxim Lieber, had already sent tentative proffer letters to Condé Nast and *Harper's Bazaar* when he wrote Caldwell to see what sort of interest there might be in "an article by you on Mrs. Chiang Kai Shek and her sisters. Does this interest you?"[15] Plans had progressed so far that on August 23, Theodore Roosevelt's eldest son, then working as an editor at Doubleday, wrote a letter of introduction for them to Hu Shih, the Chinese ambassador to the United States.[16] Nonetheless, all these plans were tabled when Bourke-White's overseas *Life* assignments and their joint *Say, is this the U.S.A.* project took precedence. But the lure of Soviet Russia lingered.

The West Coast

Between 1939 and 1941 the globe's political climate had dramatically transformed. Actual war was at hand. Germany had consumed France and much of Europe and was wreaking havoc through the air on Britain. The Axis was now a tripartite menace with Italy and Japan in support of the Nazis. But as the Caldwells were arranging the logistics of their imminent departure to the Soviet Union, the United States still remained on the sidelines.

In "The American Century," a dramatic 6,600-word broadside in the February 17, 1941, issue of *Life*, the magazine's publisher, Henry R. Luce, fired a challenge at the people and leaders of the United States by answering his own rhetorical question, "Where are we?": "We are in the war. All this talk about whether this or that might or might not get us into the war is wasted effort. We are, for a fact, in the war."[17] A self-made media mogul, Luce was strongly supportive of international cooperation against the Axis with the hope that American involvement in a physical war could be averted, to *Life*'s and America's profit.

His and *Life*'s message then and throughout the war was a mix of corporate activism and moral responsibility backed by the vigorous middle-class consumerism to which *Life* would dedicate its pages. Understandably, Luce also advocated for the relevance of the press in this anti-isolationist project: "Journalists, too, of course, are implicated. But if Americans are confused it is not for lack of accurate and pertinent information. The American people are by far the best informed people in the history of the world. The trouble is not with the facts. The trouble is that clear and honest inferences have not been drawn from the facts. The day-to-day present is clear. The issues of tomorrow are befogged."[18] Although Luce did not mention the Soviet Union in this essay, he and *Life* were enthusiastic about Bourke-White's and Caldwell's forthcoming Russian project, plans for which were progressing at full throttle.

On February 21 Hicks wired Bourke-White in Connecticut that all was set to go:

> THE ANSWER IS YES ON RUSSIA FOR YOU AS PHOTOGRAPHER. THE MATTER OF POSSIBLE TEXT BY MR. CALDWELL TO BE DETERMINED LATER ALSO YOUR ROUTE ETC. SUGGEST YOU COME IN FIRST OF WEEK. I AM DELIGHTED AND KNOW YOU WILL BE AT THIS HISTORIC MESSAGE. REGARDS.[19]

A month later, and just before their departure, Caldwell received a "to whom it may concern letter" from *Life*'s associate editor, Noel Busch, verifying that "Mr. Caldwell has been retained by LIFE Magazine, a TIME Inc. publication, to write a series of articles. In this capacity he is a member of LIFE's editorial staff and is authorized to represent it in his journalistic activities."[20] On March 24 Hicks sent a much longer, and far warmer, letter ("Dear Miss Bourke-White") to Bourke-White through the American embassy in Hong Kong, stroking her ego. In it he assured her: "I am sure you will have no difficulty in convincing the persons whose approval for your activities you must obtain that we anticipate the most effective results from your present expedition. I venture to say that many of those you will see already are aware that you are one of the United States' outstanding photographers and that LIFE has published your work at frequent intervals since its first issue appeared more than four years ago."[21] On March 5 the State Department mailed the couple their passports, warning them in a cover letter, "It is assumed that you have a full appreciation of the dangers involved due to the present situation in Europe, and of the possible scarcity of return transportation to the United States."[22] With these final letters of approval and introduction, Caldwell and Bourke-White could finally embark for Asia, officially sanctioned.

But of what their journalistic activities would consist was not clear. When they reached Los Angeles on their way westward, a stringer for the *Hollywood Citizen-News* interviewed Caldwell and reported on March 20, "He will observe the effect of war's blighting touch upon a people, individually and collectively. . . . 'It is our purpose,' he [Caldwell] said, 'to study at first hand the effect of war upon a people forced to undergo it. Once we have done that I think the nature of the book will take care of itself.' . . . After touring the Orient, they will probably visit in the Near East, Africa, and Mediterranean points." The *Herald-Express* was more cleverly succinct: "[The Caldwells] were in Hollywood today visiting friends and making final plans for a takeoff to visit the 'tobacco roads' of the Far East."[23]

When Caldwell and Bourke-White traveled together, they did so as celebrities. Fueled by the remarkable extravagance their literary successes and fame enabled, they almost always traveled first class, were feted by the press and the public at most of their stops, and rarely saw themselves as merely humble members of the Fourth Estate. Although neither remarked on the attention and adulation they received, contemporary newspaper accounts almost always accorded Caldwell the lead role. Headlines appearing in the Los Angeles press on March 19—as the Caldwells arrived from Reno on their way to the Matson Lines' flagship SS *Lurline* and the first leg of their Pacific crossing—indicate the semblance of a pecking order: "Tobacco Road Author Here, China-Bound" (*Herald-Express*) and "'Tobacco Road' Author Here on Orient Trip" (*Hollywood Citizen-News*). For the *Herald-Express,* Bourke-White was "authoress and photographer" and "ace camerawoman," while in the *Citizen-News* she was simply "the photographer." She was either not interviewed or just not quoted.

Furthermore, Caldwell's authorial preeminence generally accorded him some credibility in matters of national interest. Before they embarked, the *Los Angeles Times* headlined its piece on the travelers: "Poverty in South Declared Increased by War Work." The article opened: "Caldwell is not in Hollywood to write scenarios as he did some years ago or in the interest of the cinema production of his 'Tobacco Road.' With his wife, Margaret Bourke-White, famed photographer, he is on his way to China. He will write some articles, she will take pictures for 'Life,' and together they will do a book." The declarer was Caldwell himself, but his opinions about the South were reserved for the deep body of the article.

With two $149.95 one-way United Airlines tickets in hand, good for passage from New York to Los Angeles, the Caldwells departed on March 14, 1941.[24] After overnighting in Chicago due to inclement weather, they arrived in Reno where they paused for a couple of nights at the Riverside Hotel for a commemoration of their wedding vows two years earlier. They checked into the Hollywood Knickerbocker Hotel on March 19, where they readily accommodated the press. Apparently a dockworkers' strike forced a change in boarding plans, so the Caldwells had to take a lighter out to the *Lurline* anchored in San Pedro Harbor.

Hawaii

From there the *Lurline* proceeded to San Francisco, where more newspaper interviews ensued. The *San Francisco News* noted that in addition to Caldwell and the "camera genius" Bourke-White, the passenger manifest included "a group of 20 Portland businessmen, members of a Chamber of Commerce 'good will' tour, with their wives," as well as "H. W. Jackson, San Francisco stove manufacturer, and [Mr. and Mrs.] L. M. Du-Commun, president of the Pacific Paint and Varnish Co." That the Caldwells' travels were newsworthy is further evidenced by both the *Syracuse Herald-American* and the *El Paso Times* printing a wire service release on March 23 to the effect that "Margaret Bourke-White, celebrated photographer, and her equally celebrated author husband, Erskine Caldwell" were off on a "round-the-world trip."

Arriving in Honolulu five days later, they checked into a twenty-dollar suite at the Royal Hawaiian Hotel on Waikiki Beach to await their connection with the Pan American Airways Pacific Clipper the next day. But weather problems had kept it grounded in San Francisco for over a week, so they had to cool their heels in Hawaii during the interim. They were not without things to keep them busy. In addition to a day trip to Hilo on April 1 to visit "a friend of ours [with a] lovely home" (*SRW* 6), Caldwell purchased his most necessary item for the trip, a Corona Sterling portable typewriter and a half-dozen ribbons for $38.25.

As was usual in Hawaii, celebrities in town were always news, and the Caldwells were no exception. The day they arrived, reporters were at the

Matson Line terminal ("573 Tourists, Isle People Arrivals Aboard Lurline") getting Caldwell's opinions on important issues. He had in mind already his political aims: "'The pressure of events is forcing America to become the leading nation of the world,' he maintained. 'The United States has abandoned its traditional role of isolation,'" the *Honolulu Star-Bulletin* reported him opining. The *Honolulu Advertiser* nominated him as a "writer and authority on matters south of the Mason-Dixon Line" whose wife was "the famed photographer."

Both papers covered a talk the Caldwells gave on March 28 at the Honolulu YWCA before about a hundred members of the Inter-Professional Association (*Honolulu Star-Bulletin:* "Social Gains Threatened, Caldwell Says"): "Mr. Caldwell, instead of giving a prepared talk, invited questions from the audience," wrote Lawrence Nakatsuka. Bourke-White, a "commercial photographer" of note, spoke about photography in the Balkans. The article was accompanied by a photo of a smiling Bourke-White in a pillbox hat with kukui nut, maile leaf, and hibiscus leis.

Earlier that day Bourke-White had finally gotten an interview of her own, though it was on the features page, not in the news section of the *Star-Bulletin:* "Well Known Lady Photographer Visiting Honolulu This Week." Lynn Thomas's piece, accompanied by a photo of Bourke-White in her trademark pillbox but without leis, introduced her as "one of the finest woman photographers in the world." That must surely have rankled Bourke-White, who disliked that qualifying adjective. "The little lady couldn't get a job as a waitress, so she got mad! And when Mrs. Erskine Caldwell, better known as Margaret Bourke-White, gets mad, things begin exploding in all directions. Her usual even temper held full sway, though, as she sat on the beach fronting the Royal Hawaiian Hotel and looked back upon her past experiences. . . . She is naturally very demure and petite, but that Yankee spirit once left the king of Egypt somewhat crestfallen."

This vignette recalled Bourke-White's photographing the king while he was "eating chocolates": "The king was still patiently trying to tell her of the good luck she was having, when she thanked him very politely, turned her back (which just isn't done with kings) and walked away with the words ringing in her ears, 'Well, young lady, you are really very lucky to photograph me!'" The following day Caldwell got his own features piece by the *Star-Bulletin*'s literary editor, Dr. A. W. Slaten. "Why Erskine Caldwell Wrote 'Tobacco Road'" began: "Erskine Caldwell talks with a shy earnestness that is humorless and naïve. He feels that he has a mission. There is about him a restrained evangelistic fervor that keeps him from being a sophisticate, an ironical bystander or an art-for-art's sake malingerer in the battle of life. He is still bucking the line, the son of a Presbyterian minister, and a chip off the old block."

By the time they checked out of the Royal Hawaiian, the Caldwells had run up a $472 tab that included—as usual for wherever the Caldwells encamped—telephone, postage, and cablegram fees, but also clothing, laundry, and beauty shop charges.

Throughout their many travels, both Caldwell and Bourke-White kept meticulously detailed expense ledgers.[25] His was a long-established practice—both as a hobby and for accounting and tax purposes; her accounts were required by the *Time* finance department. Caldwell kept such precise accounts that, while he was in Moscow, he not only itemized such obvious costs as his telegrams, physical therapy bills, and his chauffeur's and secretary-interpreter's monthly salaries, but also daily expenses for such items as subway fares, newspapers, tips, rubber glue, shampoo, and tobacco. Even more remarkably, he records such minutiae as 10 rubles for mushrooms on September 1, 12 rubles for watermelons on September 7 and 8, and August purchases of currants (2 rubles), tangerines (5.9 rubles), and pears (4.5 rubles).

Also, both Caldwell and Bourke-White always maintained personal secretaries, sometimes jointly, sometimes individually, to whom they gave a great deal of responsibility and from whom they expected a great deal of initiative. The result was that nearly complete financial and correspondence records exist for this Russian trip. Upon their departure from Hawaii, Caldwell wrote Rhoda Lynn, his secretary back in Connecticut:

> Dear Miss Lynn:
>
> I have written a check to the order of the Royal Hawaiian Hotel for $471.78[.]
>
> On the back of one of the sheets of the hotel bill you will note what this sum represents. MBW paid me in cash $265.19, and the balance represents my own expenditure. However, for the sake of expense accounts, you should credit me with the entire amount of $471.78, as I'm using the $265.19 to pay on my future traveling expenses. MBW would be making up her own Life expense a/c, and she will record the sum in her own accounts.
>
> Erskine Caldwell[26]

From these records one can calculate the cost of the Caldwells' first-class journey to the Orient, which is astonishing. The clipper fare, for example—and bear in mind the roughly 1:15 conversion ratio from 1941 to 2015 money—was $507 each. Bourke-White had actually negotiated a reduced fare with Pan American because their tickets had been issued in conjunction with the Matson Line / *Lurline* passage. Normally the rate would have been $564. Nonetheless, their excess baggage fees were a staggering $880 ($862 for her, $18 for him). Not counting excess baggage fees, their fares from New York to Hong Kong ran

$822 each. Hotel bills in Reno, Los Angeles, and Honolulu plus incidentals onboard the *Lurline* amounted to $784. Finally, after carefully separating her personal and professional expenses from her husband's, Bourke-White submitted an itemized expense list to *Time* for her portion of cables, car fares, and entertainment (including $5.50 for "entertaining Lt. Col of Marines and wife evening at Guam") covering the period March 14 to April 14 amounting to $448. Thus, the Caldwells' progress from New York to Hong Kong was accomplished at a cost of not less than $3,798, and probably closer to $4,000 ($63,650 in 2015 money). Before they embarked, *Time* had already cut a check to Bourke-White for $2,500 as an "advance for expenses Russian assignment."

The relevance of this detail makes evident that Caldwell's and Bourke-White's trip was a carefully planned and assiduously recorded expedition. Yet the journey he describes in *All-Out on the Road to Smolensk* is a selectively constructed one. In fact, *Smolensk,* after its initial paragraphs, does not pick up the tale until the couple reaches China, a month after their departure from the East Coast. Because Caldwell wrote very little about their remarkable journey through war-torn China and Bourke-White focused her memoir, *Shooting the Russian War,* on the Russian summer portion of their adventure, the details of their transpacific and cross-Asiatic adventure can be located only in the Bourke-White and Caldwell archives at Syracuse and Dartmouth Universities. The material in those collections reveals how quickly the advantages and the power they were accustomed to as a result of their fame and wealth dissipated after a few days in Chongqing.[27]

Across the Pacific

On April 3 they finally were off from Honolulu, heavily burdened with impedimenta. Caldwell had 7 pounds of excess baggage, Bourke-White 337, almost all of which was camera equipment and supplies. Despite her advance, she dutifully billed the $862.72 baggage fees directly to *Time*. Presumably, Caldwell paid his $17.92 penalty himself.

The Pacific Clipper portion of the trip included overnight stops on Midway and Wake Islands (with an extra day on Wake for bad weather) and on Guam. In many ways the trip was another idyll for the Caldwells. Although he makes no mention of this portion of their trip in *Smolensk*, the first chapters of Bourke-White's *Shooting the Russian War* fill in some missing details, though she does misremember certain particulars. For example, she reports flying to Honolulu by clipper rather than by cruising on the *Lurline*. Although she doesn't mention the specifics of their luxury PanAm clipper accommodations, perhaps because they were so well known at the time, she does provide profiles of the crew and of their fellow passengers, including the exiled Dutch "Foreign Minister van Kleffens," who "look[ed] like a high-school boy in prim spectacles" (*SRW* 7) and was on his way back to the Dutch East Indies after conferences in Washington with Roosevelt. She recalls gooney bird–watching and swimming during the overnight stops on Midway and Wake Islands, but as for the evening with the Marine lieutenant colonel and his wife on Guam, there is no mention, though she admits to "sip[ping] cool drinks with navy officers, who complained, with more prophecy than any of us could know, about Senators who refused to vote appropriations for adequate armaments, for fear of offending Japan" (*SRW* 9).

When they stepped off the clipper at Cavite Naval Base in the Philippines on April 8 (they'd lost a day to the International Date Line) they were again greeted by the press, but here they shared the spotlight. Bessie Hackett, a features writer for the *Manila Daily Bulletin*, with her photographer in tow, covered their arrival: "Novelist Caldwell, Photographer Bourke-White - - - A Working Team." After describing them as "tops in their respective fields," Hackett continued, "The Caldwells were an interesting-looking couple as they stepped off the clipper at Cavite. The broad-shouldered author of 'Tobacco Road,' 'God's Little Acre,' and other successful novels, and the attractive fashion-conscious woman whose photographs have gained her a worldwide reputation [*sic*, no verb]. Mrs. Caldwell wore a powder-blue suit with white blouse, perforated pumps, a white felt hat with a tall red feather, and a red patent leather knapsack bag slung over her shoulder."

Then Hackett got down to the history of their relationship, recording a story Bourke-White surely had told many times: "'I worked five months selling the idea [of accompanying him to photograph the South] to his agent,' Mrs. Caldwell recalls, 'and all this time Erskine and I have never met—not until we actually started out on the job. For the first five days we fought about one thing after another and couldn't agree on anything; after that we got along fine all right and by the time the job was done we decided to get married.' They have been married just two years." The following day the couple also appeared on the front page of the *Bulletin*, and there the subject was international affairs ("Americans Set for Plunge Into War, Says Noted Author"), and, as usual, Caldwell was the expert and Bourke-White, "equally known in her own right as one of the leading women photographers in the U.S.," was his companion. By now Caldwell's political message was well framed: "Americans have already taken sides in the international issue of democracy against fascism, and should the occasion for active intervention arise they would be in a determined frame of mind to take the plunge into war. . . . This is in remarkable contrast to the attitude of aloofness, even indifference, in evidence as late as mid 1940. But now that the American people have made up their mind, said Caldwell, they are grimly determined to go through with whatever path their country decides to pursue." After an evening at the air-conditioned Manila Hotel, they were off again, but not before Bourke-White got in some shopping. Before leaving the Philippines she mailed Rhoda Lynn a hastily handwritten note:

> Have written check on Home Bank for $30—April 9 to Mrs. Marcial Lichauco (address: Dept. of Finance Manila)
>
> Check may be filled in for less than $30, as I made it out for her to fill in.
>
> It is for Philippine eve. dress they are making for me. If she needs a few more $'s I have authorized her to write you for it, but in all probability it will be for less.
>
> She'll be mailing dress to you at Darien.
>
> Also an embroidered suit will come for Mr. C from Manila Writers League. That is a gift.[28]

This was to be just the beginning of Bourke-White's Asian shopping spree.

Their final Pacific stop was Hong Kong, where they were forced to spend five nights awaiting tickets and clearances for a flight to Chongqing, but fortunately they were able to enjoy the gracious luxury of the centrally located Gloucester Hotel, PanAm's hotel and headquarters. They were lucky, however, because most travelers without the connections available to the Caldwells were barred from the direct route through China, being forced to detour on the rather more arduous trek through the uncertainties of Southeast Asia.

As always, the press sniffed them out. The day after their arrival, the English-language *South China Morning Post* noted: "War Correspondents—American Author and Wife to Visit Chungking—Mr. Erskine Caldwell." The *Morning Post* denominated Bourke-White as "one of America's leading industrial photographers, well-known the world over for her photographic essays of pre–World War II European countries." Charmingly, the *Post* translated Caldwell's *God's Little Acre* as *The Earth Is The Lord's*. In any case, the article went on to note: "The Caldwell team is the third famous man-and-wife combination to visit Chungking on behalf of the American reading public recently, the others being Carl [photographer] and Shelley [writer] Mydans of *Life*, and Ernest and Martha (Gellhorn) Hemingway who arrived in the Chinese war capital a few days ago. However, the Caldwells will follow the journalistic beaten track only as far as Chungking. From there on, their itinerary covers a rambling route to the Mediterranean—wars and visas permitting."

The wait was not enervating in the least for Bourke-White. She went shopping. "The stores were spilling out into the streets with their stocks of Swiss watches, English woolens, carved ivories, and embroideries at fantastically low prices. Everything was cheap, because Hong Kong was a free port for foreign articles, and coolie labor made native products cost next to nothing," she wrote disingenuously (*SRW* 13). From April 10 through April 14 she shopped the Shanghai Kerchief Store, Bombay Silk Store, Swatow Lace Co., East Asiatic Trading Co., Fair Shoe Factory, Swatow Drawn Work Co., Sin Luen Shing Ivory Manufacturer, the Peking Company, and Wing Fong Tailor. She paid cash for fabric, purses, a luncheon set, "bracelets, skulls, etc.," kerchiefs, "cigaret cases, powder boxes," and "ornaments, fish, animals." Beyond this, the Caldwells had pants, suits, shirts, and shoes personally tailored, and Bourke-White commissioned a set of specially zippered chamois camera cases.

Caldwell, too, shopped in Hong Kong. At a lecture given at the UCLA Student Union in March 1967, he recalls having had a bespoke suit of "British woolen" made but was stuck with the only color remaining in the tailor's depleted stock: "a shade somewhere between canary yellow and hamburger mustard."[29]

At the Gloucester the Caldwells necessarily made the acquaintance of Philip Chai, the PanAm and China National Aviation representative. In addition to helping them with their passage into Chongqing and beyond, Chai arranged to have all of Bourke-White's Hong Kong purchases packed into a trunk, sent back to the United States on the S.S. *Coolidge*, then forwarded on to the East Coast by Railway Express to be picked up by Rhoda Lynn, to whom he sent the key for the trunk and all the customs documents. Bourke-White was so appreciative of Chai's help that she dashed off a scribbled note to Lynn on the back of one of Chai's business cards: "Send him copy 'Say is This ——' when it comes out. Send him a yrs. subscription Life starting now—Send a good edition of 'You Have Faces[.]' Write him note saying we so greatly appreciated his help."[30] In a letter a few days later from China, Bourke-White, always thorough, advised Lynn further: "Of course pay custom duty, if any, and have the contents unpacked & mothproofed, even if you have to pay storage somewhere, in case house at Darien is not available" (it had been leased).[31]

The gifts took a while to arrive, but five months later Chai wrote Lynn:

> Dear Miss Lynn:
>
> Mr. and Mrs. Erskine Caldwell's "Say, Is This the U.S.A.?" and "You Have Seen Their Faces" and the year's subscription to LIFE magazine have all arrived.
>
> Please extend my heartiest thanks to them upon their return from Moscow for their exceeding kind thoughts.
>
> If there is anything I can do for them in the Orient, do not hesitate to call on me.[32]

But Bourke-White was also busy professionally in Hong Kong. Because of their fame, throughout this trip the Caldwells had remarkable and unprecedented access to important and internationally renowned public figures. The first of these were the three Song sisters ("The Three Graces"; *SRW* 11). Two years earlier Maxim Lieber, the Caldwells' literary agent, had sent tenders about audiences with the Song sisters to several publishers when the Caldwells were trying to arrange a Siberian rail trip to Moscow. They met two of the sisters in Hong Kong, where the women maintained residences as "refugee guests of the British government" (*SRW* 11). Bourke-White, respecting their modesty and shyness, was able to photograph both.

Song Qingling, the widow of Sun Yat-sen, the founder and first premier of the Republic of China, was at the time the head of the China Defense League and was then trolling for American money. She was the first to agree to sit. She then convinced her sister, Ailing, the wife of Dr. H. H. Kung, the Chinese minister of finance, to agree to a photo session. To be photographed by Margaret Bourke-White was a considerable honor. One evening, at a sumptuous and formal dinner, Caldwell refused to eat the Chinese delicacies, insisting rather on simple rice, which the Chinese thought of as "peasant food." In the end, Madame Kung, who actually was schooled at Wesleyan College near Macon, Georgia, and had a southern accent, joined him in his rice-only meal (*SRW* 12–13).

Later, in Chongqing, Bourke-White completed her portraits of the sisters. The third Song sister was Meiling, the wife of China's leader, Chiang Kai-shek. Soon after the Caldwells arrived, Madame and Generalissimo Chiang Kai-shek extended a formal invitation for tea and sent a Buick to chauffeur the Caldwells to their "house [that] might have been built for a well-to-do resident of Kansas City, Missouri" (*SRW* 16). In *Shooting the Russian War,* Bourke-White lingers on the intricate detail of Song Meiling's clothing, appearance, and even the timbre of her voice, in addition to offering a few details of the evening's events. Soon, Bourke-White was behind her camera photographing Madame Chiang while she and Caldwell had an animated conversation (Song spoke elegant English) in which he encouraged her to go to America to promote her cause (the need for American aid to China). When the generalissimo arrived, Caldwell chatted with him about the current status of American and British aid, describing the crated fighters and bombers he had seen in Los Angeles's port. Song Meiling, a Wellesley College graduate, served as interpreter. Later, Bourke-White had a portrait session with him as well.

Finally, just before departing Hong Kong, Bourke-White took the precaution of forwarding some extra equipment to herself. She wrote Lynn from Chongqing, "One batch of heavy things were sent from Hong Kong to Bagdad by ship and the bill was supposed to go to Hicks [*Life*'s photo editor and her boss]. I only mention this in case he speaks of it. These are a reserve which I hope to [meet?] up with but unsettled conditions may prevent."[33]

One of the remarkable features of Caldwell's and Bourke-White's books and writings about their Asian passage is how little attention they give to the real war that was taking place right before their eyes. Of course, at this juncture in their trip they did not view themselves as news correspondents. Little mention is made of China's truly precarious political, social, and military circumstances in 1941, other than Caldwell's comments that their pilots feared attack by Japanese fighter planes and that the city of Chongqing was experiencing periodic Japanese bomber raids. Perhaps because he recognized that he was not prepared to enter into a knowledgeable commentary on a very complex and fraught state of affairs, Caldwell does not even mention their social interlude with Chiang Kai-shek and Song Meiling. Later, as ground delays changed from hours to days to weeks, they may have recognized that war shortages and priorities were to blame, but they never mentioned this.

China had been at war with Japan since July 7, 1937, when the first skirmishes between Chiang's Nationalist forces and Emperor Hirohito's army occurred at Marco Polo Bridge in Wanping near Beiping. But before that Nationalist China had had, since September 1931, to bear the unpleasant burden of Japanese occupation of Manchuria in the far northeast. By late November 1937 Shanghai, one of China's most important ports, had fallen under Japanese control, thereby threatening Nanjing, the national capital two hundred miles inland. In early December Chiang and Song evacuated Nanjing to Chongqing in the mountain fastness nine hundred miles to the southwest, where the provisional administrative government had been established. The military headquarters had also moved to Wuhan, about halfway to Chongqing. But by the end of 1938 Wuhan and its airbase also had fallen into Japanese hands, thus easing the way for regular bombing sorties by the imperial Japanese air force over Chongqing.

Complicating these war matters for Generalissimo Chiang was that Nationalist China was not a unified nation. In early 1940 Wang Jingwei, a devotee of the freedom fighter Sun Yat-sen, had established a collaborationist government, a kind of Chinese Vichy, headquartered in Nanjing in Japanese-occupied eastern China.

The Chinese Communist Party was now entrenched in the north China province of Shaanxi in the city of Yan'an, and Mao Zedong had risen to power. During the early 1930s the Kuomintang under Chiang had attempted to suppress armed Communist factions throughout the country and almost succeeded. In October 1935 the Reds, following a providential sixteen-month retreat ("The

Long March"), finally recoalesced in the north. By 1941 the Red Army, ostensibly still under Nationalist control, had become fractious and added to Chiang's woes. He was beset with the difficult task of holding his fragile nation together while simultaneously fighting a well-equipped invader.

In 1941 Nationalist China was in a desperate situation. It was running out of money, it was running out of armaments, millions of its people were internal refugees from the war, and millions were starving as a result of crop failures and Chiang's often perverse domestic policies. All this was evident in Chongqing where many of the poor had come to escape the war and built vast shantytowns. Chiang must have been heartened by Caldwell's comments about the warplanes he had seen in San Pedro Harbor in late March being prepared for shipment west, because in February Lauchlin Currie, Roosevelt's personal emissary, had come to Chongqing to let Chiang know that soon Lend-Lease matériel would be arriving. Nevertheless, one can only wonder what Chiang must have thought of these two wealthy Americans passing through his war-torn country—and demanding special privileges—headed toward the Soviet Union, a regime he considered an adversary.

China

After a wait of almost a week, the Caldwells finally obtained all the requisite documents and were cleared for travel into China. Caldwell describes the start of this phase of their trip in an unpublished manuscript, "Transit China," which he later composed in Moscow: "At four a.m. we took off from the dark airfield. There were three other passengers on the plane, all Chinese, and the remainder of the space was taken up by bales of newly-printed banknotes for the Central Government, the main cargo of every flight to Chungking, and by cases of medical supplies."[34]

The trip was a necessarily dangerous one because of the war; the airspace between Hong Kong and the Chinese capital frequently was infested with Japanese aircraft. Caldwell recalled that "[t]he pilots had laughed and joked with us on the field, but once in the plane they were grim-faced and silent," but in the end the trip proved to be "as uneventful as a routine flight between New York and Chicago." His principal interest in Chongqing, he wrote, was in "at once trying to get out of the city." In *Smolensk*, he crisply sums up the first month of the expedition: "We reached the provisional capital of China in mid-April after many weeks of delay in Los Angeles, Honolulu, and Hong Kong. Flying weather in the Pacific was not at its best during that season of the year" (*Smolensk* 4).

On the other hand, he did pen a letter from Chongqing to his parents, with whom he kept in regular if intermittent contact throughout his life, describing Chongqing as "a very quiet place" where "the only thing that disturbs the peace [are] firecrackers that go off every five minutes from 5 am to 8 pm. The coolies building a road above the hotel shoot off squibs to blast a bucketful of earth, and that is the nearest thing to machinery they use." He adds with a touch of wistfulness, "The country looks like the Blue Ridge Mountain Country without trees."[35]

"Transit China" is a remarkable 7,585-word traveler's tale from which Caldwell later extracted about 2,800 words and reworked them into the bulk of the first chapter of *All-Out on the Road to Smolensk*. Because he did not see its relevance to his *Smolensk* project, he ignored their time in Chongqing and their marvelous tea with Madame and Generalissimo Chiang about which Bourke-White waxed so ecstatic. Caldwell picks up their journey in the central Chinese outpost of Lanzhou. There they were marooned for over a week because of aircraft problems and aborted efforts to get to Hami, a town ever deeper into the continent, near the Mongolian border. In "Transit China," the reader meets Caldwell's travel persona, as distinct from his Popular Front foreign correspondent persona. Caldwell-as-traveler is a mix of the supercilious and condescending British travel writer of the interwar period, Mark Twain's sardonic reporter in *The Innocents Abroad*, and a country bumpkin.

In contradistinction to Bourke-White's description of their sumptuous tea with the Chiangs, here is an example of Caldwell's description of life in Chongqing. This vignette concludes one of the couple's many fruitless trips to the airport: "In a confused state of mind we retired to one of the recesses in Chialing House, a Chinese version of a pigeon coop, which is an eating and sleeping establishment for foreigners. Then we sat down and attempted to cool off with alternate swigs of hot tea and Chungking's version of un-iced lemon pop. Hot, humid, and sweaty, Chungking is no summer resort from April to October."[36] In this passage from "Transit" included in *Smolensk,* Caldwell writes of his negotiations in Chongqing for air passage west: "When we first applied for passage on Eurasia to Hami, we were told there were no seats available, but that reservations would be accepted pending the close of hostilities. We took a short ricksha ride and came back and said that it would be impossible for us to wait in Chungking for the war to end. That settled the matter for all concerned, and we were promised passage on the plane scheduled for the first week in May. We held out firmly for the plane scheduled for the last week in April."[37] He adds as a codicil: "After several days of false starts, caused by air raids, foggy weather, and motor trouble, we finally took off for Hami via

Chengtu and Suchow. Ordinarily it is a flight of about eleven hours; we arrived there exactly twelve days later" (*Smolensk* 5).

Caldwell, usually a very careful planner during his travels, was clearly at the mercy of others for whom all his celebrity and reputation had little meaning.

Bourke-White is at her best in the Chongqing section of *Shooting the Russian War*. She writes with a kind of honest yet embarrassing naïveté, quite distinct from Caldwell's ironic Twainian posture. In Chongqing the Soviet embassy sat atop the highest hill and was reached by a trudge up "446 steep steps," but, observes Bourke-White, "some of the luckier ones were riding in sedan chairs carried up the breathlessly steep streets by two human beings." Later she describes their own harrowing trip, during which "it seemed that our swinging sedan chairs might be pitched off our coolies' shoulders at any instant into the gorge below." After claiming their Russian visas, which were waiting at the embassy for them as Ambassador Oumansky had promised, they climbed into their sedan chairs for the trip back down the mountain, but the Russian consul observed, "None of us in the Soviet diplomatic service ever use sedan chairs, because we do not feel that it is right to exploit the back muscles of other men" (*SRW* 16). Bourke-White was chastened and followed suit at the next opportunity.

Next on her agenda was a trip to one of Song Meiling's many orphanages. More photographs were taken, and Bourke-White wrote a long newspaper piece about the people and children of war-torn Chongqing ("Children in Chungking Use Symbols of War in Learning How to Count"), which she dated April 21 and posted to the North American Newspaper Alliance, to which both she and Caldwell were then sending dispatches.

Then, just before they were scheduled to fly out, there was an air raid. With a nonironic touch of orientalism, Bourke-White describes the scene: "When the warning sounded, the great staircase suddenly overflowed with what looked like little black ants, so densely matted that it seemed as if an enormous black curtain were being pulled down the white steps to the river." For Bourke-White, except when it came to luminaries, China seemed dehumanized: "It is this constant moving on coolie back, moving things in river sampans and in hand cars, moving everything from a dismembered dynamo to the family teapot; it is this constant excavating, mending, and building that tells the story of China at war" (*SRW* 20). This sense of man as machine had long been one of the themes of her photographic oeuvre.

In her next chapter Bourke-White's gives a personal and feminine touch to the fiasco of the airplane trip into the USSR that included a forced ten-day layover in Lanzhou because of equipment problems the Chinese were experiencing

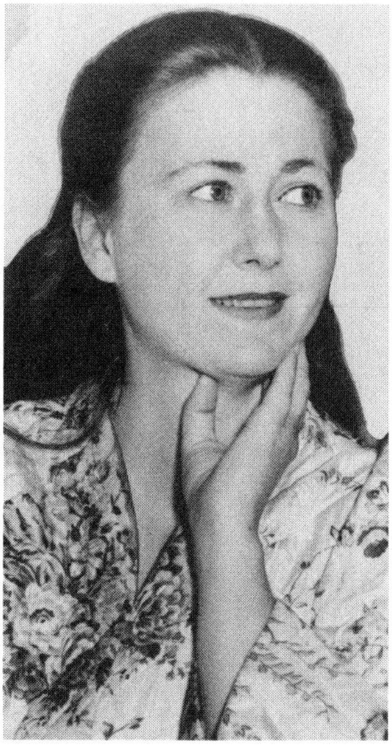

FIGURE 7. Alice-Leone Moats (1942) (*World Telegram* photo by Fred Palumbo, Library of Congress, www.loc.gov/pictures/item/00651659)

with their airplanes. She lingers over the details of sifting through a local bookstall in Lanzhou, buying intricate trinkets and hand-painted gourds, and Caldwell's attempt to teach the Chinese to play Chinese checkers while they are sequestered in a plane on the tarmac of Süchow, "just across the border of Inner Mongolia" (*SRW* 25). She is resigned to the rugged primitiveness of their living quarters and the general lack of sanitation but takes pleasure in telling of the efforts of their cook boy, Show King as she calls him, to please them. Rather than succumbing to boredom, she begins to learn some Russian. She even finds humor in the extended search of her camera equipment at customs in Alma-Ata, on the Russian border.

Neither Bourke-White nor Caldwell mentions the intrepid American socialite-cum-journalist carrying credentials from *Collier's* who joined them toward the end of their extended layover in Lanzhou. But Alice-Leone Moats was not at all reticent to describe *them*. In *Blind Date with Mars,* she writes a gadfly gossip columnist's recollection of her own seventeen-month round-the-world journey that included a harrowing traverse of the perverse Burma Road as well as several summer months spent in Moscow. In *Blind Date,* she takes pleasure in her self-portrayal as "an ordinary mortal just traveling about."[38] Typical of her often-patronizing journalistic style, she offers this observation of the Japanese not long after she arrives in Yokohama: "Of course it's illogical to loathe a race because it is ugly. The fact remains that I loathed the sight of their nasty little bowlegs, duck bottoms, and prominent teeth. I hated the sound of their polite hissing. Their slow-wittedness and lack of intuition angered me. They not only were incapable of learning a foreign language, but they also had no instinct for understanding what one was trying to say to them" (Moats 39). Moats's schadenfreude over the Caldwells' plight in Lanzhou is evident as she first encounters them when she disembarks from her own Chongqing flight:

> Margaret Bourke-White was standing on the field with her husband, Erskine Caldwell, entirely surrounded by two hundred and eighty kilos of luggage. I had met them casually in Chungking, where they had picked up their Soviet visa. There was a great difference between their experience and mine, for, as Oumansky had made all arrangements for them from Washington, they didn't have to wait at all. They were treated as very big shots indeed, got a ticket on the plane with no difficulty, and were allowed to carry all the excess baggage they liked. Trailing clouds of glory, and very pleased at being the first Americans to travel to Moscow over the air route, they left Chungking ten days ahead of me. At Lanchow their plane broke down and they spent what I gathered were nine very boring days there. (Moats 156)

Nonetheless, Moats's description of their crossing of China is certainly more thorough than either of the Caldwells' and possibly more reliable. She expresses a kind of ambiguous displeasure at the couple's haughtiness, while admiring their chutzpah. She introduces herself in *Blind Date* with this snarky, jealous, and backhanded dig at the Caldwells, and at Bourke-White in particular: "In Chungking I didn't become an intimate friend of the Generalissimo and Madame Chiang; in fact I never met them. In Russia I didn't interview Stalin" (Moats 4).

At their first overnight stop, in Süchow, accommodations were rudimentary, "an adobe resthouse," as Moats describes it.

> The Caldwells and I were shown into a room with four beds. I called the manager and explained that only two of us were married to each other and that we needed two rooms. The request astonished him. We were all three Americans; why shouldn't we want to share a room? Anyway, he didn't have another vacant. But after supper he came up and announced that there was one very small, dirty room available. Caldwell politely offered to take it, leaving the better one for Peggy and me. At that she cried, "Oh no! I want to sleep with you, Skinny darling!" Never one to come between a husband and wife, I reassured her with, "That's all right. You sleep with Skinny darling, and I will take the little room." (Moats 157)

Though neither Caldwell nor Bourke-White mentions their vain attempt to charter a plane privately during the four days they were marooned in Hami, that clearly seems to have been the case. They even got Moats to agree to go in on the cost. Moats shakes her head in wonder at the Caldwells' willingness to bargain over a $3,000 charter. But that plane never materialized.

Moats provides an unforgettable image of Caldwell and Bourke-White there: "Erskine set up his typewriter on a balcony and spent the afternoon composing telegrams to his Russian publisher and other important people in Moscow, asking them to use their influence to get us a private plane. As he finished each wire he handed it to Peggy, who would read it over with gasps of wonder. 'Splendid, Skinny darling, simply splendid!' she would exclaim. 'What a great writer you are!' The admiration she felt for her husband was quite awe-inspiring" (Moats 159). On the other hand, Moats does admire the Caldwells' harmony, even if it excluded her: "With few books to read, I had to depend principally on the servants for entertainment. Both the Caldwells were engrossed in work most of the day. Aside from that, they moved in an atmosphere of such connubial bliss that I didn't like to intrude" (Moats 160). She does confirm the Chinese checkers anecdote, however. Fashion reporting was a Moats forte, and she offers a startling and contrasting portrait of Bourke-White and herself in Hami:

> Wearing an out-at-the-elbows suit, a white shirtwaist, clodhopper brown shoes, and my hair skinned back in a knot, I'm sure that I was taken for Peggy's rather inferior lady's maid; particularly after she opened several of her twenty-odd bags and came forth wearing slacks—a symphony in almond green, from the antelope Dutch cap, placed far back on her iron-gray curls, to green and red shoes. (Moats 160)

The USSR

After days of delay and boredom, and after a refueling stop in Urumchi, the entourage ultimately reached Alma-Ata on the south-central border of the USSR on May 7. But now it was Caldwell who was attired like a peacock, presenting "a picture of such sartorial perfection that he took my breath away" (Moats 161). "He had on powder-blue gabardine trousers, very wide in the leg and with seams hemi-stitched in navy-blue thread; a blue-and-white striped shirt; a white tie; a jacket with huge navy and light blue checks, and navy suède platform-soled shoes cut out at the sides" (Moats 161–62). Moats recalls even Bourke-White, wearing merely "her great traveling suit and red topcoat" (Moats 161), as being impressed: "Skinny darling, I bet you're the best-dressed man who ever traveled on this route" (Moats 162).

After a night's stay in a "grand, but . . . grim and shabby" Alma-Ata hotel (Moats 167), they had enough clout to obtain tickets for the following day's Aeroflot flight to Moscow. The plane, Caldwell wrote, was "a USSR-made

Douglass DC3-type, complete with stewardess and all the accessories of U.S. airline travel,"[39] about whom Moats amplified: "[The stewardess] had food for sale and even produced some hot dishes cooked on an electric grill" (Moats 169). The DC-3 stopped briefly in Tashkent, four hundred miles to the west, where Caldwell described the central Asian spring as warm and pleasant (*Smolensk* 16), and Moats recalled its depiction in *Anna Karenina*. It seemed to her diminished in stature to just "a sprawling village" (Moats 169). But for Caldwell, Tashkent compared to western China seemed a Shangri-la: "The airfield restaurant was surrounded by a garden of roses in full bloom. Inside there were white ruffled curtains over the windows, embroidered pillows in the deep chairs, and piles of fresh strawberries on the table" (*Smolensk* 16).

During their final overnight stop, in Aktyubinsk a thousand miles to the northwest of Tashkent, Moats was again chagrined at how she was so readily identified as the Caldwells' maid or secretary. "I had been sure all along that my shabbiness compared to their splendor would give that impression. When I denied that [Alexander, a fellow traveler from Alma-Ata] asked, 'Are you a governess?'" (Moats 170). Taking off at 6 a.m. on May 10, they flew nonstop another thousand miles farther northwest to Moscow, arriving just after noon. "The plane flew low over the city, circling above The Kremlin and Red Square, and landed at a plane-filled airport beside the Dynamo Stadium" (*Smolensk* 16), but only after aborting the initial attempt when a small plane crossed the runway directly in its path. The DC-3 briefly recircled the city, skimmed over the rooftops, before finally touching down in front of a throng of flower-tossing well-wishers. But in fact, the cheering crowd, much to Moats's chagrin, was not for them but rather "was in honor of a famous Russian pilot who was just back from a flight to the Arctic" (Moats 172).

Indeed, even the American ambassador, Laurence Steinhardt, whom both Caldwell and Moats had cabled about their anticipated arrival that day, was too busy to meet them, instead sending one of his clerks on his official behalf. Moats quickly left with the embassy staffer en route for the Hotel Metropole, while the Caldwells, burdened by many hundreds of pounds of luggage—mostly the photographic equipment and supplies but now also a fair number of souvenirs from China—were taken to the swank Hotel National on Red Square, directly across from the Kremlin.

After about ten days in Moscow, Caldwell wrote his parents, bringing them up to date on their travels: "We came through China over a route few people have used. We saw every means of transportation in use, from coolie to camel, and I am afraid we would have been six months getting through China if we had used Chinese transportation." He complained of the cold in Moscow but tells them of the pleasures of Alma-Ata, where "it was warm and springlike. Everyone was eating strawberries and flowers were blooming everywhere." Caldwell and his father frequently corresponded about monetary matters, and so such a discussion in this letter—the first they had received directly from their son in a month and after at least one newspaper article published in their hometown paper reported the couple missing—would not have been unusual: "The rate of exchange is unfavorable for dollars, and if we did not have royalties in roubles [*sic*] we couldn't last very long. Three books have been published here already, and two more will be published this summer. That will pay most of our expenses for the three months, possible [*sic*] all of them."[40] He dispatched the letter via official U.S. diplomatic pouch.

That same day he typed a letter (misdating it April 19) to his secretary, Rhoda Lynn, on Hotel National stationery, advising her that he was sending her two copies of a seven-thousand-word "China letter."[41] In a subsequent June 3 note he tells her the piece was sent "about May 20th." Because *Life* had the right of first refusal, he wrote her, she should first submit it to Noel Busch, the magazine's associate editor, but if it needed to be shortened, "then call in Mr. [Julius] Weiss [Caldwell's attorney]." In any case, he does not want it cut more than a thousand words. Only if *Life* rejects it should she give it to his literary agent, Maxim Lieber. But he implores her in an intercalated handwritten line, "get it into print, Busch or Lieber, as soon as possible."[42] This apparently never happened, and today "Transit China" languishes in a folder in the Syracuse Special Collections Library.[43]

Barely installed in their room, Caldwell writes in *Smolensk*, he began trying to make arrangements to leave Moscow as soon as possible to travel south through Ukraine toward the Caucasus and the Black Sea. It took a few weeks, but with the invaluable assistance of the Union of Soviet Writers and VOKS (Society for Cultural Relations with Foreign Countries), with which both Caldwell and Bourke-White remained on cordial terms throughout their stay, unprecedented permission for their trip was granted, including authorization for Bourke-White to take pictures.

Bourke-White did not recall those prewar days with such halcyon nonchalance, and as is clear from her memoir, their first month was not as single-mindedly focused on travel as Caldwell implies in *Smolensk*. "During our early weeks in Moscow we had many visitors and we made many Russian friends. We were singularly fortunate in the kinds of contacts we had with the Russian people because it is not easy, as a rule, for foreigners to mix with Russians" (*SRW* 34–35). There is surely a great deal of Pollyanna in that Bourke-White recollection, but there *had been* ample opportunities for socializing. One evening

Sergei Eisenstein, the famed Russian filmmaker, invited them to his house for a private screening of the then-banned anti-German *Alexander Nevsky*. Bourke-White went to fashion shows, attended and photographed a Red Army soccer game at Dynamo Stadium, visited a downtown bar where she photographed (and recorded the recipe for) a remarkable Kowboy Koktail featuring a raw egg layered between differently colored liquors (see figures 12 and 13), bought discount chocolate at a grocery store reserved for the Moscow privileged, and relished the hospitality extended by the diplomatic community, extolling Mrs. Steinhardt's skill at the interior decorating of their country dacha, all the while noting the strained and complex social and political protocols among members of the Axis and Allied consular coteries.

On the other hand, though she never published her thoughts, she wrote in her Moscow notes that she was dismayed at her husband's withdrawal into his own world of writing while so much was going on around them. Much to her consternation, Caldwell spent what she considered to be an inordinate portion of his time in their hotel room writing. And he was busy. Before they left for the Black Sea he had completed and sent off to his agent several vignettes for his semi-autobiographical short-story cycle, *Georgia Boy*, which would be published after their return to the States, and he also worked on an ambitious project he had undertaken before the couple left the United States. He was the editor in chief for a series of books of regional lore to be published by Duell, Sloan and Pearce, titled the American Folkways Series, and his first job had been to recruit authors for the three-dozen volumes initially envisioned.

On June 5 U.S. ambassador Steinhardt, somewhat archly, wired the State Department in Washington: "The Soviet authorities have granted permission to Mr. and Mrs. Erskine Caldwell to visit Kiev, Odessa, Sochi, Yalta, Batum, Tiblis and Baku if they so desire as well as Rostov. All these are in areas which diplomats are forbidden to enter."[44] Such favoritism and celebrity both dogged and benefitted the Caldwells throughout their Russian summer, affording them unprecedented privileges and access to people and locations around Moscow at the cost of some professional jealousy and discontent on the part of the other, less-favored members of the Western press.

Five days later they were off for a twelve-day tour south of Moscow during which they were feted, dined, and lionized. But by then the Kremlin must have been aware of the dangers of war because the Baltic states, Ukraine, and the White Russian districts suddenly were placed off-limits to them and the Caldwells were required to drive directly toward the Caucasus, though they did get a reprieve that permitted them to head straight to Kharkov, Ukraine.

Accompanying them on this tour were two Russian guides, perhaps minders with responsibilities to one or another official surveillance agency. Caldwell refers to them only as "two interpreters," but Bourke-White names them: Elisaveta, the assistant to the editor of the foreign-literature department of the Writers' Union who spoke "almost perfect English," was their secretary-interpreter, and Eugene Petrov their driver (*SRW* 35).[45]

But Petrov was much more than that. Four days younger than Caldwell, he was the editor of the photojournal *Ogonyok* and the satirical magazine *Krokodil* and was on the editorial board of the important literary newspaper *Literaturnaya Gazeta*, the official organ of the Soviet Writers' Union, founded by Pushkin in 1830. He was an admirer of Caldwell's but was renowned in the USSR in his own right. He and Ilya Ilf, a fellow reporter, had written a pair of well-received satiric novels, *The Twelve Chairs* (1928) and *The Little Golden Calf* (1931), creating a much-enjoyed conman character, Ostap Bender.[46] In 1935 he and Ilf had visited the United States to travel the country, photograph it, and write about it. Bourke-White had met him when the pair passed through New York. The result, *Little Golden America*, a publication of the same photo-text genre as *Say, is this the U.S.A.*, was hugely popular in the Soviet Union.

Petrov was in the ideal position to afford them "access to a Soviet Union rarely seen and even more rarely reported and photographed by foreigners at that critical time in the USSR's history."[47] Once the Soviet Union moved to a full war footing, Petrov was assigned as a war correspondent to various military newspapers, providing him the access to the front lines Caldwell and Bourke-White so desperately hoped for. Later the Kremlin appointed him to be the official Soviet reporter to the North American Newspaper Alliance (NANA), the news agency to which Caldwell also contributed. He remained close friends with Bourke-White and Caldwell throughout the summer, often including them within his own social and professional circles. On July 2, 1942, he died in a plane crash on his way back from a war assignment in Sebastopol.

Caldwell barely mentions the outbound portion of this Black Sea trip in *All-Out on the Road to Smolensk;* in fact, he disposes of it in a mere dozen words. He picks up the story when he learns of the Nazi invasion. Caldwell gives the impression that the Russian people, though thoroughly surprised by the suddenness of the war, were nonetheless, without reservation, completely ready to pitch in. He admits that at least part of the popular optimism stemmed from the Kremlin's complete control of the news. He writes, "By the close of the third day the country had put itself on a full and complete war footing, both military and civil" (*Smolensk* 21). While the "foreign population of Moscow was aggressively pessimistic during those first weeks of war," nonetheless the "native population was strikingly optimistic" (*Smolensk* 23). For someone wholly unfamiliar with the Russian language, such conclusions had to have been based on his interpreters' translations. But now that the country was on a war footing, the gravitas of Caldwell's tale grew. "Military traffic filled every semaphore block of the railway, and yet civilian passenger trains were able to maintain a fairly rapid rate of speed. We reached Moscow only one day later than scheduled" (*Smolensk* 22).

To know anything of this sojourn, one has to turn to Bourke-White's memoir because Caldwell doesn't describe it. Once on the road, they were honored at collective farms, banqueted by local writers' groups, and featured in newspapers. Caldwell's only comment on these indulgent occasions is a typical and cryptically wry but revealing one made later in the context of a description of Russian eating patterns: "I was the unhappy guest at a dinner that began at nine-thirty in the evening and lasted at the rate of a course an hour until exactly five-fifteen the following morning. This was an extraordinary experience, because prior to that occasion four hours flat was the longest stretch I had spent at a dinner table in the USSR" (*Smolensk* 78). Bourke-White, always looking for a personal touch, takes pleasure in describing the Russians' sympathetic reaction to Caldwell's broken toe, suffered in a postvodka bedroom accident, even placing him in a wheelchair at one point.

Once the war begins, civilian train tickets are at a premium, but capitalizing on his own as well as the Caldwells' celebrity and privileged status as visiting Americans, Petrov readily secures return tickets to Moscow for all four of them. After noting endearingly the poignancy with which Russians listened to a translated speech of Churchill pledging British support against the Germans, Bourke-White observes how quickly and efficiently war news spread by word of mouth: "And at last, when we were within a few hours of Moscow, we saw our first newspaper. We still had not been able to buy one, but soldiers in a troop train moving in the opposite direction on the next track passed their paper through the window of our train. The newspaper traveled through our entire train, where it was read aloud in every car" (*SRW* 54).

Returning to Moscow on Friday, June 27, "in a pouring rain," they discover the National has reassigned them "the vast corner suite that had been occupied, during the time of the nonaggression pact, by the leading German trade representative in Moscow," one which smacked of "czarist magnificence" and had been occupied in the past by Leon Trotsky and Charles Lindbergh (*SRW* 55). For Caldwell, strangely, the upscale National was "old, run-down, and second-rate" (*Smolensk* 82).

Chronology of the Caldwells' Celebrity Progress (February–May 1941)

FEBRUARY	
21	Hicks cables approval of Bourke-White travel
MARCH	
5	Passports sent by State Department
14	New York → Chicago (by air)
15	Chicago → Reno (by air)
15–18	Riverside Hotel (Reno)
19	Reno → Los Angeles (by air)
19–21	Hollywood Knickerbocker Hotel (LA)
21	S.S. *Lurline* (→ Honolulu via San Francisco)
26	Arrival in Honolulu (Royal Hawaiian Hotel)
APRIL	
1	Day trip to Hilo (by air)
3	Honolulu → Midway (by Pan American clipper)
4	Midway → Wake Island (by Pan American clipper)
6	Wake Island (extra day, weather) → Guam (by Pan American clipper)
7	Guam → Manila (by Pan American clipper)
8	Manila (Manila Hotel)
9	Manila → Hong Kong (by Pan American clipper)
9–14	Hong Kong (Hotel Gloucester)
14	Hong Kong → Kowloon (by ferry) (Hotel Peninsula)
15	Hong Kong → Chongqing (by China Northern Air)
15–22	Chongqing (Chialing House)
22	Chongqing → Lanzhou (via Chengdu)
30	Alice Leone Moats arrives from Chengdu
MAY	
1	Lanzhou → Süchow
3	Flight to Hami aborted due to weather
4	Süchow → Hami
7	Hami → Alma-Ata (via Urumchi)
9	Alma-Ata → Aktyubinsk (via Tashkent) (by Aeroflot)
10	Aktyubinsk → Moscow (by Aeroflot)

FIGURE 8. Chronology from New York to Moscow, 1941

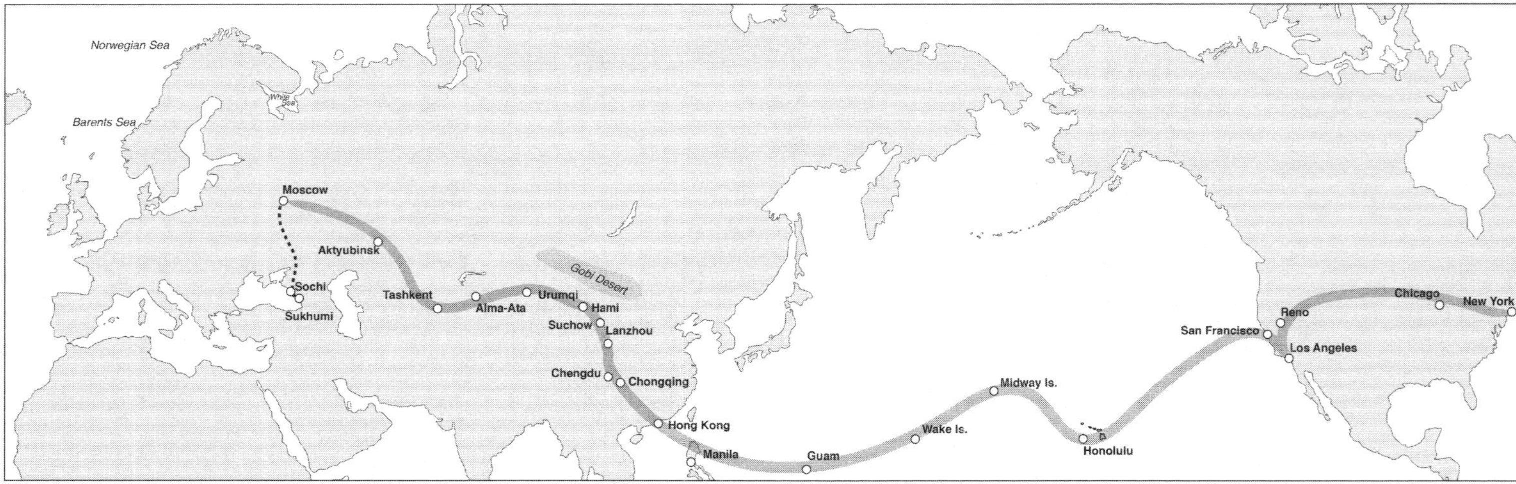

FIGURE 9. The outbound trip (Map by Charles Lindemuth, www.mepainter.com)

Within hours Caldwell was fielding telegrams from U.S. newspapers requesting on-the-scene reports from Moscow. His first radio transmissions would begin after the weekend. Whatever May funk Bourke-White might once have perceived in Caldwell had lifted, and for the next ten weeks both of them worked literally almost around-the-clock to convince Americans that the Russian war effort would be successful and that the Russian people were worthy of support. Their task was complicated by Soviet censorship and news manipulation, methods of control the Kremlin used to manage the war narrative originating from the Soviet Union. The heavy-handed restrictions placed on the media hamstrung all the Moscow correspondents over the summer and kept them well away from the war fronts to the west. Nonetheless, Caldwell and Bourke-White went about reporting what news they could despite these restrictions, and over time, they were able to bolster the Roosevelt administration's, the Popular Front's, and *Time*'s anti-isolationist, pro-internationalist positions.

CHAPTER 3

Margaret Bourke-White ★ Moscow, 1941

When Margaret Bourke-White stepped off a Russian-built DC-3 in Moscow one May afternoon in 1941 with her husband, Erskine Caldwell, she was on an assignment with a complex set of goals and rationales. She did not disembark merely as Caldwell's wife. She was Margaret Bourke-White, the famed American photographer, well furnished with friends and contacts within the Soviet Union. She had courted and developed them a decade earlier when she had photographed, with the encouragement of her employer, Henry Luce's *Fortune* magazine, the accomplishments of Stalin's first Five-Year Plan. In 1941 she was also a social advocate and supporter of the leftist Popular Front. Since 1936 Bourke-White had been working enthusiastically with her husband on a series of photo-text books documenting socioeconomic problems in the United States, particularly in the Deep South. She had become an active advocate for reform through the platform of her social realist photography.

Since her marriage to Caldwell in February 1939, she had also become a news photographer. In October 1939 *Life* had dispatched her on a five-month assignment that sent her to England, central and southern Europe, and the Middle East. Tired of the grind and distressed by a series of professional and personal issues, she resigned from *Life* in March for a higher-paying job at New York's *PM* newspaper, which was to debut in mid-June. She quickly realized that the exposure her photography received via *Life*'s multimillion circulation was far more satisfying to her than the money at *PM*, whose circulation was at best 1 percent of *Life*'s. By October she had resigned and returned to the Luce publishing empire. One of her first assignments was a cross-country tour with her husband to document America's post-Depression recovery. The trip lasted into early 1941, but *Life* declined to use any of her work, and so together the couple put together *Say, is this the U.S.A.*, which was published, with modest reception, after they departed for the Soviet Union. By 1941 Bourke-White had secured remarkable influence and importance in a man's profession, which hadn't been achieved through happenstance or luck, nor easily or quickly.

Bourke-White, Modernist Photographer

As a girl Bourke-White had idolized her father, but despite his enthusiasm for photography and his tinkering with and inventing optical devices, her interest in the field did not begin until after his death in 1922. In her autobiography she recalled, "It is odd that photography was never one of my childhood hobbies when Father was so fond of it. I hardly touched a camera and certainly never operated one until after he died."[1] In the spring of 1922, however, as a freshman at Columbia, she enrolled in a two-hours-per-week photography class taught by Clarence H. White. Her mother bought her a used 3¼" x 4¼" Ica Reflex camera to use in the class. It had a cracked lens (*Portrait* 29).[2]

Professor White was famous. He had been one of the original members of the Photo-Secession group established by Alfred Stieglitz in 1902 that promoted a new style of photography known as pictorialism. Pictorialism sought to have photographs acquire some of the properties of painting in order to better express the imaginative vision of the photographer, as opposed to "straight" photography, which emphasized realism and minimal artifice. Bourke-White had enrolled in White's class not to learn to take pictures but to study "design and composition,"[3] and so predictably her earliest photos were pictorialist. Aiming her camera mostly at buildings on the Cornell campus, where she earned her bachelor's degree in 1927, she created commercially marketable, gauzy, romantically soft-focused images shot from unusual angles that emphasized the aesthetic.

By the late 1920s and early 1930s Bourke-White found herself among the photographic avant-garde. She made acquaintance with many pioneers and remained in contact with them throughout her life. Modernism in the arts, though difficult to define because it burst into many fields and scattered in various directions, was born of an urgency emerging in the late nineteenth century to represent the world in new ways. The tectonic cultural shifts that followed World War I permanently altered the landscape of the arts, including photography.

Nascent modernism was strongly aligned with the rapidly evolving age of the machine. Robert Hughes suggests that one of the earliest important works of modernism was the tower built by Gustave Eiffel for the Paris Exposition of 1889.[4] Not only did it provide evidence of the capacity of man and his machines to overcome verticality, but it offered a fresh view of the earth. Early works of such modernists as Fernand Léger, Robert Delaunay, Francis Picabia, Pablo Picasso, and Marcel Duchamp often represent people as animated constructions of machine parts, and many even feature images of the Eiffel Tower. Bourke-White similarly shifted her style from pictorialist romanticism to the industrial aesthetic of the machine.

Because technical problems dealing with optics and chemistry took some time to work through, photography's participation in the modernist movement was delayed a decade or so, but again Stieglitz was in the vanguard. In November 1905 he opened the 291 Gallery in New York to promote the work of his fellow Photo-Secessionists, but within a half-dozen years 291 became the recognized epicenter of the avant-garde arts movement in the United States. There Stieglitz hung exhibitions of works by Matisse, Rodin, Toulouse-Lautrec, Braque, Marin, O'Keeffe, Picasso, and even some of the early practitioners of the machine aesthetic.

Within the world of photography, however, Stieglitz dramatically shifted his position in 1916, when he hosted a showing of the work of Paul Strand. Strand's carefully constructed black-and-white photographs, many of which were of architectural and industrial structures, were almost cubist in their style and, with their strong visual contrasts and disorienting vantage points, were of the "straight" variety Stieglitz earlier had abhorred. Their success arose not from manipulation of the print or fuzzing the lens but from their dramatic composition. At the same time Italian modernist painter Giorgio de Chirico was displaying architectural townscapes featuring soaring buildings and tiny, shrunken, faraway human figures to provide scale.[5] As a result of these innovations and models, photography would never be the same, and Bourke-White eventually was a beneficiary.

European and Russian photographers were at the forefront of the burgeoning industrial aesthetic that officially made American landfall at the May 1927 Machine-Age Exposition in New York. Bourke-White was living in Cleveland at the time, and through native Clevelander Ralph Steiner, an early documentary photographer and avant-garde filmmaker who had also studied with White, she was introduced to this flourishing global arts movement.[6] In 1930, when Soviet authorities realized the propaganda value of showcasing in the United States the dams, foundries, and other large industrial projects of the first Five-Year Plan, they recruited Bourke-White for the assignment. Based on her work published in *Fortune* magazine, they saw her as a perfect fit for the Soviet-inspired monumentalist arm of modernism in vogue at the time there.

Bourke-White and the Legitimacy of the Photographic Image

Photography is a form of discourse not dissimilar to writing. It had emerged over the previous half-century with a uniquely symbolic language that Bourke-White would master through years of interaction with the modernist movement. But photography has distinctive requirements, one of the most obvious of which is its requirement for direct access to its subject matter. A writer can fantasize and fictionalize, while a photographer can only record. This is not to say that the photographer is merely the passive operator of a machine, as she must compose, dictate, and select the subject, the timing, and the *mise-en-scène* of the photograph.

Photography fundamentally is the art of capturing shifting and manipulable patterns of light reflected from or emitted by an object. Whether it is art or machine-generated imagery was once a contentious controversy. Critic André Bazin, writing in 1945, makes the point that with the invention and maturation of photography, painting was freed from the need to attempt mimesis and could focus on aesthetics. Photography, on the other hand, was grounded otherwise: "For the first time, between the originating object and its reproduction there intervenes only the instrumentality of a nonliving agent. For the first time an image of the world is formed automatically, without the creative intervention of man."[7]

This is, however, not to say that the photographer is a mere automaton, or is less creative and relevant than the painter to her product. A painter achieves art through a kind of fiction; the result is that we can "admire the painting as the thing in itself whose relation to something in nature has ceased to be the justification for its existence."[8] The photographer is necessarily working in the service of nonfiction: "In spite of any objections our critical spirit may offer, we are forced to accept as real the existence of the object reproduced, actually re-presented, set before us, that is to say, in time and space. Photography enjoys a certain advantage in virtue of this transference of reality from the thing to its reproduction."[9] But this transference of reality always demands a photographer's access to a subject. The resulting print's relation to something in nature remains the justification for its existence and cannot be separated wholly from this object. As Bourke-White's career flourished and her fame grew, access to people, places, and events became easier for her to achieve. *Fortune* and *Life* could provide her all the necessary credentials, underwrite her expenses, and provide a ready platform for publication of her products, but her creative skill and her many-faceted personality were in the end the indispensable elements that brought her success.

Bazin's argument for the necessary credibility, the fact-based reality of photography, proscribes a photographer's free pass to manipulate an image without ethical consequence. This point has been argued for decades, almost since the advent of photography itself. What appears (or does not appear) in a painting, and the context it imparts to it, is clearly the choice of the painter. It does not necessarily detract from the honesty of the result since that result is mostly artifice; the viewer of a painting assumes that wrinkles and moles have been removed from the queen's face, that frayed and soiled tatters in her raiment have been omitted. But a photographer alters these at her own peril. This matter haunted Bourke-White throughout her career, and as time went on and critical attitudes shifted, the latitude of manipulation permitted a photographer shrank to the detriment of a reputation. Bourke-White was a master of presentation and manipulation. Her forte was the oxymoronic posed-yet-candid photograph.

Bourke-White, Commercial Photographer

Although Bourke-White had already successfully navigated the same paradigm shift Stieglitz had a decade earlier, she never forgot White's lesson that "any picture that was important enough to make was one that the photographer should work on until he had made it as perfect as he could possibly make it."[10] Bourke-White rarely cropped her photos. At *Life* she insisted that her negatives be printed to the edge, just as she had composed them in the viewfinder. Such perfectionism made Bourke-White a spectacularly successful photographer, both artistically and financially, almost as soon as she shifted her attention to her photographic work full time.

Following her first successful freelance work for Cleveland's Otis Steel Co. in early 1928, she began landing commissions for industrial, architectural, and commercial advertising work. In May 1929 Henry Luce, having seen great promise in some of this early work, hired her to be chief photographer at *Fortune* magazine, the first issue of which was published in February 1930. But Bourke-White, still courting lucrative commercial work, would agree only to a half-time contract. Between 1930 and 1933 she maintained a private studio on the sixty-first floor of the new Chrysler Building, ten floors above the Time-Fortune offices on the fiftieth to fifty-second floors.[11] In keeping with her modernist tastes she decorated her office in glass, wood, and aluminum; one of the famous stainless steel art-deco gargoyles was right outside her window.[12] She employed a staff of eight and for a time kept a pair of pet alligators on the terrace, while turtles roamed the studio freely.[13]

Within four years of college graduation, Bourke-White was earning, according to *Time* magazine in December 1931, $50,000 annually, equivalent to over $750,000 in current dollars. In 1933 she added color photography to her commercial repertoire and two years later began doing aerial photography, a daredevil enterprise that garnered her even more notoriety. The United Press named her to its 1936 list of the ten most notable women in the United States. Her biographer Vickie Goldberg noted, "Fame was an integral aspect of Margaret's career and her self-promotion an integral part of her character."[14] Goldberg adds that Bourke-White began fashioning her own legend when she was in Cleveland and continued to augment it throughout her professional life. She was a woman working in a historically man's world, so that both toughness and a tough hide were invaluable. Alfred Eisenstaedt, the German-born photographer who began his thirty-six-year career at *Life* in 1936, recalled in an interview many years later, "[N]obody liked her. She knew only a few people. She did not bother to talk to people very much, very aloof, knew only a few photographers. She overlooked other people."[15] Goldberg paints a picture compatible with Eisenstaedt's: "No other photographer had an office, or a darkroom, or a printer. For years, the *Life* ace photographers all shared a kind of bull pen, a large open area crammed with desks, directly outside Margaret's small but private office. That office was furnished with her specially designed desk and couch, her tropical fish, and the woman who was thought of as the queen bee herself."[16] Such notoriety, and of course her own forceful personality, contributed to her successfully arranging a photo collaboration with Caldwell, who at the time was looking for a photographer with exactly her clout and chutzpah.

Bourke-White, Social Reform Photographer

Yet it was *You Have Seen Their Faces*, a book designed to bring to the light of day a sordid socioeconomic tragedy long in the shadows of the public consciousness, that fueled the criticism Bourke-White would endure for decades. In 1935 the *New York Post* commissioned a series of nonfiction articles by Caldwell to address the Depression-exacerbated southern agricultural implosion. His pieces appeared as a four-part series between February 18 and 21 ("Georgia Poverty-Swept, Says Caldwell," "Landowners Find Help Gives Them Edge on Laborers: Negroes Chief Victims of Account Juggling," "Georgia Land Barons Oust Dying Girl and Her Father," "Starving Babies Suckled by Dog in Georgia Cabin"). The last of the four is a remarkably descriptive exposé of the heartbreaking squalor he had found. Reading it is difficult:

> IMAGINE THIS SCENE
> In the other room of the house without chairs, beds, or tables, a woman lay rolled up in some quilts trying to sleep. On the floor before an open fire lay two babies neither a year old, sucking the dry teats of a mongrel bitch. A young girl, somewhere between fifteen and twenty, squatted on the corner of the hearth trying to keep warm.

The articles suffered from a lack of photographic support. Imagine is all that one could do, but Caldwell's descriptions are so graphic that one's imagination need not work very hard. Nonetheless, it was just Caldwell's word, and in 1935 many vocal southerners considered that word suspect, inasmuch as he was now a New Englander.

In April the *Post* ran a second four-part series ("Caldwell Declares AAA [Agricultural Adjustment Administration] Ruins Thousands in South," "Landlords Chiseling South's Poor on FERA [Federal Emergency Relief Administration]," "Negroes Who Ask Pay Beaten in Alabama," "Georgia Tenants, Ousted by Landlords, Eat Dirt as Change From Bread and 'Lasses"), noting that the initial "revelations . . . met with wide hostility throughout the South." The *Post*'s editor explained, "Following this criticism, Mr. Caldwell went back, this time accompanied by his father, the Rev. I. S. Caldwell, of Wrens, Ga., to make a more complete investigation, not only in Georgia but also in Alabama and Mississippi. The photographs which accompany the series were taken personally by Mr. Caldwell and are the subjects and scenes of his story." But Caldwell's own photographs did not deliver his message as well as his impassioned prose.

Running alongside the April 19 article, under the headline "Share-Crop Life a Bed of Roses, Senator Holds," the *Post* published South Carolina senator Ellison D. Smith's rebuttal to Caldwell's articles. The *Post*'s correspondent, Charles Malcolmson, reported that Smith, identified as a "plantation owner," "insisted that only Southerners can be trusted to report such conditions as they truly exist." Caldwell, a southerner by birth and conscience, was irritated by this criticism, and so he set about finding a photographer who could capture the truths of his writing.

From Caldwell's point of view, having Margaret Bourke-White document his descriptions of the plight of the southern tenant farmer could make his case airtight. And it initially seemed to. They traveled in the South in July and August 1936, made a second shorter trip the following March, and then worked feverously through the spring to select the pictures and finalize the captions that would accompany them. In November 1937 *You Have Seen Their Faces* appeared in print to mostly rave reviews, with dissenting ones appearing mostly in newspapers of the Old South or written by critics originally from there. The book was successful, critically and commercially, and it also generated a groundswell of public concern for the impoverished in the benighted agrarian backwoods of the South.[17] Such calls for reform had been Caldwell's and Bourke-White's goal from the outset; sections of Caldwell's text were given over to specific recommendations for public and government interventions.

You Have Seen Their Faces seems to have been the perfect book for its time and served as a loose model for all their future collaborations, including the one they anticipated writing upon returning from their 1941 Russia assignment. Bourke-White's *Faces* photography received positive reviews, and most critics approved of Caldwell's essays. Furthermore, text was not necessary for one to grasp its meaning, with the result that it lost little impact in its foreign editions. *Faces* was also commensurate with the period's general concept of what documentary photography should be and do: it should move its viewers, be a call to action, and be, in short, beautiful propaganda—Bourke-White's specialty. It was not until a quarter-century later that critical judgment of *You Have Seen Their Faces* shifted 180 degrees to Bourke-White's and Caldwell's disfavor.

Beaumont Newhall of the Museum of Modern Art, one of Bourke-White's contemporaries, was an influential proponent of this social construct for documentary photography. In 1935 MoMA hired Newhall, a student of art history at Harvard, as its librarian, and later promoted him to be director of its Photography Department. Noting in a 1938 essay in *Parnassus* that the root meaning of "documentary" is the Latin *docere* (to teach), Newhall insisted that one of the goals of documentary photography is to serve as "sociological propaganda." Nonetheless, "It is undeniable that the documentary method, as opposed to the abstract desire to produce Fine Art, has resulted in significant photographic art."[18] Contending that a documentary photograph "is an approach rather than an end," he disputed the formalist critique of photography wherein only the elements within the print itself are to be considered: "The documentary photographer is not a mere technician. Nor is he an artist for art's sake. His results are often brilliant technically and highly artistic, but primarily they are pictorial reports. First and foremost he is a visualizer. He puts into pictures what he knows about, and what he thinks of, the subject before his camera."[19] For much of the first half of the twentieth century, documentary photography in fact had generally been message driven. Just as Upton Sinclair's *The Jungle* (1906) had brought about important changes in the meatpacking industry, so too Jacob Riis's photographic study of the poor in New York City, *How the Other Half Lives* (1890), and Lewis Hine's documentation of immigrant and child labor abuses (1904–13) had brought about significant social reforms.

Moreover, Newhall believed, photographs in the age of mechanical reproduction must be evaluated within their own print milieu, because the photographer often is disarticulated from the print's final display: "The prints for publication are chosen by a second person, are captioned by a third, are laid out by a fourth."[20] In *Faces*, Bourke-White retained complete control over all these decision points, even insisting on high-quality paper for the book. But when *Life* later ran a feature on the book, she had no input over which photographs were used, how they were laid out, or what editorial text accompanied them.

Caldwell's and Bourke-White's messaging did finally land them in hot water. They frequently lent support to a variety of leftist journalistic enterprises—their names on the masthead, articles, money—facts the FBI would add to the dossiers it was constructing on them as evidence of their potential danger to the United States. Indeed, just after their departure for the USSR, the FBI added their names to its Custodial Retention List, first Bourke-White,[21] then Caldwell.[22]

Bourke-White, *Life*, and the 1941 Russian Venture

On June 27, back in Moscow from the sojourn to the Black Sea, Bourke-White was ready to go to work, her real work. Combining her artistic skills as commercial, social, and news photographer, she was once more in the business of promotion. This time her goal was to promote a wartime alliance with the Soviet Union. But by Kremlin *diktat*, all photography had been embargoed: "anyone caught with a camera should be shot on sight," she recalled in her memoir.[23] Not atypically, she took matters into her own hands by calling on and telephoning officials in the Commissariat of Foreign Affairs, writing letters in English and Russian to a variety of people of influence, always emphasizing the point that since the Russians were at war with the Nazis, they would benefit from favorable press, including photographs, in the United States and the West. On July 15 the Soviet Press Office reinstated her permit.

Although small handheld cameras were just coming on the market, Bourke-White was not an early adopter of them, preferring instead the equipment she had grown up with. In *Shooting the Russian War*,[24] she provides a careful inventory of her gear for the trip, which included five cameras:

- 3¼" x 4¼" Speed Graphic with five lenses from 9 cm. to 30 cm.
- 3¼" x 4¼" Linhof View Camera with multiple lenses, including wide angle and telephoto, and two tripods
- 3¼" x 4¼" Linhof (spare)
- 2¼" x 3¼" Plaubel-Makina with three lenses, 7.3 cm. to 19 cm.
- 3¼" x 4¼" Soho reflex camera (damaged in the rain during trip to the front)

She shot exclusively on Eastman Super-XX Panchromatic film that fit her large-format cameras. During the seven-month trip, she developed all her own negatives in the bathtub of her and Caldwell's suite in the Hotel National but did no printing, except for the portraits of Stalin taken at the end of July.

Over the course of the summer, Bourke-White made and developed hundreds of exposures. Ultimately, about three hundred of these were published. Bourke-White's personal memoir of their summer, *Shooting the Russian War*, contains 93 photos; the book she published in England with Caldwell, *Russia at War*, another 79. But neither of these books reached the public until the United States had already been at war for over half a year, and even then they sold modestly. Thus, their suasive impact on public opinion, other than as examples of the photographic documentary aesthetic, was minimal. Of far greater significance for Bourke-White's promotional project were the 121 pictures published in *Life* between August 11 and December 1, 1941.

In 1940 *Life* had a paid circulation of 2.86 million, but it had a high "pass-along rate" (Vials 74),[25] which meant than in 1938 *Life* could reasonably claim a *readership* of a staggering 17.3 million (Elson 1:343).[26] In fact, *Life* was the uncontested primary source for visual information in the United States.[27] By its own 1940 audit ("Bigger'n We Thought!"), *Life* claimed to reach a quarter to a third of the available upper-middle- and middle-class reading audience and 41 percent of what it labeled the prestigious "A" group, comprising those who "lived in a 'substantial house' and didn't 'have to pick and choose between the luxuries common to his community.'"[28] On the other hand, James L. Baughman notes that these circulation figures, while valid, overstate *Life*'s impact because many of these "readers" were actually "thumbers" who browsed the magazine not for its serious content but for the fluff and scandal in its pictures.[29] Be that as it may, Bourke-White's contribution to *Life* was exactly that: the photography.

The abiding principle of the magazine was the advancement of American interests through consumerism, which was in keeping with Henry Luce's unique brand of internationalism that sought to merge the foreign policies of conservative isolationism and leftist internationalism into a kind of conservative internationalism.[30] *Life* achieved this worldview through the construction and presentation of a lifestyle of consumption that it promoted through expansive illustrated advertisements. The journals of Time, Inc. were pro-American, pro-consumer, pro-interventionist, but by no means overtly leftist, despite their many left-leaning contributors. Luce's extolling of the values of international corporate progress and stability on the pages of *Fortune* was in concert with the photographic capitalism of the 1930s, "the selling of business goods or ideas through the persuasive medium of the photographic print,"[31] of which Bourke-White was an exemplar. As a result she had been an obvious choice as an early hire for Luce. Not only was she steeped in the modernist approach to photography, so that she might immediately infuse *Fortune* with a sense of the artistic and the aesthetic, but she also was a proven adept at understanding the qualities necessary for successful commercial advertising projects. That she insisted on a part-time contract, which allowed her to maintain her skills at product promotion, was something Luce could appreciate and accept without hesitation.

In 1941 the "product" Luce was selling was cooperation among the Allies—and admission of the Soviet Union to the group. For several years Bourke-White and Caldwell, though both insisting that they had few political interests, had been supportive of left-leaning organizations within the world of the arts. They contributed their names, their products, and their encouragement. Goldberg writes of Bourke-White that, although she was a subscriber to the *Daily Worker* and provided photomurals for the Soviet consulate in Washington, "[s]he had a conscience but not an ideology, a moral position but insufficient angst or political fervor to be a party member."[32] The same could reasonably be said of Caldwell.

Thus, Bourke-White's arrival in Moscow readily can be seen as the beginning of another promotional project. In 1930, just twenty-six and captivated by what photography could contribute to the machine aesthetic, she had traveled to the USSR to record on film the massive construction projects financed during the first Five-Year Plan. Without realizing it, she was selling the Soviet Union to the American public as a nation worthy of the status that official diplomatic recognition by the United States would bring. Her images, published in *Fortune* and the *New York Times Sunday Magazine*, reached an influential audience. In 1936–37 she and Caldwell promoted social reform in America in *You Have Seen Their Faces*. In 1941 they had come to validate the Soviet Union for the American public once again, this time as a potentially worthy ally, should hostilities erupt. Serendipitously for Bourke-White, Caldwell, and *Life*, they soon did.

After she received official clearance from the Kremlin in mid-July for her photography, Bourke-White immediately set about her work. Before then she had helped Caldwell with his late-night CBS shortwave broadcasts from the Moscow Radio Center, occasionally taking over the microphone herself. But *Life* was getting increasingly anxious about the delay in receiving her earlier material. It was not clear to the editors in New York when or how she had shipped all her prewar film. On July 12 Wilson Hicks, *Life*'s photo editor, urgently cabled Bourke-White at the American embassy about this. She must have replied promptly because four days later Hicks cabled her again with a mixture of pleasure and displeasure. He was pleased to learn that her pictures had been dispatched and that she was attempting to get to the front, but was very unhappy with her radio sideline:

> WE SERIOUSLY QUESTION ADVISABILITY YOUR RADIO WORK WHILE IN MOSCOW AT LIFES EXPENSE. MORE IMPORTANT STILL I FEAR BROADCASTING INTERFERES WITH PICTURE WORK AND URGENTLY RECOMMEND ITS DISCONTINUANCE. WHILE RADIO NOT COVERED IN CONTRACT OUR UNDERSTANDING WAS YOUR FIRST INTEREST WOULD BE IN GREAT PICTURE SCOOP.[33]

In short, *Life* was reminding her that she was its full-time employee and so should abstain from any freelancing. The pressure for a "frontward trip" would become a continual drumbeat during their stay, not to be finally realized until a few weeks before they departed. In any case, Bourke-White had sent her film with E. Alan Lightner Jr., the U.S. consul who had been transferred from Riga to Moscow after Latvia was overrun by the Wehrmacht in June and was then on his way back to Washington.

A few days later, Caldwell cabled *his* contact at *Life*, Senior Editor Noel Busch, first to confirm an upcoming interview with Ambassador Steinhardt, but then, recognizing the importance of Bourke-White's missing film, to offer some suggestions about how to track it down. The sense of frustration continued as cables crossed and direct communication was impossible.

In the meantime Roosevelt's emissary, Harry Hopkins, had arrived in Moscow for meetings pertaining to Lend-Lease matters and had gotten Stalin to agree to a historic photo session with Bourke-White. She had printed several of those pictures, a selection of which had been wired to New York, because the next day, August 1, she heard from John Billings, *Life*'s managing editor:

> LIFE RUNS STALIN HOPKINS PICTURES AS LEAD THIS WEEK. ALSO YOUR REPORT AS SIGNED TEXT PIECE. YOU ARE MAKING REPUTATION BY FINE MOSCOW WORK. KEEP IT UP. ALL CONGRATULATIONS AND BEST REGARDS

Two days later Hicks let her know that calmer heads had prevailed and that *Life* would wait for the actual negatives, and that Lightner's missing film had been delivered finally. This photo spread would be Bourke-White's first presence in the magazine since June 23, when four of her photos from their trip through Chungking in April accompanied an article about relief efforts in the United States on behalf of China. A week later, the June 30 cover photo was her portrait of Madame Chiang Kai-shek.[34] The Stalin photos did not run until September 8.

But then, just as everything seemed to be settling comfortably into place, Bourke-White heard from Walter Graebner, *Life*'s London representative, on

August 8 that a new set of photos had arrived. He deplored that her handwriting was like "hieroglyphics," causing a delay in their transmission to New York. After an exchange of cables with Edward Thompson, *Life*'s assistant picture editor in New York, she heard again from Graebner, miffed that she had apparently blamed his London office for the delay.

Bourke-White, never one to allow herself to be pushed around, wired Graebner back the same day:

> FACTS ARE MATERIAL ARRIVED LONDON JULY 27 IF YOU DIDNT RECEIVE PROMPTLY FAULT LIES OTHER QUARTERS MY ONLY AIM WAS GET MATERIAL INTO YOUR HANDS QUICKLY POSSIBLE AND RECEIVE AKNOWLEDGMENT. AFTER NO RESPONSE 3 CABLES TO YOU FEARED MATERIAL LOST . . . SORRY YOU HAD SO MUCH TROUBLE REGARDS

Fortunately for *Life* their relationship improved, and London became the point of transfer for her film for the rest of the summer.

Bourke-White's 1941 Soviet Photographic Oeuvre

The first 32 of Bourke-White's 121 *Life* photographs appeared in the August 11 number. Two weeks earlier, on July 28, *Life* had published a full-page dispatch from Caldwell ("Behind Russian Lines") that had not needed any photo support beyond the capability of the wire services. Caldwell had wired this column on July 17, and it had served Luce's interventionist position well by portraying the Russians as calm, confident, prepared, determined, and capable. Caldwell offered special praise for the partisans fighting behind the German lines and the civilian People's Army on the home front. In a way he laid the groundwork for his wife's photography by describing several of the sites where she had shot.

But in other aspects, the August 11 spread must have been anticlimactic. The war was almost two months old; well-publicized and well-reported Luftwaffe raids had been going on for three weeks. Bourke-White's photos were peacetime images. *Life* did its best to hype them, using an orientalist motif of the Forbidden East by calling Moscow "this huge mysterious city," an Asian metropolis that "represents something for which uncounted millions of Russians have shown their willingness to die." The editors then excused the tameness of the photo-essay with a disclaimer that put the pictures in context: "Her pictures are not a typical cross-section of the city's life because her Russian hosts were anxious for her to record the improvements which they had made and of which they were very proud. Omitted from her report was the seamy side of the proletarian life." The price she had to pay for her journalist's *propusk* (passport) was now clear. Censorship had begun even before the war started, and Bourke-White would be duped by more than one Potemkin village before she left.

In accordance with *Life*'s standard practice, except when Bourke-White was actually in the Chrysler Building, the photo and layout editors determined how a photographer's essay would be presented in the magazine. The editorial staff accepted input from the photographers, but it wrote all the captions and the accompanying text. In this August 11 piece ("A LIFE Photographer Looks at Moscow a Week Before the Nazi Invasion Began"),[35] Bourke-White would have the byline, but only that. The New York editorial staff would supply the text.

The three-quarter-page lead photo (see figure 10) is a quintessentially Bourke-White vertical image with strong diagonals: a docile queue of ant-sized people enters Red Square precisely in the lower-right corner of the photo, then serpentines across it to the left. In the distance can be seen three smokestacks emitting a soft plume of incinerated industrial waste. As is typical of many Bourke-White photos, the people provide an awesome sense of scale as they are dwarfed by a line of castellated kremlins and towers that fills the central two-thirds of the image. The patient file resolutely exits the picture about a quarter way up its left edge, marching slowly toward the opportunity for momentary homage at Lenin's Tomb, which is not seen in the photo. A clock tower shows it to be exactly 2:19 in the afternoon. This is monumentalist photography at its finest with a touch of industrial aesthetic, but the picture works because of its human element: the stolid, enduring, patriotic Russian people have gathered peacefully, without guards, to offer their devotion to the Soviet state. Ergo, at its core Russia must be a peaceful, law-abiding nation. And if the buildings and the tradition that they imply physically dominate the citizens, this is not an accidental message. The Soviet Union, Bourke-White and *Life* are saying, is massive enough that it can pump literally millions of bodies into the struggle to keep itself intact. And from the ancient sixteenth-century architecture presented, there is no reason to believe that the Soviets cannot be successful and continue on for more hundreds of years, though perhaps a little economic largesse from their friends in the West would be helpful.

In a formalist-influenced study, *The Photograph*, Graham Clarke argues that the documentary image "uses a highly charged and controlled photographic space. Far from being a 'witness,' it is often a director of the way events are seen." He observes that in many of her photographs in *You Have Seen Their Faces*, "Bourke-White constructs a reading for us and much of this is produced through the deliberate use of obvious codes and symbols."[36] This coding is particularly evident in her Moscow photos, though when they were initially published in *Life*, their print milieu was again out of her control. In *Faces*, however,

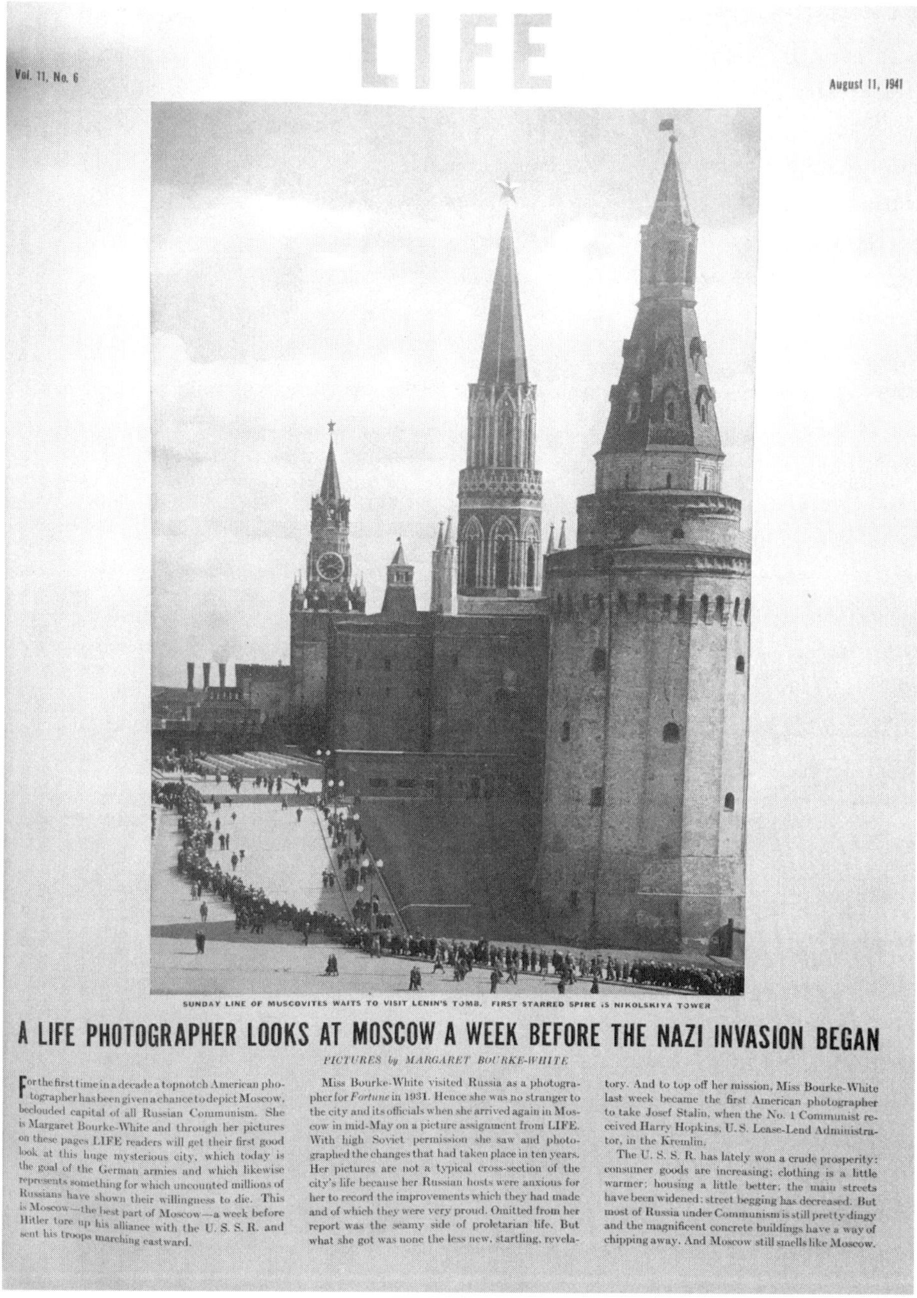

LIFE

Vol. 11, No. 6 | August 11, 1941

SUNDAY LINE OF MUSCOVITES WAITS TO VISIT LENIN'S TOMB. FIRST STARRED SPIRE IS NIKOLSKIYA TOWER

A LIFE PHOTOGRAPHER LOOKS AT MOSCOW A WEEK BEFORE THE NAZI INVASION BEGAN

PICTURES by MARGARET BOURKE-WHITE

For the first time in a decade a topnotch American photographer has been given a chance to depict Moscow, beclouded capital of all Russian Communism. She is Margaret Bourke-White and through her pictures on these pages LIFE readers will get their first good look at this huge mysterious city, which today is the goal of the German armies and which likewise represents something for which uncounted millions of Russians have shown their willingness to die. This is Moscow—the best part of Moscow—a week before Hitler tore up his alliance with the U. S. S. R. and sent his troops marching eastward.

Miss Bourke-White visited Russia as a photographer for *Fortune* in 1931. Hence she was no stranger to the city and its officials when she arrived again in Moscow in mid-May on a picture assignment from LIFE. With high Soviet permission she saw and photographed the changes that had taken place in ten years. Her pictures are not a typical cross-section of the city's life because her Russian hosts were anxious for her to record the improvements which they had made and of which they were very proud. Omitted from her report was the seamy side of proletarian life. But what she got was none the less new, startling, revelatory. And to top off her mission, Miss Bourke-White last week became the first American photographer to take Josef Stalin, when the No. 1 Communist received Harry Hopkins, U. S. Lease-Lend Administrator, in the Kremlin.

The U. S. S. R. has lately won a crude prosperity: consumer goods are increasing; clothing is a little warmer; housing a little better; the main streets have been widened; street begging has decreased. But most of Russia under Communism is still pretty dingy and the magnificent concrete buildings have a way of chipping away. And Moscow still smells like Moscow.

FIGURE 10. Line of Russians along street in front of the Kremlin (From *Life*, August 11, 1941; Margaret Bourke-White/The LIFE Picture Collection/Getty Images; © 1941 Time Inc. All rights reserved. Reprinted from LIFE and published with the permission of Time Inc. Reproduction in any manner in any language in whole or in part without written permission is prohibited. LIFE and the LIFE logo are registered trademarks of Time Inc. used under license.)

Bourke-White, working with Caldwell, used a code that she drew into her actual photographs to better drive home their message. Clearly, by using the "highly charged and controlled photographic space" above Red Square, Bourke-White is far from being merely a witness to this patriotic display; she is also directing the way these events are to be interpreted.

Of the remaining thirty-one photos, seven are exterior shots: two taken at street level looking up, then down Gorky Street, Moscow's central artery, along which are to be found the major hotels and the upmarket shopping district; two are of the crowd at a soccer game in Dynamo Stadium (message: Despite the war, Russians are so comfortable that they can still leisurely turn their attention to sports); two are of colossal statues (one of a Red Army soldier and one of Stalin wearing a military greatcoat, taken from the rear);[37] the seventh is of an unusual building at the permanent Agricultural Exhibition. The leitmotif here is of a nation of power and peace, able to participate in both commerce and play, but always at martial readiness.

The remaining twenty-four photos originate from eight different venues, all of which broadcast the message that Russians are similar to Americans, doing the things they do, taking solace in the same simple pleasures: cherishing and spoiling their children, taking pride in their educational system, enjoying the fruits and leisures of their economy. The venues of her pictures include:

- Public spaces (3): hotel lobby, subway
- Commercial establishments (6): grocery store, dress store, cocktail lounge
- *Pravda* offices (3): reading room, editorial staff meetings
- Moscow University / Technical Institute (8)
- School and kindergarten (4)

Life selected two photos for full-page presentation. They are vertically oriented, meticulously lighted, their *mise-en-scène* carefully staged. The central feature of each is a massive staircase.

The first of the two (see figure 11) is at the University of Moscow and depicts two dozen students conversing while they descend a long, balustraded stairway descending from a mezzanine, where statutes of Stalin and Lenin peacefully oversee the students' activities. Between them is a large plaque commemorating the 185th anniversary of the university, on which appears the only hammer and sickle evident in the entire set of photos.

The second staircase (see figure 12) is at the downtown cocktail lounge, where Bourke-White also meticulously composed a photograph of a "Kowboy Koktail" being mixed, which involves a pair of hands that has just cracked open and poured an egg and four liquor bottles, each with its label fastidiously turned

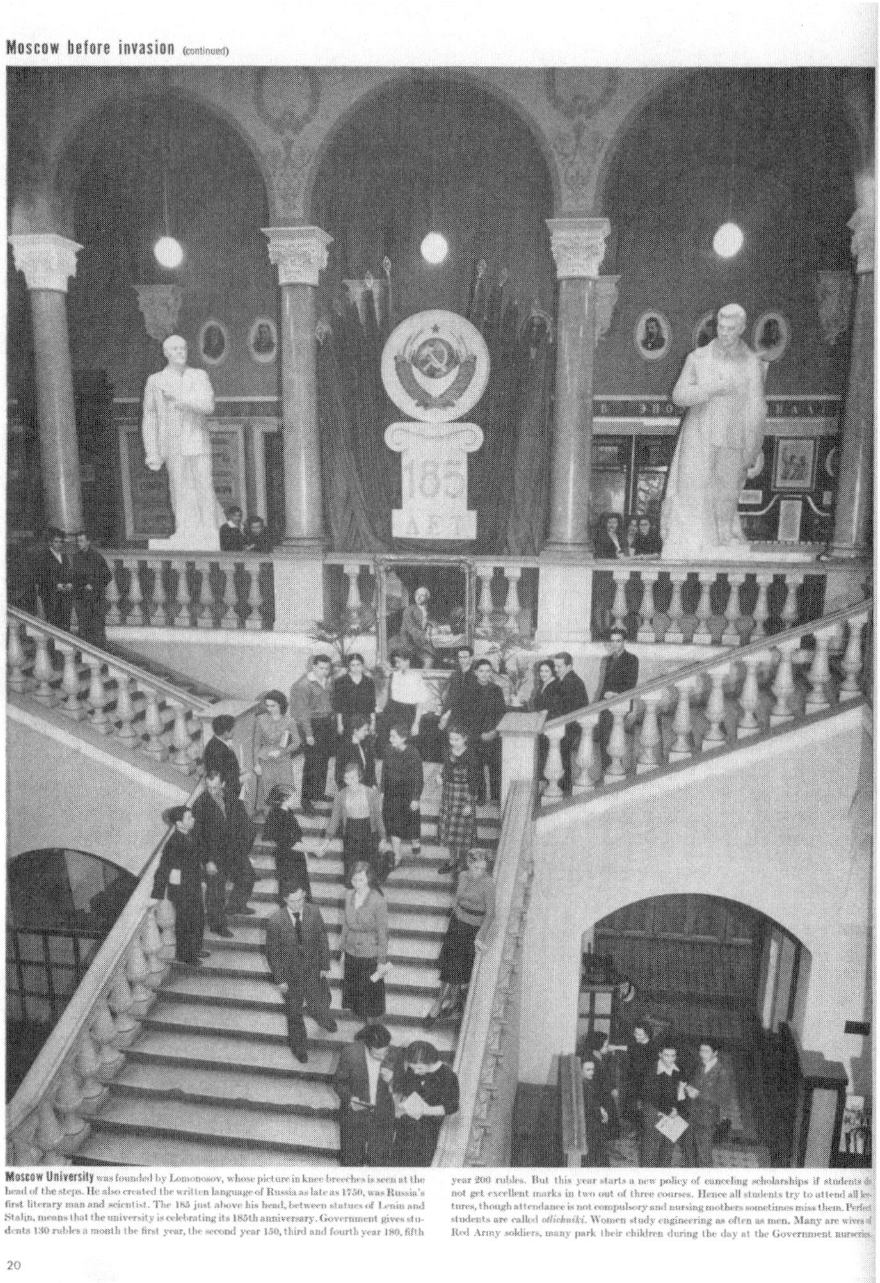

Moscow before invasion (continued)

Moscow University was founded by Lomonosov, whose picture in knee breeches is seen at the head of the steps. He also created the written language of Russia as late as 1750, was Russia's first literary man and scientist. The 185 just above his head, between statues of Lenin and Stalin, means that the university is celebrating its 185th anniversary. Government gives students 130 rubles a month the first year, the second year 150, third and fourth year 180, fifth year 200 rubles. But this year starts a new policy of canceling scholarships if students do not get excellent marks in two out of three courses. Hence all students try to attend all lectures, though attendance is not compulsory and nursing mothers sometimes miss them. Perfect students are called *otlichniki*. Women study engineering as often as men. Many are wives of Red Army soldiers, many park their children during the day at the Government nurseries.

20

FIGURE 11. Elevated view of students on a staircase at Moscow University (founded by Mikhail Lomonosov, whose portrait is visible on the landing), Moscow, Russia, August 11, 1941. At the top of the stairs, a flag display celebrates the university's 185th anniversary. (From *Life*, August 11, 1941; Margaret Bourke-White/The LIFE Picture Collection/Getty Images; © 1941 Time Inc. All rights reserved. Reprinted from LIFE and published with the permission of Time Inc. Reproduction in any manner in any language in whole or in part without written permission is prohibited. LIFE and the LIFE logo are registered trademarks of Time Inc. used under license.)

toward the camera, iconography all reminiscent of a high-end spirits ad in a glossy American weekly (see figure 13). A spiral staircase climbs the central two-thirds of the print, set off by ascending rococo columns. A rug with its linear pattern curving gently up the lower half of the image runs between two groups of well-heeled drinkers: four on the right at the arcing bar, behind which stands a female bartender; four on the left sitting in arched-back chairs at round tables cluttered with fruit, pastries, and opulent china. Four more customers descend on two of the staircase's three segments, while a waitress occupies the middle flight. That such luxury exists in "this huge mysterious city" is meant to be reassuring. Bourke-White's attention to stylistic details here is breathtaking.

Even a cursory scanning of these nearly three dozen photos displays all of Bourke-White's hallmark photographic styles and tropes. Her pictures taken at the cocktail lounge artistically combine many of her themes: the art deco modernism of the stairway and bar, the commercial art of the Kowboy Koktail, the social propaganda of the upscale clientele and bounteous amounts of food, and the artistic positioning of the curving architectural details of the room.

But also central to these two photographs is the staircase itself, the elephant in the picture. Bourke-White had been highly influenced, both personally and professionally, by the iconic Russian filmmaker Sergei Eisenstein, as is evident in the style and nature of many of her photographs that emphasize strong lines, contrast, and embedded meaning. On several occasions that summer she and Caldwell had been entertained by Eisenstein and his wife in their Moscow flat. For Eisenstein the photographic or cinematic image was a powerful signifier. One of his most famous sequences is the slaughter of civilians on the Odessa Steps in *Battleship Potemkin* (1925). This film, commissioned by the Kremlin, is an emotionally wrenching study of the 1905 populist uprising against the rule of Czar Nicholas II and was intended to portray it as a foreshadowing of the more successful 1917 Communist Revolution. A central visual of *Potemkin* is the Odessa Steps, an expansive marble staircase that leads to the harbor where, in the film, mutinous czarist sailors have just seized the battleship *Potemkin*. As the citizenry gathers to celebrate this moment, czarist troops appear at the top of the stairway and proceed to descend them, slaughtering along the way dozens of distraught people, many of whom are disabled or otherwise helpless. This image was so ingrained in the psyche of the Russian people that Bourke-White necessarily evoked Eisenstein in selecting staircase images for her book.

Not only is a staircase inherently a destabilizing and potentially awkward space, as is evident in *Potemkin*, but it is also a metaphor for power and hierarchy. Hence, the czarist forces first appear at the top of the Odessa Steps and, at the University of Moscow, the steps descend from the mezzanine where the

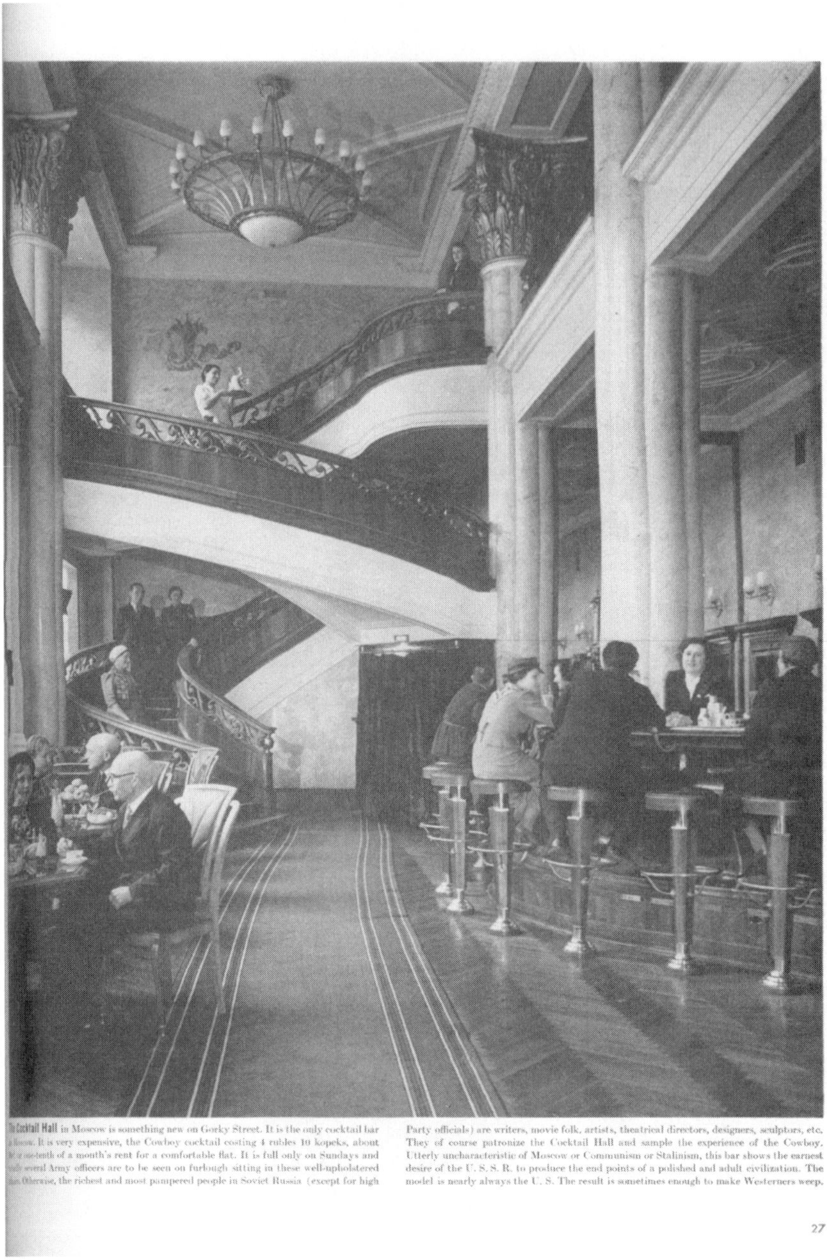

Cocktail Hall in Moscow is something new on Gorky Street. It is the only cocktail bar … It is very expensive, the Cowboy cocktail costing 4 rubles 10 kopeks, about … tenth of a month's rent for a comfortable flat. It is full only on Sundays and … several Army officers are to be seen on furlough sitting in these well-upholstered … Otherwise, the richest and most pampered people in Soviet Russia (except for high Party officials) are writers, movie folk, artists, theatrical directors, designers, sculptors, etc. They of course patronize the Cocktail Hall and sample the experience of the Cowboy. Utterly uncharacteristic of Moscow or Communism or Stalinism, this bar shows the earnest desire of the U. S. S. R. to produce the end points of a polished and adult civilization. The model is nearly always the U. S. The result is sometimes enough to make Westerners weep.

27

FIGURE 12. New, expensively elegant Cocktail Hall on Gorkey Street (only one in town) where the richest and most elite including writers, artists, designers, sculptors, and movie and theatrical people can experience a pricey Cowboy cocktail (one-tenth of a month's rent) (From *Life*, August 11, 1941; Margaret Bourke-White/The LIFE Picture Collection/Getty Images;)

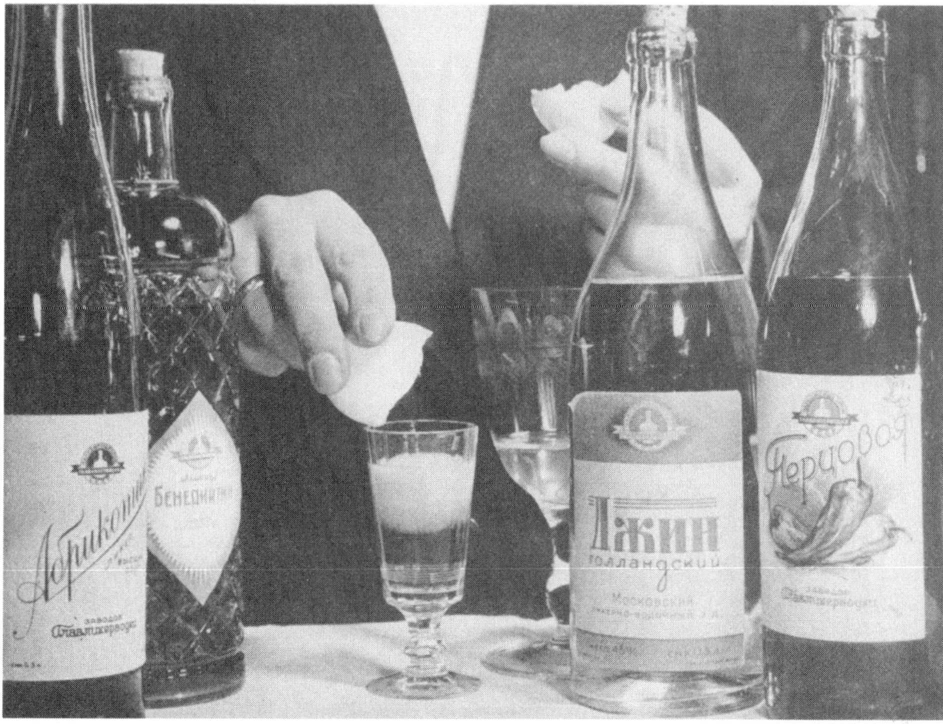

FIGURE 13. "Kowboy Koktail" (From *Shooting the Russian War*; photo © Estate of Margaret Bourke-White/Licensed by VAGA, New York, N.Y.; courtesy of Syracuse University Libraries)

busts of Stalin and Lenin are situated. The staircase has a long history in literature as well, being especially well developed in English Victorian fiction. In a psychoanalytic study of the staircase, Ann Kaplan notes that while "the meanings and crucial changes in relationships are conveyed through the image of the staircase," so too "the staircase . . . symbolizes how Victorian culture regulated class, gender, and race"; in particular, its symbolism expresses "repressed, forbidden, and unconscious desire."[38] Harry Stone, in an analysis of Charles Dickens's *Dombey and Son*, writes that on this central architectural feature of the Dombey mansion "the characters wend their lives; one end of the staircase descends into hell, the other ascends to heaven."[39] Bourke-White seems to invoke this heaven-hell dichotomy in her cocktail lounge shot. The liminality of the staircase is crucial to its power as a visual and emotional metaphor.

Beyond these symbolic meanings exists the simple visual harmony of the staircase itself, with its regularly spaced risers and its curves and straight edges that can be lit in such a fashion as to create dynamic, imposing, and aesthetically pleasing shadows. Such contrasts were central to Bourke-White's photographic aesthetic.

Other than a photo of a huge statue of a Soviet soldier at the Agricultural Exhibit, there is only one image suggesting martial activity during this prewar Moscow idyll. Photographed at kindergarten, four boys—two seven- and two eight-year-olds—have taken up positions behind a barricade of overturned chairs, hoisted toy rifles to their shoulders, and now stand at wary guard, though the eight-year-old at the top, whom Bourke-White identifies as Genya Vax, has his eyes clearly on the camera, not the enemy (see figure 14). The caption for this picture in the August 11 *Life* spread sums up the often heavy-handed pro-Soviet position that Bourke-White had unabashedly adopted:

> War games, long discouraged, lately back in fashion, are played in kindergarten by (from rear) Jena Kabanov, 8, Vladimir Levin-Press, 7, Genya Vax, 8, and Ura Grushin, 7, who wear miniature army caps with red star [*sic*]. Another game is to build a battleship out of blocks and fight in mimic of war for the Red Navy. The children had long since gathered from their parents, even during the Nazi-Communist Pact, that the U.S.S.R.'s enemy is Germany. Their parents groaned whenever Britain met a disaster. For such superior families as the parents of these children felt that the alliance with Germany was merely for convenience until the U.S.S.R. should have put new weapons into mass production. Both parents of all these children work in office, factory, school or university. Judging from the faces of the children, they do not seem to miss the full-time attention of their mothers.

These were to be the last of Bourke-White's peacetime images.

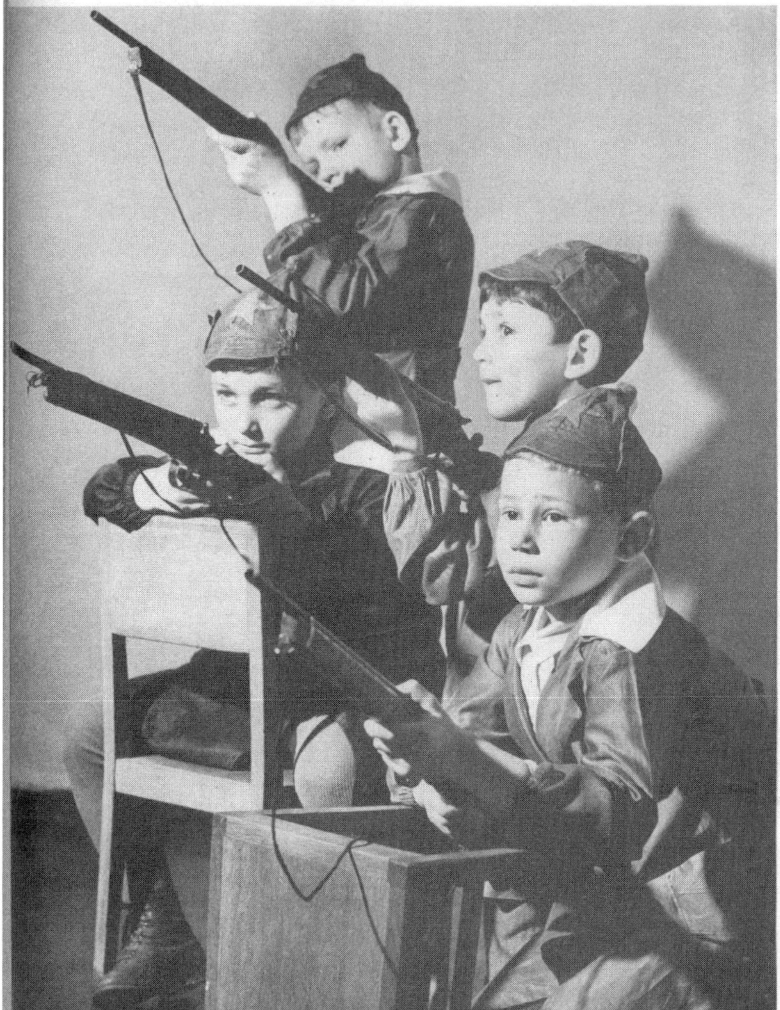

[illegible], long discouraged, lately back in fashion, are played in kindergarten by (*from* [illegible]) Kabanov, 8, Vladimir Levin-Press, 7, Genya Vax, 8, and Ura Grushin, 7, who [illegible] miniature army caps with red star. Another game is to build a battleship out of [illegible] and fight in mimic war for the Red Navy. The children have long since gath[illegible] their parents, even during the Nazi-Communist Pact, that the U. S. S. R.'s enemy is Germany. Their parents groaned whenever Britain met a disaster. For such superior families as the parents of these children felt that the alliance with Germany was merely for convenience until the U. S. S. R. should have put new weapons into mass production. Both parents of all these children work in office, factory, school or university. Judging from the faces of the children, they do not seem to miss the fulltime attention of their mothers.

CONTINUED ON NEXT PAGE 23

FIGURE 14. August 1941: Russian kindergarten boys clad in miniature caps with red stars, aiming toy rifles, barricaded behind classroom furniture, while playing war game (From *Life*, August 11, 1941; Margaret Bourke-White/The LIFE Picture Collection/Getty Images;)

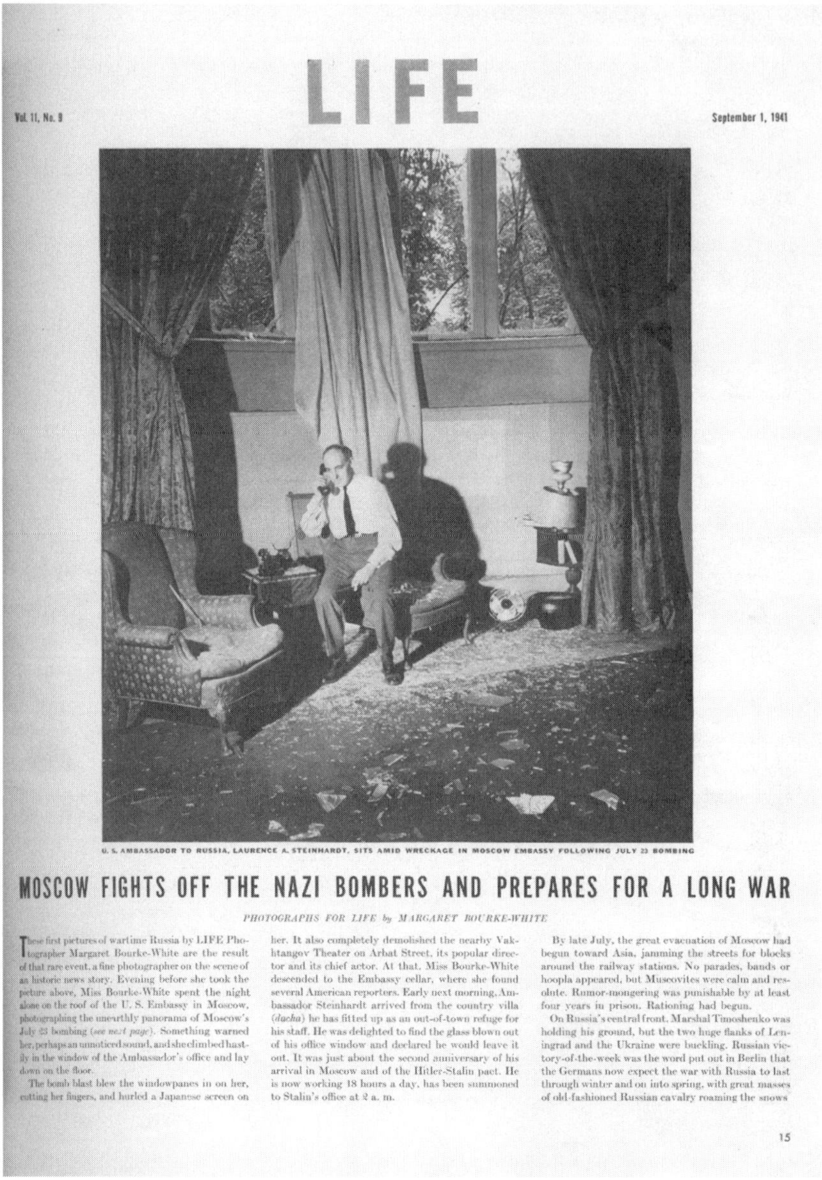

LIFE

Vol. 11, No. 9 September 1, 1941

U. S. AMBASSADOR TO RUSSIA, LAURENCE A. STEINHARDT, SITS AMID WRECKAGE IN MOSCOW EMBASSY FOLLOWING JULY 23 BOMBING

MOSCOW FIGHTS OFF THE NAZI BOMBERS AND PREPARES FOR A LONG WAR

PHOTOGRAPHS FOR LIFE by MARGARET BOURKE-WHITE

These first pictures of wartime Russia by LIFE Photographer Margaret Bourke-White are the result of that rare event, a fine photographer on the scene of an historic news story. Evening before she took the picture above, Miss Bourke-White spent the night alone on the roof of the U. S. Embassy in Moscow, photographing the unearthly panorama of Moscow's July 23 bombing (*see next page*). Something warned her, perhaps an unnoticed sound, and she climbed hastily in the window of the Ambassador's office and lay down on the floor.

The bomb blast blew the windowpanes in on her, cutting her fingers, and hurled a Japanese screen on her. It also completely demolished the nearby Vakhtangov Theater on Arbat Street, its popular director and its chief actor. At that, Miss Bourke-White descended to the Embassy cellar, where she found several American reporters. Early next morning, Ambassador Steinhardt arrived from the country villa (*dacha*) he has fitted up as an out-of-town refuge for his staff. He was delighted to find the glass blown out of his office window and declared he would leave it out. It was just about the second anniversary of his arrival in Moscow and of the Hitler-Stalin pact. He is now working 18 hours a day, has been summoned to Stalin's office at 2 a. m.

By late July, the great evacuation of Moscow had begun toward Asia, jamming the streets for blocks around the railway stations. No parades, bands or hoopla appeared, but Muscovites were calm and resolute. Rumor-mongering was punishable by at least four years in prison. Rationing had begun.

On Russia's central front, Marshal Timoshenko was holding his ground, but the two huge flanks of Leningrad and the Ukraine were buckling. Russian victory-of-the-week was the word put out in Berlin that the Germans now expect the war with Russia to last through winter and on into spring, with great masses of old-fashioned Russian cavalry roaming the snows

15

FIGURE 15. American diplomat and U.S. Ambassador to the Soviet Union Laurence Steinhardt (1892–1950) makes a phone call amid shattered glasses and damage following a German air raid (on July 23), Moscow, Russia, September 1, 1941. (From *Life*, September 1, 1941; Margaret Bourke-White/The LIFE Picture Collection/Getty Images;

"Moscow Fights Off the Nazi Bombers and Prepares for a Long War" led the September 1 issue of *Life* with a dozen photos Bourke-White took between July 23 and 26, during and just after the Luftwaffe's first few air raids on Moscow.[40] These were the ones she had dispatched into Graebner's care in London, and which she feared had been lost. The lead photo (see figure 15) is the only interior shot of the lot, that of Ambassador Steinhardt sitting in his office in Spaso House, the American embassy. The three large windows behind him are completely blown out, the curtains shredded and hanging awry, a lamp shattered on a table, the floor and chairs littered with glass shards. Bourke-White has carefully lit the picture from the left front with a strong light that casts a dark shadow behind Steinhardt, who is shown busy at work, speaking animatedly with someone by telephone. The unmistakable message is that despite the havoc the Germans wrought that evening in Moscow, the city remains functioning, as do America's diligent diplomats, working in concert with the Russians. In effect, *Life* is saying, like it or not, America is already in the war.

The next three photos are some of Bourke-White's most famous. Time-lapse night images show the walls and towers of the Kremlin silhouetted against the brilliance of a variety of Luftwaffe bombs and flares. A text block appears between two of these pictures then follows a magnificent page-and-a-half illustration. War is now an aesthetic event, both visual and, Bourke-White notes, aural: "The crash of the anti-aircraft guns and their deeper echo [were] as a classical chord in counterpoint to the jazz of the whining planes and the whistling bombs." A *Life* staffer adds: "Nothing like these pictures of Moscow bombing and defense was ever released by the British censors during the Battle of Britain. No doubt remained that the Communist State, though far from ideal in peacetime, is well geared to conduct a war. Every citizen in the U.S.S.R. had a job and did it. The fire-fighting organization was as good as London's after a year of bombing. The people were even calmer, swimming in the Moscow River by day, sitting in their shirt sleeves at their air-raid posts at night." Elsewhere in the feature the *Life* editors insist that the Russian people are "calm and resolute," but, more importantly, they summarize the first month of the war by declaring that the Red Army is "holding [its] ground" on the central front. *Life* did have to admit that the Leningrad and Ukrainian flanks were "buckling" but reassured readers that by no means had they capitulated.

Following a pair of pictures of the Kremlin, one in daylight camouflage, one in midnight blackout, *Life* placed on a single page two images Bourke-White had captured, under the scrutiny of military censors, of a German Junkers-88 bomber the Moscow air defense claimed it had shot down, killing two of the plane's four crew members. The essay concludes with three photos of peasant

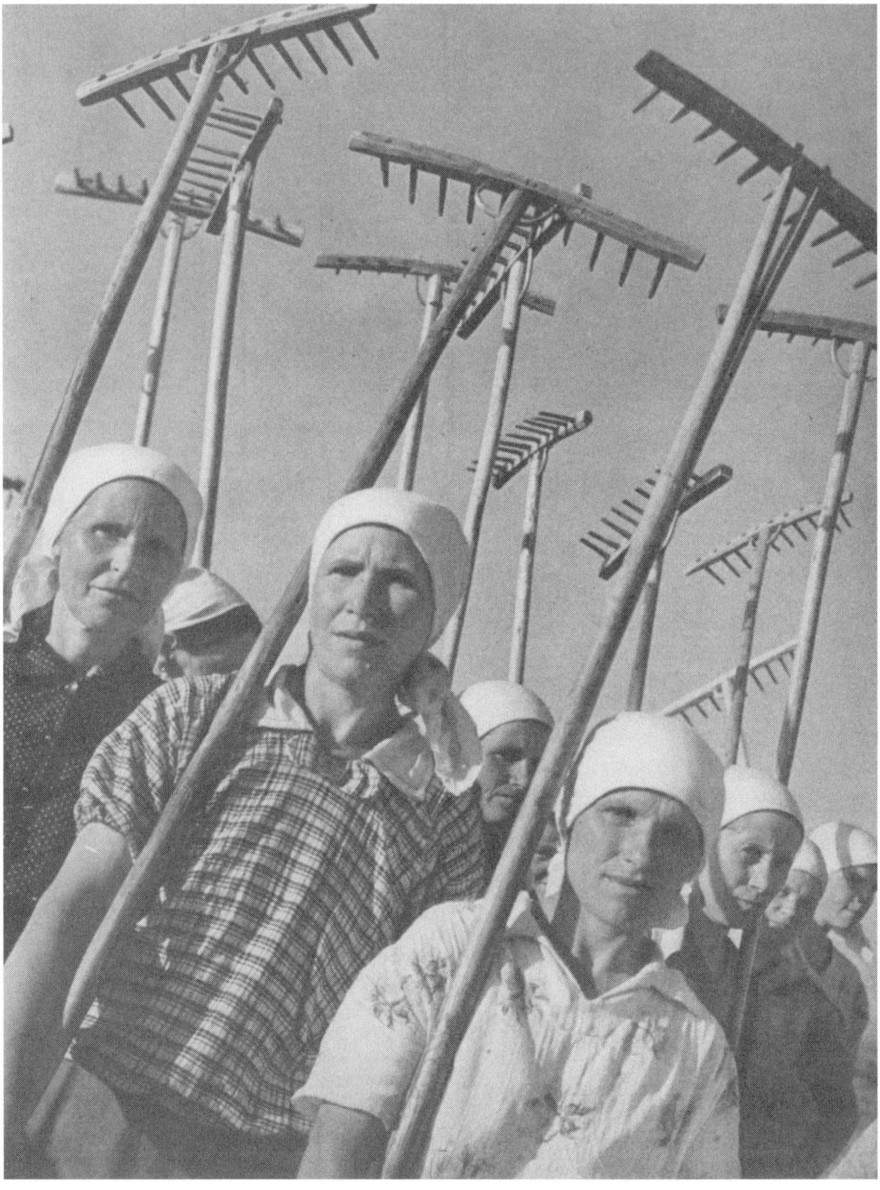

FIGURE 16. "Ukrainian Farm Women" (From *Shooting the Russian War*; photo © Estate of Margaret Bourke-White/Licensed by VAGA, New York, N.Y.; courtesy of Syracuse University Libraries)

women on a collective farm near Moscow bringing in the July wheat. These three photos are classic Bourke-White images. The first, taken at a low level with a deep depth of field, shows mounds of wheat stretching toward a distant horizon, across which a single line of peasant women can be made out, apparently hard at work. The second is a midrange shot of ten women, each with a rake over her shoulder, looking like a cast preparing a dance number for a Broadway musical. A better-known image of these same women simulating weapon-toting militiamen appears in *Shooting the Russian War* (see figure 16). The essay closes with another Bourke-White trope: two farm women, shawls over their heads and each carrying a large sheaf of wheat, are seen from the waist up. The camera is held from below, thereby venerating them with power and prestige.

A week later, *Life* again gave Bourke-White the lead, publishing a few shots from her Stalin portfolio, an exclusive it advertised extensively.[41] The images strangely provide no clear message beyond the opportunity to show an American diplomat, Roosevelt's envoy Harry Hopkins, in Moscow in the company of Steinhardt, British ambassador Sir Stafford Cripps, and Premier Stalin. Several captions are oddly disarticulated, with lines appearing out of order and failing to explain the photos under which they are placed.

Three of Bourke-White's Stalin portraits appeared during the war. The first is the September 8 full-frontal image cropped just below the chin.[42] *Life* used a second Stalin portrait on a 1943 cover, which she shot upward from just below shoulder level and then cropped at the collar. In both her photo collaboration with Caldwell and in her own memoir, she printed a third picture, cropped slightly differently in each book (see figure 17).

This last was to be her most iconic image of Stalin, one shot from well below his waist, at about a three-quarter angle. In this picture Stalin grins ever so subtly. Bourke-White explains the origin of his enigmatic smile in a two-page, first-person piece in this same *Life* issue, "How I Photographed Stalin and Hopkins Inside the Kremlin": "When I dropped to my knees to get a low camera angle, he began to laugh. And when I pressed his interpreter into work changing flashbulbs and holding reflectors for me, he practically chuckled. Otherwise he stood like a stone, like a piece of granite." She retold this story many times for the rest of her career. In *Shooting the Russian War*, she adds the touch that she had picked out a pair of red shoes to wear with her blue linen suit and put a red bow in her hair. ("I never found out whether Mr. Stalin noticed it or not.")[43] Seemingly oblivious to any erotic thoughts Stalin might have entertained, she humanizes the dictator further:

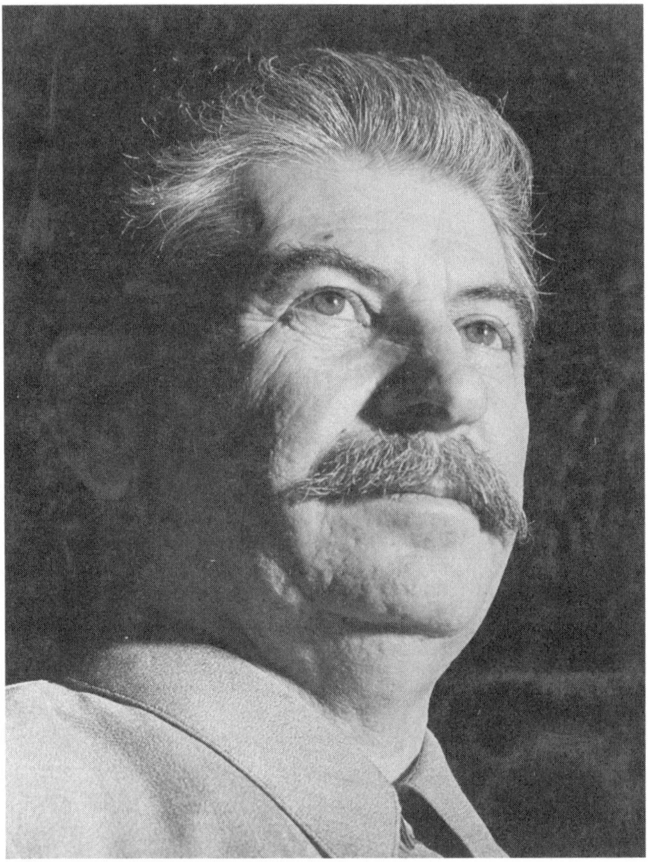

FIGURE 17. "The People's Commissar of Defense" (From *Shooting the Russian War*; photo © Estate of Margaret Bourke-White/ Licensed by VAGA, New York, N.Y.; courtesy of Syracuse University Libraries)

> As I crawled on my hands and knees from one low camera angle to another, Stalin thought it was funny and started to laugh.
>
> When his face lighted up with a smile, the change was miraculous. It was as though a second personality had come to the front, genial, cordial, and kindly. I pressed on through to more exposures, until I had the expression that I wanted.[44]

In her autobiography, many years later, Bourke-White adds still more detail:

> As I sank down to my knees to get some low viewpoints, I spilled a pocketful of peanut flashbulbs, which went bouncing all over the floor. The Kremlin interpreter and I went scrambling after them. I guess Stalin had never seen an American girl on her knees to him before. He thought it was funny, and started to laugh. The change was miraculous! It was as though a second personality had come to the front—genial and almost merry. The smile lasted just long enough for me to make two exposures, and then, as though a veil had been drawn over his features, again he turned to stone.[45]

Although she developed all her other film packs in her bathtub at the Hotel National, on this night, fearing an air raid that might cause the hotel wardens to interrupt her delicate procedures, she packed her entire operation over to Spaso House and set up shop in its basement. This was a fortuitous decision because indeed the Luftwaffe, perhaps wanting to impress Hopkins, bombed Moscow that very night. Even so, "The negatives of Stalin were so irreplaceable, should anything go wrong, that I did not have the courage to plunge them in, sink or swim, a whole film pack at a time, as I usually do. I began processing them one by one." Thinking she might need prints rather than just negatives, she created a makeshift printing shop that included "a hand-held flashlight wrapped in [a] dustcloth" and a soup plate as a developing dish. By morning she had her full set of Stalin prints.[46]

In this same September 8 essay, in addition to these diplomatic portraits, there are three photos of Theater Square. There Bourke-White took simple snapshots of people clambering over and around the remains of a downed German bomber that authorities had trucked over. There is even a strange (for Bourke-White), paparazzi-like telephoto image of Steinhardt and Hopkins walking outside Spaso House deep in conversation, and a funny photo of Hopkins's embassy automobile with a flat tire.

Meanwhile, in mid-September Bourke-White, Caldwell, and nine other American and British correspondents had finally been given permission to travel to, or at least toward, the front, the long sought-after "frontward" trip about which they had been pestered by their editors for months (see chapters 6–7). Bourke-White was not pleased with the photographic results of the junket because of the nearly constant rain. The water ruined one of her cameras, and she complained continually about the lighting. Rarely could she fashion her usual style of photograph. She wired Hicks on September 21 that she had just returned from the front where her photography had been "VERY LIMITED DUE UNUSUALLY BAD WEATHER AND CONSISTENT ARRIVALS MOST INTERESTING POINTS AFTER DARK." These pictures finally appeared a couple of months later in *Life*'s November 17 issue.

In any case, five weeks after her Stalin spread, on October 13 Bourke-White was back in *Life* with a thirteen-page, thirty-photograph essay entitled "Religion in Russia: Red Godlessness Fails to Empty Churches."[47] *Life*'s headnote explains its rationale for the long piece. After noting that, while state "Communism, the only official religion in the U.S.S.R., has been trying more or less desperately to stamp out the idea of God among 190,000,000 Russians," nonetheless "as a people the Russians are the most mystically religious on earth." But now, *Life* implies, Bourke-White's photographs, all of which were taken without Soviet censorship, reveal the true current status of churches in Russia. Unmentioned is that she had been able to visit facilities only in Moscow. All of Bourke-White's images are interiors, and, typically, most are painstakingly lighted, staged, and posed. The first dozen depict the Old Orthodox Church, the next eight the Renewed (or New) Orthodox Church. Next, *Life* presents six pictures of Protestants and then four of people described as atheists. If the magazine's readers had formerly hewn to the isolationists' argument that the Soviet Union was a godless nation, *Life*'s intention was to significantly weaken that contention.

By this time, however, *Life*'s position had become anomalous. Caldwell and Bourke-White had left Russia at the beginning of October and were now in England, and the Soviet government and the Western press corps had been evacuated to Kuibyshev by the middle of the month. Still, *Life* was publishing photo-essays shot well over a month earlier. Its October 27 piece, "Muscovites Take Up Their Guns as Nazi Horde Approaches Russian Capital,"[48] seems especially dated. It includes sixteen photographs, all of which appear oddly and stiffly posed: three of soldiers in training; single ones of a poster shop churning out anti-German propaganda, students at a first-aid school, and people in an apartment bomb shelter; six torso or head shots of German prisoners of war; and three of people relaxing at the Park of Culture and Rest.

The last of these, and the final in the set, is a full-page image of a crowd listening to a public address system. Shot from above, over a hundred people fill the frame from edge to edge, from top to bottom, most of whom (but not

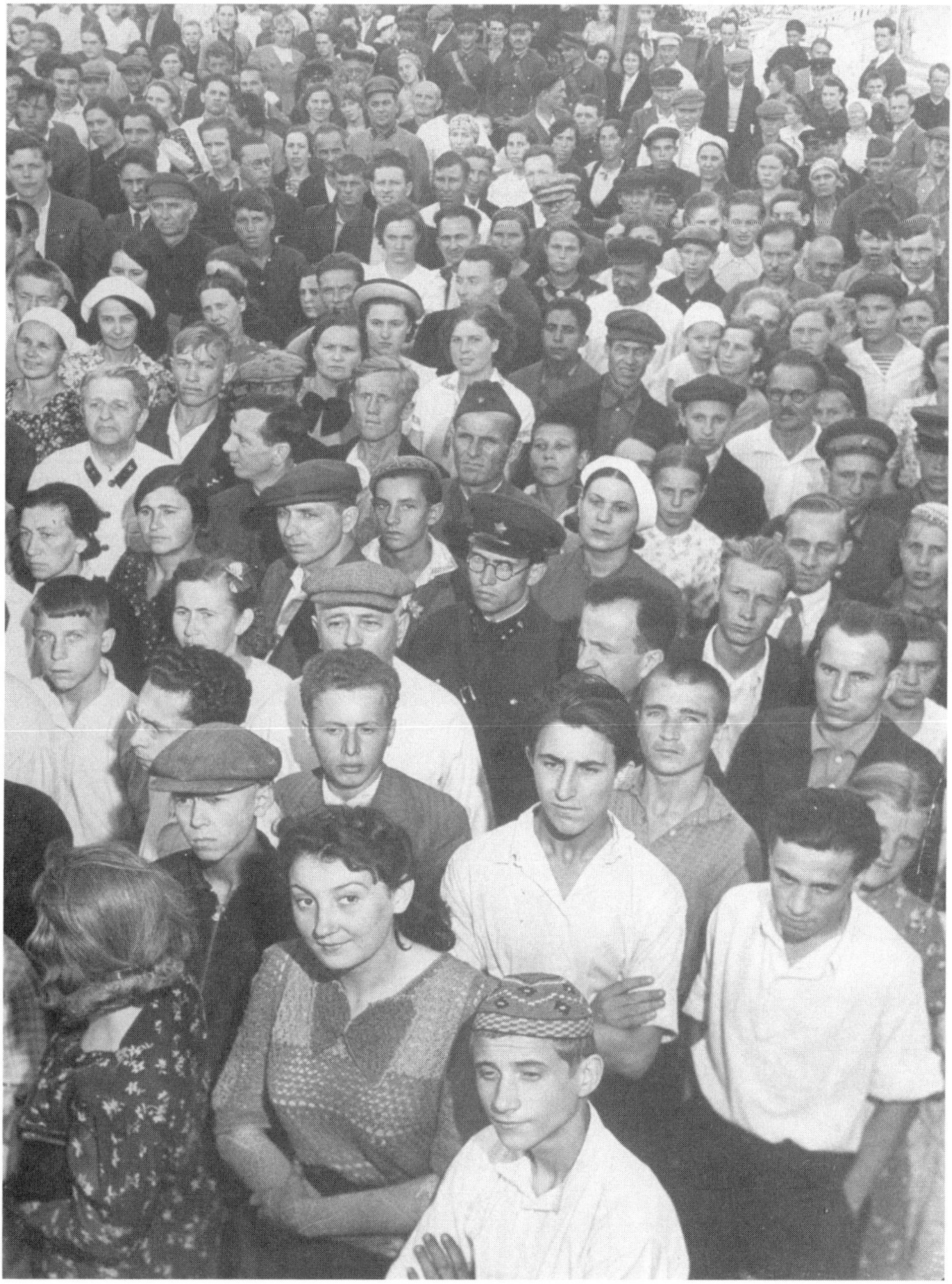

FIGURE 18. August 1941: Muscovites listening to war speakers in the Park of Culture as they relax outdoors (From *Life*, October 27, 1941; Margaret Bourke-White/The LIFE Picture Collection/Getty Images)

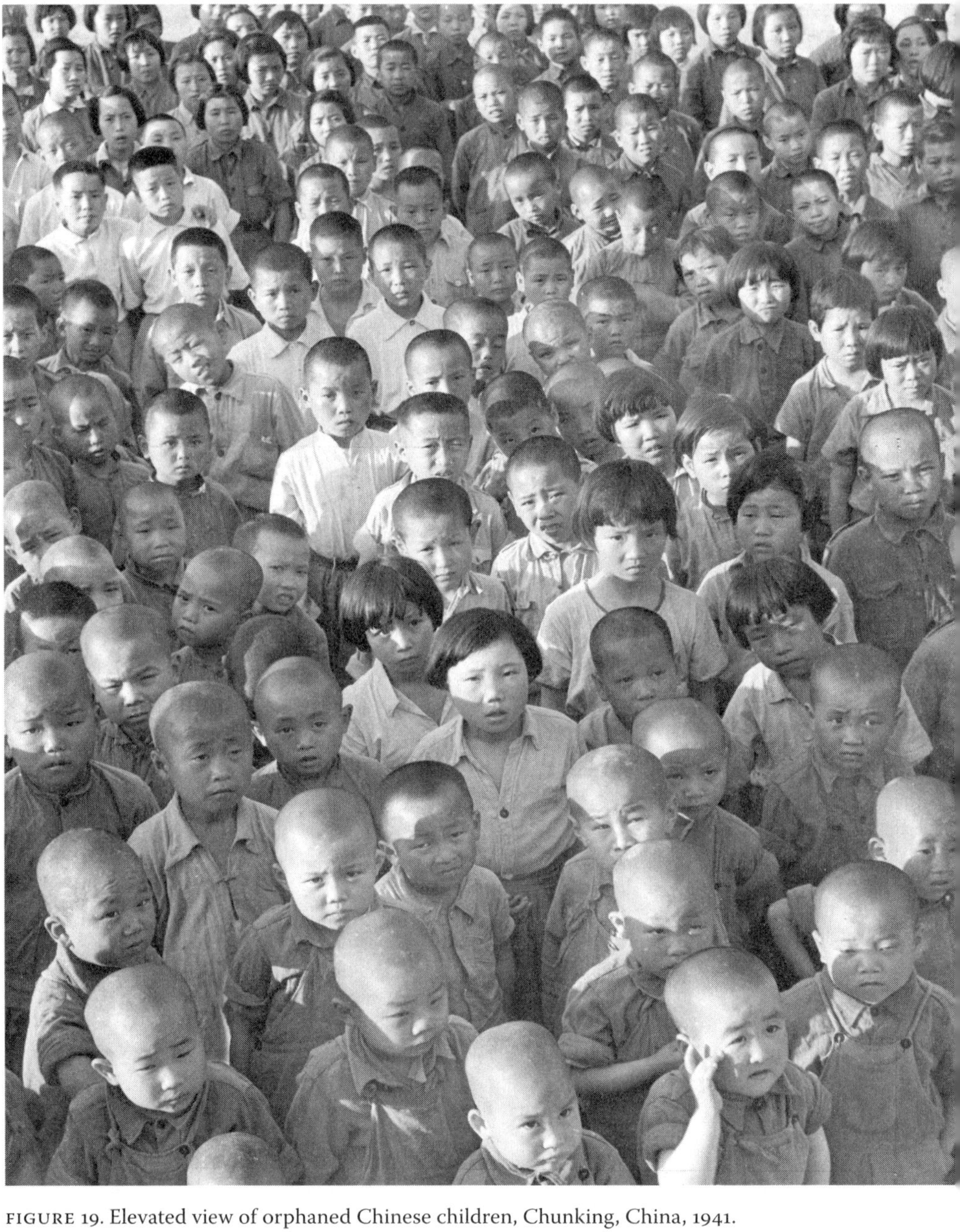

FIGURE 19. Elevated view of orphaned Chinese children, Chunking, China, 1941. The children had lost their families during World War II. (From *Life*, June 23, 1941; Margaret Bourke-White/The LIFE Picture Collection/Getty Images)

all) seem intent on the loudspeaker: the elderly, youth, soldiers, civilians, women, men, students, workers. A few are sneaking peaks at the photographer who has uncannily arranged them all for maximal facial exposure. The headnote for this piece has lost its rosy optimism. The war now has become an "intense personal tragedy," and *Life* admits that now "Moscow was in terrible peril" (see figure 18).

This group photograph is a Bourke-White trope. She arranges a large group of people such that they fill her viewfinder and such that as a group they relay a message. In this case the lesson is that the Russian people—and here you see them, she says to us—are a stalwart group ready to protect themselves and their way of life. They are confident and prepared and need only instructions (and some more Western supplies). They are, Bourke-White tells us photographically, worthy allies against our mutual Fascist enemy.

In figure 19 we see another set of people pictured in an almost identical way, but here the expressions, clothing, and general appearance are completely different. We see sadness, dirty faces, and raggedy clothes aplenty, and since the models are children the pathos is even more striking. Here, Bourke-White says, is a group of pathetic orphans, children torn from their mothers and fathers who may well be dead, children who have been displaced by fascism (in this case by the Japanese) and war. They need help, and Americans should be ready to provide cash to any of a variety of charitable relief funds; the June 23 *Life* article is headlined "China Relief: U.S. Opens Its Purse."

Even figures 16 and 31 are constructed in a similar fashion; Bourke-White has just selected a smaller group of people: hardy Ukrainian field-workers ready to feed a nation and devout churchgoers showing us that the Soviet Union is not the godless country as some would have us believe. Bourke-White's photographs almost always carried a message beneath their aesthetic surface.

Bourke-White at the Front

Finally, on November 17, two months after Caldwell and Bourke-White had returned from the battlefields near Yelnya and east of Smolensk, and weeks after they had both embarked on separate American lecture tours, *Life* published eleven photos from that trip to the front as its lead story, "Russian Mud and Blood Stall German Army."[49]

By this time there seems to have been some mission creep on *Life*'s part. While the opening image (see figure 20) is a startling one of the five cars of the correspondents mired in shin-deep mud along a road somewhere near

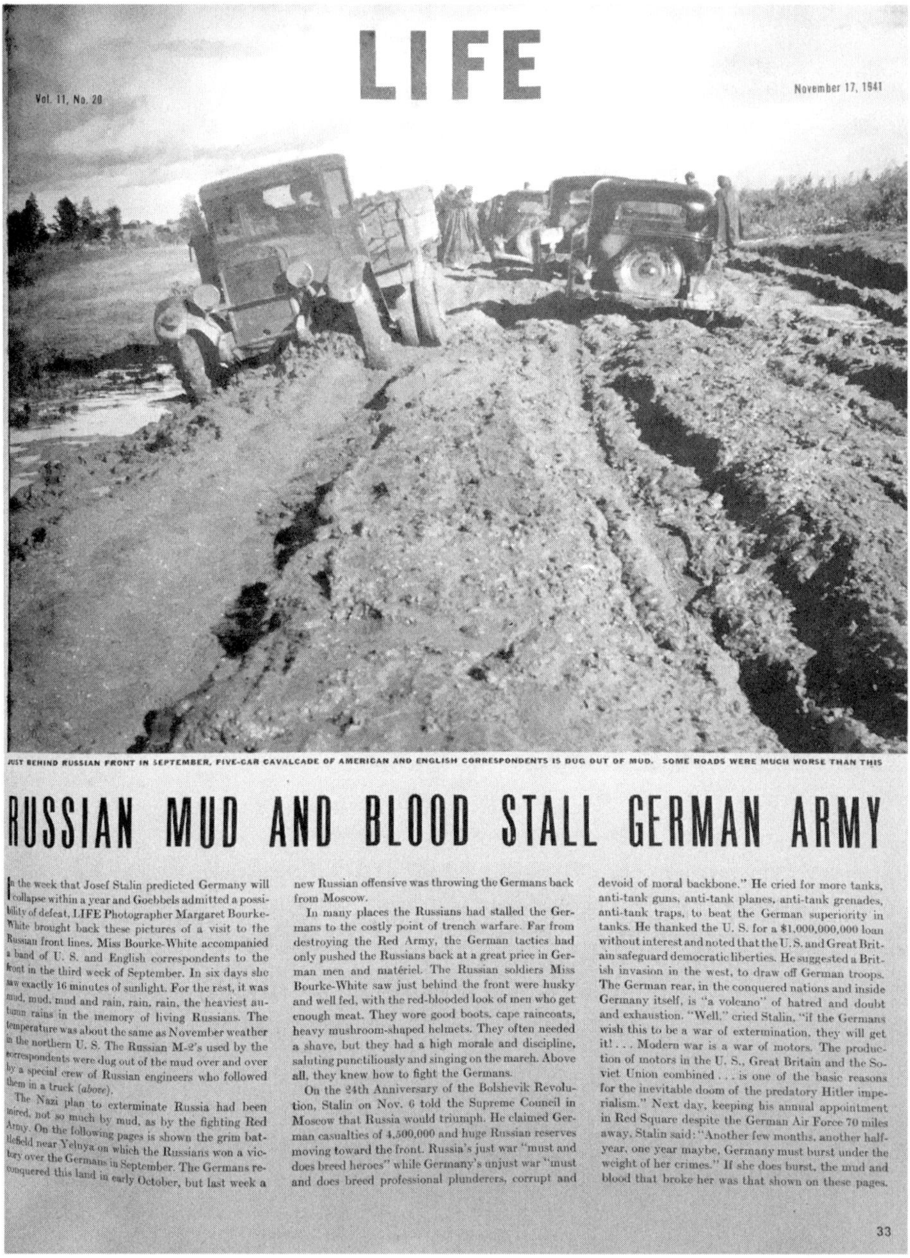

LIFE

Vol. 11, No. 20

November 17, 1941

JUST BEHIND RUSSIAN FRONT IN SEPTEMBER, FIVE-CAR CAVALCADE OF AMERICAN AND ENGLISH CORRESPONDENTS IS DUG OUT OF MUD. SOME ROADS WERE MUCH WORSE THAN THIS

RUSSIAN MUD AND BLOOD STALL GERMAN ARMY

In the week that Josef Stalin predicted Germany will collapse within a year and Goebbels admitted a possibility of defeat, LIFE Photographer Margaret Bourke-White brought back these pictures of a visit to the Russian front lines. Miss Bourke-White accompanied a band of U. S. and English correspondents to the front in the third week of September. In six days she saw exactly 16 minutes of sunlight. For the rest, it was mud, mud, mud and rain, rain, rain, the heaviest autumn rains in the memory of living Russians. The temperature was about the same as November weather in the northern U. S. The Russian M-2's used by the correspondents were dug out of the mud over and over by a special crew of Russian engineers who followed them in a truck (*above*).

The Nazi plan to exterminate Russia had been mired, not so much by mud, as by the fighting Red Army. On the following pages is shown the grim battlefield near Yelnya on which the Russians won a victory over the Germans in September. The Germans reconquered this land in early October, but last week a new Russian offensive was throwing the Germans back from Moscow.

In many places the Russians had stalled the Germans to the costly point of trench warfare. Far from destroying the Red Army, the German tactics had only pushed the Russians back at a great price in German men and matériel. The Russian soldiers Miss Bourke-White saw just behind the front were husky and well fed, with the red-blooded look of men who get enough meat. They wore good boots, cape raincoats, heavy mushroom-shaped helmets. They often needed a shave, but they had a high morale and discipline, saluting punctiliously and singing on the march. Above all, they knew how to fight the Germans.

On the 24th Anniversary of the Bolshevik Revolution, Stalin on Nov. 6 told the Supreme Council in Moscow that Russia would triumph. He claimed German casualties of 4,500,000 and huge Russian reserves moving toward the front. Russia's just war "must and does breed heroes" while Germany's unjust war "must and does breed professional plunderers, corrupt and devoid of moral backbone." He cried for more tanks, anti-tank guns, anti-tank planes, anti-tank grenades, anti-tank traps, to beat the German superiority in tanks. He thanked the U. S. for a $1,000,000,000 loan without interest and noted that the U. S. and Great Britain safeguard democratic liberties. He suggested a British invasion in the west, to draw off German troops. The German rear, in the conquered nations and inside Germany itself, is "a volcano" of hatred and doubt and exhaustion. "Well," cried Stalin, "if the Germans wish this to be a war of extermination, they will get it! . . . Modern war is a war of motors. The production of motors in the U. S., Great Britain and the Soviet Union combined . . . is one of the basic reasons for the inevitable doom of the predatory Hitler imperialism." Next day, keeping his annual appointment in Red Square despite the German Air Force 70 miles away, Stalin said: "Another few months, another half-year, one year maybe, Germany must burst under the weight of her crimes." If she does burst, the mud and blood that broke her was that shown on these pages.

33

FIGURE 20. View of the cars of American and British war correspondents on a deeply rutted, muddy road behind the eastern front during World War II, Russia, 1941. Original caption: "Just behind Russian front in September, five-car cavalcade of American and English correspondents is dug out of mud. Some roads were much worse than this." (From *Life*, November 17, 1941; Margaret Bourke-White/The LIFE Picture Collection/Getty Images; © 1941 Time Inc. All rights reserved. Reprinted from LIFE and published with the permission of Time Inc. Reproduction in any manner in any language in whole or in part without written permission is prohibited. LIFE and the LIFE logo are registered trademarks of Time Inc. used under license.)

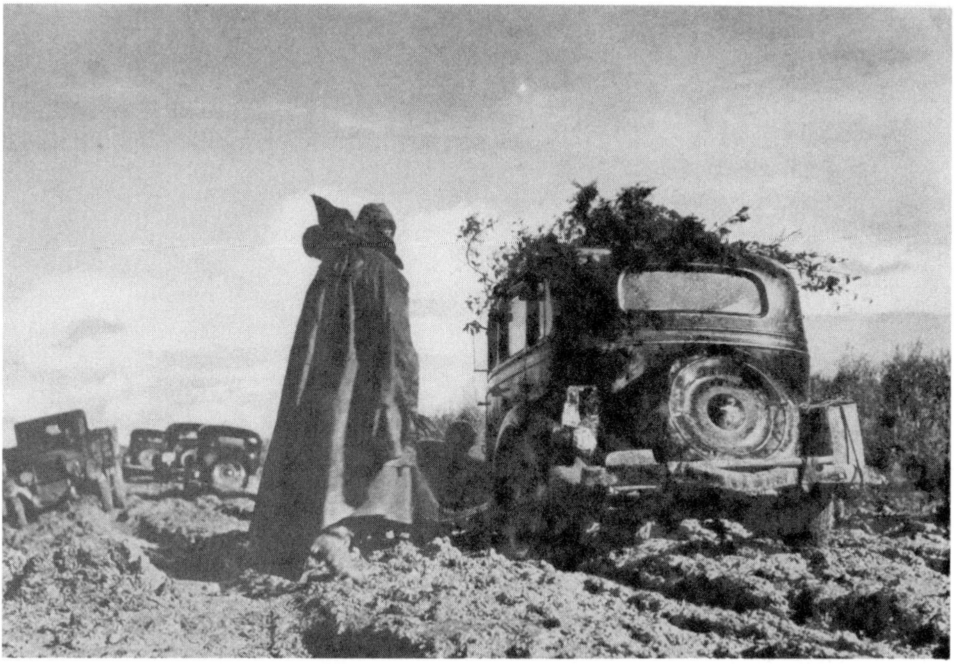

FIGURE 21. "Plowing Through the Mud" (From *Shooting the Russian War*; photo © Estate of Margaret Bourke-White/Licensed by VAGA, New York, N.Y.; courtesy of Syracuse University Libraries)

the front, the next four are panoramas of deserted, blasted, muddy steppe, across which some of the press can be seen picking their way. Bourke-White also took an extraordinary series of stark pictures of bombed-out villages in which only hearths and chimneys had remained standing, but none of these appeared in *Life*. These photos did find a prominent place in her two picture books, and perhaps that had been her plan. She submitted another first-person story, "Trip to the Front: Correspondents Get Plenty of Mud and Vodka,"[50] and alongside it is a posed photo of one of the makeshift evening banquet tables to which they grew accustomed, surrounded by a hearty crowd of Russian officers and Western press and crowned with ample viands and dozens of bottles of wine and vodka (see figure 22).

Life did attempt to put a happy face on the problems of Russia's western front by pointing out, a bit prematurely as circumstances developed, that the Wehrmacht "reconquered this land in early October, but last week a new Russian offensive was throwing the Germans back from Moscow."[51] Then,

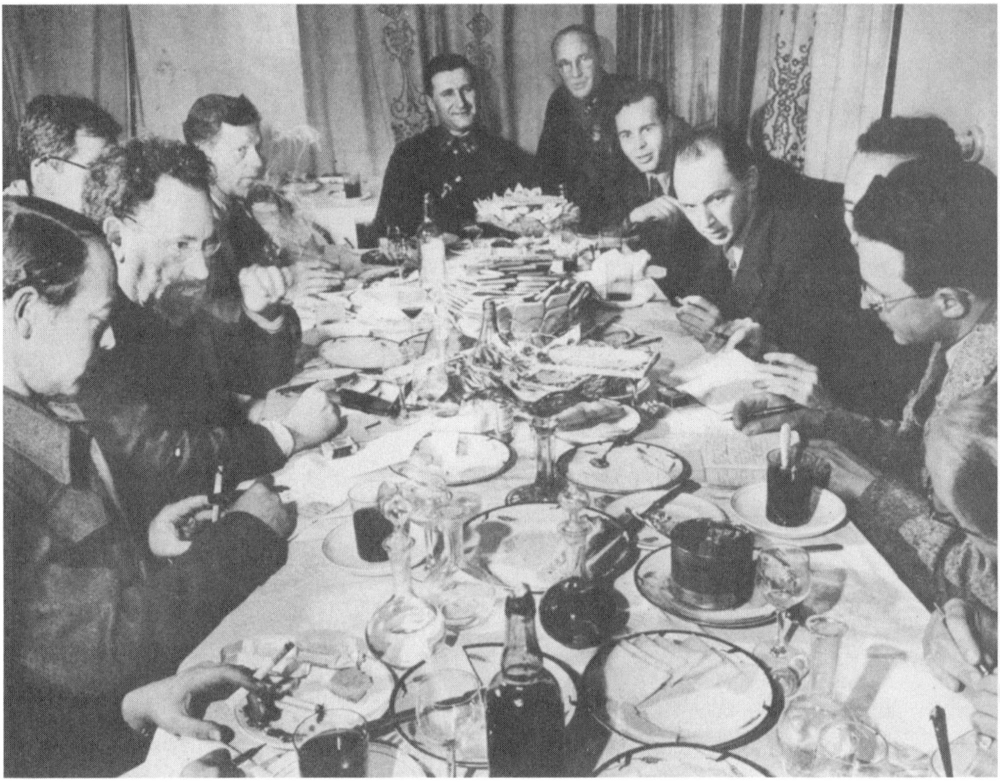

FIGURE 22. Bourke-White's original caption: "Supper for Correspondents in Vyazma, the Night before the Bombing. Left to right: Philip Jordan of the *London News Chronicle;* [A. C.] Cholerton, British correspondent longest in Moscow; Cyrus Sulzberger of *The New York Times;* Erskine Caldwell; General Sokolovsky, Chief of Western Staff under Marshal Timoshenko; Colonel Sudakov, the tank colonel who was our guide and interpreter (Sudakov served three years ago in Washington, D.C., as secretary to the Military Attaché at the Soviet Embassy); Anurov, one of the censors from Narkomindel, who accompanied the correspondents so as to be able to censor their dispatches upon return; Henry Cassidy of A.P.; Arch Steele (covered up) of the *Chicago Daily News;* Wallace Carroll, of U.P.

"General Sokolovsky, like many Soviet military officials, was young for his rank. He was forty-three and a former peasant. The three stars on his collar indicate that he is a general. He was a modest, pleasant man, brisk and intelligent." (From *Shooting the Russian War,* 227; photo © Estate of Margaret Bourke-White/Licensed by VAGA, New York, N.Y.; courtesy of Syracuse University Libraries) risking the embarrassment that the press junket was but a quick swing through a Potemkin countryside, *Life* references its intrepid photographer: "The Russian soldiers Miss Bourke-White saw just behind the front were husky and well fed, with the red-blooded look of men who get enough meat. They wore good boots, cape raincoats, heavy mushroom-shaped helmets. They often needed a shave, but they had a high morale and discipline, saluting punctiliously and singing on the march. Above all, they knew how to fight the Germans." The last two pictures, however, were startling because, for the first instance in these Bourke-White dispatches, a corpse is shown.

The Soviet Press Bureau had arranged for the correspondents to spend the first night of the trip at a small pension in the rail hub of Vyazma.[52] Early the next morning, at 7:32 recalls Bourke-White, a German bomber dumped its load of munitions across the street from the press hotel, much to the consternation of the reporters, many of whom were still in bed. Within minutes, this same bomber had been brought down by anti-aircraft fire, and later the press had a chance to observe the Russian interrogation of the three surviving crewmen. But in the moment, the Caldwells, who had been at their morning ablutions while the others slept, sprinted out of the lodge across the street to the area hardest hit, Bourke-White with her camera in hand.

Bourke-White took dozens of photos that morning, of which *Life* chose to print but two. In the house most directly hit, three had died: a young woman, her father, and her grandmother. They had been tossed about the shattered room by the explosions as only the helpless dead can be. The girl had come to rest atop her grandmother, the back of whose head was all that could be seen. She had landed propped up in a semisitting position, her legs splayed open so that the rents in her stockings were visible, her neck and head twisted at an impossible angle. Her father lay sprawled on his back a few feet away, shoeless, bloodied, and mangled. Bourke-White printed the complete photo in *Shooting the Russian War*,[53] but it is such a dreadful image that *Life* chose to crop it extensively. All that the American reader saw was the juxtaposition of the heads of the two women amid a cacophony of rubble, but that was enough for *Life* to make the point that the lives of these simple people had been snuffed out suddenly by a ruthless war (see figures 23 and 24).

In the picture at the bottom of the page we see the grief-stricken mother and the surviving son who sit stunned on a bench, comforted by neighbors. This scene capped Bourke-White's assignment. *Life* had now brought the full tragedy of the Russian war into millions of American households.

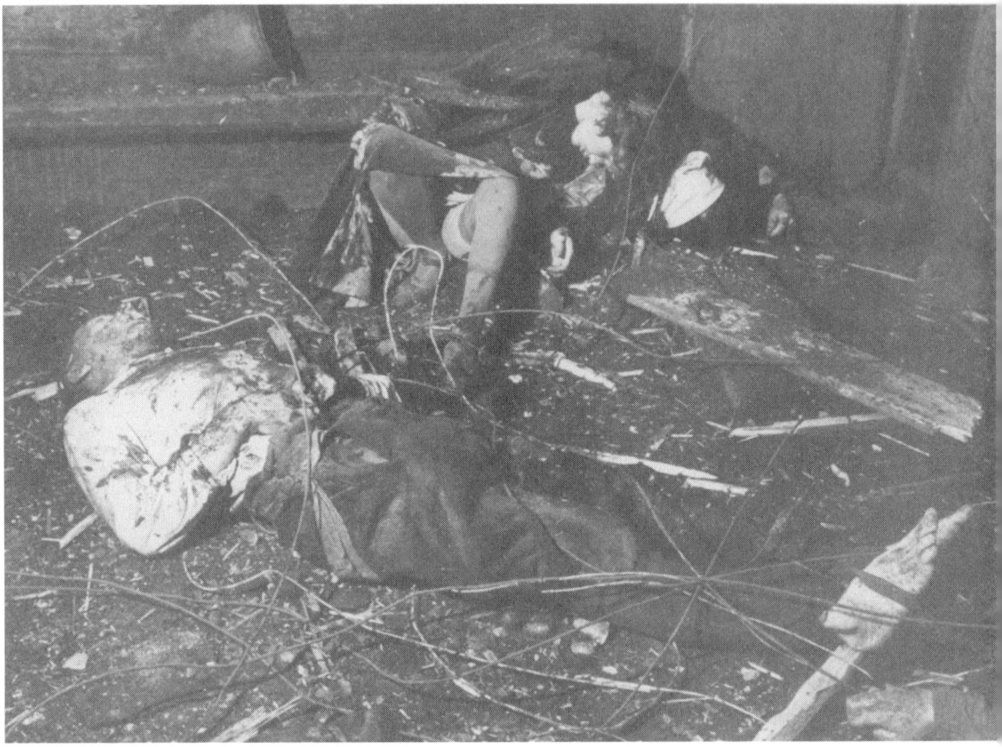

FIGURE 23. Death visits Vyazma (From *Shooting the Russian War*; photo © Estate of Margaret Bourke-White/Licensed by VAGA, New York, N.Y.; courtesy of Syracuse University Libraries)

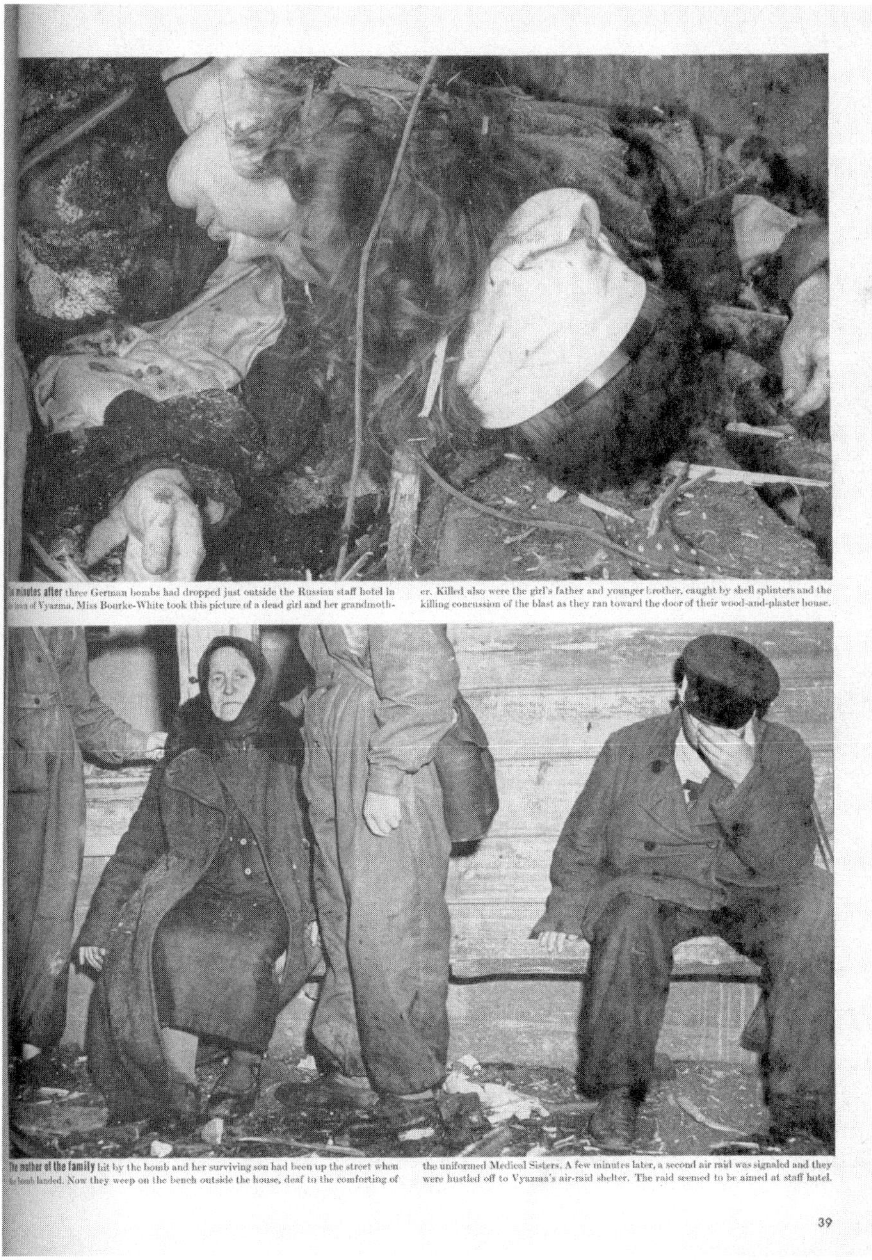

FIGURE 24. [*Upper photo*] View of the bodies of a girl and her grandmother killed on a street during a German air raid in World War II, Moscow, Russia, 1941. [*Lower photo*] As soldiers stand between them, a mother and her brother sit in shock after learning of the death of the rest of their family during a German air raid in World War II, Moscow, Russia, 1941. (From *Life*, November 17, 1941; Margaret Bourke-White/The LIFE Picture Collection/Getty Images; © 1941 Time Inc. All rights reserved. Reprinted from LIFE and published with the permission of Time Inc. Reproduction in any manner in any language in whole or in part without written permission is prohibited. LIFE and the LIFE logo are registered trademarks of Time Inc. used under license.)

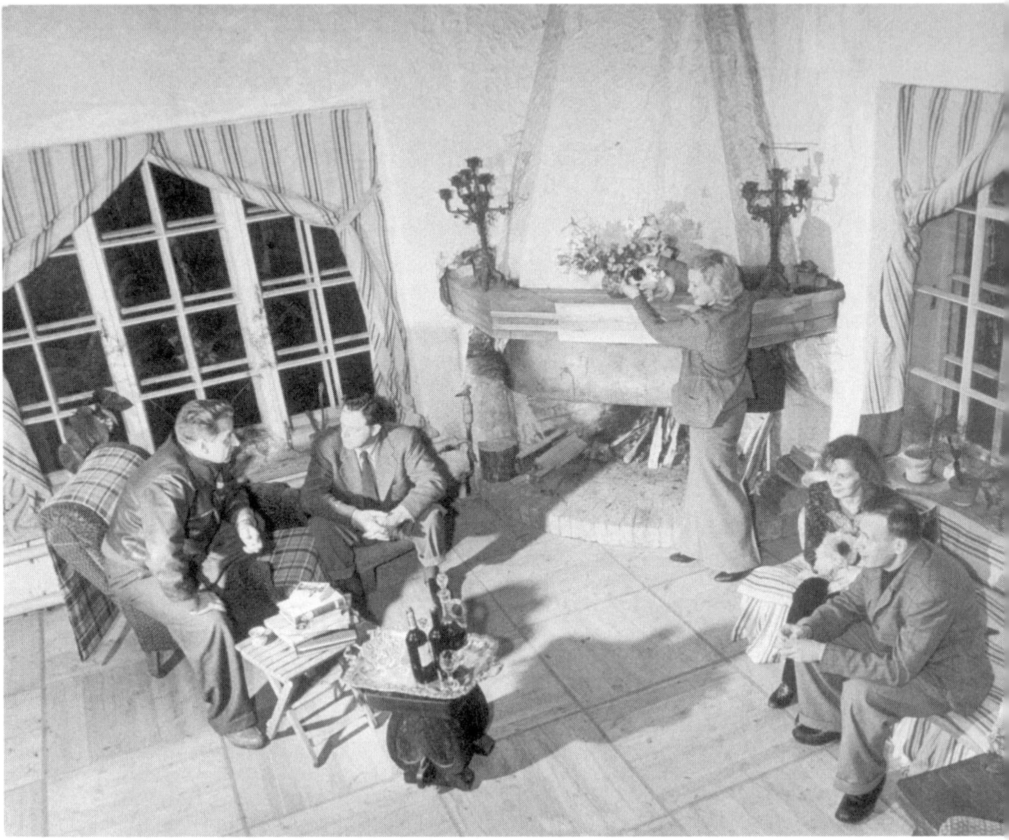

FIGURE 25. Circa 1941: Russian movie actress Lynbov Orlova (*center*) standing at the mantle while her husband, film director Gregory Alexandrov (*left*) speaks with novelist Erskine Caldwell (*second from left*) at a dinner party at their country house thirty miles outside the city (From *Life*, December 1, 1941; Margaret Bourke-White/The LIFE Picture Collection/Getty Images)

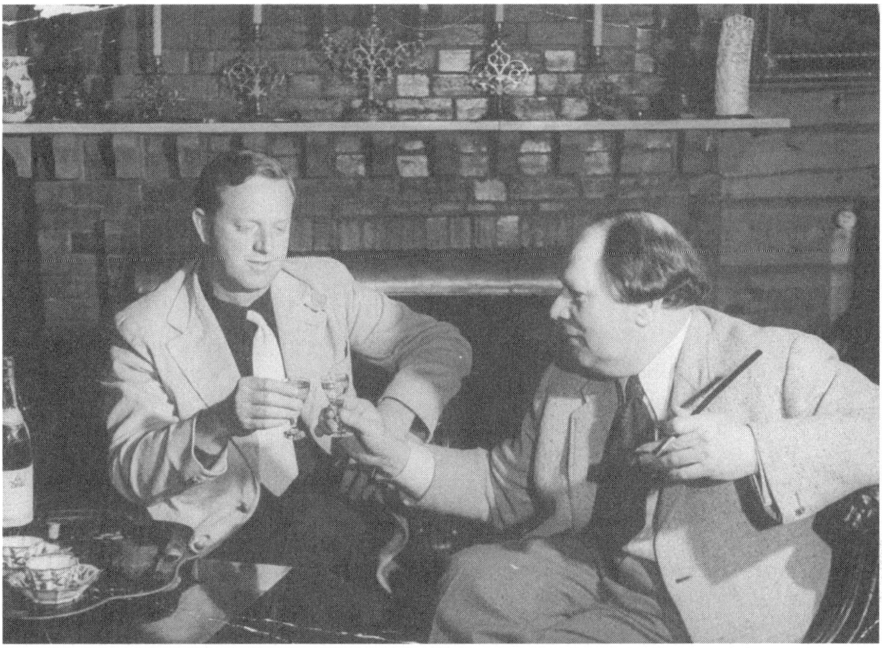

FIGURE 26. American novelist Erskine Caldwell drinking a cognac toast with his famous Russian novelist host Alexei Tolstoy in the cozy comforts of his summer home outside the city (From *Life*, December 1, 1941; Margaret Bourke-White/The LIFE Picture Collection/Getty Images)

But the magazine had not yet exhausted its Bourke-White material. One of *Life*'s regular features was its weekly foray into the social world with its "LIFE goes to . . ." reports, which usually appeared on the last few pages of an issue. In its December 1 issue it ran a "LIFE Goes to a Party" piece featuring six Bourke-White photos of Russian movie star Lyubov Orlova and her husband, film director Gregory Alexandrov ("Russia's Darryl Zanuck"), and four more of author Alexei Tolstoy and his wife.[54] Both couples are at their dachas, and Bourke-White captures them there sumptuously feting her husband (see figures 25 and 26). "Life Calls on a Russian Movie Star" opens: "To most Americans the U.S.S.R. is a vast, dreary, egalitarian poorhouse in which every worker and peasant receives exactly the same allotment of shoddy garments, bad vodka and overcrowded living quarters. Actually Russia, a land of surprises, has not only its 'millionaires' but its 'town and country set' to boot." Even in its society pieces, *Life* was still hawking the idea that the USSR was not very different from the United States.

After the Shooting Was Done

By December, Bourke-White and Caldwell, having exited Russia first by train to Archangel and then by British naval convoy to Scotland, had been back in the States a month. They had done all they could to advance Western cooperation with the Soviet Union from *within* the USSR. Her photography frequently had been stunning, its audience vast. By 1943 *Life*'s circulation would grow to 3.7 million, and *Time*'s exceeded a million.[55] Her work's shortcomings—the time gap between the original film exposure and its publication, the often fractured captions, the less than ideal selection of prints and their harsh cropping, the often heavy-handed editorial prose, and her lack of availability to control the artistic process—were not under her control and so were often not up to her own standards. Nonetheless, the tide of American public opinion had indeed turned, and this, after all, had been her, and Caldwell's, goal. Luce and his magazine empire had been much behind all this. And then came the Japanese attack on Pearl Harbor.

After leaving the Soviet Union, Bourke-White and Caldwell spent about two weeks in Britain, organizing material for their photo-text collaboration, dining out, sightseeing, shopping, and visiting Lord Beaverbrook, also just back from Moscow.[56] Caldwell, in particular, was churning out a prodigious amount of newspaper copy for the *Daily Mail* while reworking his Moscow diary into *Moscow Under Fire*. For *Russia at War*, Bourke-White selected eighty photographs: one for the cover, the remaining seventy-nine to be placed following the material Caldwell was reconfiguring from his *PM* newspaper articles. Only one photograph, that of Ambassador Steinhardt conducting business amidst the shattered glass from the Spaso House windows, had appeared in *Life*. About half the photos were completely new; others were variations of shots that had already been published in *Life*. The differences were often not subtle—faces obscured, intrusive shadows, people in group photos clustered inharmoniously, a general lack of cohesion—and always the *Life* photos were qualitatively superior.

Bourke-White apparently was saving her best work for her own book. She took great care in compiling the photos for *Shooting the Russian War*. This was to be her book and hers alone. She used ninety-three pictures, including one of her dramatic night photographs from a Luftwaffe attack that she placed on the dust jacket. Three of the photos are identical to ones *Life* published, and another ten are from the same negative set used by *Life*, but in every case in *Shooting* she prints the full-frame image she initially had composed in her camera's viewfinder. Twenty-two of the *Shooting* photos are completely new. All the

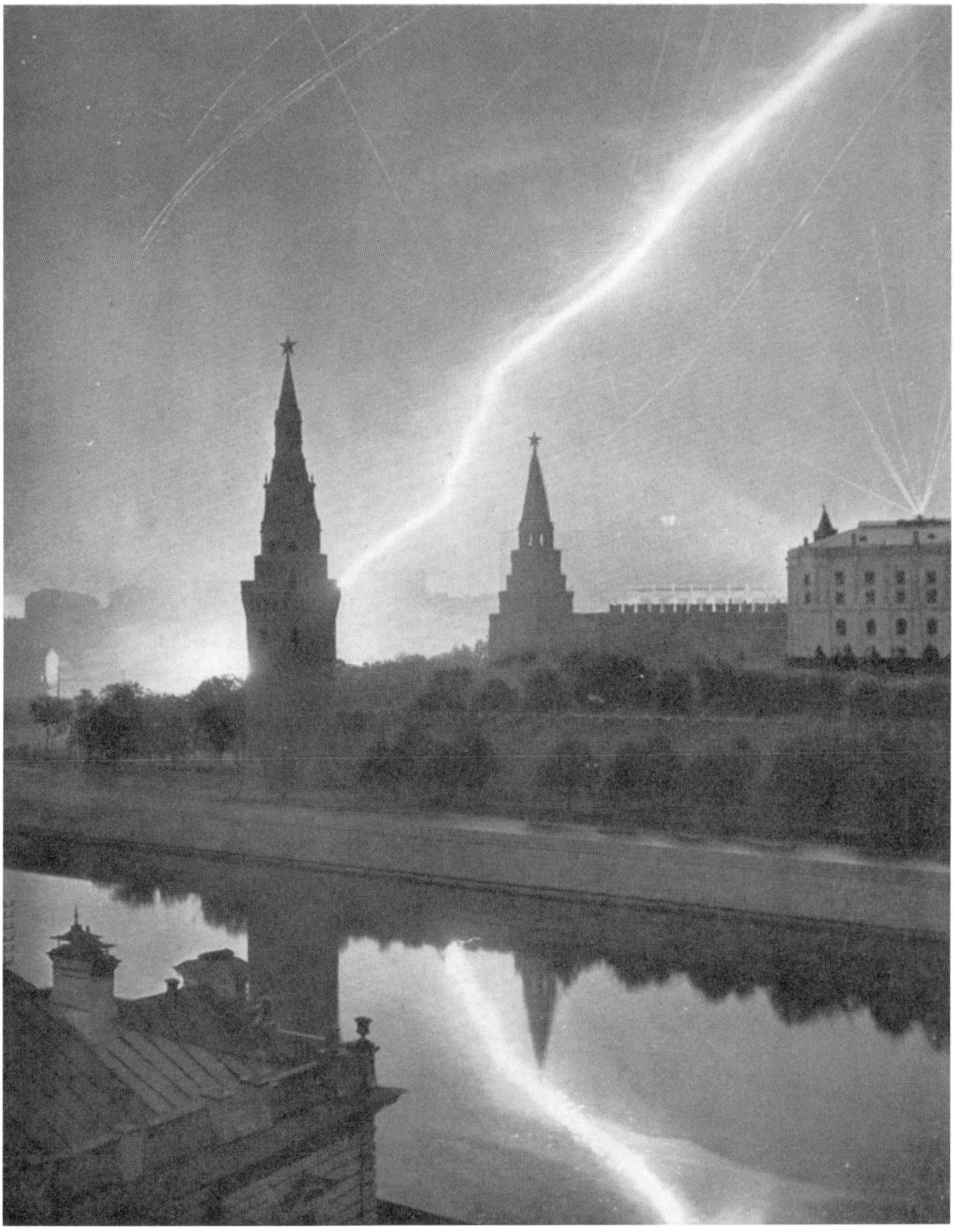

FIGURE 27. Compare with figures 28 and 29 (From *Russia at War*; photo © Estate of Margaret Bourke-White/Licensed by VAGA, New York, N.Y.)

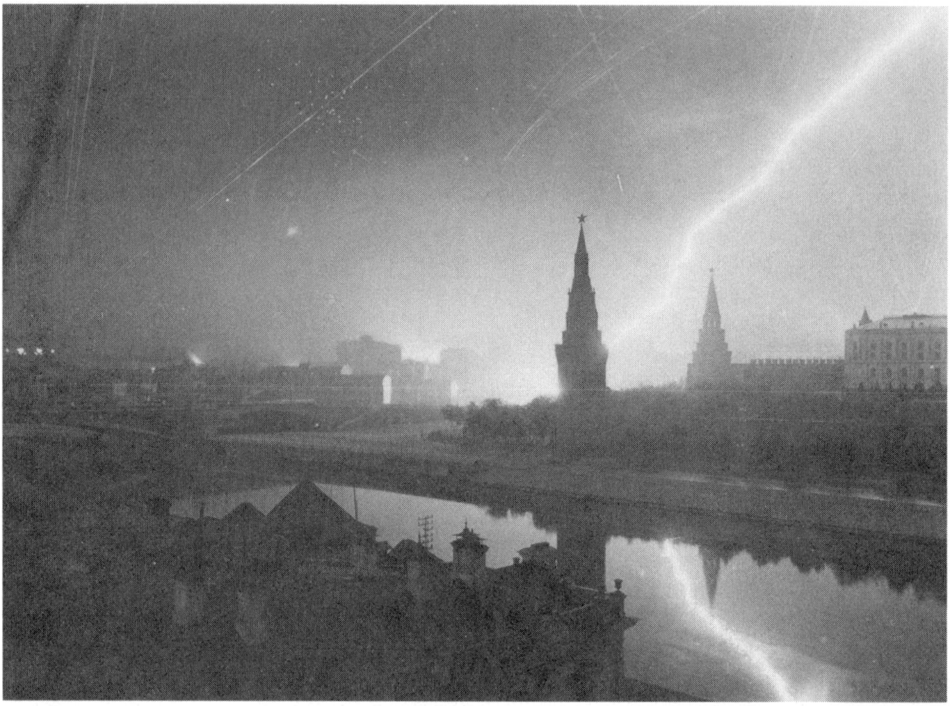

FIGURE 28. "Path of a Parachute Flare" (From *Shooting the Russian War*; photo © Estate of Margaret Bourke-White/Licensed by VAGA, New York, N.Y.; courtesy of Syracuse University Libraries)

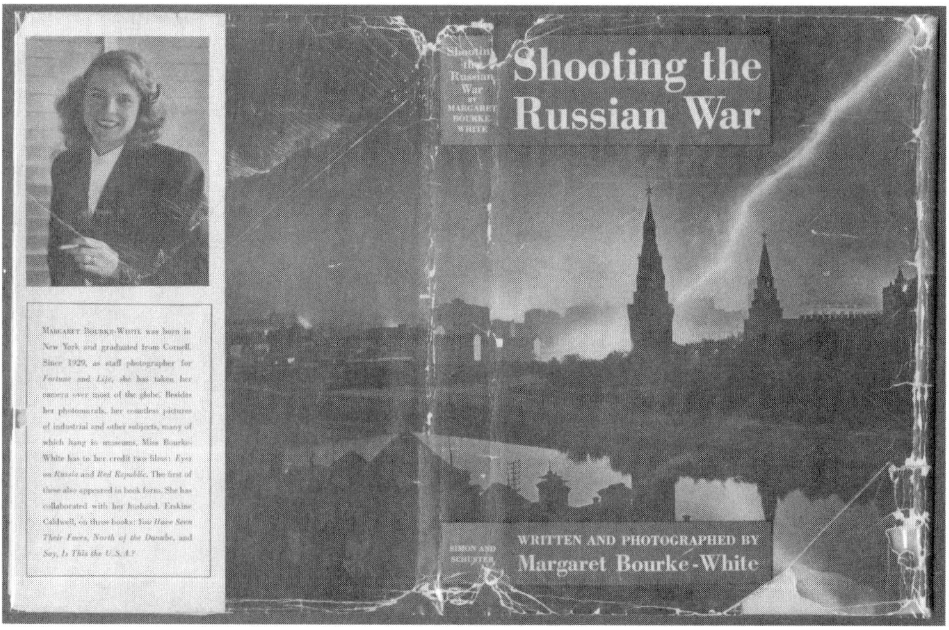

FIGURE 29. Cover of *Shooting the Russian War* (Photo © Estate of Margaret Bourke-White/Licensed by VAGA, New York, N.Y.; courtesy of Syracuse University Libraries)

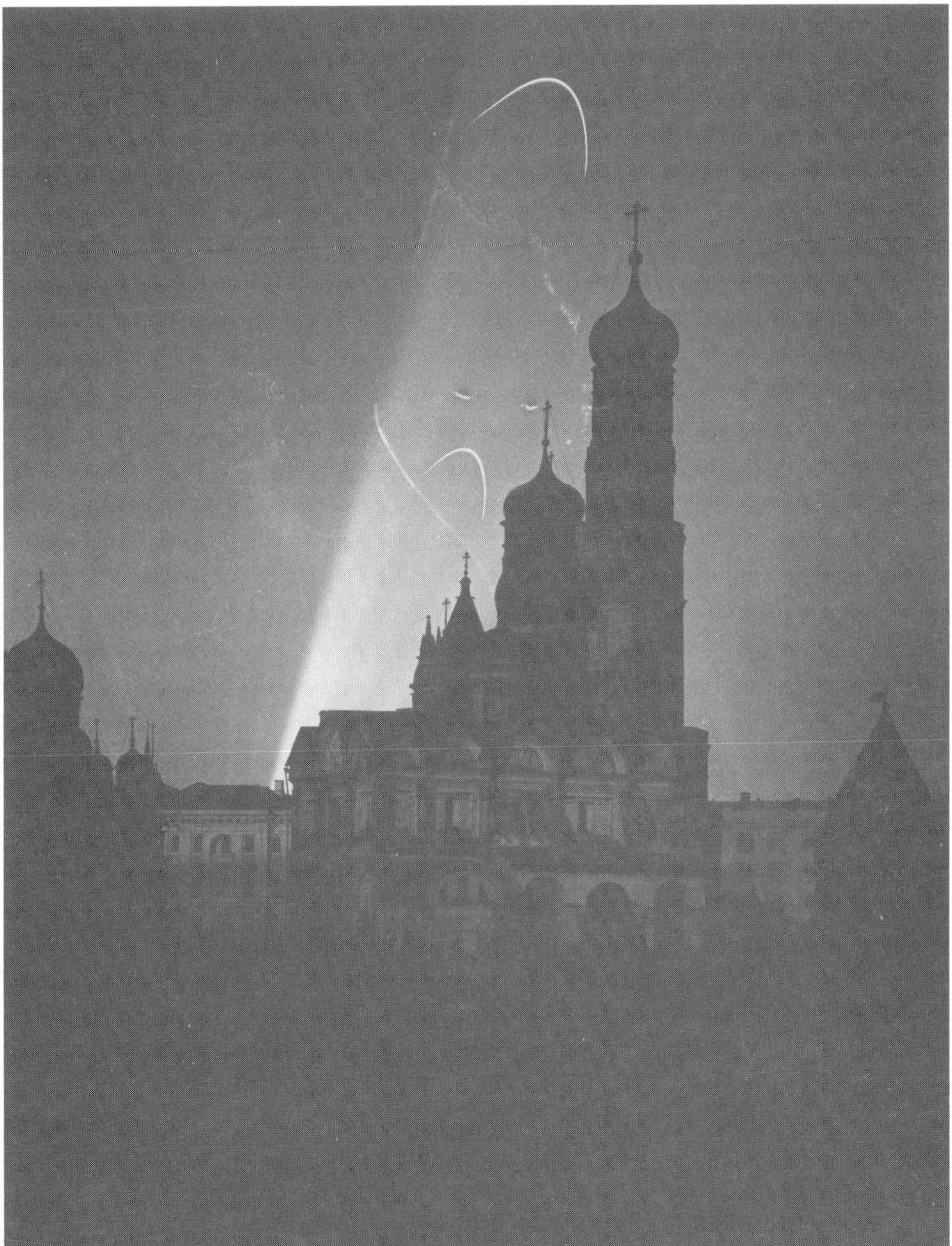

FIGURE 30. "Belfry of Ivan the Great During an Air Raid" (From *Shooting the Russian War*; photo © Estate of Margaret Bourke-White/Licensed by VAGA, New York, N.Y.; courtesy of Syracuse University Libraries)

other prints represent alternative exposures—different angles of view, different people at the same venue, different positions of the subject, different lighting, etc.—of the *Life* images.

In most cases, the images she chooses for *Shooting* are more dramatic, more evocative of time and place, and present more readily "readable" coding than those *Life* published. As an example, in the October 13 *Life* spread on religion in the Soviet Union, there is a picture of a group of about seventy-five Old Orthodox worshipers gathered behind a balustrade. It bears the caption: "Moscow countrywomen (with kerchiefs) crowd around bishop's cathedral platform in Moscow's Bogoyavlenia Cathedral for acting patriarch's blessing." There is little emotion visible across the faces of these women, men, and boys, all of whom seem to stand mesmerized by the camera; many appear more interested in Bourke-White than in the patriarch.

In *Shooting the Russian War* (see figure 31), Bourke-White uses a slightly different and more tightly cropped image for which she employed a narrow depth of field, so that the frame shows only three women in the front row, each in tight focus, and each of them openly displaying emotion. Two have placed a hand before their eyes and appear to be sobbing. Bourke-White's characteristically informative caption reads in part: "The parishioners cross themselves constantly and automatically from the moment they enter the church. After each prayer uttered from the altar the people break in with a '*Gospodi pomilui*,' God have mercy. The congregation is made up largely of women, usually old. Few young people go to church."[57]

Although the pictures in *Shooting the Russian War* are not directly keyed to the chapters into which they have been bound, their captions, which often nearly fill the facing page, serve as a supplemental text. For this reason *Shooting the Russian War* is readable, refreshingly detailed, highly informative, pleasingly visual, and there remains little doubt as to Bourke-White's purpose. At one point she summarizes the Russians' response to being attacked: "With each month of the conflict, unity became more pronounced and dread lessened. Citizens had so many new tasks to do, tasks which demonstrated their loyalty, that they no longer had to fear whether their patriotism might be open to question."[58] In essence, whatever one may have thought of the Russians before this war, they are now citizens of the free world and deserve American assistance.

Soon after they returned to the United States, both Bourke-White and Caldwell undertook extensive speaking tours, passionately promoting alliance with the USSR. They preached not only from their lecterns but also in the newspaper interviews they readily encouraged. In a 1974 article in *Historian*, Melvin

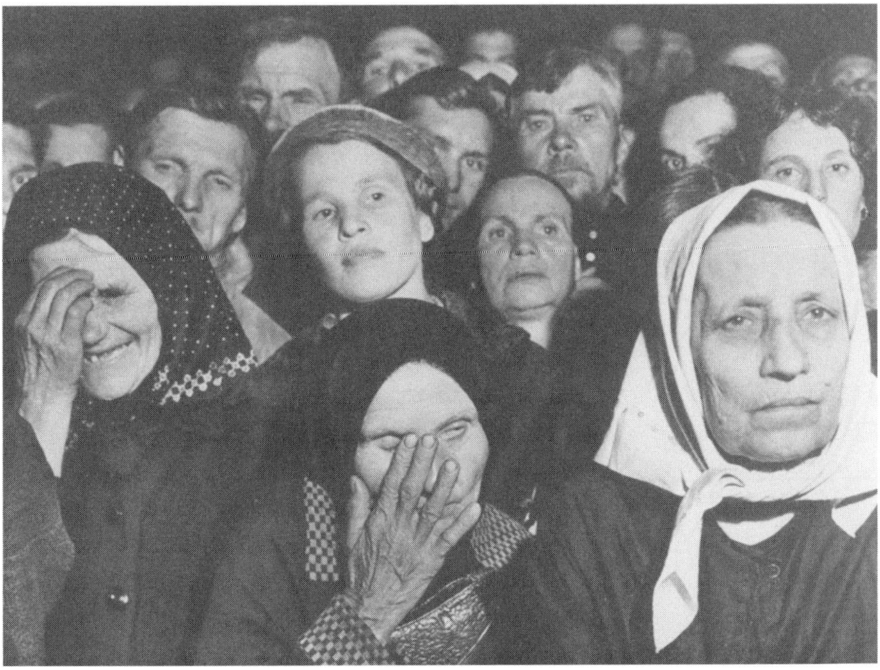

FIGURE 31. "Old Orthodox Worshippers" (From *Shooting the Russian War*; photo © Estate of Margaret Bourke-White/Licensed by VAGA, New York, N.Y.; courtesy of Syracuse University Libraries)

Small showed that the editorial practices of the liberal press during this era had a far greater public relations impact than did those of the conservative media. The combination of magazines, newspapers, newsreels, radio, fiction and nonfiction books, and movies had a profound influence on public attitudes toward the Soviet Union.[59] By the summer of 1942, Caldwell and Bourke-White enjoyed a substantial presence in all these outlets.

Bourke-White's professional relationship with Caldwell was drying up as rapidly as their personal one. Within a year they divorced, never to see each other again. Neither of her Moscow books sold well, and neither she nor Caldwell even mentions *Russia at War* in their list of works published. Although *Shooting the Russian War* received few reviews, these were generally positive in praising both her photography and her simple prose styling. Nonetheless, as always, Bourke-White's most effective promotional platform remained *Life*, as it would continue to be for the remainder of her professional career.

CHAPTER 4

A Motley Crew ★ The Other Moscow Correspondents

Only a handful of Western journalists were in residence in Moscow on May 10, 1941, when Caldwell and Bourke-White arrived with Alice-Leone Moats of *Collier's* in tow. A. T. Cholerton of the London *Daily Telegraph*, the doyen of the Western press, had been in the city for well over a decade, having arrived on assignment in 1925. Henry Shapiro of the United Press syndicate had been there almost as long. Formerly a Reuters agent, Shapiro, a Carpathian native who spoke Russian flawlessly, had been in Moscow since 1933. He'd originally come fresh from Harvard Law School but was never able to obtain the necessary credentials to practice before the bar there, so he became a correspondent.[1] Henry Cassidy of the Associated Press, the only other American, had arrived from France just the previous summer. Maurice Lovell, Reuters' current representative, had arrived earlier from Greece, having been expelled from Romania in March 1940 for displeasing Nazi authorities.[2] Moats offers a striking portrait of Lovell on June 28:

> We were sitting in the press room when Lovell, the Reuters' correspondent, appeared in the doorway looking rather self-important. Lovell was a nice fellow, but he suffered from a delusion that he should combine the functions of a diplomat with those of reporter. I was always surprised not to find him dressed in striped trousers and Anthony Eden hat.
>
> He had a slow, precise way of speaking and under no circumstances could be induced to make a flat statement of fact. His conversation teemed with references to "a certain great man," "someone who must remain nameless," and so on.[3]

But that was it. Even the venerable *New York Times* was without representation since earlier in the month.

Why the *Times* no longer had a correspondent there is worth exploring, because its former reporter's controversial status vis-à-vis the Kremlin was instructive for succeeding Western journalists. For two decades, beginning in the summer of 1921, the *Times* had been represented by the flamboyant and controversial Walter Duranty, who was one of the first Western reporters credentialed by the USSR. Prior to this, foreign journalists had not been allowed in the Soviet Union, but in 1921, in response to reports about a devastating famine along the Volga, President Warren G. Harding created the American Relief Administration to oversee food aid. This opened the door for selected journalists to report on the ARA inside the USSR, and Duranty quickly took advantage.

During his long tenure he had managed to lose his left leg from gangrene following a train wreck, acquire two prostheses, gain a reputation as an inveterate womanizer, present the striking image of a man in a long topcoat with a beaver collar and a snap-brim hat, and finally become an active alcoholic. During his heyday, when he won a 1932 Pulitzer Prize for his coverage of the Russian Five-Year Plan, Duranty's word was so solid that whatever he wrote became received fact by other reporters and even the diplomatic corps, who ought to have known otherwise. Unfortunately, as Duranty's lavish lifestyle became showier, the quality of his reportage began to slip. In May 1939, when Stalin replaced Commissar of Foreign Affairs Maxim Litvinov with the then-premier Vyacheslav Molotov, Duranty missed the significance this had for Stalin's political maneuvering. Consequently, when the Molotov-Ribbentrop Pact was signed on August 23, guaranteeing a temporary détente, if not peace, between the USSR and the Third Reich, Duranty had no inkling. His stock began to fall soon thereafter.

By the end of the decade Duranty was spending less and less time in Russia. Around 1937 the *Times* sent Harold Denny to spell Duranty during his increasingly frequent absences, and in 1939 it replaced Denny with G. D. Gedye. Duranty took personal offense at both of these stringers and, because he retained significant clout, continued to report intermittently from Moscow, infuriating the *Times* editors in New York, who finally refused to accept more than one wire report per day from Moscow.[4]

Though Duranty's personality and presentation, and even his writing style (honed in the English manner at Harrow and Cambridge, heavy with classical allusions, fairy tales, and historical references), irked many of his fellow correspondents, what bothered them most was that they believed he had traded a reporter's commitment to the facts in return for access within the Kremlin. They charged him with being a Russian sycophant or, worse, a supporter of Stalin's "Revolution from Above" philosophy. In fact, Duranty had developed and published his thesis that Stalin was to be exonerated from wrongdoing in the purges and show trials of the 1930s. Because he had had to root out a "Fifth Column" of "Nazi saboteurs from the ranks of the Communist Party. . . .

Stalin had to destroy his country in order to save it."[5] But the final straw was Duranty's failure to report on the reality of the devastating Ukrainian famine of 1937. In several dispatches to the *Times* after he had actually toured the famine area unrestricted, he denied that the peasants were starving. Earlier, in 1933, he had already established his position on Stalin's forced collectivization: "But—to put it brutally—you can't make an omelette without breaking eggs, and the Bolshevik leaders are just as indifferent to the casualties that may be involved in their drive toward Socialism as any General during the World War who ordered a costly attack in order to show his superiors that he and his division possessed the proper soldierly spirit. In fact, the Bolsheviki are more indifferent because they are animated by fanatical conviction."[6] This infamous and callous egg-omelet proposition was to haunt Duranty to his grave.

By the time the Caldwells arrived, Duranty was just a distant memory to the press corps, many of whom had never met him. Indeed, after the Soviet Union invaded Finland in late November 1939, the *Times* had removed all its staff from Moscow. Duranty had been in Romania until September 1940, when he was expelled at the insistence of the occupying Germans. Duranty's overtly pro-Soviet past finally had caught up with him. The *Times*, too, dismissed him that autumn, though their separation wouldn't be final until May, just as the Caldwells and Moats were arriving.

In a sense there was little reason for the Western press to be in Moscow at this time as it was not a focal point on the horizon of the international news front. The Soviets were viewed as strongly allied with Hitler's Germany, a belief promoted by Joseph Stalin. The diplomatic history of the 1939–41 period is complex, fraught, and contested, but from a journalist's point of view Moscow was not then a coveted assignment.

Alice Moats was in Moscow because she was an indefatigable traveler and a sometime stringer for *Collier's* magazine. She had gotten the wheels rolling for this trip to Russia almost a year earlier when by chance she had encountered Laurence Steinhardt, an old acquaintance, but more importantly the U.S. ambassador to the Soviet Union, in a New York restaurant on July 3, 1940. In her memoir, *Blind Date with Mars*, she recalls that she innocently suggested to him, "When you go back to Moscow, will you take me with you?"[7] She didn't get to actually go with Steinhardt, but he had helped with the red tape. On August 20, 1940, she embarked on the *President Taft* for Yokohama with a promise from Steinhardt that a Russian visa would soon reach her along with press credentials and an assignment from *Collier's*. Traveling through Tokyo, Shanghai, Saigon, Hanoi, Singapore, Rangoon, and then along the rustic and dangerous Burma Road, she finally arrived in Chungking in mid-February

1941, still lacking a visa. When she chanced upon the Caldwells on April 30 in Lanchow finally *with* a visa, she was already nine months into her eighteen-month round-the-world excursion.

Lacking journalistic experience, she knew she never could be a hard-news reporter: "Suffering from no delusions of statesmanship, I could only give a picture of everyday life as it is led against a background of world-shaking politics and war." Thus Alice Moats staked out her terrain. Her candid observations of the members of the Moscow press that summer are invaluable. That she had other self-described qualities only adds to her charm: "determination, curiosity, a phenomenal memory, much experience in traveling, great fluency in five languages, and an uncanny instinct for spotting phonies, and a talent for bringing out the worst in the best people."[8]

In June 1941 Moscow truly was a backwater for journalists. Henry Cassidy, the AP man who had arrived in the summer of 1940 from Paris after its collapse, noted that although visitors came through now and then, the only permanent Western correspondents were Cholerton, Shapiro, Lovell, and Jean Champenois. Champenois represented Havas, the rump news organization that survived after the Nazis nationalized AFP (Agence France-Presse), the French press agency, at the time the oldest news organization in the world. Cassidy's memoir, *Moscow Dateline*, shines some light on the enigmatic Cholerton. In the first edition of the book, Cassidy makes no mention of him in the section on journalists in Moscow at the start of the war.[9] The later American edition describes Cholerton as "a legendary figure in Moscow."

> For sixteen years, he had stomped around outside the Kremlin walls, tugging nervously at his stubby black beard, jingling keys in his pockets, dancing impatiently on the little feet that seemed hardly capable of carrying his heavy body, and raging against the régime. A Cambridge don, he had come to Moscow as a sympathizer. He remained to become a violent opponent.
>
> After sixteen years, he still could not speak Russian. He accumulated a vast store of information and misinformation, all of which became hopelessly muddled. I have heard him describing to newcomers two of the best-known Russian dishes, Borsch and Kiev cutlets, and getting them all wrong. Yet he was of great influence.
>
> Everyone liked him, even the Russians whom he denounced. They considered him a relic of the nineteenth-century Russian intellectuals, which made him dance all the more in anger. The embassies respected him for his long service, were flattered when he called, and heeded his utterances.[10]

Apparently, Cassidy's choleric comments were more than his British publisher was willing to brook, even in 1943.

As usual, Alice Moats draws a more personal portrait of him. Here she describes Cholerton in the days just following the German invasion, when she had moved in with him for her own safety:

> He had taken the black-out orders very seriously and somehow had managed to find a few dark shades which he nailed onto the windows. Besides this precaution he screwed blue bulbs into the lamps. For the first ten days Chol couldn't figure out how to hang the blinds so that they could be rolled up in the daytime, and he lived in a perpetual black-out. It is a miracle that he didn't break an arm or leg during this period, for, what with the obscurity added to his already bad eyesight, he kept blundering around falling over tables and chairs. He also had trouble finding his clothes, and every day he appeared dressed in a weird assortment of garments.[11]

But not only was the Moscow beat a backwater, it was one in which the "experts" were hardly that. The Soviets saw to that. "The experts had few, if any, personal contacts," Cassidy writes, "either officially or unofficially, with the people of the country they were trying to judge. The foreign colony of Moscow lived a life apart, behind walls which were invisible but as impregnable as the ramparts of the Kremlin. Within those walls came a few Soviet secretaries, cooks and maids, an occasional ballerina or a frequenter of the Hôtel Métropole, but among the great mass of the common people, the experts knew no one."[12] A January 1943 *Time* magazine article suggested that the situation had not changed much even a year and a half later:

> Correspondents live circumscribed routine lives in Moscow, have their most excitement trying to beat each other to the wire. After breakfast (tea, toast, and cold sausage, cold fish, occasionally an omelet), in their dimly lit, chill rooms at Moscow's squat Metropole Hotel each morning, they hurriedly compose stories culled from four Moscow papers—*Pravda, Red Star, Izvestia, Komsomolskaya Pravda.* They get their stories reviewed by Russia's sharp censors, then they race to the cable office. For a time Reuters' Harold King had the edge because he hired a motorcyclist. Nowadays U.P. and A.P., employing two fawn-fast girl runners, Venus and Zena, usually win. But mere speed is not enough for the real scoops. They come as reward, or as lightning surprise.[13]

Cassidy, in 1942, had been a beneficiary of one of those surprises. Unable to gain an audience with Premier Stalin despite repeated efforts, and being pressured by the AP in New York, he used a direct approach. Following Winston Churchill's visit in mid-August and Wendell Willkie's mission in September, on October 2 he typed out a letter to Stalin posing three questions. Later, he would write, a bit sheepishly, "Had I thought the letter would be answered, I should have taken a lot more pains over it." The following day he was summoned to the office of Nikolai Palgunov, chief of the Press Department at the Foreign Commissariat. "Palgunov was standing behind his enormous desk, his eyes bulging farther than ever. He emerged to the centre of the room, shook hands, waved me into one leather armchair in front of the desk and sat himself in the other. He squinted at me through his thick glasses, and, with an expression that might have been either suspicion, or awe, or both, said: 'The document that you are waiting for is here.'"[14] He handed Cassidy both the original Russian and an official translation, both dated October 3:

> Dear Mr. Cassidy,
>
> Owing to pressure of work and consequent inability to grant you an interview, I shall confine myself to a brief written answer to your questions.
>
> (1) QUESTION: *What place does the possibility of a Second Front occupy in Soviet estimates of the current situation?*
>
> ANSWER: A very important place: one might say a place of first-rate importance.
>
> (2) QUESTION: *To what extent is Allied aid to the Soviet Union proving effective, and what could be done to amplify and improve this aid?*
>
> ANSWER: As compared with the aid which the Soviet Union is giving to the Allies by drawing upon itself the main forces of the German-fascist armies, the aid of the Allies to the Soviet Union has so far been little effective. In order to amplify and improve this aid only one thing is required: that the Allies fulfil their obligations completely and on time.
>
> (3) QUESTION: *What remains of the Soviet capacity for resistance?*
>
> ANSWER: I think that the Soviet capacity for resisting the German brigands is in strength not a whit less, if not greater, than the capacity of fascist Germany, or of any other aggressive Power, to secure for itself world domination.
>
> With respect,
> (Signed) J. Stalin.

Of all the reporting Cassidy did during his career, this exchange of letters, and a follow-up correspondence in November dealing with the war in North Africa, are his most enduring contributions to war journalism. They made him famous.

Although in May 1941 there wasn't much news coming out of Moscow that would merit full-time Western correspondents in the city, the events of June 22 changed everything, quickly. As Charlotte Haldane, one of the late summer arrivals, wrote in her memoir, *Russian Newsreel:* "Here was I, out of the dozens of British correspondents who had been frantically seeking to get to Moscow, one of the exclusive five who made it—and the only woman into the bargain. I knew the tremendous thirst for news of Russia at home; I could have sat down and written a daily story for a month without slaking that thirst. I knew the tremendous issues at stake; straight news apart, the value of good propaganda."[15] Credentials were the easy part because most news outlets were starved for firsthand information. Visas and passes, on the other hand, were stingily restricted by a secretive and distrustful Soviet bureaucracy, and the exigencies and dangers of war made travel a challenge. In fact, it was this official Soviet policy of keeping all information within carefully controlled circles of power that ultimately made news collecting a charade, a game in which all the Western journalists became unlikely players. Even the Soviet policy of confiscating private radios for use by the Red Army and the substitution of a vast outdoor loudspeaker network over which official communiqués were broadcast daily became a part of the game. Because most of the Western press corps did not speak Russian, these regular public address announcements had to be translated for them. Even if they had possessed the requisite language skills, they were not permitted to speak with soldiers or civilians on the street or in restaurants.

For example, in the last few weeks of springtime peace in the USSR, Cassidy had gone on vacation near the Black Sea. In his memoir, *Moscow Dateline*, he explains how so many could have been in the dark: "But, in the censor-tight cylinder of Moscow, no one knew, not the foreigners, not the Russian people, not the Soviet leaders. The reason we did not know there would be war was that we did know the Soviet Union wanted peace at almost any price, would make almost any concession, even unasked, to escape war. What we could not know was that Germany was determined, in any case, to attack."[16] In fact, Cassidy learned of the invasion only secondhand through a pair of telegrams. On that warm, fresh Sunday morning in Sochi, while sitting on "the peaceful, sunlit terrace of the Riviera Hotel," he had received a mysterious telegram telling him to return to Moscow immediately. Later, strolling back up from the beach, he heard Molotov's droning announcement of the hostilities over an outdoor loudspeaker in front of the Riviera. In the afternoon Cassidy's suite was suddenly invaded by plainclothes policemen ransacking his room, looking for camera film he'd exposed of Sochi a day earlier from a hill above the town. He'd been roughly interrogated by the police at the time, but now tensions had clearly escalated.

The other telegram was a misdirected one the hotel manager asked him to open:

> It was addressed in English to Intourist, Sochi. Since Intourist, the travel agency for foreigners, no longer existed there, and since I was the only foreigner in town, and English-speaking, it probably was for me. Actually it was for Erskine Caldwell

> and his wife, Margaret Bourke-White, who were in the nearby town of Sukhum, from Ambassador Steinhardt in Moscow. It informed them he was advising all Americans to leave the Soviet Union immediately unless they had compelling reasons to stay. That didn't make my prospects look any better.[17]

Compelling, indeed. The three of them—along with those in Moscow—were sitting on what might just turn out to be the news story of the century. But they needed to get back to Moscow as soon as possible. Planes were out of the question, and even train tickets were at a premium, but Cassidy, after great effort and pleading, finally wangled a ticket the following day using his foreign press pass and arrived back in Moscow the day before the Caldwells on June 26.

The Caldwells had been touring and photographing collective farms in the Sukhumi area, and all that Sunday they had seen workers clustered around village and farm loudspeakers awaiting an official announcement, one that didn't come until late in the day. The Caldwells traveled in style. Through the largess of the commissar of the district party committee, they had use of a car that Eugene Petrov, the influential Writers' Union representative, had arranged and chauffeured. They enjoyed the benefits of a personal interpreter/secretary as well. They drove back to Sochi, where Bourke-White took photographs while Petrov obtained Moscow tickets. Bourke-White later observed that the ease with which they'd gotten tickets "was evidence of the influential place which writers were accorded in the Soviet Union."[18] Or of Petrov's personal clout. They arrived in a rainy Moscow on June 27 only to discover that Ambassador Steinhardt had issued a statement that all nonessential Americans should be evacuated immediately, particularly all women.

The intrepid Moats took to hiding in various correspondents' rooms and apartments so that Steinhardt couldn't issue the edict directly to her. She grandiosely began to refer to this as the "affaire Moats" but had the presence of mind to get *Collier's* to cable her official press credentials to authorize her stay in Russia, though they would be invalid until the Russians issued her a press card. When she saw Steinhardt that evening, she asked, "What are the Caldwells going to do?" to which she says he answered, "They are leaving immediately. You're the only one who was mad enough to want to stay on. In a few days you won't be able to send any cables out of here."

Steinhardt apparently had not spoken to the Caldwells. Moats writes, "When Henry [Cassidy] called the Caldwells that day they were their usual mysterious selves. 'We are making no plans,' they said. 'These are extraordinary times, and we're just living from day to day.'"[19]

And stay they all did, establishing as best they could, despite Soviet censorship and everyone's apparent ill-preparedness for these momentous days, multiple lines of communication with the West.

Alexander Werth

Werth was the first of the Western journalists to get into Russia after the war began. He was particularly well qualified for the job. He had been born in Saint Petersburg and spoke fluent Russian. For Werth, the assignment was not just that of a correspondent and a Reuters agent. "I felt I had to go to Russia," he wrote in his *Moscow War Diary*, "[s]o I went . . . with an open mind, but, at heart, rejoicing at the thought that my first country and my second country were allies."[20] Joining a military mission being airlifted to the USSR, he left London on July 3. His plane refueled in Scotland, then flew north and east, arriving in Moscow on the evening of July 5, the briefest journey any of the journalists would have getting to the Soviet Union. He had no qualms about voicing his nonneutral position: "We must fight the filthy Germans. We and the Russians are two immense forces which, between us, ought to crush Hitler and all that scum. What does it matter what I liked or disliked about the Soviet régime?"[21] The next day, after settling into the Metropole Hotel, he immediately set to his task of newsgathering and getting to know the resident press corps.

Philip Jordan

Philip Jordan, working for the London *News Chronicle*, followed Werth's route eight days later. He alighted in Moscow on July 14. He read *War and Peace* most of the way there, worrying all the while about what was in store for him. He had an open mind, though, ready to accept the USSR as a worthy ally: "If the Soviet Union had really triumphed over all those liberal principles that are the mainspring of human life, then I could not possibly deny it any longer to myself or those who trusted what I said."[22] Jordan, apparently discounting Charlotte Haldane, later wrote that he was the first and only "special correspondent of any British newspaper" until the London *Times* sent out its "special correspondent" on November 20.

Once established in Moscow, Jordan's dispatches, while reflecting the tone of Russia-as-great-fighting-machine, never reached the level of national self-criticism that appeared later in his 1942 memoir, revealingly titled *Russian Glory*. In it he rhapsodizes about the morale of the fighting men: "The Red Army is extremely well cared for. . . . It is superbly clothed, well fed, and every effort is made to develop the minds of its men rather than to let them rot. Every man is equipped with small arms of the latest pattern. His health is the perpetual care of a medical corps devoted more to prevention than cure." Jordan depicts the political commissar of each unit, rather than as the eyes and ears of the secret police as was generally suspected, but instead as a social director: "Right up to the front line he organizes soldiers' clubs; and the measure of his influence and popularity is always the profusion of amenities he is able to provide." And behind the front, the Red Army is well oiled also: "The maintenance of supplies to the front is highly organized and skilfully conducted." But Jordan carries his praise even farther: "Maintenance work generally is excellent: guns, tanks, trucks, and weapons of all sorts were cared for with a devotion and an understanding that I have found lacking elsewhere, particularly in our own Army and Air Force." And why is all this so? Jordan surmises, "I attribute his [the Red Army soldier's] care also to the fact that his discipline is better than ours."[23]

Jordan was a careful apologist for the Russian war effort. His pieces telegraphed back to London were a balanced combination of masculine war rhetoric and the domestic virtues of loyalty, devotion, and kindness. But he saw the war through rose-tinted glasses of his own devising. He also believed that he and the other correspondents were underappreciated. He makes the astounding, and apparently serious, comment, "If the British and French Governments, of the last ten years, had listened to the journalists who travelled from their respective countries and saw something more of contemporary life than did their diplomatic colleagues, there would have been no war in Europe today."[24]

But he also has barbs for the Americans. Ambassador Steinhart he labels a "defeatist" and a member of the "'it's all over' school." He describes the embassy's military attaché as a "delightful and kindly person, who would have made an admirable farmer," but one who mislead Steinhardt with "fantastically inaccurate reports."[25]

Jordan was also a stickler for the job of transmitting only hard news while avoiding the social interactions behind the scenes. "Journalists who write books are apt, in my opinion, to write too much about their colleagues, who are, for the most part, unknown to the public." He insists that his fellow reporters will remain anonymous in his book, and for the most part, they are. But, his fellow journalists *are* fine chaps: "[I]n all the countries where I have worked I have never met a more competent, more patient or kinder body of colleagues; and it is a tribute to their quality that, in spite of the notorious temperaments of travelling newspapermen, we never quarreled."[26]

Nonetheless, despite his nine months of quarrels with the authorities and dissatisfaction with his role as a journalist, squelched as he was at every other moment by Soviet censorship, when Jordan returned to the British Isles from the bitter-cold Kuibyshev in early February 1942, he was able to draw a detailed social portrait of the life and times of Russia during that long autumn and winter. He found the people almost stoic in their resolve to carry forth the war in defense, if not of communism per se, at least of *rodina*, the motherland. Having begun his assignment as an acknowledged leftist, he was dismayed by the extent of party control over almost every facet of the lives of Russians: access to food and housing, mobility within the country, freedom of choice in occupation and education, but especially to information. He was shocked at how little the Russian people knew about the world outside their borders: the years of bombing England underwent, the worldwide extent of the war, but especially the progress of civilization and prosperity in the capitalist world. He saw that the Soviet state had essentially locked its people into an opaque time capsule. It had become a nation of internal censorship and internalized fear.

Jordan is especially eloquent when it comes to his experience in Moscow during the German air raids, the first coming about a week after he'd arrived in the city. Initially he was incensed that Muscovites believed that no city had ever undergone such intense shelling as Moscow had, because he saw these raids as small potatoes compared to what England had suffered, labeling the Russian raids as "child's play." After a while he gave himself up to their seeming harmlessness ("I not only never went into an air raid shelter voluntarily in Moscow, but I never felt inclined to go") and relished the memory of the sheer beauty of the very first raid, the one of July 22:

> The noise was indescribable, and the sky as full of flame and splendour as the Crystal Palace sky used to be on Thursdays. . . . There was not about that night what could fairly be called the permanent and indestructible loveliness of London's horror, so compelling and so sad that it has become a sight which all who then saw it can see again when they shut their eyes and remember: this was an artificial night, splashed with the long ribbons of the tracers and the primrose bursts of flaming onions. . . . It was an elemental terror that came to London, but to Moscow it was a terror created by man for his own satisfaction.[27]

The Russians had been practicing for just this night for the previous month with dry-run tracers and mock public warnings, but then came the real thing and they were ever so ready: "When the sirens went, and the first machines appeared over the city, it was though someone had at last told a child that it might play with the toy which had hitherto been withheld from it."[28]

Cyrus Sulzberger

At the end of the month the *New York Times* put itself back in the picture by pulling Cyrus Sulzberger from his previous war assignments in Yugoslavia and Greece and getting him into the country by train through Turkey on July 29. Sulzberger had a wry, contentious style of writing, and he could be quite funny, as in this description of a Red Army officer on a cold winter day: "He [Lt. Gen. A. A. Vlassov] had a long up-turned nose and thick glasses. When one stood talking to him outside, his nose rapidly acquired a small snowdrift of its own and his glasses fogged."[29] As for the staff of the Soviet press bureau: "A batch of censors, including a pleasant young man named Kozhimyakho, conspired to hamper our journalistic efforts." He summed up his fellow press corps: "The foreign press corps was a strange motley, ranging from Erskine Caldwell, the novelist, and his photographer-wife, Peggy Bourke-White, to assorted Communist correspondents for party papers around the world." He realized Bourke-White had particularly tough sledding: "Security regulations were excessive, famous museums were unvisited and cameras banned."[30] Other members of the press rarely mentioned him, suggesting that his personality may have been as aloof as his writing style. On the other hand, his reporting to the *Times*, especially his reporting from the Smolensk trip in September, is cogent, detailed, and, for the time, remarkably neutral in tone, exactly what a reader would expect from the *Times*.

Ralph Ingersoll

On August 16 Ralph Ingersoll appeared in Moscow. At the start of the war Ingersoll had arranged press credentials for Caldwell with his New York newspaper, *PM*. *PM* was a newcomer in the New York market, with its first issue published June 18, 1940. It considered itself a cut above the other dailies. Unlike them, it was stapled along the fold, magazine-style, and depended heavily on photography for its impact. Ingersoll, its publisher, was a veteran not just of the *New Yorker* magazine but of several Henry Luce publications as well: *Fortune* and *Time*.

PM's obvious liberal orientation reflected Ingersoll's politics. Ingersoll was rabidly anti-Fascist, pro-Roosevelt, but *not* anti-Stalin, and he made no bones about it in his signed editorials (another *PM* innovation) and in his choice of contributors. In a word, he was one of the most influential supporters of the Popular Front. *PM*'s printing costs were about double those of standard

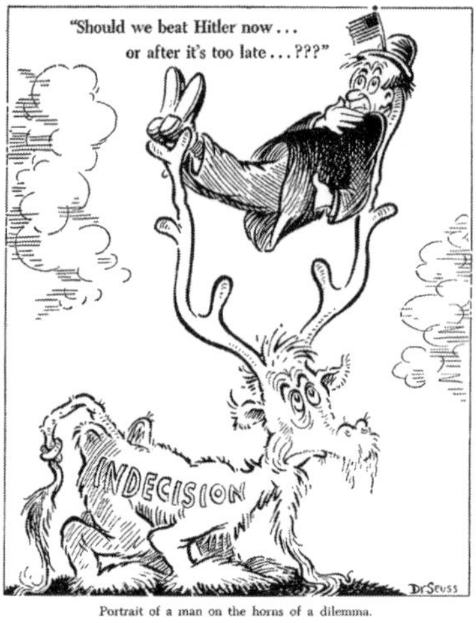

FIGURE 32. "Portrait of a man on the horn of a dilemma," *PM* newspaper, May 12, 1941 (Dr. Seuss Political Cartoons, Special Collection & Archives, UC San Diego Library)

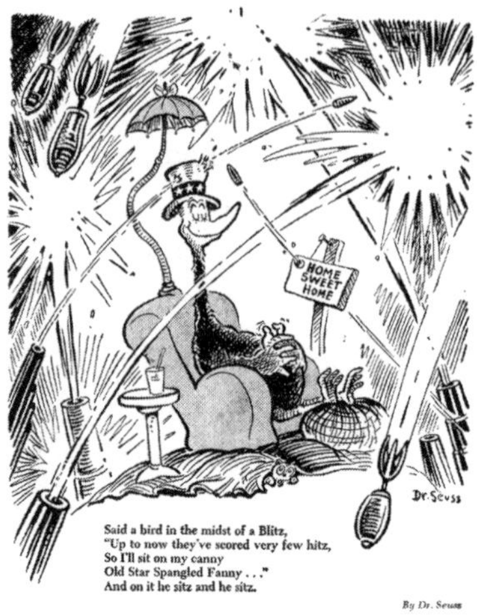

FIGURE 33. "Said a bird in the midst of a Blitz, 'Up to now they've scored very few hitz, so I'll sit on my canny old star spangled fanny . . .' and on it he sitz and he sitz," *PM* newspaper, June 23, 1941 (Dr. Seuss Political Cartoons, Special Collection & Archives, UC San Diego Library)

papers, yet for its first six years it accepted no advertising. Although its revenue never could keep it afloat, *PM* benefited from the seemingly inexhaustible coffers of Marshall Fields III, though when the war ended and the decade drew to a close, even Fields's support dried up. *PM* printed its last issue in September 1948.

But in its heyday, during its first two to three years, *PM*'s cachet was imposing. One of its most popular contributors was Theodor Geisel, who between 1941 and 1943 submitted over four hundred passionately political cartoons under his pseudonym, Dr. Seuss, such as those of May 12 and June 23, 1941, shown in figures 32 and 33. *PM* was also well known for its advanced technology for printing photographs, so it was not surprising that photographers like Weegee (Arthur Fellig), known for his stark black-and-white street photos, and Margaret Bourke-White were featured regularly.

Ingersoll, one of the most peripatetic of editors, decided—after reading Henry Cassidy's initial dispatch that the surprise onslaught of Operation Barbarossa did not necessarily spell doom to the country in five days or three weeks, as some had predicted—that he had time to get to the USSR before its collapse.[31] Moscow was clearly where the news—if not the action—was, and he wanted to be there. Ingersoll was not without influence in the chambers of government, and he immediately traveled to Washington to arrange the necessary papers with the Soviet ambassador, Constantin Oumansky.

Oumansky, Stalin, and the Soviet establishment had not been pleased when Ingersoll had opposed Stalin's temporary détente with Hitler. Nonetheless, Oumansky quickly realized that a left-leaning New York newspaper's founder and publisher could be a valuable asset in Soviet attempts to curry favor in the still-isolationist United States. In addition to the necessary travel papers, Ingersoll also got Oumansky's promise of a personal interview with Stalin and a trip to the front. He did meet with Stalin.

Because *PM* already had Caldwell "on the spot, to send us daily cables from Moscow," Ingersoll wouldn't have to wrangle with the censors.[32] He could spend his three weeks there (he finally arrived in Moscow on August 16; on September 5, he boarded a train south to Iran) soaking in the ambience and atmosphere of Moscow and assessing the attitudes of Soviet citizens and officials with his own eyes and ears.

Remarkably, after departing New York on July 7, he had followed nearly the same route across the Pacific and through China as had Caldwell and Bourke-White three months earlier, except that he had to make the same detour that Alice Moats had through Singapore, Bangkok, Rangoon, and up the infamous Burma Road. In Chungking, he, as had the Caldwells, enjoyed an audience with Generalissimo and Mme. Chiang Kai-shek. And again like the Caldwells, Ingersoll found himself in the company of a fellow traveler, in this case Archibald Trojan "Arch" Steele, the veteran correspondent from the *Chicago Daily News* who had been in China and Japan for years and was fluent in the languages of both nations. Steele was trying to get in the back door to Moscow, and "[m]iraculously, he had gotten a visa—miraculously because all Asia seemed to be full of American correspondents who had applied and been turned down."[33] On August 18 Steele filed his first dispatch from Moscow.

Steele came to be greatly admired by his colleagues, especially the Caldwells. In *All-Out on the Road to Smolensk*, Caldwell made this evident:

> The ablest correspondent in the Soviet Union was Archie Steele of the *Chicago Daily News*. Steele's dispatches, which were syndicated in a number of American papers, were as heavily censored as anyone else's, but in spite of that he was always able to interpret the news and report events more clearly than most foreign correspondents unhampered by restrictions. . . . [H]e entered into his work with admirable will and enthusiasm, and within a short time his objectivity and honesty won the respect and admiration of the Russians.[34]

Ralph Ingersoll, who kept a diary on hotel and airline stationery because he thought a notebook might seem suspicious and be confiscated, came quickly to perceive the frostiness of the Russians and one of the barriers the journalists faced: "Coming from the outside world, you are not simply a foreigner—you are the representative of a class that has been disenfranchised in Russia and the life you live is that of a specially privileged outcast." But the correspondents were the members of such a small foreign colony that "everyone knew everything everyone else was up to, and daily we exchanged notes on what we knew and did not know."[35] The problem, of course, was that the reporters were there to deliver the news back home as fully and as dispassionately as possible. Because the attitude of Soviet officialdom was staunchly anchored in secrecy and distrust, it and the news commentariat were at natural loggerheads. Ingersoll writes that this mind-set explains "why the rest of the world was so inadequately informed on the subject of the Soviet Union that its success against the Germans came as a breath-taking surprise."[36] As a result of this information fog, American isolationism remained more entrenched, and for longer than it might otherwise have, had the public been more fully informed.

After Ingersoll got settled into the National Hotel in a much smaller and less ornate room than the one his *PM* correspondents had been provided, he wasted no time in putting his plans into action. Within a week or so he had talked his way into a personal tour of one of the Russian anti-aircraft batteries to the west of Moscow, out along the six-lane Smolensk road. He wrote extensively on his impressions of Moscow society, and though he was surprised at the people's pluck and willingness for sacrifice, which he admitted he viewed with a jaundiced liberal eye, he was not "prepared . . . for the dead level of poverty that spread like a spoiled blanket from one border of the country to the other—or the low level of Soviet workmanship, which can't help but scandalize a Westerner."[37] The obverse of this was that "[f]rom what I could get in conversation with them, the average Russian thinks of America as a land in which a few thousand people lead the life of Riley and the rest are made to starve in breadlines—or slave all day tilling someone else's land—or weave clothes on someone else's machinery for someone else to wear."[38] Ironically, one source for these perceptions was the literature of Erskine Caldwell, Ingersoll's man in Moscow.

As he had in China, once again Ingersoll got to experience the Luftwaffe air raids from multiple vantage points. Though he had one of the precious "all-night" passes issued to journalists, he made a point of visiting the metro underground stations, which he found to be crowded and uncomfortable. But on other occasions he had a better vantage point: the Caldwells' suite at the

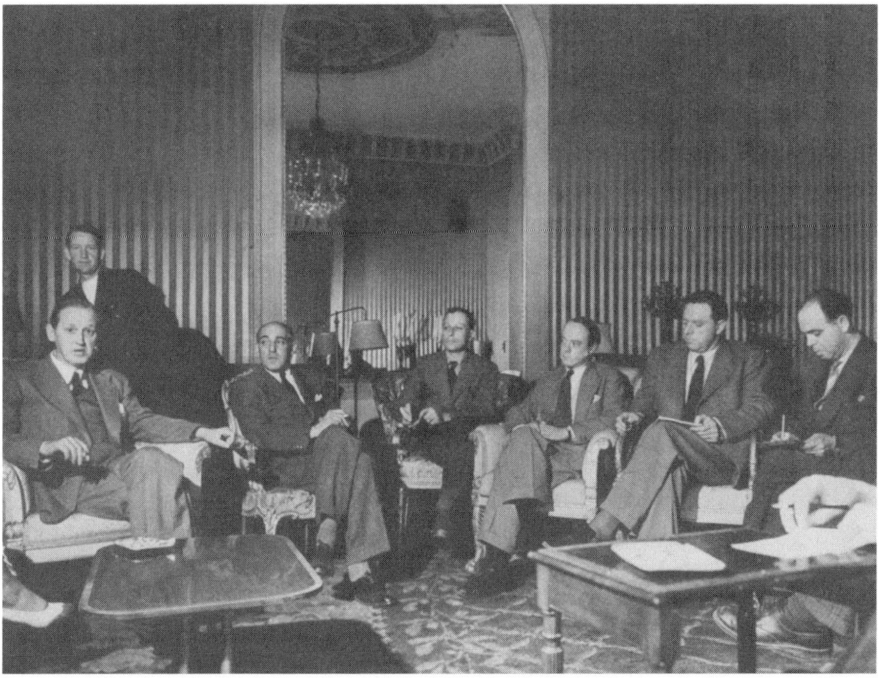

FIGURE 34. A gathering of selected correspondents in August 1941. Original caption: "Mr. Hopkins called this conference after the first meeting with Stalin. From left to right: Hopkins, Llewellyn (Tommy) Thompson, one of the embassy secretaries, Mr. Steinhardt, Alexander Werth of Reuter's, Philip Jordan of the *London News Chronicle*, Erskine Caldwell, and Harry Shapiro, U.P., dean of the American newsmen—there longer than any other American" (From *Shooting the Russian War*; photo © Estate of Margaret Bourke-White/ Licensed by VAGA, New York, N.Y.; courtesy of Syracuse University Libraries)

National. The first air raid came at two o'clock in the morning his first night in the city. "I had gone back to my room down the hall and was fast asleep when the sirens woke me. They made an old familiar sound. I liked it no more in Moscow than in London."

> It would begin way out on the edge of the city, and sometimes you could see the flick of the bursting shells before you could hear any sound or see any searchlights. These must have been fired way off over the horizon. It was always exciting when they came nearer, for the searchlights would go on and the firing would grow from a rumble to a bedlam of barks, crashes, whines and roars. The big square made everything echo. The barrage was very heavy. If a plane got in over the city the Russians seemed to let the whole thing go at once—guns on top of every building for miles. They fired so continuously that all the noises got mixed up—the crash of

> the guns, the plop of the shells from the sky, the screech of the shells going up and the clatter of the shrapnel coming down, the echoes of all these sounds, and the rat-tat-tat of the machine guns. It all blurred into a continuous roaring and crashing and whirring and tinkling. When a piece of shrapnel fell close to the balcony it made a noise like a bat flying through the air.
>
> Then you had to decide whether it was safe to stay on the balcony, even if you wore the special helmet the government had given Erskine. It had a wide steel skirt on it which protected one's shoulders. It was so heavy no one wanted to wear it for more than a few minutes.[39]

Caldwell's night gear was noted by many. Sulzberger wrote that the Caldwells had been issued "weird, broad-brimmed basin helmets that looked like the head armor of medieval Japanese ronin."[40]

And the Polish sketch artist Feliks Topolski was captivated as well, as can be seen in figure 35. Caldwell's own explanation for this gear and his description of it are more laconic. He explained to his CBS radio news audience during an August 1 transmission:

> Contrary to practice in England, where citizens have unrestricted freedom during air-raids, the population of Moscow goes to shelters at such times. This will account for the relatively small number of persons killed and injured since bombing began. The only persons permitted on the streets during raids are the militia, fire-fighting brigades, and other protective groups. Shrapnel from shell-bursts has a way of falling *kerplunk* without forewarning. I have found from experience, during those times at night when I travel by special dispensation from one part of the city to the other, that the eaves of buildings offer the best protection obtainable and I have found that I am less hesitant about making these trips when I am wearing a tin hat.[41]

But Ingersoll wasn't in Moscow to observe air raids. He would leave that to Bourke-White and Caldwell. He was there to interview Joseph Stalin.

The problem was that despite Oumansky's promise, nothing materialized, and no one seemed to know much about it. Then the day before Ingersoll was scheduled to depart, he received a call while at the American embassy. Within an hour he was at the Kremlin, mission accomplished, though with the understanding that while he could report on the substance of their talk, he could not quote Stalin directly.

He found the premier an imposing figure despite his diminutive stature—distant, reserved, then suddenly smiling, as he had for Bourke-White earlier: "The effect was startling. His whole face changed. The austere, static, deadpan quality absolutely disappeared and his expression became warm and alive."[42]

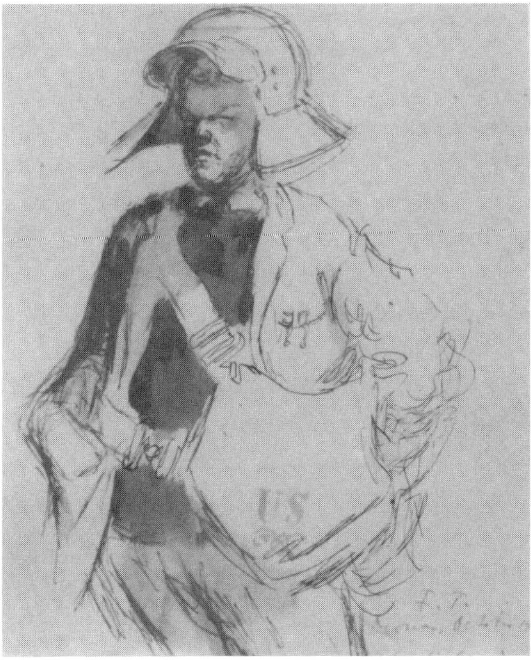

FIGURE 35. "An American broadcaster during an Air-raid," by Feliks Topolski (From *Russia in War*, 42; courtesy of the Topolski estate)

Ingersoll's anxiety dissipated. For over an hour they chatted. Ingersoll opened by lobbying for the press corps to be given access to the front but worried, "I doubt if I made myself clear." But after the smile their talk became wide ranging: "U.S. help. U.S. public opinion. How the war was to be won. Plant capacity. Tanks. Planes. Military defeat only way to beat Hitler. Food in Germany, in U.S.S.R. Oil in Germany. Replacements. Japan. Italy. Norway. France. [pro-Vichy Maxime] Weygand. Turkey. U.S. production. Sweden. Winter. F.D.R. Laurence Steinhardt. More about the press and working outside Moscow. The political situation at home." Ingersoll declared it "[a]n eminently successful talk."[43]

After leaving the Kremlin in the early evening following dinner with Steinhardt, "Erskine and I [went] to broadcast to the U.S.—about food in Moscow—if the broadcast went out at all—the control light didn't light and we couldn't find out what was the matter." Ingersoll decided to stay an extra day and like the average tourist went shopping but also visited Solomon Lozovsky, the head of the Soviet Information Bureau, with whom he thought he "finally got over a coherent argument for U.S.S.R. co-operation with the U.S. press." After hopes for hopping a flight out with the Polish embassy fell through a half-hour before his own train was to depart, Steinhardt drove him to the station. "The NKVD [secret police], Jenny ["my little blonde interpreter"], and our nine pieces of luggage followed. Erskine and Peggy (Caldwell) got to the train just as Larry left."[44] Six weeks later, a fortnight before the Caldwells, on October 17, Ingersoll finally got back to New York, working his way through the Middle East, to Egypt, across the Mediterranean and eastern Atlantic to Scotland, then finally back to the United States courtesy of the Royal Air Force's Ferry Command.

He returned a conquering hero, as journalists go. His first stop after getting back to the States was to visit President Roosevelt and fill him in on the Russian front. Then he wrote a series of daily articles in *PM* recounting his travels, pieces that would be reworked the following spring into his travel memoir, *Action on All Fronts.* His biographer, Roy Hoopes, writes that Ingersoll was gifted with a photographic, almost camera-like memory for detail. It was also a style ripe for satire, and the *New Yorker* did just that in its November 22 issue with "Alf Stringersoll's Report on Brooklyn":

> The biggest news I bring back from Brooklyn is this:
>
> Brooklyn is not lying down. It hasn't all the answers yet, but it's working them out.
>
> The man on the street is not standing still. He is going places.
>
> Ralph Ingersoll, with whom I had an audience just before I left, is not a chain smoker.
>
> I got my first glimpse of Brooklyn from Manhattan Bridge. It was dusk, and my pretty blonde interpreter and I were riding in a Sunshine Cab. I lit a cigarette. Then I said:
>
> "Why are there so many red lights ahead?"
>
> The red lights were strung out along what seemed to be a main thoroughfare. They looked like a string of ruby beads.[45]

Ingersoll was Stringersoll's Stalin, and the parody continued to be spot-on.

Following Ingersoll's departure, an eclectic quartet of correspondents arrived by ship from England: Vernon Bartlett, a member of Parliament working for the BBC; the American Wallace Carroll, representing the United Press news syndicate; the rather notorious Charlotte Haldane, a stringer for London's *Daily Sketch;* and the repatriating Polish artist Feliks Topolski.

Vernon Bartlett

Vernon Bartlett had once been virulently antiwar. Exposed to poison gas in World War I and the fortunate survivor of a massive bomb attack on his foxhole, he was invalided out of the army to enter the world of journalism. He found himself to be equally adept at writing and broadcasting. For several years in the 1930s, the BBC employed him full-time until a political brouhaha arose over broadcast comments he made that were considered insufficiently anti-Nazi after the Germans abruptly walked out of a League of Nations conference. He broadcast that he didn't particularly blame them: "I believe the British would have acted in much the same way as Germany has acted if they had been in the same position."[46] In the event, he resigned from the BBC. In time he became stridently anti-appeasement, opposed the official Chamberlain policy, and ran for an open House of Commons seat as an independent progressive in 1938. He won and held the seat until 1950.

In August 1941 he was on his way to Moscow as a British press attaché and as the voice of the BBC. Later, as the war was winding down, he produced an unusual retrospective, *Tomorrow Always Comes*. Not published until February 1944 and so not intended to meet the public clamor for up-to-the-moment Moscow news, Bartlett provides a background to the 1942–44 political situations in the United States, Britain, Germany, Japan, and Russia. He also offers a brief glimpse of the Russia he saw along with the correspondents with whom he traveled: "I was in a convoy that brought the first British airmen up the Archangel River in September 1941," he begins, "and we had not anticipated that the inhabitants would be so little pleased to see us. Mile after mile we passed grim, glum people."[47] As were all the correspondents, he was frustrated by his inability to speak with regular Russians, to move about freely, or to provide the BBC uncensored broadcasts. He sensed the cause lay with the Communist leaders' fear of exposing their citizens to the outside world and its capitalist mores. But he found military officers to be more candid:

> These occasional contacts must have destroyed some illusions about the bourgeoisie, and the Red Army has fewer inhibitions than the civilian citizen of the Soviet Union. It was a genuine relief to escape from the silences of Moscow to the talkativeness of officers in the Red Army. During a week in the Smolensk sector in September 1941 I found these officers extremely hospitable and friendly; if a sentry with a fixed bayonet would always follow any one of us who wandered off for a few moments into the surrounding wood he was only taking a laudable, if embarrassing, military precaution. On the whole, the Russian soldier is destroying the inhibitions of the Russian politician.[48]

The remainder of the book is a fictionalized war diary in the pessimistic "what-if" tradition. A contemporary *Kirkus* review concludes, "[Bartlett] forecasts the defeat of the democratic ideals, lost in a morass of bickering, irresolution, mistrust and discord," then warns: "More truth than fantasy here, and a warning, popularly presaged." [49]

Sometime later, long after his parliamentary career was over, nearly twenty years after his brief visit to Moscow that wartime summer, Bartlett published another memoir. He remained bitter about "that unhappy visit to Russia." "My mission in Russia," he writes in *And Now, Tomorrow*, "was to arrange for a better exchange of information between that country and the British Commonwealth. Never was the failure of a mission more complete." He adds, "In a country where the press prints exactly what it is officially desired to print, a Press Attaché is considered either as a spy or as the lowest form of human life—or probably both." He bridles at the censorship, at how the populace was quarantined from the journalists and vice versa, and at the attitudes of the Russian Information Commissariat. He objects to Commissar Nikolai Palgunov in particular, with whom the press had to interact on a far more regular basis than they desired: "[T]here was so little that we were allowed to do. Most shops were boarded up, and there was little incentive to wander about the streets. There were no lounges in the hotels, so that most of the newspaper correspondents spent all their time in their bedrooms or in the Press Bureau of the Foreign Office." He sees the Russians as totally self-serving, noting that the sudden change in heart of the minister of information, Solomon Lozovsky, about sending reporters to the front came about only after Lord Beaverbrook and Averill Harriman had arranged to meet with Stalin to hash out the details of the Lend-Lease Program.[50]

Upon his return to Moscow from the Smolensk press junket in September, by which time the Beaverbrook-Harriman mission was just getting under way, Bartlett achieved his greatest notoriety. At a lavish reception at the conclusion of the conference, hosted by Stalin himself and attended by most of the press corps, Bartlett rose to give a toast, one of almost thirty that night. Perhaps emboldened by the vodka he had already consumed, he raised his glass to the idea that "you could not have a free people unless you had a free Press." After this remark had been translated for him, Stalin turned to Lord Beaverbrook and commented, according to Bartlett, "That young man talks too much." As Bartlett was departing, about 4 a.m., Stalin was shaking hands with each of his guests, but "[i]nstead of dismissing me with a mere handshake, he held my hand between his for a moment. Then he said: 'English journalist. Ahhh!' and he shook an admonitory but benign finger in front of my face. He smiled, but I felt it was just as well that I was leaving for England within twenty-four hours."[51]

Wallace Carroll

Wallace Carroll perceived his role to be not just a news stringer but a correspondent with the responsibility of promoting the cause of anti-Fascism, a motive similar to that of the Caldwells. He titled his memoir *We're in This with Russia*.[52] Carroll, an American, had managed the United Press bureau in Switzerland since 1934, before returning to London in 1939. He writes that in late July "I received instructions to leave my post in London and go to Moscow."[53] He took the midnight train to Liverpool where he boarded the *Llanstephan Castle*, an 11,000-ton passenger liner requisitioned for Lend-Lease war duty. Onboard he met the vibrant Charlotte Haldane, at the time the semi-estranged wife of the British chemist J. B. S. Haldane and on assignment with the London *Daily Sketch;* Vernon Bartlett; a fighter wing of the Royal Air Force; and an American pilot named Hubert Zemke. These airmen were on their way to Archangel to teach the Soviets how to assemble and fly the British Hurricane and American Tomahawk fighters that were crated aboard the other five merchant vessels with which they were to convoy to Russia. Carroll cannot suppress his excitement: "I was bursting with inoculations against all known plagues and I carried, besides my typewriter and a suitcase full of clothes, a bag full of books on Russia and the Far East and a haversack with my helmet and gas-mask, some chocolate bars and concentrated foods—and two louse belts."[54]

Most of the social time aboard the *Llanstephan Castle* during its uneventful three-week voyage seems to have been filled with discussions of current events, topical lectures, shoptalk of the airmen, and discussions of the politics of socialism, since also on board was a contingent of Polish military staff who had been in exile in England until suddenly they had become Soviet allies and were now returning to take up the cause of world socialism. Carroll firmly places Mrs. Haldane, as most of the journalists referred to her, in the leftist camp: "If not a communist, [she] was at least a fellow traveler, first class."[55]

Carroll finally reached Moscow on the first of September and found quarters in the apartment of Henry Shapiro. Carroll had been in Moscow barely a fortnight when he was tapped to join the Smolensk press group, a trip others had been waiting for three months to take. Several weeks after that he was evacuated along with the rest of the press corps and much of the Soviet government by train, which he wryly named the Kuibyshev Komet, and from there beat a hasty retreat out through Iran on October 25. Although Carroll does devote some attention in his memoir to the Moscow around him, at one point providing a small table of the costs of food rations, he mostly reports on the war effort. The central forty pages of the memoir concern the events of the

Smolensk trip, but Carroll quickly moves on to the Beaverbrook-Harriman conference at the end of the month, relates the increasingly mixed climate of panic and stoicism as Hitler moved toward Moscow, and concludes the travel portion of the book with his otherworldly escape to the Volga and over the Caucasus Mountains to Persia.

By the time Carroll put the finishing touches on *We're in This with Russia*, Japan had attacked Pearl Harbor, and truly the United States *was* in this with Russia, along with Great Britain and all the other Allies. Before his memoir could be published, because the public demand for information about the USSR was so fervid, the United Press hustled out a diminutive and unpaginated paperback compilation of eleven of Carroll's wartime dispatches, *Inside Warring Russia*. The first half-dozen date to mid-November and are datelined Manila; they are said to be "uncensored." The remaining five are reprinted from his time in Russia, presumably censored by the Soviet Information Commissariat. *Inside Warring Russia* is an interesting study in how a journalist in the Soviet Union had to be circumspect about his pieces, making them invariably upbeat and favorable to the Soviet regime and to Stalin in particular: "Everywhere the troops appeared well fed, well equipped, well clothed and in excellent spirits." Carroll succeeds in making the war seem more like a boy's romantic adventure rather than the bloody and brutish affair it really was.

In the last communiqué, one describing the press pool's session with Lieutenant General Vassily Sokolovsky, who reported that the Germans were on the defensive and were going to be under extreme duress once winter arrived, Carroll makes his pitch: "Gen. Sokolovsky said Russia would welcome every tank, plane, gun and shell the United States and Great Britain could send."[56] This sentiment was one most of the Western correspondents shared.

Charlotte Haldane

The woman in the group was not just another beat writer. Yet she seems often to have been viewed disdainfully by the other correspondents. Charlotte Franken Burghes Haldane, an experienced journalist, feminist intellectual, and committed socialist, was the only member of the 1941 Moscow press corps, except for the Caldwells, about whom a biography was later written. Whether she countenanced renown or ignominy was a matter of a commentator's ideological compass. She had been a cause célèbre a decade earlier when she had successfully divorced her first husband, Jack Burghes, a man described by Haldane's biographer as one "who had returned to civilian life as aimless as he had left it in 1914" to enlist for World War I duty.[57] Haldane, on the other hand, had been burdened by her past: her parents were of German extraction, and although she was born in a London suburb, her father, a furrier, was an undocumented alien. In 1905, when she was eleven, the family moved to Antwerp for four years, before returning to London. But when the war began, her father, Joseph Franken, was declared an enemy alien and his assets were confiscated. He moved to the United States in 1915, then back to Germany, where he died a ruined man ten years later. In the meanwhile, to protect herself, his daughter unofficially changed her last name from "Franken" to the more Anglicized "Franklyn." Unfortunately for her, because she grew up in a German-speaking household, she forever retained a slight accent.

In any case, at about the same time, and perhaps as a measure of rebellion, she fell in love with Burghes, the "attractive but penniless" cousin of a bohemian friend from the music world.[58] When they married in 1918 she was already into the second trimester of a pregnancy and just starting out in the world of letters, whereas Burghes, to use Charlotte's delicate terms, "as the result of the first world war, in which he served with distinction in the frightful battles of Arras and Ypres . . . was permanently incapacitated, and prevented from aiding these ambitions of mine."[59] After the birth of her only child, Ronald, she began a career at Lord Beaverbrook's *Daily Express*, first as a gossip columnist but finally, around 1920, as a reporter. She used her position to aggressively promote women's issues, especially equality in divorce rights, but more generally, fairness in gender issues including access to contraception and work-rights improvements for pregnant women and mothers, all framed within an antiwar tenor. For the remainder of her life, these causes remained her focus.

In 1924 she met the famous and contentious Cambridge geneticist John Burdon Sanderson Haldane, two years her elder, and her world pivoted. She had just begun research on her first novel, the thoroughly dystopian *Man's World*, and she knew that she needed a deeper scientific background than she had acquired in school.[60] Fortuitously, another *Express* reporter gave her a copy of a magazine containing one of his own articles, but also (serendipitously) an excerpt of a lecture by a Professor J. B. S. Haldane entitled *Daedalus, or Science and the Future*. In it Haldane makes the argument that the future of the world would be determined through applied biology, especially through what he called ectogenesis, the forerunner of "test tube babies." This concept was perfectly congruent with Charlotte's science fiction, so she immediately began to press the *Express* staff to allow her an interview with him. It took place in May and for her it was magical, for him a professional opportunity. As Charlotte's biographer, Judith Adamson, writes, "teaching was Haldane's supreme hobby, as learning was hers."[61] Of course, they hit it off splendidly, politically (both were confirmed Marxists, soon to be members of the British Communist Party), professionally (they created the Science News Service, a syndication agency for getting articles by Haldane and his colleagues into the general press), and romantically.

By then Jack had returned to drinking and gambling, and Charlotte took to living away from home for extended periods of time with her son, Ronnie. Her marriage had become one in name only. But to sue for divorce in the 1920s required permission from the husband who himself could file on the grounds of adultery, unless the wife could prove extreme abuse, and in any case, a stigma of ill repute usually followed all the parties involved in the court proceedings. Arrangements were finally worked out such that on February 16, 1925, a private detective would be at a hotel where Haldane and Charlotte were to spend a night, thus providing Burghes sufficient dirt on Charlotte so that he could file for divorce on the grounds of adultery. To add to the drama, Charlotte insisted that the nominated hotel was inadequate and demanded that she and her lover move to the Adelphi, her usual residence away from home. She even had Haldane ask the detective, whom she'd spotted right away, to help them move their luggage to the Adelphi, which he did.[62] The die had been cast. Eight months later the case was taken up in court and settled finally in December, seemingly fully in Burghes's favor, even down to court costs and the custody of Ronnie, although Burghes allowed him to continue to live with Charlotte and Haldane. Charlotte had to resign from the *Express,* and Haldane's situation was touch and go at Cambridge because this was, after all, a morals case and the university had its image to protect, but in the end it all worked out and they were married on May 11, 1926, two years after they had met. *Man's World,* bearing Haldane's considerable handprint, appeared in print six months later.

The ensuing fifteen years saw the Haldanes become increasingly involved in socialist issues. In 1928 the couple visited Russia where they became even more enthusiastic converts to the Bolshevik cause. Then, for five years, 1933–38, they became fervid leftist activists in Spain on behalf of the anti-Franco, anti-Fascist Republican and Populist forces, raising money and recruiting troops for the British Battalion. At the age of sixteen, Ronnie enlisted and went off to fight on behalf of the Popular Front. Despite being wounded seriously in battle, he remained for the duration of the conflict. In 1937 Charlotte became a member of the Communist Party and was soon recruited by the British Comintern to represent it in China. Once there, the *Daily Herald* hired her to report on the rapidly developing political ferment in the Far East. Not long after she returned to England, Britain entered World War II. She soon channeled her enthusiasm back into writing but also into civil defense, becoming particularly involved in the Air Raid Precautions Emergency Committee, though her marriage by this time had soured as the two Haldanes were each involved in the arcs of their own careers, a scenario Caldwell and Bourke-White would experience in 1942.

It is important, then, in understanding Charlotte Haldane's situation within the Moscow press corps, to remember that when she left England on the *Llanstephan Castle* (she incorrectly calls it the *Windsor Castle*), her communism was a deeply held belief: "I was filled with a passionate urge to help the Russian comrades in their great and glorious resistance."[63] Once she garnered an assignment to cover the fighting for the *Daily Sketch* (ironically, later to become a right-wing newspaper)[64] as the first British female war correspondent, her party connections helped her land a visa almost immediately, but more importantly, "before my rivals appointed by the editors of the *Herald* and the *Express* received theirs; they did not, in fact, arrive in Moscow until after I had gone home."[65]

She quickly realized that she was regarded as an outcast, but one of her own making. On the convoy over "I was conscious of my great responsibility to my Party and my cause, and had no desire to 'fraternise,' either with the Poles [who were now returning to Russia to fight side by side with their former enemies] or with my 'reactionary' fellow-Britons. The latter, naturally, were profoundly bored by my propaganda and priggish intransigence, and reciprocated my lack of enthusiasm."[66] One of those Poles, the war artist Feliks Topolski, remarked that she wore the "truculent costume of a leftist-suffragette gypsy."[67] Her only friend seemed to be Vernon Bartlett, himself on the left political margin of the group. She described him, as well as British ambassador Sir Stafford Cripps, as "like myself, idealists and perhaps, very slightly, prigs."[68] Some years later, recalling this period with embarrassment, she wrote ironically, "I had only one desire, to get to Russia as quickly as possible, and to begin my job of arousing the passionate sympathy of my fellow-countrymen for the glorious fighters of the Soviet Union."[69]

As the *Llanstephan Castle* steamed into Archangel and prepared to make fast to the shore, Wallace Carroll, echoing Bartlett, recalled, "Mrs. Haldane was usually a very shrewd observer but now she was in ecstasies." Bartlett remembered that same arrival less enthusiastically: "Poor Charlotte Haldane, who had lectured to us all about the exhilarating welcome we should receive, was in despair—she was later to write a courageous confession of her disillusionment—and I still remember her relief when a small child, far too young to know about politics, waved to us as we passed."[70] At the time, he writes, she was "an outspoken sympathizer with Communism."[71]

She was ostracized by her fellow correspondents not only for her socialist fervor but also because they were insanely jealous that, being a Communist Party member, she might be the one to get the coveted first interview with Stalin. What they didn't realize, and she came to understand only later, was that Soviet authorities had no interest in coddling and favoring those who were already committed to their cause. The Russians were out to convert others, not to stroke the already transformed, including her:

> The Russians have, in fact, an almost cynical disrespect, as well as fear, towards all Western foreigners. If such foreigners become Communists and thus place themselves under Comintern discipline, they become even less respectworthy in Russian eyes, if only for the reason that they are known and despised as propagandists in their own countries. From the Russian point of view, it would have been utter waste to have given the Stalin interview to one who was already suspect in her own capitalist-imperialist country as a Soviet supporter.[72]

Haldane's Communist sympathies soon waned, however, for several reasons. Like Bartlett, she was dismayed at the amount and the style of censorship carried out so heavy-handedly by the Soviet information establishment. Not only were the Western journalists kept in the dark and toyed with as if they were Russian pawns, but so too was the populace. She was appalled to discover that the Russians had never been told about the horrific air blitz London had been weathering the last couple of years. Furthermore, the NKVD, the Soviet secret police, very carefully quarantined the Western press such that they could never meet with a Russian civilian except in tightly chaperoned situations.

The final blow to Haldane's party loyalty came after the press had been evacuated to Kuibyshev in October. She writes about this moment tellingly:

> In Kuibyshev the local food supply disappeared almost overnight. The first day of our arrival, the food shops were stacked with loaves of bread and other provisions. From the second day onwards, the queues began to form outside them. They grew longer and longer. The supplies disappeared, and were not replaced. The authorities opened a special shop for the foreigners only. The windows were piled high with bread, cheese, butter, cold meats, sausages, provisions of every kind, with caviar [*sic*], vodka, champagne by dozens of bottles. The manager was provided with the book containing the names of all those entitled to buy there. Outside the door stood a guard, a uniformed N.K.V.D. soldier, with rifle and fixed bayonet. I went there to buy my ration of chocolate, to take with me on the return journey. As I came up to the door, an old Jew paused, to peer at the rich spectacle displayed in the window. The soldier moved him on, roughly. "Not for you," he said, "only for foreigners." I felt ashamed of being one.

> I was already feeling shame and remorse. On the way to the shop, I had encountered a crowd of women in white shawls, gathered around a *droshky*, an open carriage, pulled by a tired old horse, with a traditional Russian coachman on the box, huddled in his thick cape, a drop on the end of his red nose, running into his matted beard. In the carriage sat two weeping women—one elderly, the other young, fair, common and pretty. I mingled with the crowd and let myself be jostled to the edge of the carriage. The sobbing younger woman carried on her lap a small cardboard box, similar to those in which large Christmas dolls used to be sold in the London shops. It was festooned with a wreath of wired white and red paper flowers. In it lay the doll, the waxen corpse of a small child of about two, neatly and carefully dressed in his best suit of pale blue woollies. The young mother was carrying her child, dead from starvation, to the graveyard. It may well be said that I could have seen far worse sights than this in China. It just happens that I did not. I am well aware of the fact that dead babies, especially during the war, were plentiful everywhere. I know, also, that man's inhumanity to man, the callous indifference of the "haves" to the desperate need of the "have-nots," exists in all places and at all times. I cannot excuse my sentimental reaction to this trivial incident on any of the above grounds. I can only explain it as due to the extreme sickness of my oversensitive conscience, the revolt of my sense of morality, the re-awakening of my mind and ratiocinatory faculties from a deep, drugged sleep.
>
> Standing by the side of that dead baby, I swore a silent oath that never again would I get on any platform, anywhere at any time, to use my oratorical or persuasive gifts to convince an audience of working-class men, women, and children, that the Soviet Union was the hope of the toilers of the world.[73]

Charlotte Haldane was much more than merely Mrs. Haldane, a somewhat derisive formality the others accorded her. She was a deserving literary light in her own right. Furthermore, in addition to her avant-garde feminism, her politics, her notoriety, and her extensive and legitimate literary credentials, she was also a person wrestling with the loss of her foundational faith that dated to her 1927 visit to the USSR. Communism, she came to understand, was a doomed philosophy, if only because "the political and economic theories of Marx and Engels have their roots in Western European historical and economic events, and arose as the result of their own personal observations of conditions which were nearly all of them the direct result or indirect results of the Industrial Revolution. But there has never been an industrial revolution in Asia; neither in China nor in Russia."[74] Haldane concludes, "It is enough to say that I returned to England filled with hatred and contempt for those Party leaders whom formerly I had respected and befriended as trusted comrades."[75]

When she left for the Soviet Union, she did so with high Marxist hopes. Unfortunately, she seems to have arrived totally ill-equipped for the insulation and isolation she experienced, partly because of her own lack of preparedness (she could neither read nor speak the language: she called this her "deaf and dumb" period), partly because of the heavy censorship and the complete control of information by the central Soviet authorities. She became so sorely disillusioned by her experience that upon her return to London in November 1941, she resigned her Communist Party membership. It was not until well after the war in her second memoir, *Truth Will Out* (1949), a kind of negative conversion tale, that she publicly disavowed communism. But in the earlier *Russian Newsreel* (which she dedicated "To the RED ARMY and THE HEROIC DEFENDERS OF MOSCOW") she writes that she "purposely refrained throughout this book from discussing the social, political, and economic system which prevails in the Union of Soviet Socialist Republics" because of "my own ignorance" and "the briefness of my visit."[76] Nonetheless, in *Truth Will Out*, after Haldane had decommitted from communism, she changed her position:

> In *Russian Newsreel* I tried to give the British people at war a word-picture of the Russian people at war, as I had seen it. I scrupulously refrained from raising any controversial points. When it was impossible to describe certain events without being transparently dishonest and propagandist, I treated them lightly and humorously. It was neither the time nor the place to furnish the Nazis with gratuitous material for anti-Soviet propaganda, nor to enter into a polemical argument with regard to the Soviet way of life.[77]

(*Russian Newsreel* is in fact a remarkable document of contemporary ethnography and, like the Caldwell/Bourke-White collaborations, includes photographs of citizens and even the occasional wrecked Luftwaffe fighter, some of which Bourke-White had bestowed on her.)

Russian Newsreel includes remarkable descriptions: roads and transportation, language, hotels, food and drink, rationing, clothes, even a chapter on shopping and the infamous queues. Haldane then gets down to the business of reportage and broadcasting, portraying the onerous censorship but providing delightful thumbnail portraits of her fellow journalists, including their illicit back-channel trade in radios. As with most of the Russian memoirs, her recollection of the press junket takes center stage. But after she discusses the problematic aspects of Moscow life, she returns to cultural matters: opera, ballet, theater, cinema, and especially literature, about which she offers many cogent insights. Not surprisingly, she incorporates her thoughts about women, including women on the home front, women at war, women with children, and women during air raids. She was set up to do twice-weekly broadcasts on Radio Moscow back to London, through the Writers' Union she met Sergei Eisenstein, and she had a fur coat and was ready for a trip to a farm collective. In October everything changed. "[A]s the Nazi locusts slowly and then more rapidly ate their way towards Moscow,"[78] fueled in part with drugs and alcohol,[79] she, like the other correspondents, and a just-arrived British Trades Union Congress delegation, were whisked off to Kuibyshev. A couple of weeks later, on October 25, the same day Wallace Carroll reached Iran, she hitched a ride on the Trades Union plane headed toward Archangel, to a promised rendezvous with a returning British convoy.

However disenchanted Haldane may have been with her sojourn to the *rodina*, the motherland of Marxism, in the conclusion to *Russian Newsreel*, she dashes on perfume, puts her best foot forward, and swallows her true feelings for the Western propaganda effort. Russians, she admits, are different, but they need us and we need them. Haldane smiles her one last romantic smile: "She is an unconquerable nation, with a glorious future ahead of her."[80]

Feliks Topolski

Also aboard the *Llanstephan Castle* was the Polish ex-pat artist Feliks Topolski. Born in Warsaw in 1907, he received his art education at the Warsaw Academy of Art while also attending the Polish Officers' School of Artillery Reserve. Traveling to London in 1935 to record the silver jubilee of George V for a Polish journal, he fell in love with British architecture and the nation's social scene and never returned to Poland. In 1947 he became a naturalized British citizen, but not before rejoining the Polish army to fight in Italy during the war. Long before then he had become well established and appreciated as an artist, though many thought his hectic pen-and-ink style unruly and impressionist. By the time he left for Russia in August 1941, he had on his résumé illustrated editions of several George Bernard Shaw plays, including *Pygmalion*, *Geneva*, and *In Good King Charles's Golden Days*. He had also published a selection of his drawings of the Blitz, *Britain in Peace and War* (1941). He was famously wounded during an evening's bombing, spending at least six weeks in Middlesex Hospital, where he was commissioned an official war artist.

Following his recuperation a coveted opportunity to travel to Russia came his way. As the London newspaper the *Picture Post* crowed: "He goes to Russia to draw for the PICTURE POST. He goes as official artist with the Polish Military Mission sent to help organize the Polish Army in Russia." The *Post*'s anonymous correspondent explained further, "Vivid photographs of the Russian battlefront are few. The war moves at a great pace. The Russian censorship is strict. Many things are seen which may not be photographed. In such a war an artist has a big advantage. He can see, remember and record. We chose our artist, sent him to Russia."[81] As with the other press in Moscow, Russian officials were to become more of a problem than either the *Post* or Topolski had anticipated. He wrote later about the book of drawings he published in 1942: "With my drawing permits apathetically and insufficiently provided, thus most of the book [was] drawn either from secret notes or from memory."[82]

In *Fourteen Letters,* Topolski reproduces the diary, later published in *Nowa Polska,* he kept aboard the *Llanstephan Castle* between August 11, when he and his fellow Poles left Euston Station in London, and August 31, when they took flight from Archangel for Moscow. He described his fellow passengers with an artist's sensibility: Charlotte Haldane ("the 'matushka' of British revolution"), Wallace Carroll ("stability and a child's tongue"), and Vernon Bartlett ("Pickwickian—John Bullish—confidant"). Although he alone among the journalists feared an attack by the German cruiser *Tirpitz* rumored to be on the prowl for the convoy, like the others he was moved by the Arctic. Haldane bears the brunt of Topolski's (and presumably everyone's) sarcasm: "Menace and bitterness. 'Matushka / babushka' excites herself by gossip, weaves theories, who with whom. Bored and panicky (I suspect an 'approach') I refuse to watch the sunset with her."[83] The next evening, "'Babushka' insists: I must declare whether I am an enemy or a Communist—for her, no middle way." But Topolski also feels hounded by almost everyone onboard. They soon discover him to be an artist and demand his attention. But he always returns to Haldane for comic relief: as they approach Archangel, "A lighthouse beacons from the darkness. 'Babushka of the British Revolution' quotes, the devout, Stalin—'Russia—the lantern of the world.'"

Topolski's time in Russia was unique among the correspondents. On his first morning, caught sketching at an open-air café, he and his shipboard friend Ksawery Pruszyński, the Polish embassy's press attaché, were hauled off by the NKVD to "The Militia Station" before being grudgingly released. But thereafter, he had almost unlimited access to the Polish war contribution. He flew with Generals Władysław Anders (just released from Lubyanka Prison) and Georgy Zhukov to Kuibyshev, where the newly minted Polish regiments were to be ceremoniously invested. It was in Kuibyshev that Topolski sketched some of his most moving scenes: peasants and militiamen at and around the train station. It was also Topolski's luck that the British ambassador, Sir Stafford Cripps, who later contributed a flattering introduction to Topolski's *Russia in War*, was able to get him on to one of the last Allied planes to leave Moscow before the forced evacuation of the diplomatic and press corps to Kuibyshev in mid-October. He was whisked back to Archangel, where he got passage on the cruiser HMS *Suffolk*.

One product of his ten weeks in the Soviet Union was *Russia in War* (1942), a remarkable book that in many ways stands as a direct pictorial counterpart to the photojournalism of Bourke-White's Moscow books, *Russia at War* (1942) and *Shooting the Russian War* (1941). Where her photographic work was intended to seem a perfect representation of reality—but was actually well lighted, carefully posed, its *mise-en-scène* meticulously constructed—Topolski's medium was pencil and ink and fully impressionist. His drawings are frenetic, full of energy and movement. Topolski draws faces, buildings, street scenes, country scenes, battle scenes, but because of the abstractness of the finished (or, in many cases, unfinished) creations, his representations are never mimetic of the person, place, or action shown. His drawings instead become typologies, but typologies drawn from life. As such, he characterizes what he believes to be the spirit the Russian people embody, though in no way does he glorify them as Stalinist art posters did. In fact, his drawing of an actual propaganda poster is so scrawled and diffuse that none of the bravado of the original comes through.

As the reader pages through *Russia in War*, it soon becomes evident that Topolski has placed his drawings in chronological order. He admits that many of his pieces were drawn later from memory, but it is clear that the book's layout is not similarly haphazard. More remarkably, he and Bourke-White must have visited many sites together because their drawings—for example, of wounded German airmen in a Moscow hospital—are strikingly similar. In other cases, he and she visit similar sites, ones which have the same general features, but at different times. Topolski was not on the press junket to Smolensk, but he *was* on a similar one arranged in early October for those journalists who missed the earlier one. Thus, as does Bourke-White, he depicts downed German planes, captured soldiers, burned-out villages, and soldiers, nurses, and matériel at or near the front lines.

After Topolski returned to London in November 1941, he organized an exhibition at the Thos. Agnew and Sons Gallery in London, supported by the Polish Relief Fund, Poland's Armed Forces Comforts Fund, and the British Committee for Polish Welfare. It ran August 6–20, 1942, and most of the drawings exhibited there appear in *Russia in War*.[84]

Fellow Travelers?

In addition to the Western press corps and the militarily linked Soviet journalists, a shadow group of correspondents, those representing the Communist International, were also among the crowd with whom Caldwell and Bourke-White worked. In general, these reporters had little interaction with the other Western journalists. They were afforded separate living facilities and assigned opposite sides of the press conference table. Nonetheless, the disparate groups *did* see each other at the twice- or thrice-weekly news conferences chaired at the Ministry of Information by Vice-Commissar Solomon Lozovsky. Haldane recalled the setup well:

> The bourgeois world Press representatives sat at one side of the long table. Lozovsky was at the top, and around the room, unobtrusively, sat various Security officials who watched, listened, but never spoke a word. Opposite, at the other end of the table, also sat a row of correspondents. They came always together, in one or two cars, we knew not whence, and left together. For a few moments, in the ante-room, before the conference, some of us might exchange a word or two with some of them. Most of the bourgeois correspondents were wholly mystified by this other group, and by the fact that they were obviously discouraged from fraternising with us[.] . . .
>
> The situation of the Communist International members in Moscow was one of secrecy and mystery. They were housed by the Russian Government in certain hotels set apart for the purpose, or, in the case of the more distinguished of them, whose movements even their own countrymen did not know, in small private apartments.[85]

Secret and mysterious indeed. Although it was not recognized at the time, Janet Weaver, the Moscow correspondent for the *Daily Worker* (the news organ of the Communist Party of the United States), was also the wife of Nat Ross, the U.S. representative to the Comintern in the Soviet Union. She was actually an informant for the Comintern. As a credentialed American reporter, she was able to attend gatherings, official and social, of American diplomats and correspondents. She then forwarded the information she gleaned from these "American only" gatherings to her Comintern handlers, who would then pass it on to higher-ranking officials.[86]

Alexander Werth, recalling the map of the United States on the wall of the press room, a map with American city names transliterated into Cyrillic, depicts the foreign correspondents. Besides "a Jap here called Hatanaka," he wrote, there were:

> a few foreign correspondents "of the Comintern variety," as somebody described them, and they don't mix with us. One is a young American woman, Janet Weaver, I think, is her name; an old boy called Epstein, with a fabulous nose, who works for the Jewish press in New York; a tall Negro; and a Spaniard, who writes for South American papers, and whose face was at once familiar to me. He turned out to be Jesus Hernandez, the Minister of Education in the Negrin Government, whom I had met in Madrid in '37.[87]

Among the least well known, Homer Smith was an interesting case. While he was a student in the University of Minnesota journalism program, he worked for the post office, "the safe, secure job for a Negro in the thirties,"[88] but realizing that he was unlikely to be hired by an American newspaper, he became excited about the Soviet Five-Year Plan, the same one whose achievements Margaret Bourke-White had gone to Russia to photograph in 1930. He applied directly to the Moscow post office for a job and was immediately hired on. At the same time he approached several representatives of the American Negro press about being their stringer in Moscow under his pen name, Chatwood Hall, and they accepted his offer. Entering Russia through Leningrad in June 1932, he was able to start work immediately. Over the next three years he personally experienced "the jungle of terror" of Stalin's USSR and decided not to renew his postal service contract when it expired in 1935, instead venturing into journalism full-time.[89]

In January 1938 he married a nineteen-year-old Russian beauty, Marie Petrovna, a bold move that soon put both her and her family in the crosshairs of the secret police. By mid-1941 Smith was well on his way to complete disillusionment with the Soviet system. On the decisive and historic morning of June 22, he was twice hauled in by the militia, who demanded to see his documents. Over the next six weeks, he came to believe that it was Stalin who was singularly to blame for the current Russian predicament because of his failure to heed international warnings about precipitous Wehrmacht movements eastward. One of Stalin's first reactions to the early Red Army setbacks had been to purge the defeated military leaders and to quarantine as potential traitors men who had been trapped by the lightning-fast German pincer movements along the western front. Smith noted that in mid-July Stalin changed his rhetorical position from urging the people and the Red Army to stand fast in their defense of communism to standing fast in defense of *rodina*, the Motherland, "sacred Russian soil."[90] When the Western press was ordered evacuated to Kuibyshev, as the Germans approached the western approaches to Moscow on October 16, Smith and Petrovna missed the train. They did not live in one of the hotels of the central city as did most of the Western press; they owned a private flat in the suburbs north of Moscow. When they attempted to take the metro to the central railroad terminal, it had been closed down. Not until October 19 were they able to obtain passage east.

Smith remained in Russia another few years, covering several important stories, most famously the Katyn Forest massacre. In April 1943 the Nazis announced they had found a huge mass burial pit just thirteen miles west of Smolensk, filled with the corpses of over 4,400 Polish officers, and blamed the Russians for the slaughter.[91] When the Red Army retook Smolensk in September 1943, the Soviet government immediately indicted the Germans for the atrocity. Smith was among the first Western journalists allowed on the scene four months later in January 1944. He immediately suspected that the truth was not as the Soviets had been advocating, a hunch that became evidently true over the ensuing few months of the war. His reportage had important ramifications during the postwar Nuremberg Trials.

Finally accepting a job as an editor in the Ethiopian Press and Information Office, Smith departed through Leningrad in November 1946. A year later, Petrovna and their two children were granted exit visas. The family remained in Ethiopia until 1962, when they relocated back to Minneapolis. In 1941, however, for the Western press corps in Moscow, who had written him off as a mere fellow traveler of the Comintern press, Smith was barely a shadow.

The Russians

War is difficult to visualize for a noncombatant. It is especially so when the only information about it is spoon-fed and sanitized by the authorities whose sole purpose is to make the Soviet war machine appear invincible, to give the impression that ultimate victory is inevitable, and to minimize bad news. Although official communiqués came directly from the Press Department of the Soviet Information Bureau, the Western reporters quickly came to realize that, official though they may have been, they almost never were newsworthy. Ideally, the best way to write about a war is to be in it or, if that is not possible, to know colleagues who have been. In *All-Out on the Road to Smolensk,* Caldwell describes visiting Soviet writers just back from the front in their apartments, interviews arranged through their friend Eugene Petrov's influence. But again, not everyone had Caldwell's credentials as a novelist and his connections in the Writers' Union to facilitate access to the Soviet military community.

Instead, reporters universally turned to the Moscow newspapers for information, because their news usually came from Russian reporters in the field, many of whom were actually assigned to military units, even units at the front lines, and these journalists, though obviously patriotic and under strong censorship control—and wary of the Stalinist purges of artists and intellectuals in the late 1930s—had more facts at hand than the Sovinformburo was usually willing to divulge. Furthermore, as Maurice Lovell notes in his memoir, *The Soviet Way of Life*, published in 1948, "Russians are accustomed to reading and understanding their own newspapers. Censorship was a highly developed instrument in Russia even before the Crimean war, one might say even at the time of Pushkin. . . . Enough to say that observably the Russian is expert in reading between the lines."[92]

Izvestia was the proxy for the Supreme Soviet of the Soviet Union and thus the official organ of the government. *Pravda*, on the other hand, was the voice of the Communist Party, while *Komsomolskaya Pravda* represented the Communist youth organization. Reporters read these papers daily—or had them read to them, since most were not fluent in Russian—but most of all they relied on the Red Army's official paper, *Krasnaya Zvezda* (*Red Star*). Haldane, for example, remembered "the daily stories by Ehrenbourg [*sic*], one of the greatest Soviet novelists, who is given a free hand to interview German prisoners, read their diaries, and describe them in his own superb style."[93] Decrying the lack of access to information, Henry Cassidy observed that they were forced to rely on the "unofficial newspapers, containing an unbelievably small amount of news. *Pravda*, . . . *Izvestia*, . . . and the lesser newspapers published only stereotyped editorials, following eternally the tone of Stalin's latest utterance on the subject being discussed; cautious stories and articles, containing a minimum of information, and foreign news reports, reproducing precisely the terms of the Associated Press, Reuters, or whatever servers originated the news."[94]

Soviet writers—Ilya Ehrenburg, Konstantin Simonov, Vasily Grossman, and Alexander Bek, among others—had accomplished postwar literary careers. Several of these men were poets at heart, and all later wrote novels of their experiences, novels that served, gradually and grudgingly, to tear open the scabs of Stalinist idolatry that had been festering in the Soviet Union since the war began and even before. Of these four Russian wartime authors, Bek and Ehrenburg were full-time writers. Simonov, on the other hand, was a soldier at heart who received several awards for valor as the fighting went on, but he was also an apologist for Stalin and a member of the Communist Party. Ehrenburg was clearly the lyricist, Bek the documentarian. Grossman most fit the model of a participant-observer, rather than an embedded journalist, but often, perhaps because he was a Jew, was not in good stead with the newspaper establishment.

Nonetheless, of all the writings to emerge from these Soviet writers, the work with the most lasting impact was Grossman's *Life and Fate*, initially completed in 1960 but suppressed. It is a rugged tale about the war on the western front, particularly the siege of Stalingrad, written in the spirit of *War and Peace*. A copy was secretly spirited out of the Soviet Union so that in 1980 it was finally published in Switzerland, and an English translation followed in 1985.[95]

On the other hand, there is no doubt that members of the Soviet press were allowed a greater degree of expressive freedom than that granted the tightly censored Western press, and were permitted better access to source material. As long as they did not transgress the guidelines of the socialist realist arts movement, which mandated that Soviet literature, including journalism, must promote the ideals of the USSR and the Communist Party, their prose could be as purple as they wished.

Ehrenburg's famous Christmas dispatch of 1941 (*infra vide*) is an example. He incorporates direct quotes from interviews and overheard conversation as well as snippets of diaries and official communiqués. Not only is the piece viciously anti-Fascist, but it demonstrates through its details the vacuum within which the Western news corps had been trapped by Soviet secrecy, distrust, and censorship. In the end this sort of exclusion from source material backfired and played a role in maintaining the justified distrust the West had for the Soviet Union in 1941. Furthermore, it disaffected many of those journalists who had once been friends of the regime, or who at least had been its apologists.

THE GERMAN CHRISTMAS

A German soldier lay under a snow-clad fir-tree. His white, dead eyes were rolled towards the West. A letter from Wernigerode was found in his pocket. "Dear Willi" it ran, "our German Christmas will soon be here. We shall celebrate it without you. Martha and I hope you won't forget us and will send us some nice little presents from Russia for the Christmas tree."

And now their German Christmas has come. Darkness looms over Wernigerode and Brocken in the Hartz Mountain country, and it seems as though the witches are holding their sabbath there. No, it is the wind howling in the chimney. Martha and Anna are standing in front of an empty Christmas tree. It is adorned with three candle-ends and a tarnished star from last year. And here's Father Christmas with the presents. He has a postman's cap on his head. What is he taking out of his bag? A fur cap, a Russian ham, some stockings for Anna? No, it's a letter. "Your husband died the death of a hero on the eastern front."

Hang up the official notification on the Christmas tree under the tarnished star of your Führer. There won't be any ham or any stockings. Far away, somewhere near Tula, the blizzard is covering up the corpse of your darling Willi. The postman has whole batches of letters and he knocks at one house after the other. This Father Christmas won't pass anyone by. He won't forget Hilda, Emma or Frida.

So this is your German Christmas! You thought you were going to celebrate it in a different style. You thought you were going to illuminate merry Christmas trees in the middle of bludgeoned Europe and dance a German cancan in the huge graveyard. Drunk with schnaps and blood, you thought you were going to sing "Peace on earth." Your world is a world of wolves—your Christmas is the Christmas of Herod.

We do not wish to mock the tears of Anna or Martha, but we have in front of us, in precise Gothic script: "Send us some nice little presents from Russia." We can see this greedy German hyena licking her lips and we will say briefly: "Madam, you expected presents. You have got what you deserved. Weep, if tears can lighten your black conscience."

We were a peaceful nation. At Yasnaya-Polyana which you have desecrated, Leo Tolstoy thought only of peace. On that stormy October night when the people were silent, drowning in blood, the workers of Petrograd, the city which you had mutilated, shouted, "Peace to the world." We did not want other people's property, nor did we covet other people's happiness. We acclimatized wheat in the Far North and we opened canals like wonderful arteries. We loved books and the warm clasp of brotherly hands. You mistook our love of peace for weakness. You attacked us and you have awakened our hatred and wrath. We no longer regard you as human beings. We have neither pity nor condescension for you. We have bullets and fir-trees for you. Under our fir-trees you will sleep the last sleep.

Burn on, three candle-ends on the Christmas tree in Wernigerode! Weep, German women! Your Christmas will become an endless fast. And if you don't wish to weep, then dance, jesters, pipe away and thank the Führer for your German Christmas! In the spring the snow will melt and you will smell the stench of corpses. In the spring Hans the drummer will come to Wernigerode and play a Hitler march. The death-drummer of Germany will beat his tattoo.

—December 25, 1941.[96]

CHAPTER 5

Summer 1941 ★ June, July, August

Piecing together Caldwell's and Bourke-White's very busy and very productive summer requires some shuffling of sources. While Bourke-White's *Shooting the Russian War* is reasonably factual—at least as factual as one of her photographs, in which the artist chooses what to put into it, what to remove from it, what to emphasize, and how to arrange all the elements—such cannot be said of Caldwell's *All-Out on the Road to Smolensk*. We would today probably categorize it within the genre of creative nonfiction. It is definitely based on the events of that summer in and near Moscow. Caldwell, the author, creates a first-person narrator, a new persona who is variously an intrepid and risk-taking journalist, a bemused tourist, a rube, or a thoughtful and perceptive observer of the people and events around him. The resulting work is then arranged as a novel such that, as do many travel-based books, it has a loose relationship to a quest. We have already seen the departure when the couple crosses the Pacific and the east Asian continent in the spring of 1941. The culmination of the book comes when they actually arrive near the front lines of Operation Barbarossa in mid-September.

The central part of the work describes, in Caldwell's own stylistic manner, that Moscow summer. Fact checking must be done, however, and fortunately we have the complete library of his newspaper dispatches (from which a great deal of *Smolensk* was constructed); transcripts of all his radio broadcasts as well as audio recordings of many of them; and telegrams and letters exchanged with his agent, his Connecticut secretary, his parents, and the staff at *Life* magazine and *PM* newspaper. Bourke-White kept careful notes as well, from which she fashioned *Shooting the Russian War*. Furthermore, we have multiple memoirs written by the couple's fellow journalists within a year or so of the 1941 summer. Finally, Caldwell, too, kept a diary, much of which was edited into a book quickly published in London, *Moscow Under Fire*, and the couple also pieced together *Russia at War*, a photo-text book. However, this contained little new in it and had little of the success afforded their other photo-text publications. In fact, neither Bourke-White nor Caldwell listed it in their own bibliographies.

Within a week of the outbreak of war, CBS began a search for a Moscow voice to join the regular crew of correspondents from around the world who teamed with Edward R. Murrow and Robert Trout on the daily news roundups, either *World News Tonight* or *The World Today*. It was Caldwell's name recognition that made him the network's first choice. On June 28, when he and Bourke-White had been back in Moscow for only a couple of days after returning from the Black Sea area, Paul White, CBS's news editor, cabled Laurence Steinhardt, the American ambassador in Moscow, to arrange for a broadcast by Caldwell. Before the month was out Caldwell had become a regular contributor with a voice that White at one point evaluated as "satisfactory," even though during the first several broadcasts there was a great deal of electromagnetic atmospheric interference that rendered the transmissions at times almost unintelligible. CBS initially agreed to pay Caldwell fifty dollars per broadcast, though it balked at paying Bourke-White the same amount because her voice was "too thin." In any case, that point soon became moot when *Life* forbade her broadcasting for CBS while she was under contract with the magazine. After a week or so Caldwell was broadcasting twice daily and running up such a tab that on July 15 White cabled Caldwell that they could no longer maintain the original pay scale. He offered three hundred dollars per week,[1] which Caldwell accepted, perhaps because White earlier had assured him that he was reaching an audience of about twenty million people.

Typewritten transcriptions of some fifty of Caldwell's broadcasts are housed in the archives at Syracuse, most of which are postcensor broadcast scripts. In content they reflect the same approach to journalism that he afforded *PM:* "soft" news. This annoyed White to the degree that he once cabled Caldwell: "PLEASE HEREAFTER ALWAYS BEGIN CUMNEWS [with news] LEAVING FEATURE STUFF SECONDARY." After this Caldwell often just read the Press Bureau's communiqué verbatim, which had the added benefit of not upsetting the censors.

In addition to this written record, an extraordinary aural record also exists. During the 1930s and 1940s KIRO, a Seattle affiliate of CBS, began recording the live New York news feeds on acetate or glass discs for delayed broadcast three hours later. Unlike other stations that destroyed their discs, KIRO warehoused its audio recordings. Serendipitously rediscovered in 1957, the discs were turned over to the University of Washington's School of Communications, where Professor Milo Ryan undertook the task of cataloging the recordings and transferring them to ¼" tape.[2] Ultimately these tapes were donated to the National

Archives, where they remain today. Some of the recordings have already been digitalized. This National Archive phonoarchive now is fully searchable by remote computer.[3] I have obtained CD copies of all the recordings that contain Caldwell's or Bourke-White's voice, and listening to them is a remarkable experience. The precision necessary to coordinate these shortwave transmissions from around the world and to integrate them into a single broadcast is a significant achievement. The voice quality, of course, is highly variable with the exception of Murrow's, whose deep baritone always seems to ring through strongly. Caldwell's diction has a kind of tortured meticulousness about it, as if he is attempting to speak across a large noisy room and not be misunderstood while at the same time veiling his Georgia accent. In mid-August White even cabled Caldwell some advice: "SPEAKING TOO CLOSE MIKE GIVING MUFFLED EFFECT WORK FEW INCHES FURTHER FROM MIKE RECEPTION OTHERWISE GOOD." Bourke-White's voice is indeed faint, and on the three recordings of her, interference makes her words almost indecipherable. That some of these recordings were probably made, quite literally, *during* the Luftwaffe's Moscow midnight air raids makes the listening experience all the more captivating.[4]

Authenticity is problematic in Caldwell's writing. Vignettes in *Smolensk* are often as engineered as Bourke-White's "candid" photographs. Bourke-White's goal had been a faithful rendition of the events of their Russian trip and their contexts. *Shooting the Russian War* reflects the faithfulness she intended, as is evident from a reading of the copious and detailed notes she kept throughout those six months. Caldwell, on the other hand, based *Smolensk* in large part on the daily articles he had published in New York's *PM* newspaper. Whereas Caldwell often was reclusive in his interactions with people, Bourke-White was gregarious, a trait that is manifest in the careful details she provides in *Shooting the Russian War* of her associates, events, food, clothing, and surroundings. Whereas Caldwell stresses the power, dread, and unease of the times, Bourke-White reports on the personalities, pleasures, and frivolities of those same moments. Facts, nonetheless, are often elusive in each author's work.

Travel writing frequently employs the paradigm of romance as its central element. To a large measure this reflects the gender bias of the genre, which has long been skewed masculine, the travel memoir serving as a means of "masculine self-fashioning."[5] This impulse is evident in *Smolensk*, a book of remarkable tension and mystery. But for *Smolensk* to be successful a reader must be willing to acknowledge its verisimilitude, and fortunately, sufficient grounding in fact and chronology remains for one to believe in the trueness of its general frame of events, if not the specifics of all the sketches.

Traditionally, the travel narrative has been reserved principally for male adventurers to assert their priority in matters of exploration and/or conquest, though clearly over the last fifty years women adventure writers have assumed a position of increasing relevance and importance. In his 2011 metastudy, *Travel Writing,* Carl Thompson notes that anthologists have identified a difference between the tone of male and female travelers, especially in the nineteenth and twentieth centuries, when women first began to enter the field of travel writing and to expand their presence therein. Whereas men generally wrote of the thrust of their travels—and the more potentially dangerous and uncomfortable the trip, the more credibility redounded to the author and adventurer—women wrote of aesthetics, domestic and social matters, and interpersonal affairs and connections. These ideologically distinct and gendered spheres of concern were bolstered by patriarchy; in men's writing, women were often portrayed as exotic (not infrequently orientalized) creatures of comfort or temptation for the hard-pressed men of adventure.

But male travel writing also has an internal function. Thompson notes a differentiation—to some extent chronological—in the degree to which a mission is internalized. Travel discourse in the Age of Enlightenment was often related to such external and empirical goals as discovery, scientific progress, or colonial expansion. Quest discourse, on the other hand, has almost always been romanticized in the sense that the traveler is also seeking self-discovery, often through a rite of passage.

In Victorian "discovery" literature the moment of epiphany is often heralded by the trope of "the-monarch-of-all-I-survey,"[6] a rhetorical moment marked by (a) a literary aestheticization of the landscape, (b) an increased "density of meaning" in language achieved particularly by employing multiple adjectives with "material referents," and (c) a sense of "mastery predicated between the seer and the seen."[7]

In *Smolensk,* the "monarch-of-all-I-survey" moment occurs when Caldwell finally reaches the battlefield at Yelnya. Although it does not entail mastery over that scene in any physical sense, it does bring about the epiphanic moment he has been striving for since the June 22 invasion. He has before himself evidence of the true horror of this war, if only in the detritus left behind. And he also carries away with him a discarded Russian and Nazi helmet, emblematizing that experience.

Moscow by Night

When Caldwell and Bourke-White set out from Connecticut in March, they were stirred by a rather ill-defined sociopolitical resolve to promote the values and goals of the Popular Front, by the professional possibilities that might lie in store for them, and by the sheer excitement and boldness of their undertaking. After June 22, their goal, and the goal of all the other reporters in residence in Moscow, was to get to "The Front"—or at least to get as "frontward" as possible in order to observe the war firsthand.

Within hours of his and Bourke-White's return to the metropolis of Moscow from Sochi, Caldwell is out on the streets. He describes how, after obtaining a nighttime permit, he was able to walk along Gorky Street, one of Moscow's central thoroughfares, for hours. It was nearly deserted, although "almost every doorway on the street was occupied by a watcher. At the corners there were always several of them, usually three or four standing in a group."[8] Then, toward morning, the city took on a phantasmagorical nature. "As it began to get lighter, buildings that I had not suspected of being in existence gradually rose from the earth and jutted like blackened icicles into the sky. The city began to take on shape and substance. I could recognize familiar-looking landmarks that brought me back to reality. I was in Moscow after all, not on some planet whose sun had expired" (*Smolensk* 29). He notes a convoy of trucks moving through Red Square toward the front with "soldiers, machineguns, and artillery shells" and muses, "Here began the road to Smolensk" (*Smolensk* 29). This is his first mention of Smolensk, and it appears so suddenly in the text that the reader is jolted from Caldwell's comfortable, even occasionally comic narrative back into the reality that this book and this story are about war, not travel.

Caldwell's text now takes an interesting turn. He adopts a rube-in-the-big-city conceit by describing how dark it is at night walking the streets, especially once the curfew is established.[9] He runs into lampposts, "wade(s) ankle deep through some unset cement" (*Smolensk* 32), and finally drops into a five-foot-deep manhole where water main repairs are underway. He trips over sandbags and people's feet. There is a brief vignette of an old lady on the top floor of an apartment house who is suspected of espionage. Watchers had seen flashing lights coming from her window. It turns out she had simply been striking matches in order to catch a glimpse of the bedbugs biting her, he writes (*Smolensk* 34–35).

Continuing on this humorous tack, Caldwell tells a series of yarns about the difficulties with his automobile. In order to facilitate moving about Moscow, he obtains a used car from a man who had gone to Stockholm just as the war began and who could no longer return to Moscow. Stateside, he reminds us, a car purchase normally is accompanied by a complimentary tank of gas, but petrol is so hard to come by in the USSR that the American ambassador personally siphons five gallons out of an embassy car into Caldwell's '35 Plymouth. Befitting his status and obligations as an American news broadcaster and journalist, he had been allowed to hire a personal chauffeur, Alexander. On their way back to the Hotel National, Alexander stops the Plymouth in the middle of an intersection:

> He got out and looked at the car critically, shaking his head disapprovingly from time to time. Soon traffic was in a snarl and the militiaman who was directing traffic came over to us, blowing his whistle a long hard blast with every step. Both the militiaman and I wanted to know what the trouble was. My chauffeur said the car was not fit to drive until it had been given a thorough polishing job. The militiaman sided with the chauffeur, and there was nothing I could do about it. The traffic officer put his whistle back into his pocket and, shaking his head from side to side, went back to his post. (*Smolensk* 40–41)

Caldwell finally sends Alexander off with ten rubles to buy some polish. A bit later the chauffeur is again incensed, believing that, because the car lacks basic accessories, Caldwell has been robbed. "I gave him a hundred rubles to make the necessary purchases and repairs, and promised to explain to him someday how it was that no American had ever yet sold a second-hand car complete with jack, pump, and pliers—and with a horn that would blow" (*Smolensk* 42).

Nevertheless, for all the humor, Caldwell never lets us forget that there is a war on. He is forced into an air-raid shelter for several hours one dark night when the Luftwaffe appears over the city. All day long loudspeakers in the public squares broadcast whatever news the Kremlin had decided is most palatable for its citizens. Carefully, Caldwell ratchets up the dramatic tension: "Out towards Smolensk the Germans were advancing steadily at the rate of twenty miles a day, but Moscow was not worried. Army supply trucks, sometimes two abreast, rumbled out of Moscow towards the west day and night carrying steel-helmeted troops, giant searchlights, and anti-aircraft guns to Smolensk" (*Smolensk* 38). Thereafter, very little humor creeps into *Smolensk*. Caldwell's long description of his trip to the radio station on the evening of July 21–22, the night of the first Luftwaffe raid, suggests the condensation of the events of several trips, and he writes it in the pulsing style of many of his best short stories:

> Then began a wild dash through the streets which were, except when incendiaries popped down around us, darker than a piney woods in Alabama in the dark of the moon. . . . We had no lights to see by, and Alexander glued his nose against

> the windshield and sent the car shooting through the night at forty-five miles an hour. . . .
>
> Along the way to the radio studio a bomb fell directly behind us in the street, the concussion hurling the machine around at right angles. We only avoided a head-on smashup into an apartment-house wall at the last possible instant when my chauffeur jerked the steering wheel around and sent us skidding sideways into the bomb crater. . . .
>
> Four blocks from the studio a thousand-pound bomb whammed into the street ahead of us. My chauffeur locked the wheels with a mighty thrust on the brake pedal, and we came to a jolting stop with our front wheels down in the crater. (*Smolensk* 65, 66)

They of course survive and right on time he transmits his shortwave broadcast to CBS in New York from a basement studio, "which had been fitted up like a padded cell in an insane asylum. The walls, floors, and ceilings were lined with thick mattresses. The basement shook when demolition bombs burst nearby, but the sound was muffled and practically inaudible" (*Smolensk* 67).

The construction of this chapter sheds some light on how Caldwell composed *Smolensk*. The chapter portrays the events of one night, that of the first Luftwaffe attack beginning just after 10 p.m. on July 21. Within the chapter, Caldwell strings together six or seven distinct vignettes, making them seem to have occurred during the course of this five-and-a-half-hour evening and early morning attack. In *Moscow Under Fire*, his daily entries for the period July 22 to July 31 enumerate and describe six separate nights of raids. Transcripts of his nightly CBS shortwave broadcasts confirm this.[10] Further, between July 22 and July 31 Caldwell cabled eight separate articles to New York for *PM*. These describe his experiences during the six raids commencing on July 22 and generally match up with the CBS transcripts and the *Moscow Under Fire* chronology. For *Smolensk*, Caldwell convincingly accordions all these into a single night of mayhem. Throughout these early chapters of *Smolensk*, Caldwell cultivates a mystique of horror: "A war was being fought on a gigantic scale somewhere in the vicinity of Smolensk, but during its first four weeks it remained a mystery to the people of Moscow" (*Smolensk* 43).

Censorship and news embargoes made Soviet truth-telling a well-appreciated joke. There were interview opportunities, field trips, and even photo ops, but the Kremlin, filtering information through such agencies as the NKVD and VOKS (All-Union Society for Cultural Relations with Foreign Countries), offered to the Western press only the most trustworthy and sanitized of contacts, and at all times they were carefully chaperoned by Communist Party operatives to ensure that interviews did not get off course. Bourke-White chafed under the restrictions and paperwork necessary for almost any public photography, though she realized that she had to muffle her displeasure since she was being given what, for the Russians, was an exceptional privilege. That only a few members of the press were conversant in Russian (longtime Moscow *Daily Mail* stringer A. T. Cholerton, Russian-born Alexander Werth working for Reuters, and Carpathian-born Henry Shapiro of the United Press) made the Kremlin's control even more successful. Thus, when Caldwell places in quotation marks a thousand-word "verbatim" interview ("He told me the following story"; *Smolensk* 52) with a Soviet tankist who, though gravely wounded, escaped annihilation in a battle near Smolensk, we quietly accept it as a standard Caldwell ploy to place dialogue "authentically" in the mouth of a character. He had done this quite effectively in his first travel book, *Some American People* (1935), and to a lesser extent in his photo-text books with Bourke-White.

Caldwell distrusted the routine communiqués from the Soviet Press Bureau handed out twice daily at its offices, documents he thought were often worthless: "'We continued to fight the enemy on all fronts'" (*Smolensk* 43). He also knew well from personal experience how liberal and unpredictable the Soviet censors were with their blue pencils. All outgoing dispatches from the international press corps first had to be vetted by the Soviets. His radio scripts could be broadcast only after formal approval, which often came at the last moment. Thus, to get a better sense of the war he so desperately wanted to observe firsthand, he spent considerable time in the apartments and homes of Soviet frontline correspondents just back from the multiple fronts. There he also occasionally met infantry, artillery, and armed cavalry (i.e., tank) officers. In the central chapters of *Smolensk,* he devotes substantial space to secondhand descriptions of monumentally horrendous tank battles. In the longest chapter of the book he writes vivid accounts of the Luftwaffe assaults on the capital, which he experienced not just from embassy rooftop and hotel balcony but also at street level as he attempted to get to the radio station while the city was under active attack.

While Caldwell was in Moscow, he filed over six dozen newspaper dispatches with *PM.* Much of this material can be found almost verbatim in his London publication, *Moscow Under Fire,* and often in minimally altered form in the Moscow sections of *Smolensk.* Caldwell was efficient in his writing. He even used some of this material for his nightly CBS radio broadcasts. Because he was not responsible for the hard news of the war—ironically, much of the most reliable information came from other world capitals where censorship was not a factor—his writing focused on his observations of life in the city and his conversations with Soviet writers.

Understandably, for a book of this nature, what Caldwell did *not* include in *Smolensk* were the intimate domestic matters of which his wife was so fond. For example, when Caldwell grumbles in *Smolensk* that because the exchange rate was so onerous "we had to be content with two meals a day instead of three because we could not afford full fare" (*Smolensk* 82), that wasn't quite the whole story. Bourke-White, even as she too objected to the cost, recalled that they didn't have lunch because "we seldom had time to eat" at midday. Breakfast, on the other hand, was often full of surprises such as "frequent gifts of shredded wheat from the embassy commissary" or "a jar of iced orange slices or a handkerchief full of peanuts" that Alexander picked up on his morning gas hunts.[11] At suppertime they could "sit back and enjoy our hundred-ruble dinner of caviar and chicken cutlet a la Kiev" (*SRW* 109). The other correspondents, in contrast, generally ate collegially in the Metropole's restaurant, chaperoned by the omnipresent Intourist staff.

Furthermore, Caldwell eschewed revealing any truly personal information. *Smolensk* was not about him; it was a war story. But from Bourke-White's offhand sketches of their staff and perquisites, one can understand why she and Caldwell were never considered full members of the press's social circuit. Their entourage by midsummer included not only Alexander and Elisaveta, their translator, but also a full-time secretary, Tatiana, a survivor of one of Stalin's purges *and* a two-year prison term in a central Asian "reeducation" camp. Bourke-White characterized Tatiana as "the kindest person who ever stepped into a human skin" (*SRW* 97). None of the other correspondents could afford such a staff. And, beyond having one of the most luxurious hotel suites available in the capital, possessing every possible pass needed to negotiate the nightly curfews, securing extra fuel coupons, and Bourke-White's unprecedented permission to use her camera, the Caldwells lived an envied and privileged social life. Bourke-White takes especial pride in her and Caldwell's personal connection with Laurence Steinhardt, the U.S. ambassador, as she details in *Shooting the Russian War:* a lavish Fourth of July celebration to which most of the Americans remaining in Moscow had been invited, though *not* most of the other members of the press corps; tea with Steinhardt in their Hotel National suite two nights before the first German raid; and Steinhardt's personal concern for their safety paired with his wink-wink attitude toward their refusal to be evacuated after the June 22 attack. And all this doesn't even factor in the press's envy over the huge amount of money the couple demanded, and received, for their services.

After a while Caldwell becomes so frustrated by his inability to get past the hurdles the Kremlin has erected that he prepares "to make a dash for" the front but is dissuaded from this rash attempt when Alexander calls at 5:00 a.m. to report that the crankcase on the Plymouth is cracked (*Smolensk* 102). Instead, he visits the home of a Soviet war correspondent, where he meets three stringers just back from the Smolensk front: Konstantin Simonov, Eugene Gabrilovich, and Lev Slavin, each of whom regales Caldwell with fanciful stories of newspaperman heroism.[12] In the novel, Caldwell uses them to keep the focus on the war at the Smolensk front.

The Luftwaffe Bombs Moscow

In late August the couple experienced a particularly spectacular air raid. Caldwell wrote about it, and Bourke-White photographed it, capturing some of the most startling images of her summer there. It was a memorable evening. They had gone to the British embassy, located just across the Moscow River from the Kremlin, to seek "a change in scenery" (*Smolensk* 111). The most remarkable feature of the night's raid was the *Luftwaffe*'s resorting to dropping dramatic parachute flares. In *Shooting the Russian War*, Bourke-White reproduces two photos from that evening at the British embassy, and as is her practice, her captions carefully describe the action (see chapter 3, figures 28 and 29):

> This was an extraordinary night when the German parachute flares, like a string of pearls, were dropped in parallel rows over the Kremlin. Drifting with the wind, they descended slowly to earth in snakelike lines.
>
> Note the short, thick, vertical lines leaving the path of the flare. These are goblets of molten magnesium which drop off the burning mass of the flare itself and fall straight to earth. (*SRW* 123)

In addition to this, in her technical appendix, she provides detailed camera specs. Knowing that her night photos required five- to six-minute exposures enhances one's appreciation of their extraordinary beauty.

Later in *Shooting the Russian War*, Bourke-White added to her recollection of that "four camera night," displaying a sense of entitlement the other journalists thought she consistently demanded. In late June the British Military Mission had been quickly established with the arrival of General F. N. Mason-MacFarlane to assume overall authority and Rear-Admiral G. J. A. Miles to command the naval component.[13] To be in their company was not something the run-of-the-mill correspondent could expect, but for the Caldwells it was de rigueur, in fact Bourke-White boasts that they had a standing invitation from MacFarlane "to drop in for air raids. This was valuable to me, for having used our splendid balcony to the utmost I needed new viewpoints for night pictures" (*SRW* 183). On this particular evening "during the third week of August," she recalls, the raid was so "spectacular" that "even [British ambassador] Sir Stafford Cripps was hurrying about in pajamas and fuzzy bathrobe, running to the windows first on one side and then the other, watching the raid" (*SRW* 184).[14] Caldwell also recalls that when he had been on his way up to the roof with his wife he had come across Cripps: "[He] happened to be on his way down to the basement shelter with book, bathrobe, and dog. He was reading a book on Chinese agriculture" (*Smolensk* 112). Before the night's raid was over, Bourke-White had recruited both MacFarlane and Miles to help her with her gear and worry over her safety (*SRW* 183, 184, 191). Even Caldwell writes that at one point he saw "[a] British general crawl[ing] along the ridge of the roof" (*Smolensk* 116).

Caldwell published three separate versions of this August night's extreme fireworks. By tracing these three iterations we again see how carefully Caldwell fashions *Smolensk*. In the hurried product, *Moscow Under Fire*, his note for August 8 is terse and focuses on the military aspects of the night sky: "Deprived of the light from fires they evidently had hoped to start, the Germans returned to the air over the same district and released parachute flares. These floated down in long string-like steps descending from the sky to the earth. Before the flares could be of any service, ground batteries shattered them one by one."[15] Next, in their collaborative *Russia at War*, in which Caldwell's text takes a backseat to Bourke-White's photos, he writes simply: "During the dark of the moon the German raiders depended upon parachute flares to light the city while searching for their targets. They presented a most impressive sight during the raids. They always drifted slowly earthwards, while hundreds of air defense guns blazed away at them with coloured tracer bullets. During one raid I counted eleven flares over the Kremlin."[16] Generally, though, in *Russia at War* he downplayed the Luftwaffe raids: "Up to the time I left Moscow, in the autumn of 1941, the German raids proved to be nothing more than a nuisance, and factories were operating day and night without interruption. The city was not reduced to ashes and life went on as usual."[17] By the time he got home to mold *All-Out on the Road to Smolensk*, he had enthusiastically recharged his memory:

> Deprived of the light from fires which they had hoped to start with incendiaries, the raiders began releasing parachute flares. The first ones came down in a string about half a mile long. They were spaced about a hundred yards apart, and as they floated slowly down from the sky over the river, they looked like enormous,

> illuminated pearls on a string. When these settled down over the city, three more strings were released. They were all still too high to light targets, but the ground-fire was not held back. It sounded as if every gun in that district of the city was directed at them. Machinegun bullets tore through the white silk parachutes, but they were unable to stop the descent of these glaring suns over the Kremlin. And when the first flare was about half a mile from the ground, it was struck by an anti-aircraft shell, and its gleaming fire was shattered into hundreds of fragments that plummeted to earth. This was the only flare that was hit, however, and the remainder floated slowly onward until they touched the ground or buildings where they were finally and effectively dealt with. (*Smolensk* 118)

As time went on his writing shifted from simple journalistic observation and reportage to the expressionistic devices necessary for the work he was creating.

Unlike Caldwell, who saw the raids as death and destruction—perhaps because he was out in the streets during many of them, but even more so because they were proof of a truly devastating war to the west from which he was being barred—Bourke-White saw the night attacks as art. She vividly recalls one particularly destructive night raid earlier in July as "one of the outstanding nights of my life" (*SRW* 86). Her viewing point then had been Spaso House, the U.S. ambassador's residence:

> I have never before seen the entire heavens filled with shooting stars, with hanging parachute flares, with dot-dashes of tracer-gun fire, with red, white, and blue Roman candles, and streamers like the tails of red comets shooting out into space. Around the complete circumference of the horizon the beams of searchlights swung restlessly, as though a horde of insects turned over on their backs were waving their luminous legs in the air. Once while we watched, the shafts of light came together in a knot and caught in their focus a plane which glowed like a silver moth against the sky. For minutes the knot of light kept the moth imprisoned as it dipped and turned, trying to escape, until suddenly it twisted violently and fell; we had seen our first German plane shot down. (*SRW* 86)

Roman candles, searchlights, tracer bullets, and the killing of a German airman are mainly artistic features for her tableaux, and by employing them Bourke-White applies the prevailing aesthetic of women's travel writing to her photography.

In addition, for Bourke-White, an air raid is not just *visual* art: "I had not realized that there is so much music with an air raid. The most beautiful sound is the echo of the guns, which returns on a deeper note, like the bass of a Beethoven chord. The total effect is as though two types of music were being played together—formal chords with overtones of jazz thrown in. The peculiar whistle, which one soon learns to recognize, of bombs falling in the neighborhood is like a dash of Gershwin against a classic symphonic background" (*SRW* 89).

It is clear that Caldwell found himself in the middle of a war but waylaid in a city far away from the front where he wanted, needed to be, whereas his wife saw herself in the middle of an artistic moment. The modernist influences that were evident in her early photography—monumentalism, mechanicalism, futurism, and her emphasis on industrial and architectural forms—were now all brought to bear on her work. In fact, when she later finally did get "frontward," she found the conditions and the weather so inclement and uncontrollable that she believed her art suffered.

At other times, Bourke-White accepted the almost nightly air raids as inconvenient intrusions into their lives. On this aspect of wartime life Caldwell was silent. According to her, often the couple would be in their suite in the National when a raid began. In order to hide from the hotel guards, whose job it was to shoo all the guests down into the hotel's basement bomb shelter, Bourke-White would hide under their bed. But Caldwell, she writes, found this undignified, perhaps also because "he has an enormous chest and large shoulders, a product of his preliterary days when he was a professional football player" (*SRW* 117). He was simply too big to get under the bed and so hid behind the sofa.

But occasionally bombs would come too close for such a cool approach. "Erskine would grab me in those strong arms of his and carry me to a little vestibule between two sets of doors, which divided our bedroom from the parlor. . . . I always felt safe when my husband carried me back in his arms" (*SRW* 121). Again, her perspective is traditionally "female."

After a while, their hotel suite became a party center: "As time went on, our routine was perfected to the point of seeing that our room was stocked with beer and sandwiches well before the alarm sounded; and later, as other journalists moved into our hotel, we used to keep open house during a raid. One after another, when the patrol had completed its round, silent pajama-clad figures would steal into our room. I believe that most of the Moscow raids described in the American press were viewed from our splendid balcony" (*SRW* 119). Most nights, air raid or no, Caldwell had to leave the National for his 2:00 a.m. CBS broadcast. Bourke-White again sees this as a romantic interlude:

> When my husband came back we would get into the wide bed that had held the Lindberghs, and the German trade commissioner, and perhaps Trotsky too,

> for all I know, and very comfortable under the yellow satin quilt we would doze off, and wake up again if the shooting picked up, watching it through our big windows.
>
> Finally at dawn we would hear the loud speaker on the roof above us call out, "The enemy has been beaten back, comrades. Go home to your rest." As confused voices rose from thousands of people leaving the subway, we would fall into a deep sleep. (*SRW* 124)

But for Caldwell—literally out dodging bombs in the street and avoiding shrapnel on his way to the radio station—a German attack was a work not of art or romance but of terror:

> As the glass began to fall from windows, a choking cloud of dust and smoke rolled across the street, covering everything like a blanket. A long period of unearthly silence followed. There were still no sounds of human voices, but it was not long before men of the rescue and demolition squads could be heard running towards the blast.
>
> Almost instantly the silence was shattered by the renewed blasts of anti-aircraft artillery, and all other sounds were drowned out. (*Smolensk* 74)

As protection from falling shrapnel, Caldwell mentions a helmet: "a tin hat was just about the most valuable possession a man could have at a time like that. I pulled my head piece down tightly and tightened the strap under my chin" (*Smolensk* 72). Bourke-White provides further background: "We had been wearing our Russian military helmets whenever we approached the windowsills or the balcony, but now [Erskine] changed his for an enormous helmet which the Mayor of Moscow [Vasili Pronin] had provided especially for going to broadcasts. It had a steel visor that projected over his face, and a metal apron that swept around the sides and back, and it might have been designed for a Martian invasion" (*Smolensk* 123). The helmet *was* surely memorable (see figure 35). Even Ilya Ehrenburg, the star embedded reporter of *Red Star*, the official paper of the Red Army, known then for his romanticizing of heroism and his pride in Mother Russia, recalls in his 1944 memoir, *The Tempering of Russia*, his forced visit to a shelter beneath the Press Bureau on July 24: "In the shelter I was surrounded by foreign correspondents. Among them was the American author Erskine Caldwell. I remember his stories—cruel and humane. There is much of the clay and of the master about him. At two a.m. he put on a helmet and went off to broadcast for America."[18] Although Caldwell's fellow correspondents were generally loathe to call attention to his celebrity, the Russians did not share this aversion.

Looking for War

The middle chapters of *All-Out on the Road to Smolensk* and *Shooting the Russian War* illustrate the difference in Caldwell's and Bourke-White's attitudes about the war and also in their approaches to writing about it. Caldwell hammers the point of military preparedness. He visits the ring of anti-aircraft defenses the Red Army has set up, describes his own adventures in the frightening world of demolition bombs, incendiaries, and shrapnel, but mostly he chafes at his inability to get to where the action is. For Bourke-White, however, the challenge is the home front, not the front lines. In Moscow she stakes out her territory locally, just as Caldwell is pulling every string he can to get to the west.

For Caldwell, Moscow could never be the focus of his story. Perhaps brought about by his and Bourke-White's inveterate letter-writing campaign to VOKS, the Soviet Writers' Union, Steinhardt, and Lozovsky, he and Alexander finally received a passport to leave the city on August 20. They discover an extraordinary, camouflaged airfield, a base to over fifty fighter planes, and the temporary home for several decorated airmen. Using a technique similar to the one he had used with a tank commander in an earlier chapter, he records extended transcripts of his interviews with an unnamed flier and with the highly decorated Victor Talalikhin, famous for ramming a German bomber and surviving, an exploit Caldwell describes with studied insouciance. Talalikhin had to parachute out of his crashing plane, but once he landed he found the German crew "blown to bits when their load of bombs was touched off. . . . There was nothing left for me to do except make out my report and get a ride back to my base" (*Smolensk* 130).

There is no evidence that Bourke-White accompanied the two men; Caldwell never mentions her. In *Shooting the Russian War*, however, she prints two photographs she took of Talalikhin at the Moscow Park of Culture and Rest where he gave a crowd-pleasing and "highly oratorical" speech (*SRW* 125). In the accompanying captions she observes: "This story has become so famous in the Soviet Union that it has even been set in verse. By this time, of course, Soviet ramming tactics are famous, but Talalikhin was one of the first of such heroes" (*SRW* 197). How much this undermines Caldwell's claim to an aerodrome "interview," to on-the-spot journalism, is unresolved. Comparing his diary entries with his *Smolensk* text, it is clear that episodes in the latter are not uncommonly adapted from multiple entries in the (more likely to be) chronologically accurate *Moscow Under Fire*. I suspect that, in this case, Caldwell met Talalikhin at the airbase and Bourke-White photographed him at a public tribute later in Moscow, but whether Bourke-White was also at the aerodrome is unclear.

Caldwell ends this chapter with a novelist's skill of foreshadowing. At this base on the outskirts of Moscow, he picks over the debris of a German Heinkel airplane lying "in a twisted mass": "Most of it had burned, and about all that was left were bits of metal. The impact of the crash had strewn parts of the wreckage over a wide area. Among other things I saw a portion of a human skull, and a mass of flesh that looked as though it once was part of a human being" (*Smolensk* 131). Whatever calm existed within the city and away from the front, here was confirmation that the horrors that lay not far to the west could readily encroach on Moscow.

Evidence that Caldwell wrote *All-Out on the Road to Smolensk* with a particular and carefully manicured narrative arc can be discerned from what appears in *Moscow Under Fire* but is absent from *Smolensk*. His lightly edited diary, *Moscow Under Fire*, as minimally retouched, blunt, and crude as it is, provides a clear idea of what was going on in Caldwell's mind during the three months after the war began. *Smolensk* was constructed later with a more literary agenda. Before the Nazi blitzkrieg fell upon the Soviet Union and turned everyone's lives upside-down, Caldwell had been working quietly and privately on some of the stories that would later appear in *Georgia Boy*, a series of linked episodes recalling his boyhood in rural Georgia and the blacks and poor whites with whom he played. But even in that Moscow August, this storytelling principle was still active. An excellent example is his diary entry for August 19, the day before his sally down the Smolensk road with Alexander. (*PM* published a slightly shortened version of this piece the same day.) This is not the diary entry of a man fixated single-mindedly on the war; Caldwell created a highly focused narrator for *Smolensk* later in his study in Connecticut. I quote the passage from *Moscow Under Fire* here in its entirety because of its unedited literary and comic value, and as evidence of how drastically Caldwell subsequently honed his focus for *All-Out on the Road to Smolensk*:

> Last night I went out looking for night life. I didn't find any. I am no mean finder of nightlife and I think I would've found it if it existed in Moscow. The place was as dead as Monck's Corners, South Carolina, on a Sunday night. The liveliest spot in town was a corner near my hotel where a woman with a pushcart was selling two kinds of coloured water, red and green. I stood around a while hoping somebody would come along and start busking (street-entertaining), but the closest thing to it was a man who walked past on the opposite side of the street carrying a violin case.
>
> While I was hanging around the juice stand, a dozen or so citizens came up and bought drinks. I was hoping that at least one of them would be the busking type,

but not one of them had any leaning in that direction. After an hour I decided there was not going to be any song and dance around the pushcart for years to come, so I crossed the square and loafed around the subway entrance, thinking that somebody with a good spiel would come along selling something. I didn't want to buy anything but was willing to take whatever was offered as long as a good act was put on. I waited there a half-hour and nothing happened. Nobody tried to sell me neckties, the latest hit songs, the *Hobo News* or even the unused portion of a round-trip ticket to Baltimore.

By that time I would have collared a clip joint tout and handed him my pocketbook for safe keeping if only one had eased up to me. I guess I must've looked like a fox in a chicken pen by that time because a militiaman who had been watching me a good fifteen minutes came over and looked me up and down. I decided he was the wrong type to give a steer to a hot spot, so I wandered off.

I looked at my watch and saw it was only 8.30. I made another move toward the door and the woman met me half-way with a forearm slam that sent me reeling down the street. I ended up on the corner at my hotel, and while I was trying to find the door to the café in the dark a stack of sandbags toppled over and hit me on the head.

I decided the café was no place for me because I had been there two hours earlier and got tired of whooping it up on a cheese sandwich and bottle of soda pop. I crossed the street, went past the hotel and climbed some steps through an archway. That put me in a place I didn't know about but was willing to take a chance on.

The blackout was closing in and it wasn't easy to see an arm's length ahead.

A lot of people were all around me and I figured that in a dark street like that somebody would stick an automatic in my ribs and reach for my pocketbook.

I stopped on the busiest corner and then moved along slowly down the street, whistling a little to let a stickup man know where I was. I discovered there were no stickup men in Moscow. I found also that there were no women making a profession of walking.

By that time I was pretty well worn out trying to find what didn't exist. The chances are I would've gone berserk if I had stumbled into a Whelan drugstore about that time.[19] But I knew when I was licked, so I made my way back to my hotel, went to bed and thumbed once more through my seven-months-old copy of the *Saturday Evening Post*.[20]

As corny as this rube-in-the-city routine is, when it came to writing *Smolensk*, Caldwell realized he had already done something similar to this in the used-car vignette.

But more than this, *Moscow Under Fire* reveals that his and Bourke-White's ninety days immured in Moscow must at times have driven them into bored distraction. *Moscow Under Fire* begins with an entry for June 26, and from the first of July through the end of September Caldwell records something for all but five days. Single episodes in *Smolensk,* such as his going to the apartment of a Russian journalist, are compressed from three or four entries that actually occurred over a several-week period of time. In *Moscow Under Fire,* he writes air-raid-related entries for fourteen different days, whereas in *Smolensk* these raids and their effects are distilled down to four chapters and composed so as to gradually increase a sense of the barbarity and proximity of the Nazi onslaught. Though he has been beset by his adversaries in Moscow, still the climax is nearing. As Wallace Carroll, the United Press correspondent who didn't arrive in Moscow until the first of September, soon realized, "The foreign correspondents in Moscow were an unhappy lot. The greatest war in history was going on two hundred miles away and they had to stay in the capital."[21]

Toward the end of the Moscow portion of *Smolensk,* Caldwell dedicates a chapter to the hazards he faced during his trips to and from the radio station in the middle of the night. Some moments are humorous, as when he "bump[s] into a large fat woman who was carrying what felt like a sack of bricks" (*Smolensk* 138), or when he "walk[s] headlong into a dray horse . . . backed up into a tobacco-shop doorway" (*Smolensk* 139). Others are strange and frightening, as when a cable from a downed barrage balloon lands on his car and wraps itself round the rear axle (*Smolensk* 135–36). But the final incident builds drama and adds to a foreboding prefiguration.

Lightheartedly pulling the reader into the account, Caldwell begins innocently enough:

> I stumbled over some street-car tracks and went off into the pitch blackness with hands outstretched. The next thing I knew I felt a sharp object pressing into my stomach. I felt it with both hands for a long time, and then reached up above my head and touched some cold stony fingers. I realized that the object was a statue, and I began wondering what statues in Moscow could be identified in a blackout by an outstretched hand. I knew that if I could visualize the statue I could orient myself and find my way to the broadcasting station.
>
> I stepped up on the pedestal and began feeling for the other hand. I could not find a second hand, but I did feel the tail of a coat. I was still baffled, so I climbed up higher and tried to feel if the coat were military or civilian. I felt what I thought was a high military collar, but the spacing of the buttons and the number of pockets felt like civilian attire.
>
> Finally, I stood on the statue's boots and reached up to feel if the headgear were military or civilian. That was when a militiaman grabbed me by the arm and hauled me down to the ground. (*Smolensk* 139–40)

Caldwell is rescued by his chauffeur, but in the morning he returns to the square. "There was nothing to be seen of the statue, and in its place was a bomb crater twenty-five feet deep and a hundred feet in diameter. The remains of the statue, I discovered later, lay on the sidewalk" (*Smolensk* 141). The war clearly was becoming more personal and very, very close.

Neunnert

Though Caldwell and Bourke-White did not know at the time how soon their long-sought-after trip to the front would materialize—indeed within the week—they visited a Soviet hospital for German prisoners. Caldwell claims he was able to arrange this through his personal diplomacy with a myriad of faceless Soviet agencies and bureaucrats. For *Smolensk,* he develops the infirmary excursion into the dramatic venture of an intrepid, persistent, never-take-no-for-an-answer journalist. Heavily armed military guards wearing "full equipment, including sidearms and bayoneted rifles" conduct him through a maze of passageways deep into the hospital (*Smolensk* 148). When some of the prisoners respond in an understandably hostile fashion, the reader can readily sense the narrator's unease. He speaks with two men who survived what they describe as "the terrible hell at Smolensk" (*Smolensk* 152), who detail the bloody and fiery horrors of tank warfare. Finally he comes face-to-face with the truth for which he has been searching in this Russian assignment, the answer to why the United States should accept the Soviet Union as an ally. The answer is provided by the bitter and unrepentant Oigen Neunnert, who seems to the narrator "more like a professional soldier than any of the others in the ward" (*Smolensk* 155). "The German people are not tired of the war. . . . They know they have to stand for it until it is won. They will be as strong as necessary," Neunnert insists. Then there is a final confrontation, in its small way a encapsulation of the war to the west, which he will experience soon enough:

> He would not answer any of my questions after that for several minutes, and during all that time he looked at me coldly with tightly pressed lips. I had the feeling that what he wanted most in the world then was a service revolver or bayonet.
>
> Finally, I asked him if he thought the war was necessary.
>
> "What is necessary for the German people should be done," he said quickly, clamping his lips tightly.
>
> "Are you sure it is necessary to have war?"
>
> "We can get what is rightfully ours only by having war."
>
> "What do you mean?"

> Neunnert raised himself on his elbow, thrusting his jaw almost in my face. A crimson glow enveloped his face. (*Smolensk* 156)

The tension is almost palpable, the physical danger evident.

> He looked at me so hard I leaned back a little. He thrust himself forward towards me as though issuing a challenge. I had the comforting feeling that the Russian sentries had undoubtedly searched him well for concealed pistols and knives when he was captured, and, moreover, that three of them were standing in the doorway with fixed bayonets on their rifles.
>
> "Does Germany want to fight America?" I asked finally.
>
> "We'll fight America!" he said loudly. "Nobody can stop us. We will beat America just like we will beat England and Russia. We will beat America when the time comes."
>
> I pushed back my chair. His breath was hot in my face. I started to ask him if he wanted to fight me then and there, but thought better of it. I stood up.
>
> "You think then that Germany is going to win the war?" I asked.
>
> "We will win the war," he said, raising his voice. "We will win it no matter how long it takes."
>
> I moved away.
>
> As I passed through the doorway into the hall I could feel Neunnert's fiery eyes following me. I turned and looked back for an instant. He was sitting up in bed glaring at me. (*Smolensk* 157–58)

For what it was worth, Caldwell now has a firm idea of what the menace at the front would be like.

In fact, Bourke-White had accompanied Caldwell on this encounter, as had their secretary as translator. Bourke-White even photographed Neunnert and the other prisoners, publishing prints of seven of them in *Shooting the Russian War*. About Neunnert she writes, "We asked him whether the German people were tired of war. He said that he didn't know, but added enigmatically that they would stand it as long as necessary" (*SRW* 111). For Bourke-White, Neunnert is simply another prisoner of war, not the adversary Caldwell saw.

Social Observations

In *All-Out on the Road to Smolensk,* Caldwell now steps back. The final chapter before his departure to the west—the maw of evil he has pictured for the reader—is a summary of his social and political observations. He visits many of the same venues as Bourke-White, summarizes many of her observations, and in effect restates many of her opinions. He discusses religious freedom (or the lack thereof), housing, queues, the subway, motion pictures, the "controlled" press, and socialism. He hints tangentially at the generally repressive nature of Soviet society: "Russians are touchy on the subject of criticism and more than two decades of training has discouraged all but the most daring from voicing disapproval of anything within Soviet borders. The generation that has grown up since the First World War and the Revolution has been trained to believe that it is a traitorous act to question or criticize the state" (*Smolensk* 161). He does not explain what this "training" might consist of.

Caldwell, the writer and political activist, now makes one final point: he remains sanguine about socialism as an enterprise and expresses his feeling that the Soviet Union isn't doing a terrible job at it: "The Soviet Union is no Utopia, but neither is it a dismal hole of rags and hunger. The country is within hailing distance of what it intended being, or at any rate it is the closest approach to a state of socialism and communism this side of abstract theory" (*Smolensk* 165). In the final analysis, he opines, it is a "question of whether a person wants socialism, security, and restricted existence, or whether he desires capitalism, insecurity, and freedom of action and speech" (*Smolensk* 166). Some will like the USSR, some won't. Caldwell accepts Russia for what it is: a worthy ally against the Axis, and after tasting the venom of Neunnert in the hospital, he is convinced that the more force deployed against Germany, the better.

Both Caldwell and Bourke-White occasionally make surprisingly naïve statements about the war, probably because they wanted to believe that the Russians would be good allies, but also because it was hard to shed their Popular Front mantles. As an example, Bourke-White summarizes the early Red Army strategy vis-à-vis the instability of the front: "No one knew where these front lines were. According to the Soviets they were far to the westward, with small forward thrusts being permitted the Germans only for the purpose of allowing the Soviets to capture the enemy in the pockets thus formed" (*SRW* 65). In fact, the reverse of this was actually taking place. Red Army battalions were being encircled by the rapidly advancing Wehrmacht.

Caldwell too seems extremely gullible at times. Perhaps because he was quarantined in Moscow, far from Ukraine and Belarus, where the impact of Stalin's collectivization polices had been the most harsh and where want and starvation had been the norm just several years earlier, he writes, "the Russians were satisfied with their economy, and there was plenty of evidence to prove that the 194,000,000 persons living in the Soviet Union were fairly well fed and housed" (*Smolensk* 83). Passages such as this suggest that Caldwell and Bourke-White shared a similar political naïveté.

Even once back safely in the United States, Caldwell remained a strong apologist for Stalin. While recognizing that he was an autocrat ("He is public opinion, and the people follow him"; *Smolensk* 86), Caldwell saw him as a benevolent one: "He is calm, wise, and unshakable. His knowledge of military, economic, and political conditions within the borders of his own country, as well as those in the countries of Europe and Asia, is superior to that of anyone else in the world" (*Smolensk* 88–89). In fact, Stalin was secretly held in contempt by many in the contemporary Soviet military leadership and solely responsible for the summer debacle on the Russian Western Front, during which the Russians lost untold millions of soldiers and civilians.[22] Calling Stalin the "supreme strategist of his age" (Smolensk 81), Caldwell gives him credit for his prewar readiness: "The government had been preparing for this [Operation Barbarossa] since the end of 1940" (*Smolensk* 88). This is, we now know, ludicrous. But at the time it was written, just after the Japanese attack on Pearl Harbor, such bald statements of propaganda arguably can be seen as constructive to the overall war cause. And they certainly did not detract from the thrust of the novel. Moreover, reflecting on the political cauldron of that summer, Caldwell would have been amenable to advancing Stalin's stature as an ally, especially since Bourke-White's July photographs of him had already contributed to a mellowing of anti-Soviet sentiment. How Caldwell himself felt about Stalin at the time is hard to know, although he did publish a very favorable profile of the premier in the London *Daily Mail* during his passage back to the United States. And it is hard to look past Bourke-White's infatuation with the man, as is evident in her many recollections about her photo session with him.

In addition to his portrait of Stalin, Caldwell wrote glowing profiles for the *Daily Mail* of Ambassador Steinhardt and Solomon Lozovsky, the head of the Soviet Information Bureau (i.e., the press office). Originally each had been a 2,500-word study written in Moscow, then adapted for the *Daily Mail* between October 18 and November 1, 1941. In *Smolensk,* he uses each sketch to keep the emphasis and focus on Smolensk. From his interviews—with soldiers who have been on both sides of the front, airmen, dark-visaged representatives of the Kremlin, fellow journalists, Russians who have returned from the front, and those who have remained on the home front—he has learned much about the world into which he is about to plunge. He has come to understand the stoic Soviet war psyche and that the war is coming closer. The culmination of the book is now at hand, the journey down the road toward Smolensk.

CHAPTER 6

Smolensk I ★ Death Comes Calling (September 15–16)

Ever since June 22, the Western press corps kept trying to figure out a way to report on the *actual* war.[1] The official Soviet war communiqués—issued once or twice daily by the Press Bureau and often read aloud only in Russian by Solomon Lozovsky, the vice-commissar of the Soviet Information Bureau, to the correspondents gathered around a large table at the Narkomindel, the Press Office—were generally self-serving, often misleading, and occasionally out-and-out fabrications. In early August, Ralph Ingersoll, the publisher of *PM* newspaper and Caldwell's employer and Bourke-White's friend, had told Stalin directly that a free press with unfettered access to the news was the only viable press. Stateside editors continually hounded their correspondents and stringers to get to the warfront. The reporters themselves also ineffectively pressed the issue, as did credentialed diplomats on their behalf.

One of the stumbling blocks was simply that no safely secured portion of the front existed that the Soviet government supposed it could permit the press to visit. After six weeks of desperate fighting to the east of Smolensk—Smolensk had fallen into German hands on August 5, and the Wehrmacht succeeded in encircling a large Red Army force farther east during the first week of August—the Kremlin believed the front was too brittle for civilian visitors (although at the time the particulars of this fragility had not been revealed to the Moscow press corps).[2] In Ukraine, to the southwest, a huge Wehrmacht encirclement of Russian forces in and around Kiev was already underway and would be complete by September 26. The German swag there included two-thirds of a million Russian soldiers and untold numbers of peasants.[3] It would prove to be a Pyrrhic victory for the Germans. Between August 30 and September 2 the Red Army retook the diminutive salient that incorporated Yelnya, fifty miles southeast of Smolensk, following a coordinated Soviet counteroffensive and a withdrawal by the German forces, who were severely debilitated from having to support an extensive front running from Leningrad in the north to beyond Kiev in the south.[4] Although Yelnya would be lost again within a few weeks, its temporary liberation had forced Hitler to rethink his direct drive on Moscow, forever altering the war. Such great cost of matériel and blood on both sides was not information the central news agencies of the USSR were about to make public or share with the Western press. But on September 8 Russian officials finally announced the Red Army's retaking of Yelnya, and the possibility arose for a chaperoned visit for the journalists to the front lines in that limited region, though the press corps didn't know this at the time.

The Banquet and Its Aftermath

On Sunday, September 14, Vice-Commissar Lozovsky hosted a luncheon at the Moskva Restaurant to which most of the international press corps was invited. The most memorable aspect of this gathering, according to several members of the press, were the large horses carved from butter and placed down the center of the banquet table, "hardly less big than a fox terrier," recalled Philip Jordan of the London *News Chronicle*.[5] The tone of this banquet was set when Alexander Werth, the Russian-born Reuters agent, offered a vodka-fueled toast. As he recalled in his memoir, after he had praised the anti-Fascists in general and President Roosevelt in particular, he bumbled on: "Tanks for Russia, I said, were much more important, from America's own point of view, than the continued manufacture of joy-ride automobiles." The response was not what he had intended: "The Moats [Alice Leone Moats of *Collier's*] was very annoyed, and so was Mr. Sulzberger, and the Russians looked—or tried to look—rather pained; and Hatanaka, the Jap, hissed and giggled and said he found my remark about joy-ride automobiles 'most embarrassing.'"[6] But Werth just chalked it up to too much vodka and thought the American reaction had been overblown.

"The Moats" *was* annoyed. Werth, she recalled, had *first* offered a toast to Lozovsky, *then* to Stalin, an order that was politically verboten. He rambled on that Americans "were too fond of their motorcars and electric refrigerators. They weren't willing to give them up to build tanks for Russia. The United States was not doing its share, and the American people must realize that they had to bend every effort and make every sacrifice for the sake of England and the Soviet Union." She says she cornered him after the luncheon, "Alexander the Agency Man, you certainly managed to make an ass out of yourself this time!"[7] But perhaps Werth's diatribe had helped the press's cause.

Later that day Nikolai Palgunov, the press chief and later the director of TASS (the Telegraph Agency of the Soviet Union), called a special news conference for a select few reporters, during which he told them to reconvene at the Narkomindel the next morning with a full kit of warm gear and minimal luggage. Moats was not invited.

In *Shooting the Russian War,* Bourke-White insists that to ensure herself a position on the travel roster, she had taken the matter into her own hands. Fresh from her photographic audience with Stalin a month earlier, a singular achievement that everyone in the entourage knew about, she clearly had star credentials. She insisted on going to the front. Lozovsky argued that the front was dangerous. Bourke-White portrays Lozovsky as another victim of her persuasive powers: "'Hmm,' said Mr. Lozovsky, enigmatically, through his mahogany beard. 'You are a very determined young lady.'"[8]

Caldwell also describes this four-hour luncheon for over a hundred guests but in even greater detail in *All-Out on the Road to Smolensk,* noting as well the seating arrangements (as did Moats, of course) and the food and beverages. Seated with Lozovsky "at the head of table," he and Bourke-White were among the "eight guests of honor."[9] Caldwell had not been offended by Werth's drunken toast. He even inserts a sense of mystery into the story: "There was no hint of what the purpose of the luncheon might be." Then, conjuring up a cloak-and-dagger image, he adds: "After the luncheon was over, an official in the Foreign Office drew my wife and me aside and asked casually if we expected to remain in the country another week or two. We told him we were planning to leave for America towards the end of September. He said, merely, that he hoped we would find it convenient to remain as long as we had planned." With his usual understatement, Caldwell mentions the hastily called meeting at the Foreign Office just before midnight where Lozovsky announced "a week's tour of the front the next morning at 6:45."[10]

In *Smolensk,* Caldwell's explanation for the Russians' change of heart about a press trip suggests that he and Bourke-White probably had their hands on at least a few of the levers. He writes that he'd detected a change in the official stance toward the press earlier in the month, such that "Stalin had been persuaded, possibly by the American and British ambassadors" to provide more access for the press corps.[11] And this may have been facilitated further in early September during Ingersoll's brief visit, when he had personally bearded Stalin over the matter of restricted press access to the war. Then there was the cable Caldwell and Bourke-White had fashioned for the foreign minister, Vyacheslav Molotov, early in the month: "Were referred by your office one week ago to Press Dept on important matter of going to the front STOP have as yet received no answer from them STOP will be here only six more days to accomplish this important mission before we return to America please assist in arranging front visit."[12] Simultaneously, Caldwell applied further pressure on the Soviet ambassador to the United States, Constantine Oumansky.[13] But obviously there were many moving parts, none more important than the vicissitudes of the war itself, with the Red Army's Western Front first collapsing, then resurging, then collapsing all over again.

Monday: Dramatis Personae

The next morning the couple arrived fifteen minutes early at the Narkomindel, having arisen at 4:45 to pack. Caldwell recalls: "We reached the Foreign Office the next morning at 6:30 and found nine other sleepy-eyed correspondents pacing up and down on the sidewalk. Fifteen minutes later we were off—six Americans, five British, a Red Army colonel, and a Foreign Office representative. There were no American communist or Japanese correspondents in the party, and several well-known American journalists were absent. It was obvious that the Foreign Office had selected only a few names from its list of accredited correspondents."[14] But the trip had not been planned nor equipped as a picnic. "Our chauffeur carried a .38-caliber army revolver strapped to his waist, and our car carried an extra spring. On the dash was a water canteen and in the glove compartment half a loaf of gray bread. He had stored also half a dozen hand grenades."[15] All the Kremlin roadblocks finally had been overcome.

Werth recalled the eclectic group:

> Bearded old [A. T.] Cholerton [*London Daily Telegraph*], and Jordan in his old war correspondent's uniform, and Vernon Bartlett [BBC], and Wally Carroll, star United Press reporter, looking the good, tidy boy that he always looks, and Charlotte Haldane [*London Daily Sketch*], with beret over one ear, and little [Henry C.] Cassidy [Associated Press], and Sulzberger, all dressed up for winter sports, and [Archibald T.] Steele of the *Chicago Daily News*, and the Caldwell-Bourke-White *ménage*, cameras and all.[16]

"Little Cassidy" added further detail: "We met in front of the Narkomindiel [*sic*] at 8 A.M., September 15, in a bewildering assortment of costumes, including Miss Bourke-White's redcoat, Mrs. Haldane's brown London fire-warden uniform, Cy Sulzberger's white ski jacket, and Wally Carroll's gray topcoat and tin hat. We were met by a staff colonel, a brigade commissar, and the censor."[17]

Charlotte Haldane's recollections of the correspondents' "special garb" are even funnier:

> Philip Jordan, as he had, of course, every right to do, had put on his British war correspondent's uniform, making the other males secretly envious and ashamed of their mere civvies. Werth had countered by producing his Russian fur coat; a

> short yellowy-white dog skin jacket, with a peculiar and penetrating odour all its own. Jordan and I, who had to ride with it for several days, christened it "Fido." Cy Sulzberger turned up in a garment that looked like a bit of a souvenir torn off of a parachute, wedded to the remainder of a Carthusian monk's habit; it was of white waterproofed silk, complete with hood and zip fastener. Cy claimed defiantly that it was a Yugoslavian ski-ing [*sic*] jacket. The rest of us were more or less normally dressed. Mrs. Caldwell and I both wore slacks; she a smart American outfit with coat to match, in small black-and-white checks; I, my faithful "sireen" suit, that had stood me in good stead in many a London Blitz, topped by my old blue leather coat, which had had its baptism of fire in the trenches in front of Teruel,[18] when I visited the boys of the International Brigade there.[19]

That she was a part of the group, she claimed, was only because of her own pluck, since she believed Lozovsky had consigned her to a second wave of correspondents that he said would take a later trip to the front. Although in her later memoir, *Truth Will Out* (1950), she admitted that she had had to tug on political strings and enlist the assistance of an Austrian friend and fellow member of the Communist International, in the earlier *Russian Newsreel* (1942) she recalls her toast at the luncheon: "I ardently hope that if, as I hear may be possible, the foreign correspondents are privileged to visit the Red Army in action, the fact that I am a woman will not disqualify me from being allowed to do my duty to my paper as my men colleagues will be doing theirs."[20] In any case, something worked, so she joined Bourke-White as one of the two women on the junket.

Later, while recalling the absurd lavishness with which the group was treated, Haldane wrote that the concept of news in the USSR was intimately coupled with propaganda. There was to be no contact with individual soldiers, only with officers handpicked to advance the Soviet agenda. Of the trip, she recollected: "The hospitality received from the Red Army was magnificent. We were entertained to banquets, with the usual enthusiastic toasts and speeches, wherever we were taken. The organisation functioned excellently. Enormous hot meals were produced in the midst of dripping forests, the tables were laden with vodka, champagne, wines, cigarettes of good quality, and chocolate, a very great luxury."[21] In return, the Soviets expected glowing reports in the Western media.

Wallace Carroll, the United Press stringer, was among the chosen few. In his 1942 memoir, *We're in This with Russia*, he attributes the thawing of the Soviet attitude toward the Western press to the ongoing efforts of the two ambassadors, Sir Stafford Cripps and Laurence Steinhardt, to convince Stalin that with a three-nation conference scheduled for the end of September where the

Lend-Lease project would be hashed out, it would be good to curry some favor with the British and American people to whom the press reported.

If Carroll is to be believed, when he and the others learned during their Sunday-evening meeting with Palgunov that two women were to be included, "The rest of us had almost rebelled when we learned that this was to be a coeducational trip, but we decided that the story was too good to miss."[22] He, too, described the motley crew that Monday morning:

> The party struck a new note in fashions for war correspondents. Miss Bourke-White wore a flowing coat of bright scarlet. If a German flyer sighted her, he would probably report that he had seen a marshal of the Red Army. Cyrus Sulzberger, the mercurial young correspondent of the *New York Times,* wore a white ski jacket and blue ski trousers under a fur-lined overcoat which flapped around his ankles. Someone alleged that he had bought it from a pawnbroker in Bessarabia. Almost as picturesque a figure was Alexander Werth, the Russian-born correspondent of Reuters, the British news agency. He appeared in a knee-length coat of white fur which he said was Siberian dogskin. A committee of veterinarians headed by Vernon Bartlett decided that it was indeed the skin of a Siberian dog, a rare breed used by the secret police, or Ogpu, and therefore known as an "ogpoodle." The most picturesque figure of all, however, was undoubtedly A. T. Cholerton of the *London Daily Telegraph,* who simply appeared as usual with the bushy black beard which gave him the air of a sinister revolutionary. I had nothing to contribute but a louse-belt, and I kept that in reserve.[23]

Bourke-White also wrote of the strangely dressed junketeers: "The most weirdly dressed of the correspondents was Cy Sulzberger of *The New York Times,* who wore his Greek battle dress, a kind of white shiny tunic of the Isadora Duncan school. The most de luxe was Alex Werth of Reuters, who wore a dazzling short coat of white dog fur. And the most natty was Philip Jordan of the *London News Chronicle,* in his khaki military outfit worn by British war correspondents in Africa. The other men wore just clothes."[24] In addition to their attire, Bourke-White also described most of her fellow junketers' personal appearances *and* their personalities. The "bearlike" A. T. Cholerton had "lived in Russia for almost twenty years—so long that he has grown a long black beard like a Russian." Philip Jordan, whom she had met several years earlier in Cairo, was "blonde, slight, [and] whimsical," while Arch Steele, whom she'd met in China, was "gaunt, sparing of words, Lincolnesque in appearance" and "justly respected by his fellow correspondents for his astuteness. We all called him the Admiral." Cy Sulzberger "always reminded me of a tightly wound watch spring. His manner was so quick and positive that everything was usually done his way before the rest of the crowd woke up to what was happening." Vernon Bartlett, “a roly-poly, elderly British M.P. . . . was even more impatient with the discomforts of the roads than Cy.” Alexander Werth was especially valuable. He was “tall, dark, with a rather gloomy face [but] was a useful addition to our party, for he was half Russian and made a perfect translator of speeches and toasts at banquets.” The two quietest members of the group were Henry Cassidy and Wallace Carroll, the former “diminutive,” the latter merely a “star-reporter.”[25] She does not mention Mrs. Haldane.

Bourke-White’s description of Bartlett’s impatience is reflected in Bartlett’s own writings. In his 1960 memoir, *And Now, Tomorrow*, he recalls, “On the whole, we were not immensely impressed. There seemed to be so little activity [at the front] and so much incompetence,”[26] but he does admit that in retrospect he, at least, had failed to recognize the many subtle signs of Russian pride and resistance. He was content to make light of his travel hosts, as in this story of the “marked sardine.” He and his colleagues, he recollected, often wondered how they could regularly be supplied with such sumptuous feasts, the ones over which Haldane gushed, and why their arrival at a distant outpost was always a matter of such pleasure for the officers in the field.

> A marked sardine provided at least part of the explanation for the enthusiastic welcomes we received. Members of our party grew suspicious after one car, which normally preceded us, broke down. We found our hosts unprepared and unhappy. We were tired and hungry, but we had to wait for hours before any food was given to us. So at lunch on the following day one of my colleagues marked a sardine, and, sure enough, it was identified at our evening meal fifty miles farther down the front. Each day, we discovered, our own party supplied the food that was offered us, and the Russian officers received a meal the likes of which the poor devils had probably not tasted for months.[27]

Certainly, the story rings true, even though no one else mentions it. Transport problems, the transient nature of field headquarters, and the Red Army’s frequent need to relocate them on short notice makes the story quite plausible.

Cyrus Sulzberger, almost always a reliable source, published his World War II memoirs, *A Long Row of Candles*, a quarter-century later in 1969, and although he too writes of the Smolensk trip in the form of a diary, the result is a mishmash of memories cobbled together with little relationship to an accurate chronology. Nonetheless, his writing is often pleasurably tongue-in-cheek, and he can poke fun at himself as readily as he can at others.

> Vernon Bartlett, always eating raw mushrooms, has to rush off after breakfast to do what the English call “a rear.” A peasant comes along and stares. Bartlett tries

to get him to go away by explaining that he is a member of Parliament. This only excites widespread curiosity. The peasant brings up an admiring throng of friends and soldiers.

We are a weary group. During his sleep, Philip Jordan, long wisps of hair falling all along his face, shouts out in an anguished voice: "Where the hell are we?" Alexander Werth, in dogskin coat, looks like a depraved madman. A. T. Cholerton, of the *Daily Telegraph*, his beard full of straw, spends most of the night searching for his handkerchief and glasses. The correspondents' "Soviet" meets and loudly disagrees every dawn and dusk. Cholerton spoils our appetite each breakfast by nibbling raw fish which he holds by the tail, getting oil and bones mixed up in his beard.[28]

Alice Moats was absolutely livid over her exclusion from the Smolensk trip. When she learned from Cassidy's assistant, Robert Magidoff, on Monday morning that the group had already left without her, she was at first placated with the excuse that only one person from each agency was to be allowed along, *and* that there would be no women. But later, when she learned the Caldwells and Haldane were on the way, she protested her "shabby treatment" in a letter to Lozovsky: "I suggested that it was due to the fact that he and Mr. Palgunov did not consider either my magazine or me important. 'I scarcely expected to encounter such a snobbishness in the Soviet Union.'" *Collier's*, she pointed out to him, had a circulation of over three million in the United States.[29]

As was typical with previous press junkets around the environs of Moscow, the Western journalists would not be allowed to investigate the front on their own. Haldane described their handlers:

> Our guide was to be Colonel Baltin, head of the military department of the Press Bureau, one of the most sympathetic and intelligent men I had the pleasure of meeting in Russia. Attached to us as well was a Political Commissar, a handsome but sullen-looking young Ukrainian, and a smartly-uniformed Major of the Tank Regiment [Colonel Sudokov], who spoke excellent English and was a most amiable bear-leader [*sic*]. Finally, one of the hard-worked censors [Anurov], a thoroughly likable chap, came too, in order to know what to "kill" in our copy when in due course we should write it.[30]

But off they went, Bourke-White in heavy tweed slacks and her only warm coat, a "bright-red one which even the Chinese had realized was not the proper thing to wear at a war. There was nothing to do but wear it, and be glad that it had a black-satin lining. All during the trip to the front, I was whipping it off and turning it inside out whenever we came within the range of guns."[31]

Arrival in Vyazma

As is often the case in travel, the first twenty-four hours produce the most unexpected, most exciting, and best-remembered moments. And so it was to be for the eleven correspondents. They headed west in a caravan of about a half-dozen or so Russian-built M-1 coupes, a version of a 1936 Ford, along the wide and smooth Mozhaisk highway.[32] Because Smolensk, 230 miles away, was in Wehrmacht hands, the group was actually headed to Yelnya, 50 miles to the southeast of it. Their first night would be at the important railway stop of Vyazma, about two-thirds of the way there, some 140 miles from Moscow, "a small town surrounding a grain elevator . . . with little plaster houses on the sloping streets . . . decorated with the elaborately carved wooden eaves and window sills characteristic of that part of Russia."[33]

The road was smooth though heavily trafficked and so was under constant repair by work gangs. Army supply vehicles, some of which had been infamously converted into surprisingly effective wood- and charcoal-burning lorries, headed frontward moving at barely twenty miles per hour. Only the occasional checkpoint stalled the traffic. The countryside was flat and sparsely populated, which made Wallace Carroll think of the great "Russian composers—Rimsky-Korsakov, Mussorgsky, Borodin, Tschaikovsky [*sic*]."[34] After an hour or so the entourage stopped for what seemed to be a picnic breakfast. "[E]normous parcels of bread, butter, cheese, sausage, and tinned fish were unpacked and we fell to."[35] Bartlett and Cholerton supplemented the fare with fresh-picked mushrooms.

Around two they arrived in Vyazma. For Carroll, Vyazma's importance was historical. It was there that Napoleon had ordered the Grande Armée's advance on Moscow, and also where he was attacked in retreat. The St. Petersburg–born Werth recalled that, when he was a boy, Vyazma had been renowned for its gingerbread, but now it was just another vulnerable town along a principal rail route, a place Werth observed "cannot have changed much since the days of Gogol." In fact, the International Hotel at which they would lodge was "much in the Gogol tradition, except that there were no books."[36] Charlotte Haldane echoes this description, almost to a tee, though with a sarcasm that belies her leftist leanings and without the literary allusions: "The place smelled as if the windows had not been opened for many months; above the stale odours of cooking and unwashed human inhabitants, was the unmistakable sweet, sickly smell which remains in a building that has recently been disinfected of bugs."[37]

But the day was just beginning. Immediately the group was treated to its first of many long and alcohol-fueled meals. Carroll recalls it lasting a good three

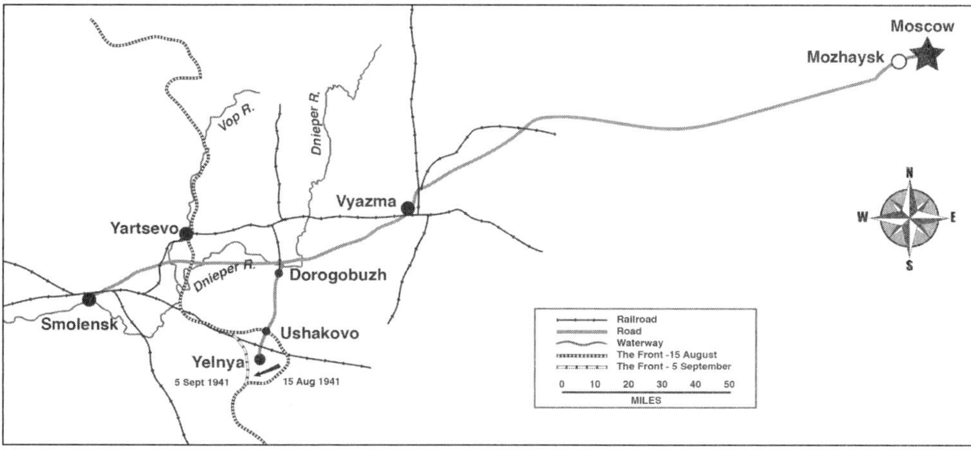

FIGURE 36. The Moscow–Vyazma–Smolensk region (Map by Charles Lindemuth, www.mepainter.com)

hours—vodka and caviar; *zakuski* (appetizers usually consisting of a variety of cold cuts); cabbage soup; chicken and rice; and finally, "I forgot what came after, perhaps because we also had three or four kinds of wine."[38] By the time the group headed out, around five, for their afternoon excursion, they were "in a mellow mood."[39] In *Smolensk,* Caldwell described it as a three-and-a-half-hour "meal of no mean proportion" that included "several varieties of cheese, sardines, and raw fish; there were biscuits, gray bread, black bread, butter, white vodka, hunter's vodka, port wine, tea, candy, chocolate bars, and cigarettes"; nonetheless, "compared to some of the banquets we were to sit down to during the remainder of the week, [this] was merely a course of appetizers. Closer to the front we were served, in addition, such dishes as turkey, chicken, goose, steaks, chops, and caviar, pressed, salted, and fresh."[40]

Werth recalled it as just "a quick meal downstairs," but it is clear that with his fluency in the language (Cholerton spoke Russian, too, but not nearly as well) and his shared cultural heritage, he was operating on a completely different plane than the other reporters. After a long and detailed conversation with an army captain during which they swapped stories about the Spanish Civil War, Werth strolled the streets of Vyazma, conversing freely with its citizens.

After a brief visit to a crater created by a fifty-kilogram bomb that seemed to impress no one and that no one realized unintentionally presaged what was to come, their hosts motored the group on toward what at first appeared to be merely a sparse forest near the edge of a large field. It turned out to be a large aerodrome—"one of the largest airfields I have ever seen," reported Jordan—home to a squadron of MIG-3s, fighters the Red Air Force claimed were superior to the German Messerschmitts then in operation in this sector.[41] From the road the reporters could see aircraft landing, but by the time they arrived on the scene the planes had already been hidden under a camouflage of tree limbs. Nonetheless, the squad's dashing commander, Major-General Georgi Zakharov, met them and enthusiastically introduced them to some of the illustrious Stalin's Hawks (*Stalinskie Sokoly*), the young fighter pilots recently made famous in the Russian cinema. ("What good, fine, strong, and yet human faces they all had!"[42]) One of them, nineteen-year-old Lieutenant Alexei Rodin, had landed with a one-foot-diameter shell hole straight through his plane's wing. Charlotte Haldane's memory of this meet-and-greet session with the young, debonair air force pilots was highlighted by their noticing her badge from the International Brigade—an organization created by the Communist Party to recruit volunteers to support the Republican cause during the Spanish Civil War. When one of the pilots started to speak with her about Spain, the watchdog political commissar "told him sharply not to refer to the matter further."[43]

Just after dark, Zakharov also briefed the correspondents on a new Russian low-altitude, air-to-ground, armor-piercing, anti-tank weapon the MIGs were carrying, one of "diabolical precision and power."[44] He had one of the camouflaged planes taxi out to give a short demonstration of its destructive power. Before they departed, Zakharov swore the reporters to secrecy.[45]

In the evening they were feted again in the hotel dining room. Major-General Vasily Sokolovsky was the principal guest. He was the chief of staff for Marshall Semyon Timoshenko, who was in charge of the rejuvenated central front that even then was attempting to advance toward Smolensk to relieve it. One of the main topics of conversation was the vital role the Russian guerillas, or partisans as they were called, were playing in disrupting German supply lines, which forced the Nazi High Command to divert forces from other areas. This was the first time the Western press had firsthand information about this vital gear in the Red Army's machine. Caldwell was so fascinated with the partisans' story that he wrote of them in all three of the books he published upon leaving the Soviet Union.

Sated and unsuspecting, the reporters retired to their rooms around midnight for their first night's sleep.

Tuesday: Mayhem

Early the next morning the journalists were brought face-to-face with real war. As Philip Jordan recalled it: "German bombs blew out all the windows of the little building where I was staying; but I had the felicity of talking that same evening with the men who had so nearly smashed us up. They had been smashed up themselves by a Soviet fighter only a few minutes after bombing the little town where I was staying."[46] Somehow Jordan completely missed the human drama of the episode. As it developed, the attack was a reprisal for a Soviet bombing of Smolensk the previous afternoon. Cassidy recalls the attack starting at about 7:30:

> The Viazma air-raid sirens whined, the anti-aircraft guns set up their roar, there came the drone of planes, and then, suddenly, the shriek of falling bombs. One fell directly across the street from the hotel, blasting in our windows. A shower of glass sprayed across my bed. In a single movement I went out of that bed, back across the room, and under another bed by the door. Cholerton and Carroll were already there. We waited, breathless, for the next bomb in that string. It never came. Instead, there came the song of fighters, rising to meet the enemy. The drone of planes faded into the distance. We could breathe again.[47]

Werth, rooming with Bartlett and Jordan, recalled the event with a kind of detached irony. Jolted awake by the noise, he first thought the innkeepers were knocking on their door. Although they consider crawling under their beds, the room is pitch-black and they are all too busy rummaging about for their socks. Jordan is "in bed, near the window, with a blanket over his nose," while Bartlett sits "on his bed, in his pyjamas, and with a tin hat on his head." The hullabaloo seems to pass and everyone "feels elated after getting safely through a bombing; and we were all very cheerful and talkative round the tap at the end of the passage, and around the breakfast table downstairs."[48]

The problem was that the bomb, which shattered the hotel windows, actually landed on a house quite nearby and with gruesome results. As was typical of the male reporters, their reaction to Bourke-White's actions throughout the junket are framed by measures of personal annoyance, professional jealousy, and sexism: "Mrs. Haldane had dashed along to look at the dead bodies, and Mrs. Bourke-White had gone to photograph them."[49] Yet there was a real human tragedy just outside the hotel, and all Werth was willing to entertain was hearsay: "[T]wo young girls had been killed by the blast just outside the house, and an old woman, and there was an old man who was wounded, and whom they saw being taken away on a stretcher. And the mother of the two girls sobbed over their bodies, and there was a crowd of people round the house, and many of them were weeping."[50] Cassidy's sarcasm was even greater: "We looked out to see a few forlorn folks digging into the wreckage of a thatched cottage, bringing out a body. Margaret Bourke-White bustled out to photograph those poor people in their moment of mourning."[51]

Moats, Cassidy's and Cholerton's particular friend, must have absorbed some of their cynicism in their posttrip conversations, but she turned it into a kind of ribbing of her fellow correspondents. "As far as I could gather, they had spent most of their time eating gargantuan meals, being pushed aside to make way for Bourke-White's tripods and cameras, and bickering among themselves." As for the bombing, her hearsay summary was unnervingly callous, concluding: "Nobody was hurt, but when they picked themselves up it took some time to brush bits of broken glass out of their hair."[52]

Wallace Carroll was more intrepid. After assuring himself that his friends were safe and unhurt and that the hotel would stand though it had "trembled like a ship in a storm," he ventured forth. He like the rest had been impressed at the condition of their censor, Anurov, whom they found lying on his bed, the window frame blown in and draped across his torso so that, Carroll thought, he looked as if were framed in a picture. If there had been a moment of true comic relief, this was it. Carroll went outside to investigate and reported on the downed telephone poles and their repair, the three houses destroyed and the clearance of the rubble, an injured old man, eight corpses, and how "a little white dog whose owner was missing ran about the courtyard looking for a friend. The ways and cares of everyday life were already pushing into the background this danger which came only infrequently and against which the town could do nothing."[53] He does not mention a photographer on the scene.

On September 22, about a week after the junket had concluded, Sulzberger filed a story with the *New York Times* in which this bombing receives the attention of but one short paragraph: "Everyone does a racing dive flat on the hallway floor, like frogs leaping into a pond at the approach of danger. Bombs are blasting all the windows out of the building. Some little ones fall and you go out to see the damage. Rescue workers are already putting the stiffening bodies of two women, a child and an old man into a truck, and other workers are searching collapsed dwellings for more."[54] The earliest to rise that morning had been Charlotte Haldane, who was rooming by herself and at about seven o'clock was performing her morning ablutions in the hall sink. At first she attributed the "thud" to military training activities, but when the glass windows slivered and the hotel shook she knew it was something more, and when her "colleagues came tumbling in various stages of dress and undress, some half-shaved, some still with the night's beards adhering to their chins, their startled eyes heavy with sleep," she realized it must have been an air raid. She recalled that at about this time Colonel Baltin happened by and she readily convinced him to go with her to investigate the scene of the bombing, and Bourke-White, whom Haldane calls Margaret Caldwell, quickly joined them.[55]

The dust had barely settled outside and they found themselves in the midst of a scene of desperate havoc. On a side street a stretcher party of four girls was carrying out "an elderly man, bald, his face chalk-white, his grey hair matted with plaster. A red stain was spreading across his chest. As the girls carried him past me, the poor old chap began to regain consciousness and to moan." They watched as "a fluffy little white puppy dog jumped unharmed from a first story window."[56] Bourke-White gathered it up to soothe it, but when it became evident that there were more serious casualties nearby, she handed it to Haldane. Showing how precise and accurate was her memory, Haldane's descriptions of these dead mirror exactly the photo that Bourke-White later published in *Shooting the Russian War*, one which Haldane had not seen: "There were four people in the yard, all of them stone-dead; a middle-aged man, a boy of about fifteen years, and two girls. The men were lying down; but the girls were sitting propped stiffly against the wall of a house backing on the yard; one, a child of about fourteen, had her arm and hand raised as if to protect her face from a blow. All had been killed by blast; death must've been instantaneous."[57] Haldane was indignant in her horror: "What a magnificent morning's work for the Nazi bombers."[58]

The Caldwells had joined Haldane at the corridor sink and were washing and shaving when the bombers struck. They hit the floor as one of the bombs fell in the hotel courtyard, splintering most of the windows. Later they discovered that "an entire window-sash was wrapped around the neck of the Foreign Office representative [Anurov]."[59] Caldwell must have gone outside with his wife because he recalled in *Smolensk* that "[o]utside the hotel, the dead lay on the ground in the queer-looking positions human beings assume when life has been blasted from their bodies."[60]

But it was Margaret Bourke-White who made the most of this moment of war horror, despite the caviling of her male counterparts. In *Shooting the Russian War,* she reproduces five full-page pictures of their twenty hours in Vyazma.[61] The first photo is a wide-angle view captioned "Supper for Correspondents in Vyazma, the Night Before the Bombing," in which the guest of honor, Major-General Sokolovsky, is at the head of a long dinner table laden with plates of Russian delicacies, innumerable empty bottles of vodka and other liquors, dishware, and cutlery (see chapter 3, figure 22). Four correspondents sit along the side of the table to Sokolovsky's right, Colonel Sudakov and the censor Anurov are to his immediate left, while three more correspondents sit to their left. All eyes are focused on Wallace Carroll, who is holding a pen in his right hand and carefully studying a notebook in which he has just finished writing. Two other sets of male hands are visible in the foreground, so that only the two women are missing from the shot. The focal point of the whole photographic exercise is the surfeit of food in front of these journalists and their Russian hosts. For the villagers the availability of food was far more problematic, to say the least.

Immediately follow three photos taken the next morning. The first is "Rescue Squad" (eight people, at least four of whom are women, and a collapsed stretcher held by one of them, all standing in front of a thatched-roof wooden house destroyed in the blast), the third is "No. 9 Trubetsov Street" (a cleanup crew of six, several with shovels, sorts through the debris in front of the house). The pièce de résistance, "Death Comes to Vyazma," occupies the middle position. The scene is ghastly. It is so graphic that Bourke-White does not elaborate the horror of the four dead peasants, contorted into the strange postures which her husband had alluded to and lying in death amid the shards of their home and their lives. It is evident that Haldane also had gotten the description spot-on. Bourke-White ascribes their deaths to an act of revenge over the previous day's bombing of Smolensk. "Undoubtedly, our hotel, where Russian Air Force officers were known to be quartered, was one of their targets. However, they missed our hotel, and this was the result."[62]

In *Shooting the Russian War*, Bourke-White reflects—perhaps as an antidote to the criticism she felt from those of her colleagues who remained indoors and away from the war on their very doorstep—on how it is to function as a photojournalist in these moments of stark drama and emotional duress: "It is a peculiar thing about pictures of this sort. It is as though a protecting screen draws itself across my mind and makes it possible to consider focus and light values and the technique of photography, in as impersonal a way as though I were making an abstract camera composition. This blind lasts as long as it is needed—while I am actually operating the camera. Days later, when I developed the negatives, I was surprised to find that I could not bring myself to look at the films. I had to have someone else handle and sort them for me."[63] Like Haldane, she had not been untouched by the tragedy. She watches as the cleanup crews scrape up the "shreds of blood and hair and internal organs and clothing" and observes that this is what has become of "one more small family that had taken its unconscious stand between Hitler and his *Lebensraum*." While she was working, a woman ran suddenly into the house, crying and distraught because these four dead people were her children and her family.

"Her desperate moans penetrated even my protective shell, and as I focused my camera on this vision of human misery it seemed heartless to turn her suffering into a photograph. But war is war and it has to be recorded."[64] She later published that photo in *Russia at War*, the book she coauthored with Caldwell, along with three of the previously published photos and a new one of a Junkers 88 bomber that the Stalin Hawks had shot down. Oddly, perhaps because she could not bear the tragedy, she cropped "Death Comes to Vyazma" for *Russia at War* so that one sees only the head of the mangled daughter.

The two women, Haldane and Bourke-White, see this moment of terror and carnage as a microcosm of the war. The men, on the other hand, Werth and Sulzberger in particular, see this event as just one inconsequential moment in a larger theater. In contrast, Caldwell, on September 25, wrote an emotional dispatch for *PM* newspaper,[65] an excellent example of the kind of war writing that he produced on a regular basis over the summer.[66] Its common words and paratactic structures enhance the verisimilitude and pathos of pastoral normalcy gone terribly wrong:

> Moscow, September 25—While at the front recently I witnessed the bombing of a town by German planes. Nine Junkers 88s swept over the horizon soon after seven in the morning and dropped their loads of 500- and 1000-pound bombs. People were doing the usual things at that hour, such as milking cows, cutting wood, cooking breakfast and walking along the streets on their way to work.
>
> In the back yard of a house 50 yards from where I was I could see an old man trudging from the woodshed to the kitchen with several sticks of wood in his hands. Two children were carrying pails of water from the well to the house. A woman in the yard was milking a cow. A 500-pound bomb dropped squarely in the rear of the house with a roar that sounded like the end of the world. There was a viloent [*sic*] upheaval of splintered timbers, shattered glass, brick and powdery plaster. Fragments of the house flew in all directions, striking other buildings and falling with crunching thuds into the soft earth.
>
> The old man with his arms full of sticks lay face downward in the muddy path, his body broken and bleeding. The woman, who had been milking, and the cow itself, had been hurled against the side of the shed and almost flattened by the impact. The two children with their pails of water lay screaming on the ground while life slowly flowed from their bodies. A woman who had been in the kitchen cooking breakfast had been blown into an unrecognizable mass. A young girl who had been in the front part of the house lay crushed under timbers that had fallen from the second story.
>
> There was a short period of absolute silence. Bombs were falling at intervals in other parts of the town, but for several moments there was a complete lull in life. Then suddenly the silence was broken by the shouts of men and women running

towards the blasted dwelling. Men tore into the wreckage, calling to anyone who might still be alive. But no one was alive. The entire family of six persons had been killed.

From across the street a woman of about seventy, evidently a relative of the family, ran toward the bombed house—her face contorted with anguish. She ran to the bodies of the children on the ground and tried to lift them into her arms. When she saw that she could not bring them to life she fell down beside them and lay there screaming and moaning.

By that time several rescue squads had arrived. One was a civilian demolition squad that went to work prying the timbers from the body of the young girl. One was a squad of demolition workers who began shoveling through the brick and plaster in hopes of finding anyone who might still be alive. A third squad was composed of six girls with Red Cross arm bands and first-aid kits. Neighbors, soldiers and other labor squads began arriving and soon several hundred persons crowded around the bombed house and its dead.

Then a truck drove up and backed into the yard. The bodies were lifted into it. The young girl's body was placed in the truck beside the body of the old man, with one stick of wood still gripped in the fingers of one hand. The last to be put into the truck was the shattered body of the woman who had been milking a cow. The upper portion of her body was lifted up first and a few minutes later the lower portion was put into the truck.

The blasted body of the other woman, the one who had been cooking breakfast, was gathered bit by bit by the girls with Red Cross arm bands and placed in a small wooden box. Someone lifted the weeping grandmother from the ground and guided her toward a shed.

In New York, *PM* placed above the piece the headline "Nazi Bomb Comes for Breakfast . . . And Wipes Out Family of Six."

Back on the Road

Around 10:00 a.m. the now subdued party begin the day's tour. Soon they are forced to detour into a makeshift air-raid shelter when their convoy is strafed. First they travel in a Smolensk direction along a primary road dotted with the usual number of active guard posts and heavy with military traffic going to and from the front, then they turn off onto narrower and narrower tracks through wooded countryside. For Caldwell, as usual, it seems a grand adventure.

Three hours later we were halfway between Vyazma and Smolensk when our chauffeur suddenly jerked the car to a stop and shouted to us to abandon-car. We piled out and dove into the ditch beside the road. Our car, like all the others making the trip, had been heavily camouflaged with fir boughs until it looked like an overgrown Christmas tree, but since we were in open country at the time there was no sense in pretending that a car could escape detection from a low-flying bomber.[67]

Bombs *were* dropped while they took shelter in a birch grove, the result being "[g]eysers of earth, roots, and stone shot upward and showered down upon us."[68]

Bourke-White and Haldane recalled this attack from a very different perspective. They had noticed that the forest floor was covered in flowers. "To my great delight I saw masses of exquisite blue gentians—the long and the short-stalked varieties—growing at my feet," recalled Haldane.[69] She had just started picking some when the bombs began to fall, but she didn't let the explosions interrupt her. Bourke-White recalled that after "we dashed out of our cars and slithered across the slippery surface to the edge of the meadow," she found herself "lying in the largest patch of fringed gentians that I've ever seen. The gentians were at a level with my eyes, and over this blue border I watched three great curtains of mud rise in the air and hang there shimmering, as though suspended on invisible curtain poles in the sky."[70] But rather than collect flowers, she pitched in and started gathering shrubbery and boughs for camouflaging the automobiles, a sufficiently strange sight that drew the attention of her camera. In *Russian Newsreel,* Haldane prints a Bourke-White image taken that second day of two of the cars being piled with branches by one of the chauffeurs while five correspondents (Carroll, Jordan, Mrs. Haldane herself, Cholerton, and Caldwell) study a map and one of the Russians looks on from the side of the second car. In *Shooting the Russian War,* Bourke-White publishes a haunting image taken several days later shot from a low angle of a soldier in a rain slicker standing beside one of the cars he's just dug out of the mud. Three other cars and a truck rest slightly out of focus in the distance, beyond and to the left of him.[71] Thereafter the cars of the caravan generally motored with pine branches on their hoods, rooftops, fenders, and bumpers.

In the early afternoon they cross the Dnieper, passing through "a wide wooden gate, decorated with red flags, with portraits of Stalin and Timoshenko, and inscriptions reminding Red soldiers that they must 'do their duty to the last'; 'Victory will be ours,' and 'The Fascist Reptile Must be Crushed.'"[72] Beyond this is more bucolic countryside where "a girl wearing a blue beret was hanging up the washing, and there were ducks in the pond, and two little boys in sheepskin coats waved at us."[73] Finally, farther toward the west and closer to the sound of gunfire, they arrive at a regimental headquarters where the first order of business was a meal: "[T]here was a great display of zakuski and vodka bottles all down the large table, and the plain-clothed female attendants served round enormous dishes of roast beef, and half-pound hunks of bread."[74] There were sufficient vodka toasts to drink one of the correspondents under the table. Henry Cassidy was the unlucky party. He admitted it freely and charmingly, good-naturedly implicating Caldwell as the source of his problems:

> Erskine Caldwell sat opposite me, beside an enthusiastic captain who was determined to engage in a duel of "do adna," meaning "in one," or "bottoms up," with vodka as the weapon and a visitor as his opponent. This, it seemed, was a time-honored tradition, and the guest challenged was honor-bound to meet every pass of his challenger. Caldwell skillfully turned his captain's attention to me and I became the correspondents' champion for the day. Afterward, I was told, I was carried out of the tent, while the captain, standing at the door, saluted his valiant though defeated opponent—and then passed out in his turn. This is possibly an exaggeration in my case, and probably in the case of the captain, but in any case, when I first became clear about the progress of that historic trip to the front, I was lying in a comfortable cot in a schoolhouse, many miles back of the front.[75]

He observes that during the banquets still to come his compatriots kindly "assumed the rôle of champions." But Cassidy's memory did remain sharp enough to recall that as the correspondents entered the tent "a soldier played an entry march on a piano."[76] Haldane writes that "throughout the meal one of the men entertained us with swing music and tangos."[77]

Perhaps Caldwell felt a bit chagrined and guilty about Cassidy's plight because, according to his wife's memoir, as the group was about to embark on that afternoon's tour, he realized Cassidy had been left behind. "So my husband raised the unconscious correspondent in his arms and placed him in the back of one of the cars, where he was brought along, quite unaware that he was being carried to the very brink of no man's land."[78] The next day Cassidy borrowed the notes of his colleagues and wrote up his own version of the story.

The one feature that all agree upon, and write about, is a twelve- to fourteen-year-old boy whom the regiment had adopted. His entire family had been killed during a German air raid on a nearby village, and so they had kitted him out in an ill-fitting uniform, given him a gun, and turned him into a combination of beloved mascot, doorman, and errand boy. Haldane was worried. "This little boy, Sasha, an orphan, had been adopted by the men. I thought he would get terribly spoilt, for the tough Red Army officers were fussing round him and showing him off like a lot of old women. But he was a very good little boy."[79] Although Caldwell does not mention this tender scene in *Smolensk*, he makes great use of it in his stem-winding tale of Russian guerilla warfare, *All Night Long*.

Haldane and Bourke-White also became interested in one of the white-overalled waitresses named Tanya. They agree that "[s]he was a tall, fine-looking girl, with large blue eyes, a schoolgirl complexion, and masses of chestnut curls."[80] She had been specially selected to be a member of the waitstaff but more usually performed observation and reconnaissance work. Before the luncheon broke up, Bourke-White asked her to sit for a photograph, and according to Haldane, she insisted that Haldane be included. The "observation and reconnaissance work" in which Tanya was engaged was this:

> She knew every footpath, and at night, as soon as it grew completely dark, she would buckle on her sidearms and go crawling on her hands and knees through the long grass and low shrubbery, across to the German lines. There, behind the lines, she would learn what she could about the movements of the enemy and location of German guns, and creep back just before daybreak to report on what she had seen. Then she would sleep a few hours, go to the hospital tent to help tend the wounded, and at night if she was needed she would be off again.[81]

Perhaps this explains why Bourke-White published no photos of this dedicated partisan. She appears in Caldwell's *All Night Long* in a barely modified form.

Much of the luncheon conversation focused on the Russians' attempts to clarify their position in the war, in careful support of the official Stalinist ideology. This war was not one against the German people, they insisted, but rather one against the Hitlerites, as the correspondents referred to members of the Nazi Party. But as usual the toasting put an end to the serious aspects of the political discussion. Not particularly interested in this sort of male camaraderie, Bourke-White would often sneak out of meals early "with a piece of black bread in my hand, loaded with salt herring or a slab of cheese" while the men were still drinking, in search of suitable photographic conquests of her own and gathering stories of partisan exploits that were featured later in her husband's *All Night Long*.[82]

After lunch the group took a walking tour of the area, but as the artillery shelling increased in intensity, so did the anxiety level of the pince-nez-adorned military commander, Colonel Kirov (the other reporters record his name as Lieutenant-Colonel Kirilov). As usual, Werth was ready with literary allusions: "He was a typical *voyaka*, a soldier of the old tradition which had produced Lermontov's lovable Maxim Maximich [*A Hero of Our Time*] and so many of the simple, brave, unassuming men whom Tolstoy drew so well in *War and Peace*, and especially in *Sebastopol*."[83] Apprehension over the press corps' proximity to gunfire worried the regimental political commissar, Nikolai Suslov, as well; in any case, the group soon left the front for a preplanned trip to a field hospital two miles to the rear.

Carroll was impressed with the accommodations:

> Like Kirilov's headquarters, it was underground, and the walls and ceilings were covered with white cloth. Operating tables, surgical instruments, and beds look as clean as any you would find in the hospitals of a big city. The operating room was lighted by electricity. The chief surgeon was a young woman dressed in a khaki tunic, navy-blue skirt, and top boots. . . . This hospital was obviously on show for our benefit. I was therefore glad the following night when we dropped into a base hospital where we had not been expected. It was just as clean, however, and its staff of doctors and nurses looked just as efficient as those we saw here.[84]

Haldane was particularly fascinated with the role women had in this forward post. Not only was the medical staff predominantly female, but so were the pilots of the ambulance planes who evacuated the more serious cases to the rear. She writes poignantly, "In their eyes was that watchful, alert, tragic expression which comes to women who have looked on much suffering but had no time to weep over it."[85]

The next stop was another dugout facility, a kind of club for NCOs and regular troops, one of many that had been established along the front. Werth thought their visit seemed staged: "We sat on benches among the soldiers and drank beer, and some of the soldiers sang, and others danced a Russian folk-dance, and the music was provided by a young N.C.O. playing a tinny piano. . . . There was something slightly incongruous and 'Intouristy' about the whole setting, and the soldiers, I felt, were about as ill at ease as many of us were."[86] Carroll describes a well-stocked library connected to this room through a tunnel. "The books on the shelves included, of course, the complete works of Lenin, but I also saw novels by Tolstoy, Dostoievsky, and Mikhail Sholokhov, the plays of Ibsen—and the poems of Heinrich Heine!"[87] After the ever-present artillery fire diminished, the group drove about five miles back from there to a large village where they were bedded down for the evening in what appeared to them to be the dormitory of a boarding school. Again Werth felt ill at ease: "The Narkomindel had certainly done everything to make us as comfortable as possible at the front, sometimes at the expense of other people's comfort, I feared."[88] Bourke-White recalled that the Foreign Office was so considerate "that a barber was even waiting to give the correspondents a shave" here.[89]

In the officers' mess, after a dinner consisting of "slices of salami and Bologna and cucumbers, served with pieces of black bread as big as a fist and portions of creamy butter the size of a deck of cards," the Russians produced three surprise

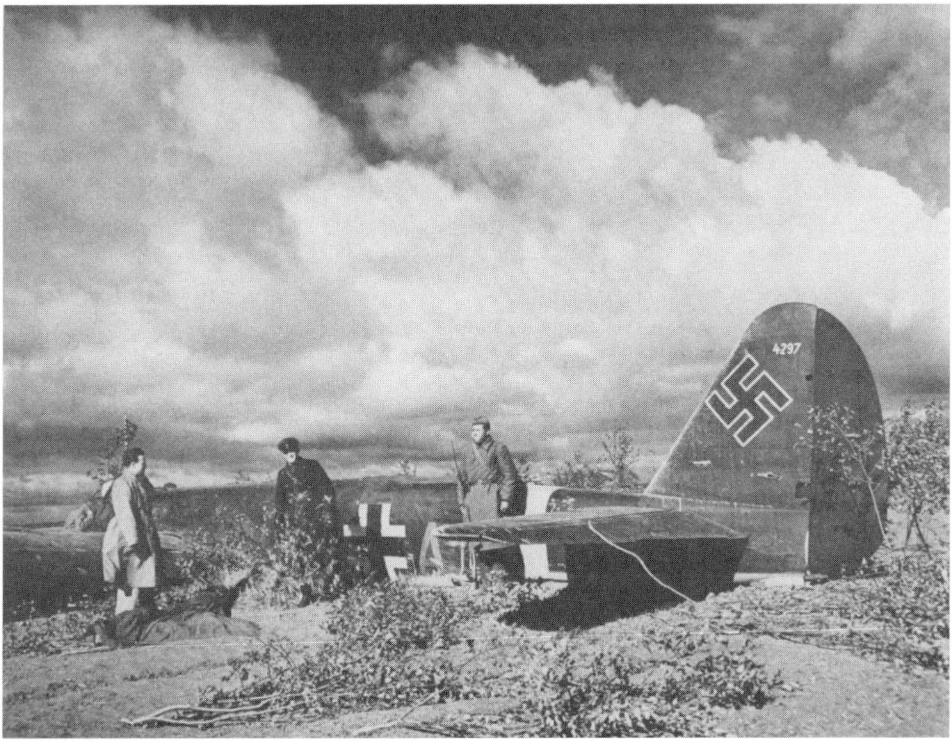

FIGURE 37. "Wrecked Nazi Raider" (From *Shooting the Russian War*; photo © Estate of Margaret Bourke-White/Licensed by VAGA, New York, N.Y.; courtesy of Syracuse University Libraries)

guests.[90] Earlier that day, the Stalinskie Sokoly had been able to shoot down one of the German planes that had bombed Vyazma that morning. Three of those German airmen were marched in, along with a German interpreter, for interrogation by the correspondents. Werth, fluent in Russian, English, and German, described the nature of them. One, Josef Trocha, twenty-six, was "the wireless operator, . . . a simple-minded and rather amiable youth. . . . He clearly tried to make a good impression, and perhaps give one the idea that he was one of the 'good Germans.'" The second, Walther Rasek, twenty-two, the navigator with the bandaged eye in Bourke-White's photo, was a "fanatical Nazi. With his remaining eye he looked at us with animal hatred." The press took the opportunity to grill them about their membership in the Nazi Party, admission of which would have been grounds for immediate execution. The third, Rudolph Taüse, twenty-five, "was the pilot of the Heinkel that had been brought down. He was as much a Nazi as the others, but he had a cold, foxy face . . . and he explained calmly that no German on active service was allowed to belong to any political party."[91] Then the questioning got down to the matter of the Vyazma raid, and the prisoners insisted they were trying to bomb the aerodrome and had simply missed. "This was too much for old Cholerton. 'Aerodrome, aerodrome,' he bubbled. 'You bombed *me*,' he cried in German, ignoring the arrangements [for no direct conversation with the airmen]; 'me, in my bed, at my hotel. Smash my window. Aerodrome, indeed!—centre of Vyazma, miles away from the aerodrome.' The Germans had nothing to say, and number two merely shrugged his shoulders contemptuously."[92] All but the surly German saluted as they were led away. The fate of the Luftwaffe airmen is unknown.

Bourke-White included a photograph of these three men in *Shooting the Russian War* (see figure 38), noting that "[t]he fourth member of the crew, the mechanic, does not appear in the picture. He was wounded too badly to be present."[93] Among all the reports of this interview it is only Bourke-White's that carefully identifies each of the crew by name. Gathering such basic information as the names of one's subjects is routine for a photographer, but by naming the men in print she humanizes them further, by making them individually responsible for the carnage and damage they had wrought. In her composition they appear dazed, bandaged, and posed. They are shot from below and from their right such that their heads and noses form a perfect diagonal downward to the lower right of the frame, a typical Bourke-White arrangement.

The following morning the group visited the site where the bomber had come to rest, riddled with bullets, having come down smoothly, "slickly, without much damage to the machine. Fox-faced number three must have been a good pilot."[94] Later, in her personal memoir, Bourke-White took great pleasure

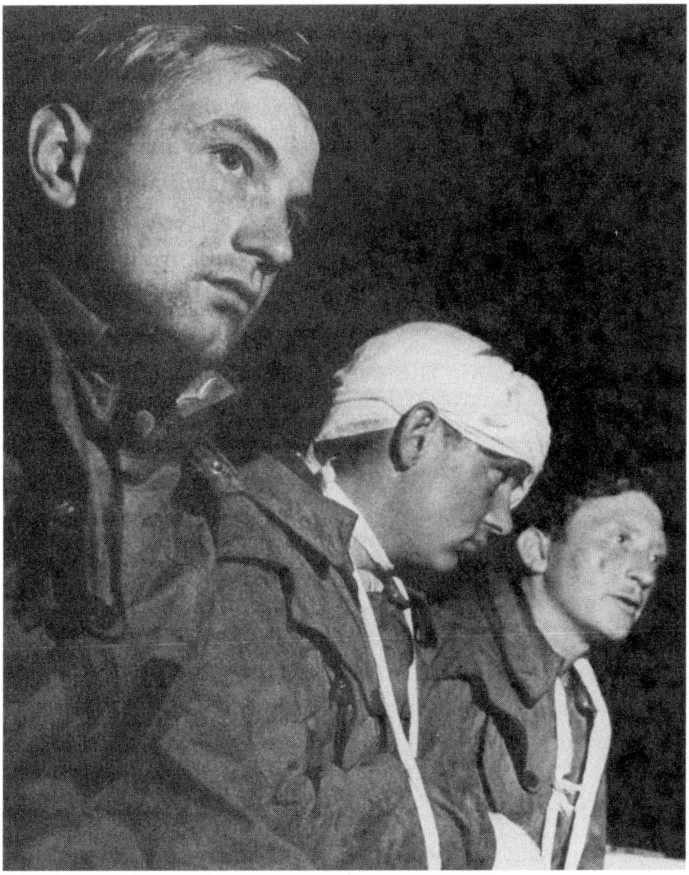

FIGURE 38. "Captured German Bomber Crew" (From *Shooting the Russian War*; photo © Estate of Margaret Bourke-White/Licensed by VAGA, New York, N.Y.; courtesy of Syracuse University Libraries)

in tattling on her husband: "Erskine, who had developed a souvenir-collecting facility that astonished his wife, filled his pockets with clips of machine-gun bullets and even took the speedometer of the plane, while I made a set of photographs."[95] She reproduces a magnificent one in her memoir (see figure 37), a shot dominated by majestic clouds, a three-quarter perspective from the rear of the fuselage, the swastikaed tail filling the right side of the frame. Three diminutive figures, Carroll, Sudokov, and a Russian sentry, stand about six feet apart in a line to the left of the plane.

Haldane, who was fluent in German though not Russian, took careful notes during the questioning and reproduced them in detail in her memoir, *Russian Newsreel*. Her descriptions of the men are very similar to Werth's. She says that the wireless operator was friendly and loquacious to the point of the comedic: "[H]e was almost cheerful and very willing to talk." The pilot, "[o]bviously a would-be gentleman and aristocrat," but in fact just the son of a butcher, displayed "the most arrogant expression I've ever seen on a human face . . . an expression of defiant nonchalance." The bandaged navigator, on the other hand, was "a much coarser type than the pilot; obviously neither of the same degree of intelligence nor so well educated." He had "the sullen, scowling features of a born bully. He, too, was clearly a Nazi."[96]

Finally, Haldane had enough. When she learns that the wireless operator, the most callow of the lot, and a former member of the Hitler Youth, had participated in the London Blitz, "I looked at this specimen of German youth, brutalized and mentally corrupted almost beyond repair; . . . I could not see any hope, in a civilized world, for such as he."[97] The session came to a close soon after.

As usual, Bourke-White was able to distance herself from her emotions by focusing on her art and her job:

> I don't know how the other correspondents felt as they gravely questioned these men who had dropped their missiles so close that it might have been the end of us instead of those families just across the street. But my habitual impersonality with the camera came to my aid, and if I had any feeling at all it was just a slight sense of gratitude that they should have let themselves get shot down so providentially close to where we were going to spend the night, so that I could have a continued story.[98]

Later, the correspondents retired to their dormitory cots. It had been a long and eventful day. Haldane reported that she slept without waking, while Caldwell noted that "[t]he roar of artillery went on all night without pause, and when I woke up the next morning, I had become so accustomed to it that I did not notice it again."[99]

CHAPTER 7

Smolensk II ★ To Hell and Back (September 17–20)

The next morning (Wednesday, September 17) was cold and the sky so often spotted with fluffy white clouds, obscuring the sun, that Bourke-White finally complained that she was having trouble with her exposures. For everyone else it was just chilly, though later in the day rain fell in earnest. In the area through which they were now traveling, an area to the northeast of Smolensk where there had been some recent Russian inroads on the once inexorable German advances, "General Mud" had joined the fray. Caldwell recorded that the caravan bogged down fourteen times in the quagmire the roads had become. But this was only in the morning; midday rains further impaired their progress.

Even so, as they proceeded north from the Yartsevo sector where they had spent most of Tuesday, the general impression was one of almost bucolic serenity. Peasants industriously worked crops of potatoes, flax, and buckwheat despite the propinquity of war, evident in the shell craters in the fields and forests and beside the rural roads, along with the periodic distant barrage of artillery. Haldane, ever on the lookout for evidence of the important role of women, rhapsodized: "Short, stocky, muscular, these round-bodied, round-faced peasant women, with white headcloths tied under their chins, barely paused in their unremitting labors to glance at us. . . . These peasant women are of a startling physical similarity, as if they were all sisters, aunts, first cousins; near blood relations. Their broad faces, little blue eyes, snub noses, and wide mouths all seem cut from one family pattern."[1] The common denominator of all the peasant scenes they came across was the near-complete absence of able-bodied men. They were all off at war. Only women, old men, and children remained. Although she was later bitterly to repudiate communism, at this time Haldane was still a Soviet champion: "Everywhere the soldiers mingled with the peasants, often helping them with the farm work." But then again, "ninety per cent of the soldiers themselves were just peasants in uniform."[2]

Caldwell observed the scene through a very different lens. Before this Russian venture, he had perceptively cataloged the ravages of rural poverty in the American South. The similarities to this Russian scene seemed evident:

> The people reflected the poverty of the soil in this area, they look drab in their dark worn clothes. I saw many adults and children wearing bound leggings, made of strips of cloth, and straw sandals, instead of shoes or boots. . . . In some of the villages tank crews and field-kitchen units were quartered in the family cowshed, detachments of soldiers were quartered in barns, and machine gun and antiaircraft stations had been erected in church and school belfries. . . . What was perhaps the strangest sight of all was the sheepherder with his dog and flock carrying his gas mask over his shoulder.[3]

But the going was so rough on the road that the Soviets finally arranged for a demolition squad to be specifically detailed to the press caravan to help in the never-ending vehicle extractions from the mud. The light coupes were no match for the potholes and slime, road conditions the heavily modified trucks and carriers and the treaded tanks could manage with minimal impairment. Each of the correspondents provided estimates of their speed for the day, all in the range of three to ten miles per hour. At one point, near a bombed-out community that once again reminded Werth of a village in *Dead Souls*, they had to cross a small ravine with a gurgling stream at its bottom. The soldiers, chauffeurs, and remaining villagers laid down "a sort of bridge of planks and bundles of straw,"[4] and the correspondents were able to proceed fitfully forward, the men often annoyed at Bourke-White for getting in the way and slowing everything down with her photography. For their purposes she was too much down in the mud, but she reveled in it. At one point, she was attempting to get shots of the cars skidding into the mud holes: "as the third car skirted cautiously around the crater rim, the door opened, and Erskine jumped out, pulled me up over the running board, and I was inside."[5] This sort of uxorial gallantry also annoyed the others.

During the course of the day's travels, the press was occasionally shown the detritus of battles in which the Red Army had been successful in repulsing the Germans. Many years later Haldane recalled one of these stops. Knowing her leftist sentiments, her two riding partners had come back to their coupe in a huff. She described the kerfuffle in detail:

> They were in a particularly black mood on account of a small incident that occurred during the morning. We had been taken to view a dump of allegedly captured German war material; gun carriages, and other small transport stuff. When we had examined it, one of my companions re-entered the car, livid with anger.

On my asking the reason for his annoyance, he replied: "Next time they show us 'captured' German war material they might have the elementary intelligence to remove the stamp of the Stalin motor factory from the hub of the wheels!"[6]

This sort of rudimentary falsification of evidence for propaganda purposes was not an isolated event as the war bore on, but just one of the many failures of the Soviet Way that finally so disenchanted Haldane that she surrendered her party membership after returning to Britain.

But Haldane perhaps was not always forthright with her own recollections. Alice Moats tells the following story, sewn together from several threads of hearsay. The context is that not all the battlegrounds the press corps examined had been sterilized, many still having "battered, bloodstained helmets, bits of fingers and legs. . . . The stench was still there." Moats writes, "Vernon Bartlett, who had fought in the last war, began to grow a bit white about the gills on having unpleasant memories so vividly recalled. He grew even whiter when Mrs. Haldane pounced on a helmet and crowed with pleasure because the inside was smeared with something that looked like strawberry jam and there was a lock of blond hair sticking through the bullet hole in the top. In spite of several protests, she carried it away with her."[7] Bartlett was so upset that he switched cars, leaving Haldane with Cholerton, but Cholerton would not allow the gore-filled helmet inside. A Soviet officer finally took custody of the helmet, whereupon it was soon lost.

> That evening Chol was approached by a Soviet officer who said, "You were disgusted at the sight of that helmet, weren't you? I suppose you are shocked at the cold-blooded way in which we take that kind of thing for granted. We aren't upset at the sight of dead Germans and we don't care how gruesome the process of killing them becomes. We are fighting too hard to spare time for finer feelings."
>
> Chol answered, "I agree with you heartily. My gesture of distaste when Mrs. Haldane tried to put the helmet in the car was not directed against you but against her. Such ghoulishness in a woman makes me sick."[8]

Wednesday Night's Party

Toward the end of the day, around six o'clock, after passing through another ravaged town, they arrived at the headquarters they had hoped to reach hours earlier, commanded by Colonel Mikhail Dudonov. They were now only about fifteen miles northwest of where they had begun the morning. Dudonov's division was mostly of Siberian origin: large, rugged men who had proven steadfast in recovering this sector and would later receive the Order of Lenin decoration for their service. But once again, before their actual tour of the front, which was barely a few kilometers distant, a late luncheon had to be enjoyed.

Before sitting down to this repast, Bourke-White recalls a tour of a two-room dugout—a visit she may well have confused with the one they had the day before—called the Red Corner, though there are enough significantly different details to suggest such recreation facilities existed at every headquarters site:

> A rubber plant stood in a pot at the head of a little flight of stairs cut out of earth and leading down into the ground. The roof of the recreation center was only a slight hump above the earth, reinforced with planks and sod, and showing two tiny windows about ten inches square with glass panes crisscrossed against concussion with strips of brown paper. . . . In the second room, which led from the music room by a narrow earth tunnel, there were three pairs of soldiers bent over the favorite game of the Red Army—chess.[9]

A "medical sister" was playing a piano, and several of the men were singing a patriotic ditty to its tune.

The meal, as usual, even in this advanced outpost, was well catered. This time, the table was in the open air within a grove of trees, not under a tent. Carroll recalled roast goose and champagne. But Werth remembered a far more spartan affair. On account of the tardiness of their arrival, Dudonov was not prepared for them and stated he had only "our ordinary soldiers' food" available. "However, he ordered a few tins of pickled fish to be opened by way of *zakuski*. But the *kasha* [buckwheat porridge] and the cabbage soup and the stewed beef were excellent."[10] A spread of such meager fare clearly was not how Bourke-White recollected it: "We began with raw fish, salt fish, and pickled fish. We had cucumbers both raw and pickled, and we ate the raw ones as the Russians do, skin and all, like apples. We had woodcock in sour-cream gravy, and slices of ham, cheese and Bologna, served with little hillocks of caviar decorated with crisp circlets of onion and hard-boiled eggs. In the center of the table were large bowls of cookies, chocolate bars, and little tissue-wrapped candies called chocolate bears."[11] Whatever they had to eat, they all recalled the sudden appearance of a German reconnaissance plane—a Focke-Wulf ("Fokker-Wolff") aircraft nicknamed the Stepladder because of its "queer shape"—overhead.[12] Anti-aircraft guns went immediately into action, "fragments from anti-aircraft shells pelt[ing] the table,"[13] a development that put all the correspondents on edge, but apparently not their Russian hosts, who kept on eating, drinking, and chatting.

To the delight of the male reporters, the principal topic of conversation was military strategy, especially the insight that the Germans were deathly afraid of night warfare. In part, this was due to Soviet partisan activity occurring mostly in the dark hours, but it was also that time of day when the Red Army moved its forces from place to place to confuse the Wehrmacht commanders. Bourke-White quotes Dudonov: "When you know the weak points of the enemy you can best them. Because they hate the night attacks, we always thrust at them in the darkness."[14] The Germans had responded to this by lighting the night sky near the front with searchlights, star shells, and other incendiaries, such that the actual forward line of hostility was at times brighter than daylight.

But while this is taking place, one of the Siberians approaches Bourke-White: "As we sat at the table talking, one of the Meat Choppers [the nickname they gave themselves] came up to invite me to waltz to the tune of an accordion. After being whirled around the trees I was breathless, but the soldiers begged me to teach them the latest American dance steps. My efforts to impart the nature of the rhumba, in my muddy slacks and earth-caked shoes, to the accompaniment of the accordion, were greeted with more enthusiasm than the performance merited" (see also endnote 62).[15] Before that a private had ventured forward to present her a bouquet of red poppies "[i]n the name of the entire Red Army, and because of our admiration for your great country."[16]

Phil Jordan had his own poetic memories, recalling: "In the dusk, when the wind came up and the slender birches were swaying like ballerinas, the commander of this division talked while white-coated mess waiters moved among the trees like moths, with hot food and cold drinks in their hands."[17] The correspondents' champion for this Wednesday's drinking contest turned out to be the *Times*'s Cy Sulzberger. On this occasion three kinds of vodka were available: "the common white variety, which has a slight gasoline taste; Georgian vodka, which is pale yellow and considered a great delicacy; and brown hunter's vodka, which feels after each swallow as though small fires are being lighted inside."[18] Sulzberger ("Fill up the gasoline glass") was matched against Anurov, the censor, following each vodka shot with one of brandy. "The censor had broken into flowery speeches in English, and soon Cy was accomplishing miraculous orations in a mixture of English, Russian, Greek, and Turkish."[19] Although he managed not to pass out, his hangover the next morning was epic.

Sulzberger recalled this bout well and rejoiced in it with a certain degree of pride but placed it on Thursday evening in Dorogobuzh, whereas Bourke-White has him passed out the night before at the field hospital near Dudno.

> That evening is my turn on the vodka rotation list. The Russians like to drink competitively and, after the usual toasts, a glass is placed before me and another before a major general, then equal drinks are measured out. We each destroy two bottles

of vodka and are well into a horrible variety of Crimean brandy when my adversary passes out. He is carried to his straw mattress and spends most of the night vomiting over himself. Some hours later he wakes up, lights a *papyrossi* [a Russian cigarette], and sets his bed on fire. I try to find my way out to take a leak, miss the door, and almost break my fist on the concrete wall before a kind sentry helps me. Thank God my turn is over.[20]

In any case, after the feast gradually winds down and dusk thickens into evening and finally blackens to night, the tour of the front begins. Everyone is warned to stay directly on the marked path as they tour several field gun emplacements because the rest of the battlefield is still heavily mined. But darkness, rain, and increasing fusillades of artillery finally curtail the enthusiasm of the Soviets for escorting the unarmed press corps any closer. Thus the tour ends, and the journalists' desire to be on the actual front line, as were their Russian counterparts routinely, goes understandably unmet. By this time it is well after sunset and the evening's light show is well underway. Haldane was realistic: "We all of us wanted to go there, but were not allowed to. The party was too large and the soldiers thought the noise we might make would attract the enemy's attention—and his fire."[21]

The night's battle was one that Caldwell would not forget, vividly recalling and retelling it in his posttrip books. Here, only a kilometer from the front, there was a continuous din of artillery and mortar fire, to which Caldwell insisted he had grown accustomed. Carefully husbanded by the Siberians, who warned them not to stray off the path, he and several of the correspondents inched frontward:

> After another half hour the night was suddenly turned into day by the appearance of hundreds of flares and rockets over no-man's-land. The Siberians said it looked as if something might be starting up and urged me to leave the grove. We crossed the pasture and went to a hilltop three quarters of a mile in the rear. From there the whole front could be seen for a distance of fifty miles in both directions. Flares and rockets by the scores were continuing in the air, and it was possible to tell time by my watch from the garish light.[22]

How long this lasts he never tells us, but Philip Jordan corroborates Caldwell's night: "I was able to watch these [star shells] until early dawn, and there is not a moment of the night when one wasn't in the sky."[23] As the day dawns Caldwell is still there, painting a mesmerizing scene: "The lights hung over the front all night, and the guns did not become silent until dawn. The earth lay strangely still and quiet when the sun rose. The only movement I could detect anywhere was that of Red Army trucks that continued to plow and plunge through the deep mud, carrying supplies of food, ammunition, and fresh troops forward, and returning with loads of wounded who had fallen somewhere along that whiteway of a front during the night."[24] It is evident that the group did not overnight at or near the Siberians' camp, but rather got back into their vehicles and motored on.

Sometime during the dark the convoy pulled out, headed for its night's lodgings, somewhere to the south. But being as far behind schedule as they were and having to travel without headlights for self-protection, it was unclear to everyone where that would be. Several of the men suggested they sleep in the cars, but the Foreign Office representatives rejected that idea. After several hours in a dismal downpour, they came to a halt around midnight, some sixteen hours after their day had begun back near Yartsevo. Haldane describes the travelers: "Stiff and weary, I got out among more dripping firs, undergrowth, and grass, in the pitch darkness. None of us had the remotest idea where we were. A short squelchy path came to an end with the opening of a tent-flap. Inside the large, roomy tent was a cozily-burning wood-stove; the air was dry and sweet with the smell of the glowing logs."[25] They had reached another field hospital and were given a tent of their own with stretchers for beds and straw-filled bags for pillows. Haldane fell asleep immediately, as did Sulzberger; the Caldwells found a private corner beneath "a blazing poster of red and black" portraying "a snake, bent into the shape of a swastika, and with Hitler's mustache, . . . being bayoneted by a looming Red soldier, and the slogan read: DEATH TO THE FASCIST VIPER"; but the more intrepid of the group stayed up several hours more with the nurses, drinking tea.

Thursday, September 18: Dissension in the Ranks

Dissension, as it turned out, had begun to rattle the ranks of the press corps. Some were getting fed up with the hardships and the lack of hard news since important diplomatic events were about to take place back in Moscow, where Lord Beaverbrook and Averell Harriman were arriving from London to meet with Stalin. Some, the Americans in particular, wanted to stick it out in hopes that there would be a crowning moment. Bourke-White, many of whose camera lenses and shutters were gradually becoming nonfunctional, still sided with the "front faction," arguing that photographers' needs were different from those of journalists. Moats heard a different story upon the correspondents' return, apparently with malicious glee: "Margaret Bourke-White, who felt she hadn't taken enough pictures, burst into tears. All in all, it must have been a pretty little scene."[26] Thursday morning at the infirmary, as one of the nurses served them breakfast, they reached a decision to stay the course and not turn east on the Moscow highway. "Everyone's spirits rose, and the vote was cast to continue on through the mud and rain and see whatever the Russians were willing to show us."[27]

Nonetheless, it *had* rained heavily all night. Werth recalled what confronted them in the morning: "the mossy ground among the trees was like a swamp, and the roads were worse than ever," and so they headed south. It was supposed to have been simply a day to get somewhere else. But it turned into another one of mud slogging. Their Soviet chaperones again prudently arranged for support services. A platoon of Siberian troops rode behind the convoy in an uncovered transport. Whenever one of the coupes got mired down the Siberians would hop out to push, pull, and heave until progress was reestablished.

Their first brief stop was the collective farm at which they were supposed to have had a meal and a good night's sleep the previous night. This particular *sovkhoz* was a vegetable farm cum dairy. Here the caravan picked up a pair of hitchhikers, two captains headed to the rail stop at Dorogobuzh, one of whom rode with Werth and implored him to spread the word that without Western aid, he didn't think the Red Army could hold out much longer. Without foreign aid, winter was their only hope. After a brief respite along the Moscow–Smolensk highway, the group headed south again toward the Dnieper. After dropping off the two officers, the convoy's next task was to cross the river, but the Germans had destroyed the bridge, and all that was available now was a temporary crossing somewhere in the night. Werth captures the mood perfectly: "Sliding, skating, and plunging into dark pools, our little car moved on. We felt it sliding down an embankment, and then it seemed to swim gently across the river. It was actually a temporary bridge, scarcely wider than the car itself. Wherever we looked, there was water, or some of it was mud, wet deep mud. But after another hysterical scream of the engine and an upward leap, we felt we were on solid ground at last, somewhere on the other side of the river."[28] In *Smolensk,* Caldwell recalls another frightening automobile moment during the trek, though he locates it no more definitively than by saying it occurred "at the front." Again, as is often the case with Caldwell's anecdotes, it seems to have been intercalated into his novel and provides a representative example of Caldwell's propensity for intertwining the comic with the deadly serious and grotesque. After observing how seriously Soviet citizens follow commands to the letter, Caldwell narrates:

> The automobile in which Margaret and I were riding with three Russians was caught between the guard gates on a railway crossing. We had passed under the

> first gate when suddenly both gates were lowered, trapping us between them. From a distance we could see a passenger train approaching at a fairly rapid rate of speed.
>
> The Russians jumped out of the car and demanded that the gates be raised so we could get off the tracks. The crossing tender, who had been instructed to lower the gates when a train approached, recited his orders with unwavering firmness and severity.
>
> Everyone ranted and raved, but the crossing tender merely repeated that he could not under any circumstances disobey orders. One of the Russians got the crank from under the seat and threatened to hit him over the head with it if he did not raise the gates. One of the other Russians ran to a car that had just arrived and found a Red Army colonel. The colonel jumped out, sized up the situation, and shouted at the crossing tender in his most authoritative voice. Another Russian came running up and pointed to his government decoration—the Order of Lenin. None of this did any good.
>
> During all this time the train was fast approaching the crossing. We started to crash the car through the gate, but the crossing tender warned that he would report all of us for willfully destroying state property if we damaged the gate. One of the Russians attempted to take matters into his own hands and raise the barrier, but we were warned that the militia would be called and that we would be placed under arrest on the spot for interfering with the duties of a state employee.
>
> The train came roaring around the bend only a few hundred feet away with whistle screaming. We pushed the car alongside the track, barely managing to get far enough to the side to escape being hit by the locomotive. As soon as the train had passed, the crossing tender raised the gates and congratulated us for having escaped with our lives and for having saved our car.[29]

The fact that this vignette did not appear as a newspaper story in *PM*—since so much of *Smolensk* is refashioned from *PM* pieces—and Bourke-White does not mention it in *Shooting* (nor does any other correspondent in a memoir) suggests that it was either dramatically embellished, hearsay, or made up.

Dorogobuzh was an infamous town in the annals of war. Napoleon had tried to entice the retreating Russian army into a battle there in 1812. In July 1941 the Luftwaffe had razed the community, and now the Red Army occupied it for strategic purposes. Where once ten thousand citizens had lived, there were now but a hundred or so remaining. Charlotte Haldane christened it Russia's Guernica. Werth's description of his surreal experience of driving through it in the pitch-dark night on the way to an army camp for the evening is steeped in rhetorical flourishes, literariness, and moodiness: "On either side of us were the black shapes of houses; but through all their windows the dark sky was showing. They were not faces, but skulls with empty sockets—burned-out houses. Houses of different shapes and sizes, but always the same—the same dark, deathly sky showing through their windows. The gun was still booming in the distance. A street, and then another street, and then another; and still it was the same; burned out, burned out, dead."[30] Werth and his companions, tromping through a heavy rain, entered a deserted house, but it proved inadequate as shelter, and so they moved on.

> It looked as though we were driving along the white walls of some giant castle; and only by concentrating did I realize that the "walls" were the night sky, with the trees outlined against it. Each tuft of trees, with the white walls towering above them, looked like the entrance to a rich country manor—to a château in France. What were all these mad optical illusions? . . . Groping over the roots of pine trees, and over some steps, we entered a narrow door. There were two small rooms there; and sacks of straw lay on the floor.[31]

Even at this late hour and in this devastated outpost there was a meal ready for them, albeit an impoverished one of "some *zakuski* and a vodka bottle and some minced-meat cutlets," or at least so Werth recalled.[32] Carroll remembered "an excellent dinner of hors d'oeuvres, minced meat cutlets, canned eggplant, and *smetana*, a rich sour cream."[33]

Friday, September 19: Into the Heart of It

Friday was to be the much-anticipated tour of the battleground at Yelnya. This area southeast of Smolensk had been quickly overwhelmed by the Wehrmacht during its blitzkrieg phase of June and July. Almost all the villages had been burned out, and the residents who hadn't fled had been rounded up and taken to German work camps. The Nazis reduced Yelnya from a town of fifteen thousand to a pile of rubble where only a several hundred survived. Then during the Red Army's late-August resurgence, this single sector had been recaptured—with bayonets and hand grenades—at a great loss of men and matériel on both sides. This had provided a great psychological lift to the Red Army, to the Communist Party, and to the Russian people; if only briefly, Yelnya became emblematic of the strength of the Russian people and its army. The last serious fighting had tapered off around September 5. The Soviet leaders in Moscow, who for so long had denied any direct Western press coverage of the war, must have seen this as a serendipitous window for a great propaganda sally. While the correspondents had been hoping to get to the actual front during the trip, and almost had, the Russian Press Bureau wanted to get them to Yelnya, which had been cleared for "tourism" barely days before. Tragically, with the onset of

Operation Typhoon, Hitler's drive toward Moscow, on October 2, Yelnya was quickly attacked and encircled once again, trapping thousands of Red Army men and women in an encircling Nazi embrace.

Yelnya lies about twenty-five miles due south of Dorogobuzh, and between the two were two nearly totally destroyed villages, Ushakovo, six miles from Yelnya, and Ustinovka, a mile farther south. Ushakovo had disappeared. Their local guide was to be a Colonel Revzin, an actual veteran of the battle, whom Haldane discovered to speak near-perfect French. He had been a professor of geology in civilian life. Except for a single wooden birdhouse in a birch tree,[34] all that remained was an extensive German trench system, a "lunar landscape." Werth described it: "There wasn't a house standing; not a fragment of a house, not a single plank standing. An old tin samovar, lying on the ground, was the only remnant of the actual village. From the bare patches along the road one could roughly imagine where the houses had stood."[35] But the detritus of war remained: "Here were scattered German tin hats, some with bullet-holes."[36] It may have been here that Haldane actually found her blood-smeared and brain-caked helmet. Bourke-White recalled the specimens the Caldwells collected as sacred relics:

> I heard Erskine shouting to me from the top of the hill. He was waving a German helmet, so I picked up one of my own. There were plenty to choose from; hundreds of them, savagely gashed and broken or riddled with bullets, were lying around in heaps. The metal they were made of was thin, much lighter than the heavy mushroom-shaped casques that protected Russian heads. I selected one that was fairly intact. The owner's name, Herbst, was lettered in white inside, and a single bullet-hole over the left ear showed how Herr Herbst had met his end. I have the helmet at home now, in Connecticut.[37]

Nearby was a large tumulus over which bloomed a blanket of purple-flowered morning glories; a coverlet of fir branches had been laid on top. A wooden fence encircled the mound and bore a tin plaque shaped like a Red Army star commemorating the fallen Russian soldiers that read, in Werth's translation: "Soldiers of the Red Army who died at Ushakovo fighting for Country, Honour, and Freedom. July 28th to September 1st."[38] The German dead had been dumped into shell holes and into their own trenches.

The German trench was remarkable in its extent and complexity. Carroll writes, "Four terraces had been cut into the side of a hill about seventy feet high. On each terrace was a row of dugouts, strongly reinforced with pine logs and sandbags. In the shelter of the hill they had put their guns and a tank which had become immobile but whose cannon they used to augment their artillery."[39] In

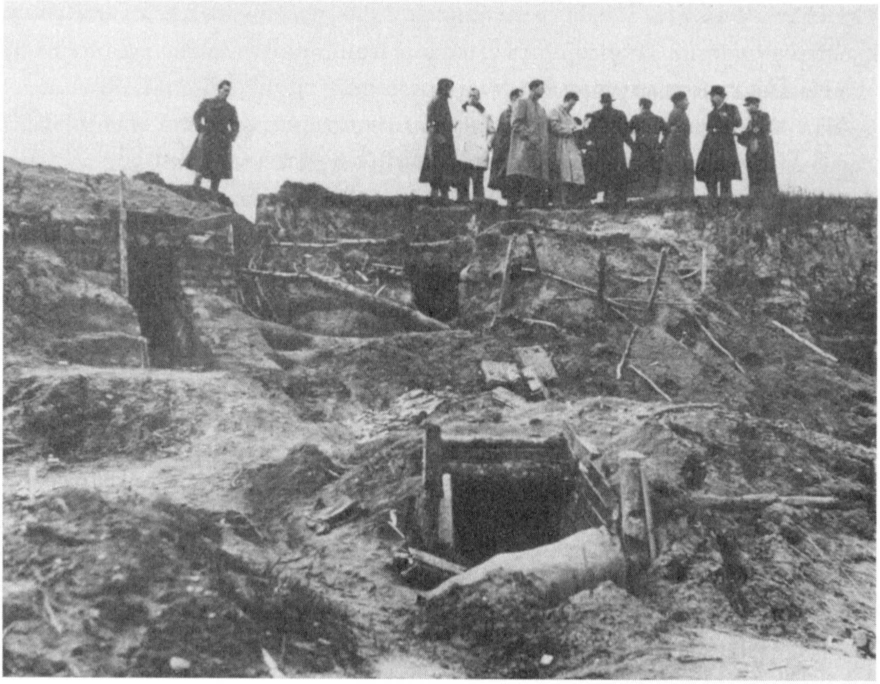

FIGURE 39. "Where the Germans Dug In" (From *Shooting the Russian War*; photo © Estate of Margaret Bourke-White/Licensed by VAGA, New York, N.Y.; courtesy of Syracuse University Libraries)

fact, these trenches must have been relatively livable. Werth again: "The insides of the dugouts had been furnished with beds and tables and chairs stolen from the neighbouring villages. A large oil-stove suggested that the Germans were already making preparations for winter conditions. Here again many German tin hats were lying about, and biscuit cartons, and empty vodka bottles, and German illustrated newspapers only two or three weeks old."[40] Bourke-White adds, "In the dugouts were telephones and supply dumps. Above on the hilltop were networks of trip wires leading to mines, and heavy cannon camouflaged under woven branches."[41] Her photograph of the scene, which she described as a Zuñi village, captures all the correspondents and two of the Russian guides gathered on the ridge above the Ushakovo warrens engaged in animated conversation during a light rain, while a single Russian stands alone to the their right, his hands in his pockets, staring grimly into these death traps.

The next village, Ustinovka, had been wiped out as well, but here several peasants had returned to dig the potatoes that had been planted before the

German onslaught. In fact, in many areas, vast fields of flax and buckwheat had started going to seed because there was no one to harvest them. In one hut Haldane found "a young mother . . . preparing a meal for three little children."[42] Bourke-White saw a woman carrying hot charcoals home from a neighbor's fire and wondered what she was toting them in: "The shape was familiar. She was bringing home hot coals in a Nazi helmet."[43] One other inhabitant of this village grabbed everyone's attention:

> A blind old woman. I saw her wandering about the road, carrying a few dirty rags, a rusty pail, and a tattered sheepskin. She would go from one spot to another, laying down her possessions for a few minutes—her only possessions—and stare with her white, blind eyes. Then she would pick up her belongings again and wander on. She was here when the village was shelled, and she went mad. "*Babushka*!" (grandmother), one of the officers with us called to her, but she paid no attention and only clutched her possessions closer to her stooping, wretched body, and wandered on, her bare muddy feet wading through the mud. One of the boys who came up to us said she slept in her shattered hut, and they gave her potatoes, and sometimes soldiers who passed through the village would give her something, though she never asked for anything. She never uttered any articulate words, except the word "*Cherti*" ("the devils").[44]

Beyond the village, they found further evidence of German presence, a posted warning: "the village of Petraninov is a zone of military operations[.] For this reason the population is ordered to leave this place by eight o'clock tonight and go to Yelnya or farther to the rear. Any civilians still in the village after that hour will be shot on sight."[45]

Their final stop was the town of Yelnya itself, now mostly ashes and chimney stacks, and a few damaged survivors. Bourke-White's two published photos of the town capture this desolation. One is of a symmetric array of three ruined chimneys; the other, shot from a low angle, is of a pair of Russian sentries guarding what remains of the Yelnya cathedral. To the left stands a chimney stack with a fireplace connected to it; in the center is a steepled tower, around the top of which protrudes an octagonal observation deck; to the right, and farthest away, crouches a low, iconic, "coppery-green" onion-topped church. It had become a dormitory for the soldiers.

In Yelnya's streets Philip Jordan found a variety of poignant items: "Here there is a samovar with a bullet hole through its jagged zinc sides, here the remains of the clock by which some child once knew when it was time to go to school, here a garden hoe or a piece of shattered bed on which some innocent lay down to rest."[46] Seeing the remains of what had once been Yelnya,

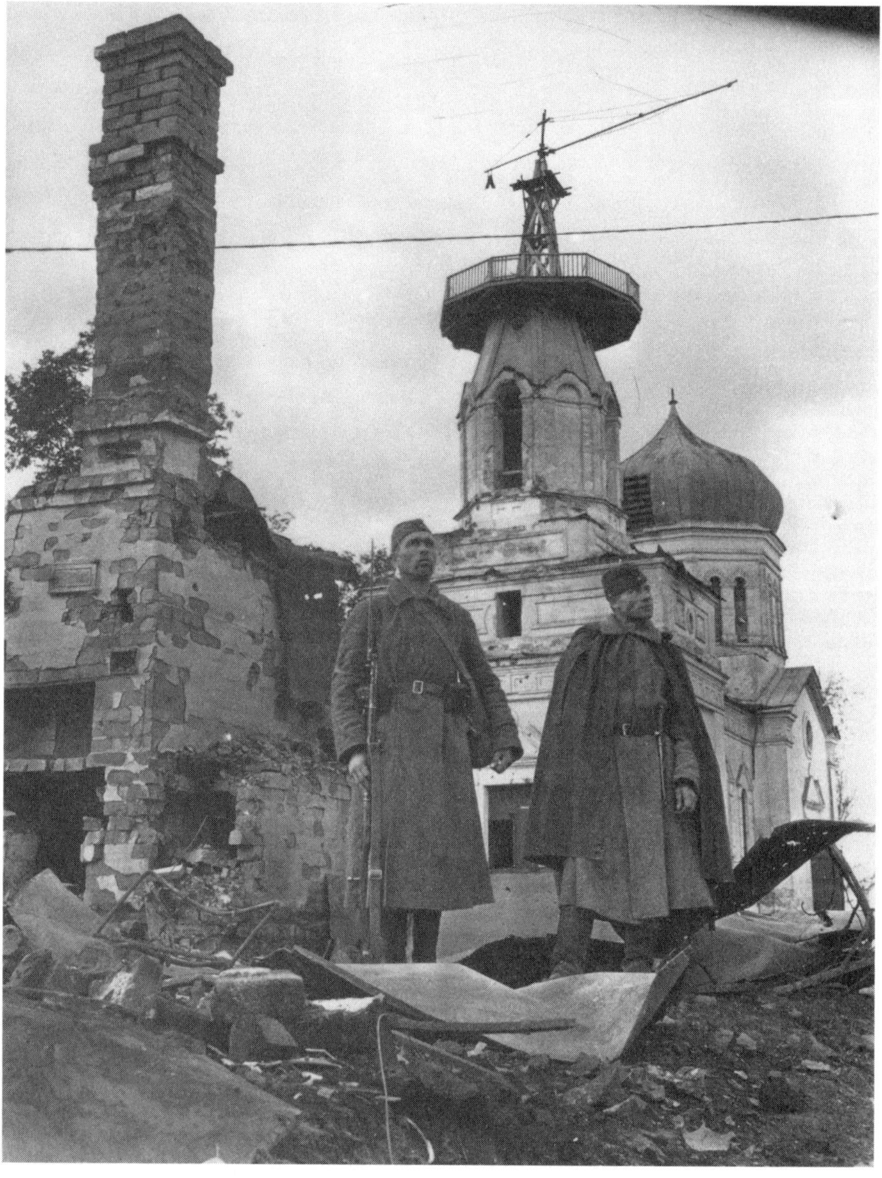

FIGURE 40. "The Cathedral of Yelnya" (From *Shooting the Russian War*; photo © Estate of Margaret Bourke-White/Licensed by VAGA, New York, N.Y.; courtesy of Syracuse University Libraries)

Henry Cassidy thought of Paris, where he'd been a correspondent when the Germans invaded in June 1940. By contrast, the Nazis had treated the area with kid gloves: "There, after the fall of Paris, I found the battle had passed swiftly and lightly over most places, punching only a few holes in the village here, wrecking a crossroads there. Around Yelnya, all was consumed in a frightful, all-devastating struggle between two giants, fighting savagely to the death."[47]

It is not possible at this remove to know how Caldwell himself behaved on the battlefield at Yelnya, whether he was an entranced tourist and relic-gatherer or an insightful and thoughtful war journalist. But the narrator of Caldwell's *All-Out on the Road to Smolensk* is devastated. He has now reached the forbidding center of this holocaust and come face-to-face with death itself. He observes, "I walked over the battlefield for several hours looking for some sign of life, but all was dead."[48] No crows. No vultures. No homeless dogs. Even the field mice in the dugouts were dead. So he takes an inventory, and in this inventory the combatants come back to life in the mind of the reader. Here, Caldwell is no longer writing of his own experiences as do the other diarists, nor attempting to create an accurate account of the trip, and he is not even a journalist at this moment. Caldwell rehabilitates the individual lives of these faceless soldiers through the detritus and impedimenta of their deaths:

> They had filled their dugouts with many of the comforts of home. All of them had wheat straw on the floors, and most of them had straw-stuffed mattresses. Some of them had books on shelves; the shelves had been carved in the clay walls. There were vodka bottles, both full and empty. There were musical instruments and games.
>
> In one trench, laundry was still hanging on a line—two shirts, several socks, and a piece of material that looked as if it had once been a tablecloth. In another trench I found a pair of boxing gloves, a harmonica, a samovar, and a wall calendar with heavy pencil marks drawn through all the dates of the month except the last nine.
>
> The battlefield was covered with all the odds and ends of war and peace. There were torn and shattered gas masks and helmets: there were Iron Crosses and regimental insignia; there were letters from home and photographs of children. There were belts, boots, swords, pistols, rifles, cigarettes, magazines, buttons, pencils, coins, diaries, bottles, first-aid kits, tins of fish, wristwatches, dispatch cases, key-rings, pocket knives, can openers, pocket books, bank books, finger rings, blood-soaked bandages, unused cartridge clips, and rain-soaked bread.[49]

The closest he is able to approach an actual human being is the only marked grave he finds on the battlefield.

> On a mound of earth under what once had been a tree I stumbled over a carefully lettered marker on the grave of a German soldier. The board had been hewn from

> a birch tree, and an inscription had been burned on it with a red-hot iron. Since the marker had been lettered and erected with such care, it was evident that the German had died and been buried before the storm and furore of battle.
>
> The birch marker was inscribed:
>
> In Memory of Max Goerighter
> Died September 2, 1941
>
> Of all the thousands of Germans and Russians who died in the Battle of Yelnya, only Max Goerighter's grave is marked. When I was there, the slender birch post over the grave had fallen down, and I pushed it into the soft earth as firmly as I could before I left.[50]

We must guess whether Caldwell pushed the grave marker into the earth to erase Goerighter's Nazi subjectivity or pushed it into the earth more uprightly and firmly so as to restore his basic humanity.

In this ambiguous act at the German soldier's grave, Caldwell embraces the reality and horror of war, leaving it for us to parse. He never tells us his thoughts. Was his act of acquiring of Herbst's Wehrmacht helmet simply one of youthful exuberance, thoughtlessness, souvenir hunting? Were the German war dead less meaningful than the Russian dead? Or was it an acknowledgment that, in the end, all war is a singularity and he was Goerighter's and Herbst's personal witness? Now, walking back across the battlefield to join his wife and fellow correspondents, he had already begun his journey home.

Friday Night and All Day Saturday: Homeward Bound

As dusk approached, the correspondents climbed back into their small cars and were chauffeured east some ten miles to the small village of Islednivo, where a final banquet was to be held, and a final night's sleep on the road was to be endured. For Werth, the accommodations suggested a scene from a Turgenev novel, "an old country house, with an old overgrown park round it, and a green, slimy pond at the other end."[51]

As usual, it was a lavish spread: "caviar, hors d'oeuvres, ham, and *chachlik*, or lamb grilled on the spit, with vodka, Soviet champagne, and Caucasian wines."[52] Werth gave a twenty-minute speech in Russian, thanking everyone he could think of. This so impressed one of the political commissars that he insisted Werth must have a *russkaya duhsa* (a Russian soul) and offered further toasts. At this point the details become conflicting, but according to Haldane's 1950 memoir, the banquet, though it had begun "in an atmosphere of the warmest cordiality, and the alcohol was unlimited," degenerated into what she called an "orgy,"[53] though it in fact was only one more drunken debauch.

Haldane, offended by the drunkenness, wrote nothing of the affair in *Newsreel*, a book clearly written as a pro-Soviet puff piece. In order to protect the leftist cause, she avoided the matter entirely by summarizing, "That night we started our trip back to Moscow,"[54] which was only indirectly true. Even Cassidy summed up the post-Yelnya tour with a curt, "From Yelnya we turned back through Viazma to Moscow."[55] Bourke-White and Caldwell each terminate their story at Yelnya. But apparently there was more to it. With razor-sharp memory, Haldane wrote of the evening in *Truth Will Out*, her later memoir:

> It was two o'clock in the morning before we were put to bed; as usual, all of us in one large dormitory. (I never undressed throughout the trip, but slept each night in my clothes.) By this time, with a few exceptions, everyone was roaring drunk. Suddenly, someone in the bed behind my cot, was noisily and violently sick. The odour was, naturally, extremely unpleasant, and several of the men began yelling for someone to come and clean up the mess. After about ten minutes, a little Russian A.T.S. [Auxiliary Territorial Service] girl arrived with a mop, a pail, and a candle. In the darkness, she could not at first find the cot and the culprit. When she did so, she explained in horrified tones: "Oh, it's the comrade political commissar!" The language of the Americans, at this revelation, can be better imagined than printed![56]

She was so discomfited that she and Vernon Bartlett found their way back to the banquet room where they spent the remainder of the night dozing fitfully while the Russians tried to apologize. They were terribly embarrassed. In the morning, before anyone else was awake, "Some military men in different uniforms, those of the N.K.V.D., arrived, very early, and took away the commissar, under arrest."[57] Clearly the Werth and Haldane versions don't agree, and since she was writing nearly two decades later and he within a few days of the event, she could have the chronology confused with an earlier drinking bout but is assured in her writing about it nevertheless.

Saturday (September 20) was to be the last push, but because the cars were so beat up, their springs sagging, and because the roads were so slow due to the effects of the last several days of inclement weather and the increased military traffic, they didn't reach Vyazma until early afternoon. After a brief lunch, this one without alcohol, they were ready for the final leg east, but they still didn't reach Moscow until after midnight.

It had been a long trip, and everyone sensed that it had, on balance, been a success. They had seen and experienced more, and spoken to more people, than they had in Moscow since the war had begun in June. And in the end, even Bartlett, the grumpy curmudgeon—if that mantle didn't belong to Cholerton—gleaned something positive from his experience despite the privations of the wet and muddy tour. He had been especially vexed about the distance he was forced to keep from ordinary Russian citizens by his Soviet minders, who prevented their attitudes about the West from drifting too far from the official party line:

> These occasional contacts [of a Muscovite man on the street with a Western journalist] must have destroyed some illusions about the bourgeoisie, and the Red Army has fewer inhibitions than the civilian citizen of the Soviet Union. It was a genuine relief to escape from the silences of Moscow to the talkativeness of officers in the Red Army. During a week in the Smolensk sector in September 1941 I found these officers extremely hospitable and friendly; if a sentry with a fixed bayonet would always follow any one of us who wandered off for a few moments into the surrounding wood he was only taking a laudable, if embarrassing, military precaution. On the whole, the Russian soldier is destroying the inhibitions of the Russian politician.[58]

It had been an exhausting trip, one that permanently altered the balance of power between the Soviet Press Office and the Western journalists. Once they had sniffed, heard, and glimpsed the smells and sounds and terrors of war—the reality of it, as distinct from the pabulum of the official communiqués—the correspondents would never again settle for less. The weeks of to-and-fro battles around Yelnya claiming the lives of some seventy-five thousand souls had forever shifted the delicate balance between the Red Army and the Wehrmacht. The German blitzkrieg had been temporarily slowed just enough that Hitler would never achieve his goal of occupying Moscow. Within weeks, further parlays of diplomats led to improved understanding and communication between the Soviet leaders and the Allies, and the Red Army gathered the necessary footholds and momentum to right the Soviet war machine, so much so that there would be less need for the self-serving Sovinformburo prevarications of the initial three months of the war.

That their journalism was held in contempt by some is evident in the observations of Curzio Malaparte, an Italian newspaperman embedded in the Wehrmacht forces in Ukraine in 1941.[59] While there is no evidence that the Western reporters in Moscow or the Soviet reporters on their front-line assignments were aware of Malaparte's work, he knew something of theirs. In the introduction to *The Volga Rises in Europe*, a 1943 collection of his 1941–42 dispatches, he observes, after first commenting that he is the only Italian war correspondent on the eastern front, from Murmansk to the Black Sea:

> Even the British and American correspondents, who were forbidden by the Soviet authorities to go to the front, had remained in Moscow, with the result that their

> writings were characterized by the forced tone, the episodic manner, the vague language and rhetoric of men who write from hearsay and not from personal experience. To confirm this, one need only read the dispatches which the American writer Erskine Caldwell, author of *God's Little Acre* and *Tobacco Road*, subsequently assembled in a volume entitled *Moscow under Fire*. (10–11)[60]

Malaparte insisted that "[t]he only objective writing on the German war against Russia came from an Italian" and that he "did not undertake to describe events of which I had no firsthand knowledge, nor did I stoop to make propaganda in favor of one side or the other."[61]

Even so, this visit by eleven members of the Western press, armed only with notebooks and cameras, to sectors of active combat near the western front was groundbreaking.[62] Not only did those nine men and two women finally experience war almost firsthand, but the trip established a precedent and created a blueprint for what Western journalists expected in terms of open access to the war they were supposed to be covering.

One of the most important ramifications, evident in subsequent news dispatches and feature articles and books, was that the Russian army was not one that would be rolled over easily. It became clear that the USSR could, with immediate and accelerated Allied aid, block Hitler's progress. These journalists' observations and reports, published in newspapers and magazines, broadcast over radio, and delivered in person on the lecture circuit, influenced decision makers—Winston Churchill, Franklin Roosevelt, the exiled Charles de Gaulle—and ultimately contributed in significant fashion to extensively ramped-up Lend-Lease aid to Russia and to the establishment of a belated second front against Hitler. In his history of the twentieth-century Western foreign press, *Foreign Correspondence*, John Hohenberg writes that until this trip the Moscow correspondents had been reliant on either the official communiqués or articles translated by their secretaries from the government-controlled Soviet press: "In view of all the limitations, it is remarkable that the world knew as much as it did about the condition of the Russian people as they approached the darkest years in their history. As for the outlook from Moscow, it was clouded with doubt and suspicion."[63]

But once on the tour, the correspondents were strongly influenced by the credibility of the Red Army officers recruited to provide on-site press briefings, such as Major-General Vasily Sokolovsky in Vyazma: "[T]hey began reporting things differently. Carroll, for one, vigorously disputed the view, prevalent at the time, that the Russians would be finished by Christmas. He wrote for the UP that the Russians by the spring of 1942 would still be resisting and gathering strength. The whole tone of the world press began to change."[64] The result,

Hohenberg concludes, is that no one of importance again asserted that the Russians were defeated.

In light of this it is odd how little Caldwell and Bourke-White made of this trip in their autobiographies. In *Portrait of Myself,* Bourke-White alludes to it only once, and briefly: "At the front, which was then near Smolensk, I made the acquaintance of what Russian war lore knows as General Mud. We traveled to the front over rivers of maple icing turned to glue, along what were once known as roads. We drove through plains scattered with helmets of the dead, and battlefields that looked like the end of the world."[65] Caldwell mentions the junket in neither of his autobiographies, *Call It Experience* (1951) or *With All My Might* (1987). Presumably, he had covered it, exhaustively in his mind, in *All-Out on the Road to Smolensk* and *All Night Long.* Apparently there was no need to rehash these final pleasant months with Bourke-White. Within a year they were estranged, never to see each other again.

CHAPTER 8

Getting Out ★ The Road Home

The final phase of this tedious and sometimes dangerous journey for Caldwell and Bourke-White began, Caldwell writes in *All-Out on the Road to Smolensk,* with a series of stirring arguments with the railway authorities in order to obtain tickets on the Moscow–Archangel line. Privations are relative. Once on the train the couple's biggest concerns related to getting enough food and achieving a modicum of comfort over the week-long trip (Bourke-White has it at three days in *Shooting the Russian War*). In *Smolensk,* Caldwell applies his well-honed skills as a travel writer to the trip by observing his fellow passengers, the makeup of the rolling stock, the land outside drifting past the windows, his adventures at the station stops along the way, the increasingly wintry weather, and their own discomfort, since only second-class accommodations had been available.

Archangel itself lay across an icy estuary from the railroad terminus, which the train reached just as the sun set. From there the passengers had to step across windswept tracks to a muddy wharf and then cross from it to a floating dock "on a narrow plank that seemed no wider than a piece of string over the icy water."[1] The lighter that was to take them into Archangel soon stopped dead in the water with engine trouble. It took a frigid hour or so to complete the repairs. *Smolensk* concludes with the Caldwells safely in Archangel in early October: "We were two degrees under the Arctic Circle and ready to begin our tussle with the arctic winter on our way to America."[2] That Caldwell had already begun to plan the construction of *All-Out on the Road to Smolensk* is evident from the fact that he transcribed this final chapter almost word-for-word from the concluding October 1 entry in his edited-for-publication diary, *Moscow Under Fire,* then tacked on the concluding phrase "on our way to America."[3]

Of course there was more to their actual return to the United States than appears in *Smolensk,* but for that we have to turn to Bourke-White's *Shooting*

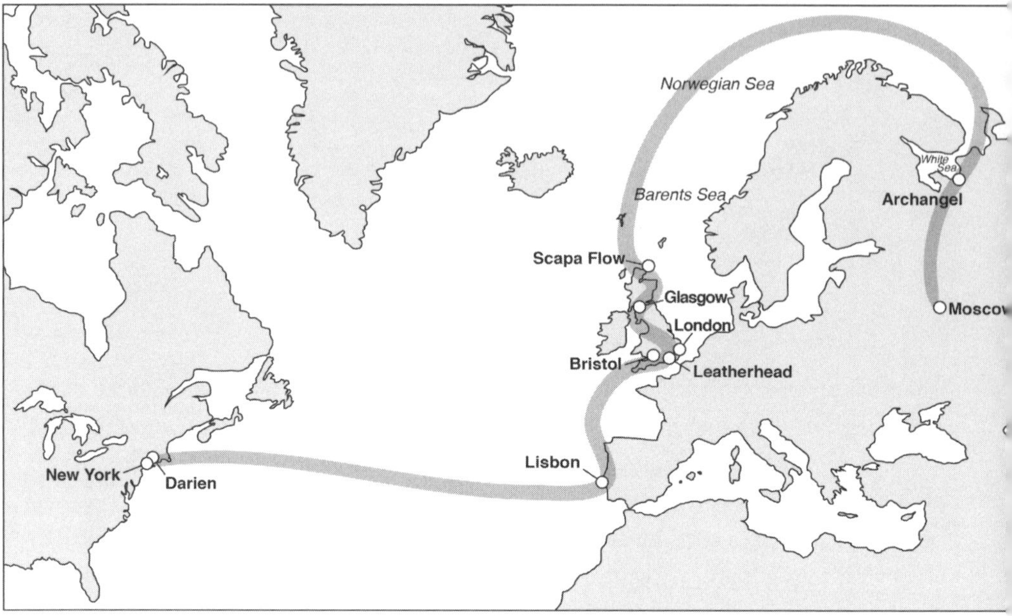

FIGURE 41. The return journey (September–October 1941), Moscow to Darien (Map by Charles Lindemuth, www.mepainter.com)

the Russian War. There is last-minute packing, hurried developing of negatives, giving away of clothing and other belongings, tearful good-byes, and the pièce de résistance:

> Then there was the last great banquet at VOKS with all our friends invited: Eisenstein, Alexandrov, and Orlova from the movie colony; Eugene Petrov, Elisaveta, and many others from the Union of Soviet Writers; the Mayor of Moscow; the director of the Art Theater; and an assortment of opera singers. Erskine was presented with the most unique gift that it was in their power to give: a collection of captured German insignia which included iron crosses of the first and second class, medals for marksmanship, the insignia of the *Luftwaffe* and Panzer, and the aluminum skull which is the sign of the Death's-Head division.[4]

Bourke-White dispenses with the railroad trip in three brief paragraphs, one of which she devotes to the floral arrangements with which she'd been gifted. But the fog-enshrouded fifteen-day sea journey aboard an 11,000-ton troopship in a twenty-two-ship convoy routed far to the north, then through Scapa Flow in the Orkneys to Glasgow, rates five pages and three photographs—as well it

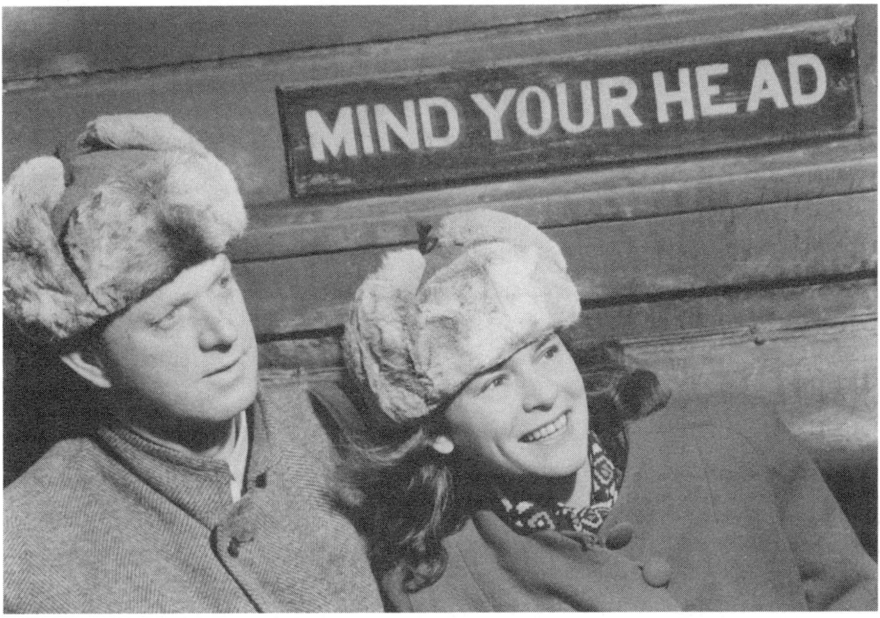

FIGURE 42. "White Sea, 1941" (Christmas card, 1941; also from *Portrait of Myself*; photo © Estate of Margaret Bourke-White/Licensed by VAGA, New York, N.Y.; courtesy of Syracuse University Libraries)

should have. Over the fortnight the convoy had to navigate minefields, suffer Luftwaffe bomber attacks, depth-charge a lurking submarine, and in the end return with only twenty-one ships.

And so *All-Out on the Road to Smolensk* concludes, a journey complete. And so, too, concludes the Caldwell–Bourke-White Moscow venture, a photo-adventure-turned-successful-propaganda-mission. There was other work to be done, other books to write, different war fronts to photograph. Not at the top of their agenda was their marriage, which would also conclude a little over a year later. The Wehrmacht never reached Moscow.

An Alternative Tale of Departure

While both Caldwell and Bourke-White create a narrative of a departure appropriate to their textual goals, there is abundant archival evidence that both accounts are fabulist and faulty. As Bourke-White has it, they hatched their exit plans very late in the game: "'Which do you think will be quicker,' puzzled

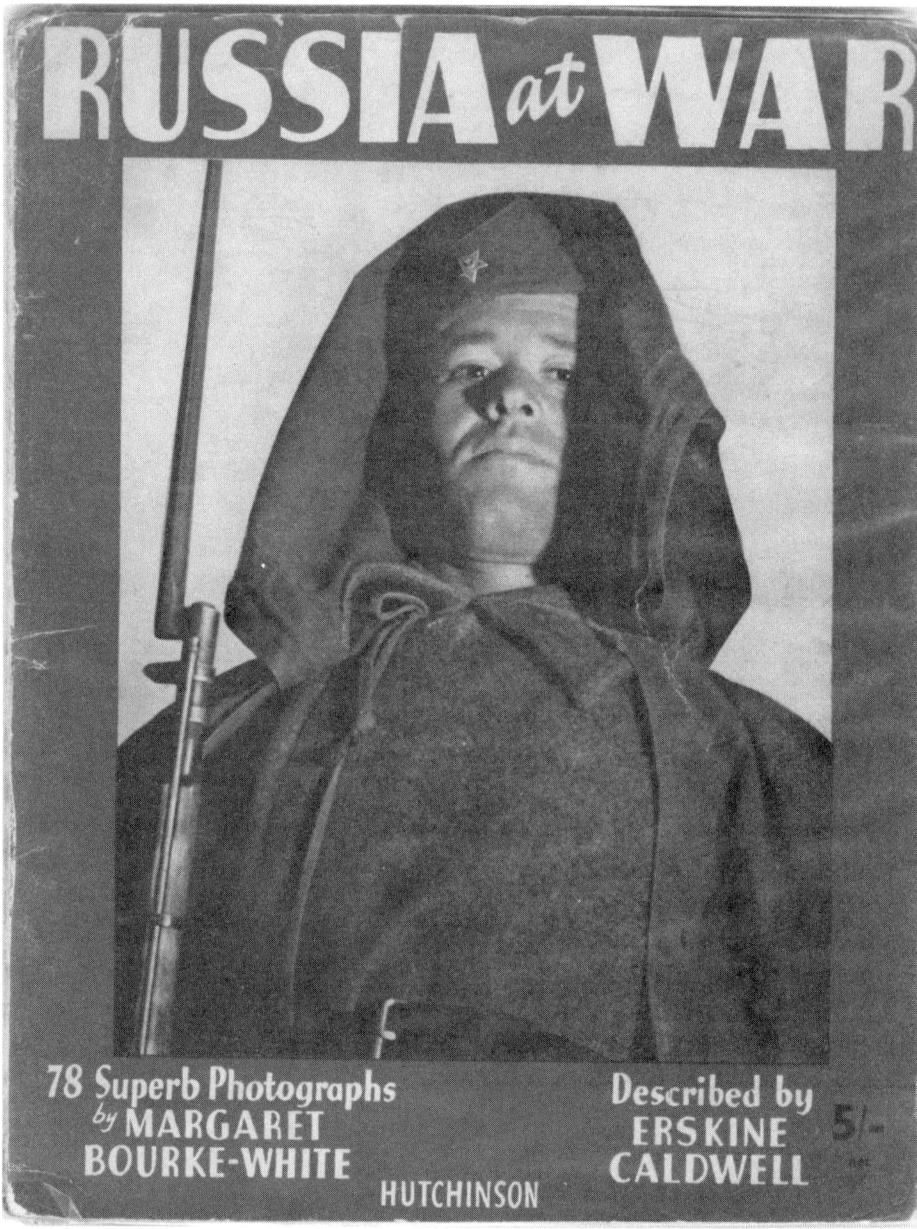

FIGURE 43. Soldier at Dorogobuzh (cover of *Russia at War*; photo © Estate of Margaret Bourke-White/Licensed by VAGA, New York, N.Y.; courtesy of Syracuse University Libraries)

Erskine, 'to go home by way of Australia, or by way of the Arctic Ocean?' We were back in our Moscow hotel suite, and he was lying on the white bear rug, studying all his available maps. . . . It was October, just after our return from the front, and we both had lecture tours starting in less than a month, so we had to get home the fastest possible way."[5] She claims to have gotten Sir Stafford Cripps, Great Britain's ambassador to the USSR, to personally arrange their exit via a British convoy and to obtain special permission to photograph along the way. Ambassador Steinhardt even chips in by cutting red tape. This story turns out to be only marginally accurate.

After the press corps' return from its Smolensk trip, the Caldwells' dazzling corner rooms in the Hotel National featuring a white bearskin rug and a direct view of the Kremlin were soon requisitioned for the use of Lord Beaverbrook. Along with Averell Harriman, he arrived in Moscow on September 28 at the head of an Anglo-American delegation to discuss Lend-Lease scheduling and logistics at the Kremlin for the next four days. Alice Moats, the Caldwells' erstwhile travel companion, had had to transfer from the National to the Metropole on September 17 to accommodate members of the Beaverbrook-Harriman mission, and to judge by her description of the move, it must have been quite an ordeal because "the rooms at the Metropole were dreadful and the food worse."[6] She adds that the chairs in the Caldwells' room were "unusually comfortable."

Actually, as early as August 20 Bourke-White had begun cabling *Life* (collect) about her dissatisfaction in Moscow and her desire to leave as soon as it could be arranged:

> WITHIN NEXT WEEK WILL HAVE PHOTOGRAPHED PRACTICALLY EVERYTHING PERMISSIBLE OF ANY CONSEQUENCE WITHIN 50 MILE RADIUS BELIEVE ADVISABLE PREPARE LEAVE THAT TIME. HAVE COVERED THOROUGHLY AS POSSIBLE CIVILIAN LIFE IN WARTIME TRAINING SHELTERS HARVESTS . . . HAVE REPEATEDLY EMPHASIZED IMPORTANCE PICTURES FRONT BUT SO FAR DEAF EARS.[7]

She suggests a possible early exit through Iran. Her exasperation that there was a hot war unfolding not that far away and that she was unable to shoot it is plain.

Four days later she was even more explicit, though considerably more upbeat, in a cable to Edward Thompson, *Life*'s picture editor:

> All efforts frontwards stalemated. Consider it highly unfortunate that authorities here do not realize vast potential American sympathy that could be aroused by using my photography to the full while eye [*sic*] am here and of course have pointed this out emphatically on many occasions. After fulfilling photographic

> program executing this week feel that any further time spent here wasted unless sudden reversal of policy going front which highly unlikely.

After not getting a satisfactory response, she elected to go over Thompson's head. On August 29 she wired his boss, Wilson Hicks, *Life*'s executive photo editor:

> WANT YOU CABLE IMMEDIATELY YOUR OKAY TO FOLLOW OWN JUDGEMENT ABOUT MEANS OF EXIT AS WILL BE UNPREDICTABLE AND UNDISCUSSABLE.

The problem was that while Bourke-White was trying to negotiate an exit, her editors at *Life* had begun a countercampaign to get her to remain in Moscow longer. On August 31 Thompson cabled her and tried to stroke her ego:

> SUGGEST YOU TRY GET PERMISSIONS DO DEFENSE INDUSTRIES BEYOND URALS WHICH COULD BE DONE UNDER CENSORSHIP SO WOULD BE NO HINT IN PICTURES OF SPECIFIC LOCATION OF PLANTS. ALSO ARRIVAL OF WINTER IN RUSSIA IS SOMETHING NO ONE EVER SEEN IN PHOTOGRAPHS WITH BACKGROUND OF WAR EFFORT SHOULD MAKE TERRIFIC STORY.

Bourke-White responded immediately, firing off a more expensive urgent collect cable both to Thompson and to *Life*'s associate editor, Noel Busch, brimming with new ideas including some secret work to be undertaken during their trip out. At this point Bourke-White seems to have moved on, at least in her own mind, to a more promising and exciting assignment. Several days later, during the first few days of September, she dropped hints about this secret work to Thompson and Busch:

> New important request. Have just received confirmation unusual opportunity secure rare story pictures and text via british. Unable to transmit details but can assure you excellent setup. Completely exclusive and then probably nobody else could have chance duplicate within six months. British wish decision not later one week as time short. Necessary you work on state department authorize us travel under british flag as working journalists as spaso house query to his home office brought routine unconsent caldwell bourkewhite

When she didn't hear back immediately, she shot off another exigent cable to all three men:

> Second important request. Opportunity secure good story pictures and text via british. Please work on state department authorize us travel under british flag as working journalists. British here have gone great pains arranging picture permissions and passage their end but state department gives routine unconsent. Imperative we know midweek caldwell bourkewhite.

A bit later she twitted them for their presumed penury: "this route cheap fast newsworthy also no good reason why rule couldnt be broken from obtaining life story."

In the meantime, Bourke-White added fuel to the fire. One of her principal arguments for leaving as soon as possible was that she was booked for a lecture tour back in the States and had no intention of breaking those engagements, but this seemed to fall on deaf ears. Thompson cabled her that he was working on obtaining diplomatic clearances through "Hyde Park," then reminded her that *Life* wanted her to remain in Moscow.

Even though Thompson had hinted he would try a direct plea to Roosevelt, in frustration on September 2 Bourke-White fired off one final detailed missive, this time adding *Life*'s managing editor John Shaw Billings to the list of recipients. She reiterated that she had no intention of breaking her long-standing twenty-eight-stop lecture tour contract that would begin in November, but compromised by agreeing to stay through September. She also offered to return: "Realize winter story thrilling. Heavy snows not until december can return then." After this lengthy cable, no more was said about extending Bourke-White's stay in the USSR. But nor were any travel arrangements or itineraries suggested.

Caldwell and Bourke-White, meanwhile, were pulling out all stops to arrange their departure. They put their Connecticut-based secretary, Rhoda Lynn, to work on ferreting out possible travel connections. On the first of September Lynn sent off the first of several not especially hopeful radiograms to the Caldwells care of the American embassy indicating that the PanAm Clippers to San Francisco via Baghdad, Cairo, or Singapore were booked until December, but she was still looking into a Lisbon or New Zealand flight. A day later, she wired more bad news that the Caldwells would have to arrange a London–Lisbon connection through the British embassy in Moscow.

The Caldwells even called on their new friend from their outbound passage, Philip Chai, the PanAm executive in Hong Kong, on whom they had lavished thank-you gifts for his assistance: "Can you assure us clipper passage leaving Hongkong about October 22 to America also connecting passage from Chungking as must be home end of October. Both much thinner now and greatly lightened baggage Cordial regards—Bourkewhite Caldwell care." Ten days later, on September 11, Chai had a set of reservations lined up.

Lynn, meanwhile, had called the State Department on September 4. Two days later Ambassador Steinhardt wrote Caldwell a letter, addressed to him just across town at the National. "My dear Erskine," Steinhardt began. "I am in receipt of a telegram from the State Department sent on behalf of Miss

Rhoda Lynn in which she requests that you be advised that it is 'not possible to obtain definite information in the United States regarding travel routes at present available from Moscow to points abroad.'" Steinhardt concludes with the advice that "if the Iran route is now open and you decide to travel that way you should advise me of your tentative travel dates so that I may advise the Department."

In fact, Lynn had been even more proactive on the Caldwells' behalf, because on September 8 J. H. Keeley Jr., the assistant chief of the Special Division of the Department of State, assured her that the cable she had wanted sent had gone through.

Life's London correspondent, Walter Graebner, had also gotten involved. On September 12 he cabled Bourke-White that he was working on seats out of Baghdad to Auckland on the Clipper on October 23, but they should try to arrive "EARLY ENOUGH TO EXERT LAST MINUTE LOCAL PRESSURE."

But by this time the Caldwells had gotten wind of a possible northern exit strategy. The problem with that itinerary was that it required passage on a British ship, which would technically violate the rules of the United States' official neutrality. This route was the secret one about which Bourke-White had hinted earlier to her *Life* editors. Thompson let Bourke-White know that such a routing still did not look promising, but he was working on obtaining special permission. He added that he might be able to obtain a delay in the start of her lecture series.

Never one not to exert every last bit of influence, on September 12 Bourke-White contacted *Life*'s editor in chief, Henry Luce himself, whom she'd known since her days with *Fortune* magazine in the late 1920s and since *Life*'s inception in 1936, and asked him to spare no effort. Perhaps feeling guilty that she'd gone over his head, she soothed Thompson in a separate cable that same day. Thompson reassured her that there was no breach of etiquette, but also cautioned her not to be overly optimistic about Luce's efforts: "LUCE WIRING PER YOUR REQUEST. STATE DEPARTMENT SOFAR UNCOOPERATIVE OTHER REQUEST BUT STILL PUSHING."

Then, suddenly, everything shifted. Two days later, on September 14, Bourke-White cabled Thompson again, smug and playing it overly close-to-the-vest:

> NEVERMIND INABILITY GET MARINE PERMISSION AS SOMETHING HIGHLY DESIRABLE HAPPENING HERE. PLEASE INFORM LUCE AND DETAILS LATER. WILL REMAIN THIS COUNTRY SHORT WHILE LONGER THEN CONNECTING BAGDAD AUKLAND ROUTE SO HOPE GRAEBNER ABLE SEW UP HABBANIYEH [airport near Baghdad] ALL THANKS REGADS—BOURKEWHITE

Early the next morning the Caldwells and nine other correspondents were off on their six-day chaperoned press junket to the western front near Smolensk.

When Bourke-White got back to Moscow she wired Hicks gloomily: "trip fascinating but photographic results very limited due unusually bad weather," adding, "most interesting points after dark." Editing herself as she writes the text of her cable, she summarizes her work: "believe material as whole makes ~~interesting~~ fair series." Then she gets down to the matter of travel arrangements:

> please use all necessary pull make two reservations Atlantic clipper for week october nineteenth and advise Rhoda Lynn also request graebner work connecting shuttle. Re first lap keep details confidential please avoid mention certain placenames either in Newyork or in cables.

Somehow Rhoda Lynn, still working tirelessly on their return itinerary, seemed to be operating in a vacuum. On September 22, after the Caldwells had returned to Moscow from the press tour, she cabled them on what she believed to be the updated plans that involved an October 5 departure from Baghdad.

Later that day, she cabled again to warn Bourke-White of the tight connections "AS TRAVELING NEARLY IMPOSSIBLE NOW." The next day Walter Graebner superseded all Lynn's work with the news that a very timely Atlantic clipper crossing had been arranged:

> CLIPPER RESERVATIONS MADE NEWYORK SO HAVE REQUESTED HICKS CONFIRM. ALL LONDON LISBON PRIORITIES UPTAKEN TILL NOVEMBER FIFTEENTH WHICH DATE YOU DOWN PRO [FOR] TWO SEATS. ADVISE WHEN DEFINITELY FINALLY CERTAIN COULL [*SIC*] UNWANT HABBANIEH [*SIC*] RESERVATION REGARDS—GRAEBNER

Ever diligent, Lynn remained in touch with the State Department. On September 24 Loy W. Henderson, at the time the assistant chief of the Division of European Affairs but from 1934 to 1938 a member of the U.S. legation in Moscow, wrote Lynn that "according to a telegram received from the Embassy at Moscow, Mr. and Mrs. Caldwell plan to leave the Soviet Union on September 23, 1941. No information has been received as yet, however, to indicate that they have actually accomplished their departure."

Clearly, the Caldwells' efforts in enlisting so many people on their behalf to arrange transportation out of the Soviet Union, beginning as early as the third week in August, do not square with their memoirs. Such bald desperation does not conform with either of the personae they had created for their books. Their anguish over airplane connections has been expunged from their travelogues. But Caldwell had been confident enough in their travel plans that on September 10 he made a payment on a pair of rail tickets from Moscow to Archangel. They returned from the Smolensk trip on the evening of September 20 and must have departed three days later, as the ticket stubs in Caldwell's Dartmouth archives are dated September 23 at 9:45, the same date the American embassy in Moscow had given Washington. In *Smolensk,* Caldwell describes their chances for an escape as so nip and tuck that he is not even allowed to purchase train tickets until after 7:00 a.m. on the morning of their scheduled 9:45 departure. For Bourke-White those last three days were hectic ones, and they would have hardly been able to get all their photo developing, packing, and partying done while also wrangling for tickets, special permissions, favors, and travel documents. But it does make for a nice conclusion to Bourke-White's upbeat story.

CHAPTER 9

All-Out on the Road to Smolensk ★ The Critical Response

In London, Caldwell and Bourke-White worked at breakneck speed. Within a week of stepping safely off their transport ship after a fortnight's run from Archangel, they had put together *Russia at War*, their last photo collaboration, disagreeing over which photos to include because Bourke-White was planning to publish her own book once they were back in Connecticut. Caldwell, simultaneously, worked on a series of half a dozen pieces for the *Daily Mail*. Just before they departed, his London publisher talked him into revising his war diary, much of which consisted of first drafts of material already submitted to *PM*. During the four days he had for the project, he had time only to improve some grammar and punctuation before submitting the manuscript to Hutchinson & Company, which the following spring published it under the title *Moscow Under Fire, A Wartime Diary: 1941*.[1]

Space on the transatlantic Pan American Yankee Clipper was at a premium in wartime. After an intermediate flight to Lisbon from an airbase in Bristol, they embarked on the final leg of their 225-day round-the-world trip. After a stopover in Bermuda, they and thirty-eight other intrepid passengers arrived in New York just after noon on Sunday, November 2, in time, they hoped, for a splendid dinner. Caldwell had wired ahead to Rhoda Lynn, their secretary: "ARRANGE SUNDAY DINNER WITH BOTH STEAK AND FRIED CHICKEN, ALSO ALL KNOWN FRUITS AND VEGETABLES BOTH IN AND OUT OF SEASON."[2]

Bourke-White was off that very evening for St. Louis to begin her lecture tour. By Wednesday, Caldwell too was gone, speaking that night in Detroit, ironically on a topic that had been arranged back in April: "The South—America's Foremost Social Problem." In any case, before they could each settle down to their planned writing projects, they had speaking commitments to fulfill. Whereas before the war their travel radiated a kind of personal excitement, now they threw themselves into it for purely professional and promotional causes. Although in their memoirs their recollections of the exact timing and sequence of events over the next several months are confusing and at odds, what is clear is that both were in high demand on the lecture circuit: she more than he, probably because she enjoyed it, had photographs to show, and was a more enthusiastic speaker. As a result she commanded fees nearly twice what he could, $500–750 vs. $300–400. Occasionally their paths crossed, such as on November 16, when both were in Boston and he spoke at the Ford Hall Forum on "What I Have Just Seen in Russia" and again in Milwaukee in March. They mostly traveled separately. In *Portrait of Myself,* Bourke-White devotes seven pages to the excitement, pleasures, and rewards of the lecture circuit, while in his two memoirs, Caldwell is silent on the subject. Nonetheless, on November 6 Maxim Lieber, his New York literary agent, wrote him, "there's no getting away from it, but you must submit to being lionized."[3]

Well Received Only on the Left

Nonetheless, the reaction to *All-Out on the Road to Smolensk*'s February 18, 1942, publication was disappointing. Reviews were lukewarm and sales were sluggish.[4] After Pearl Harbor, the American public's interest had shifted to the Pacific, and former ambassador Joseph Davies's pseudohistorical memoir, *Mission to Moscow,* published in November, had ignited a furor of criticism from the Right, causing its sales to skyrocket, ultimately to 700,000 copies.[5] In contrast, by 1965 *Smolensk* had sold only 18,954 copies worldwide. Caldwell's other Russian book, the potboiler novel about partisan warfare, *All Night Long,* which followed immediately on *Smolensk*'s heels, sold 237,400 copies worldwide in the same period.[6] Contemporary critics saw *Smolensk* not as the carefully structured creative nonfiction I have described but rather as either simple journalism or memoir, and, not surprisingly, found fault with it. The *Kirkus Review*'s prepublication blurb was noncommittal:

> Here is a picture of the Russians today,—proving their efficiency, their determination, their rigid obedience to orders, with heroism taken for granted. From January to September 1941—an anecdotal, intimate picture of the country and the people. The relief and joy when war with Germany was a reality, and the country—in three days—on a full war footing, military and civilian. Scenes behind the lines—in bombed cities and towns—getting out his story—broadcasting what he could. After seeing them in action at last, he had no doubt of victory, he sees no defeatism in the Russian make-up. Not a book for the long picture—but good reading now.[7]

But in the left-leaning, Popular Front–promoting *New Masses,* Samuel Sillen, not unexpectedly, was quite complimentary: "We may be thankful that

Erskine Caldwell was in Moscow during the early days of the war. By cable and by radio he gave America a graphic sense of what General MacArthur has called the 'scale and grandeur' of the Soviet fight. It was appropriate that one of our finest novelists should report the war to us, just as Ehrenbourg, Sholokhov, and Alexei Tolstoy reported it to their countrymen."[8] Of course, Ehrenburg, Sholokhov, and Tolstoy were completely at the mercy of the Communist Party censors and under the sway of the prevailing climate of socialist realism, so that their work at the time was almost pure Stalinist hagiography. Sillen concludes, "With the economy and concreteness of a first rate story teller, Caldwell presents the drama of an entire people mobilized in a war of liberation."[9] In fact, the sense of the war on the eastern front (from the American point of view) as being "a war of liberation" is not the thrust of any of Caldwell's war writing or reporting.

The *New Republic* was less effusive but straightforward:

> A good piece of reporting covering the reactions of the Russian government and the people to the German invasion, blackouts, air raids, etc. Includes visits to the front, conversations with German prisoners and the usual adventures of a foreign correspondent. The author, unprejudiced against the Soviet Union, was deeply impressed by the Russian resistance. The book throws no new light on Russia and is somewhat uncritically written, but it is nevertheless a convincing, and at times exciting portrait of a people resolute and undivided battling for independence behind a competent military leadership.[10]

Likewise, Ralph Thompson in the *New York Times* focused on the political aspects of Caldwell's information, noting that he writes "at points gingerly and almost ingenuously, as though the censor were still breathing down his neck." Nonetheless, "he has interesting stories to tell at that, and he has seen more of wartime Russia than anyone else who has reported in book form thus far." On the other hand, Thompson, missing the point of the book and unaware of the widening schism in their marriage, was saddened that "Mrs. Caldwell took quantities of photographs with her famous camera, but none of them is reproduced here."[11] An observation that misses the point of Caldwell's objective.

In a second *New York Times* review, W. H. Chamberlin, after noting that "Mr. Caldwell [is] himself a sympathetic observer of the Soviet war effort," touched on his storytelling craft: "Mr. Caldwell possesses literary gifts superior to those of the average reporter and conveys vividly even some impressions which he did not personally experience." He explained away some of the shortcomings of Caldwell's journalism as the result of the Kremlin's attempts to control information.[12] But it fell to Alfred Vagts, the book reviewer for *Military*

Affairs, to call out Caldwell—and his fellow correspondent, Alexander Werth, the Russian-born Reuters agent—where each was most vulnerable: "The day of the great and informed war correspondent, the man who was allowed to go to the war, see and describe it, and who knew something of the war in the bargain, seems over forever."[13] Reflecting the presumed attitude of most of his readership, Vagts continues: "The two newspaper men, Caldwell and Werth, endlessly complain that they were not allowed to see the war at the front, but we are not convinced that they would have seen its true face or significance if they had been, judging from the reports of a week's stay on a quiet sector where they were taken for a guided tour."[14] Vagts persists in his editorial assault: "What they could not see or grope for themselves in the Moscow blackout they collected from soldiers' stories which they did not always understand, or which were a little Munchausean." He then dispenses with Caldwell with one final rapier-quick thrust: "Caldwell is clearly more at home along Tobacco Road than on the road to Smolensk."[15]

Another knowledgeable critic is Caldwell's old Soviet friend, Timofei Rokotov, of the literary journal *International Literature*, whose review in *Vechernyaya Moscva*, a Moscow evening newspaper, is reported by the *Daily Worker*. The *Worker* quotes Rokotov as saying that "lack of knowledge of the Russian language and of our customs, too much confidence in explanations given him by casual acquaintances, left a significant imprint on this book." On the other hand, Rokotov continues, "If we ignore a number of regrettable misunderstandings in the description of certain events, then it must be said that Caldwell's book will play a positive role in acquainting American readers with the Soviet people in wartime."

Markoosha Fischer was a friend of Bourke-White's since the early 1930s and a well-known ex-Stalinist who had come to recant in light of Stalin's atrocities. Writing in *The Nation* in March 1942, she takes a more solemn, neutral approach to *Smolensk:*

> Erskine Caldwell writes superbly of what he has seen with his own eyes or of concrete happenings reported to him by others. His account of the tank battles, the bombings of Moscow, the splendid work of civilian defense, and his visit to the front and his description of the deserted battlefield are forceful and exciting. And he also conveys the most important fact about Russia today—the absolute unity of the people in fighting the war and their inflexible determination to achieve victory at whatever sacrifice. He does not, however, seem to be very well acquainted with Soviet history—he never saw Moscow before 1941—and when he interprets Russian mentality and politics he frequently errs.[16]

After noting several factual errors in the book and taking issue with him about his respect for Stalin, whom she finds anathema, Fischer concludes that Caldwell shows "warm sympathy" for the Russian cause and that he understands the single-minded drive of the Russian people to defeat the Nazis.

Cue magazine dismisses *Smolensk* as "one of the most superficial and inadequate of all the war-correspondence books of the last three years." In a brief note in the *New York Herald Tribune,* Stephen Vincent Benét calls it a "good and interesting job." For Alexander Kendrick in the *Philadelphia Inquirer,* Caldwell is a "crack observer" and "one who says he never doubted a Russian victory and who holds up Russia's all-out national effort as the only logical way to win a war." Kendrick, uniquely it would appear, is aware that much of the "material has in part been contained in his news dispatches and radio reports. But a great deal of it is fresh and obviously uncensored, and in the form of a book it gains cohesion, continuity and force. And the style, of course, is superb." Another reviewer who seemed to understand that *Smolensk* was not just simple journalism was Louis Gannett, also of the *Herald Tribune.* "You may have some doubts of the literal truth of such stories," he warns, but "[u]nlike most of the correspondents, he deliberately underwrites. He never dramatizes himself; he leaves his wife almost out of the picture. (She is writing her own book.) But his dead-pan, poker-face narrative style supplies its own drama. It leaves the reader wishing for more."

Even the Federal Bureau of Investigation reviewed *All-Out on the Road to Smolensk.* Caldwell, as well as Bourke-White, had been on the FBI Custodial Detention List since late 1941 because of their apparent pro-socialist, left-leaning writing and their associates, so, not too surprisingly, *Smolensk* came to the bureau's attention when it was published.[17] On April 2, 1942, the special agent in charge of the New Haven office, J. J. McGuire, drafted a three-page memorandum for the assistant director of the FBI, Louis B. Nichols, about the book, based on Special Agent Bernard M. Suttler's review of it. The report is a straightforward and noncommittal description of *Smolensk,* but is of interest in that on my copy of the file, obtained via a Freedom of Information Act request, someone has penciled in above an editorial caret between "well-known" and "American author" the single word "PINK." A year later (August 21, 1943), however, the book was again being summarized, then by Special Los Angeles FBI Agent R. Bruce Baumeister as "a glorification of the STALIN Regime," and Caldwell was labeled "an outstanding propagandist for Communism." Five months earlier (March 23, 1943), Agent C. Kirby Smithe of the Phoenix FBI office had concluded, more favorably as well as accurately, that Caldwell was "pro-Russian . . . but that he is not pro-Communist." On the other hand, one of Smithe's unnamed informants had described Caldwell as follows:

> Subject while in Tucson, engaged in no known political activity and entertained a few people in his home. He worked most of the time on a new book. The entertainments consisted of quiet dinner parties with a few friends of Tucson.
>
> Informant gained the feeling that subject had been interested in Russia purely as a reporter of news events and current interest; that he has no political feeling for Russia or Communism except from a purely objective viewpoint.
>
> Subject was described by this Informant as being an extreme extrovert who is interested in anything only so long as he can gain by it. He is completely involved in his writing which is tantamount to interest in his moneymaking. He certainly, in Informant's opinion, has nothing to gain by interesting himself politically in this Country or elsewhere in Communism. Subject is a prolific writer and occupies himself almost exclusively with his writing and gaining of material therefor. He, although apparently somewhat "over-sexed," leads a happy life and is interested in the trials and tribulations of others only to the extent that they furnish him with materials for his works.

One can only wonder what the FBI intended to do with this kind of report.

In any case, this mixed but mostly tepid response to *Smolensk* must have weighed heavily on Caldwell's mind, because his financial status was always one of his foremost concerns. That *Smolensk* was being taken seriously by many readers and that he had been asked cogent questions about the eastern war and the USSR's chances of turning back the Germans during his book promotion tour was gratifying. But sales lagged, and for Caldwell that mattered enormously. He had created a work of art and a serious book and had fulfilled his mission to promote the Soviet Union's war collaboration, but it sold poorly and became lost in the clamor over the United States' involvement in a Pacific war and a western European war. The Soviet Union no longer held the public's attention. Bourke-White's career meanwhile was taking off photographing the war in Africa and Europe. Their marriage had foundered on the shoals. He did have several lucrative advance contracts in the works for his next book about the Russian war, *All Night Long*, but beyond that his future was vague. Hollywood beckoned; the script that he had been hired by Warner Brothers to work on at $1,250/week (for a total of ten weeks) was a treatment of the very book that was dramatically outselling *Smolensk:* Joseph Davies's *Mission to Moscow*.

CHAPTER 10

All Night Long ★ Caldwell's Flirtation with Socialist Realism

In his memoirs Caldwell writes of finishing *All-Out on the Road to Smolensk* in late December and having it ready for publication by the middle of January, then starting work on the final volume of his Russian oeuvre, *All Night Long*, that same month. But he mostly seemed overwhelmed with loneliness and lovesickness, suffering intensely during Bourke-White's extended absences on her speaking tours and on her lengthy *Life* photo assignments. The bright flare of their nuptial celebrity was dimming, and he was tormented by this. It is clear that during this spring of 1942 their marriage, forged originally in the late 1930s during the heat of their joint passion for social activism, cooled and began crumbling away.

Sometime during the spring and unbeknownst to her husband,[1] Bourke-White put out feelers to *Life* for another overseas assignment, preferably one where the war would be hottest. The result was her accreditation as an official war correspondent in the U.S. Army Air Forces, an appointment that came with a specially designed uniform of which she was exceedingly proud. Thus spruced up, by August she was back in England, from which platform she would become a permanently peripatetic *Life* photographer. She had once considered having Caldwell accompany her, but she knew this really wasn't realistic. She felt burdened by his inexplicable and periodic moods of silence and withdrawal, since much of her success came from her enthusiasm for socializing.

Caldwell was desperately lonesome and torn between trying to reinterest Bourke-White in their marriage and getting on with his own life as a writer. In January he had completed the purchase of a house in the hilly desert north of Tucson, to which he hoped he could lure her back from Europe so they might set up a domestic life together. In fact, the deed with the Pima County Registrar was in both their names. That he had so completely misconstrued her aspirations reflects the growing barrenness of their relationship and their near-total loss of communication. Caldwell also had apparently forgotten his commitment to her written into their unofficial prenuptial agreement, which he had signed on their flight to Reno near where they were married in February 1939. One condition of that covenant, Bourke-White writes in *Portrait of Myself,* was that "there must be no attempts to snatch me away from photographic assignments."[2] In *With All My Might,* Caldwell recalls only a discussion about her name:

> "Is that the only condition [not to have a formal ceremony] you intend to impose?"
>
> "Well, I wouldn't want to give up my professional name. My name means so much to me in my career and—"
>
> "Now hear this, madam," I said emphatically. "As far as I'm concerned you can be Margaret Bourke-White from here to the world's end as long as you are Kit to me."[3]

Memory, of course, can be selective, especially after a half-century.

Caldwell had had several goals lined up when 1942 began, and prioritizing them was difficult. He had to finish up his Russian material and still promote the American war effort. He planned to return to his interrupted literary project of chronicling the American South in a series of novels, of which four had been completed to this point. He wanted to continue with his editorial guidance to the American Folkways series, work he had put on hold once war broke out in the Soviet Union. He needed to maintain an adequate income to ensure he could meet the progressive strain on his bank account from a foundering marriage, an ex-wife, three children, and two houses. Finally, he hoped to restore some of the romantic magic of the early days of his relationship with Bourke-White. He wrote *All Night Long* with several of these goals in mind.

Caldwell had seen his role as a journalist—then influenced by his belief in Popular Front sociopolitical policies and in the Roosevelt administration's efforts to effect a Soviet-American alliance—as rallying his countrymen to the Soviet cause. In early 1942 the attention of the United States had been consumed by the war in the Pacific, but the greater war, he believed, was still taking place in the western Soviet Union. It was there that the Axis's power and interests were concentrated, and there that Western, and especially American, support would earn the greatest dividend. Nevertheless, though no longer a credentialed journalist, he had never stopped being a novelist.

In his eyes the best way to bring a renewed focus on the Soviet-German conflict was to write a solidly pro-Soviet book that would attract a wide audience. Though they received mixed but mostly positive reviews, none of his or Bourke-White's serious Russian books had sold well. Caldwell now envisioned an adventure novel, namely, a stem-winding, patriotic thriller that might even attract interest from Hollywood, a combination that could serve both his country and his own pocketbook. He resolved to write about Russian partisans. But in 1942 all that he knew about the Russian guerilla fighters came from his indoctrination by the Kremlin's information sources during the summer of 1941. He nonetheless was convinced that a widely read tale of partisan heroism, buttressed by his own observations of the Belarusian countryside gained during the six-day press trip to the war front in September, would be a worthy contribution to the U.S. war effort.

The result was the carefully though formulaically structured *All Night Long*, which bore the subtitle "A Novel of Guerilla Warfare in Russia." He spent that spring working on it, finally submitting a completed manuscript to his publisher in late June 1942. It was completely unlike anything Caldwell had written before, filled with predictable characters, readily anticipated situations, and clichéd outcomes, all coupled with embarrassingly improbable dialogue. Released first as a serialization in *Redbook* magazine, then as a Book League of America selection, within a year it sold over 175,000 copies.[4]

Critics panned it, but Metro-Goldwyn-Mayer optioned it for $50,000 as a feature film. It never went into production. Though it was in no way intended for a Soviet readership, in retrospect *All Night Long* can be characterized as socialist realism, the now widely disparaged World War II literary genre that was the official (and only acceptable) art style in the Soviet Union until Stalin's death in 1953.

Soviet Realism

At the 1934 Congress of the All-Soviet Writers' Union in Moscow, the Kremlin and the Communist Party placed their stamps of approval on a type of literature they saw as consonant with the ideals of the October Revolution, "socialist realism." Thereafter, all artistic products—literature, art, sculpture, photography, and film—had to reflect the goal of state socialism, but especially the ideology of the Communist Party and the Communist International. Since no formal rubric for literary socialist realism was ever promulgated, its canon grew more by example than by rules. In a 1979 paper in the *Journal of Aesthetics and Art Criticism*, "Socialist Realism and Literary Theory," Gary Saul Morson outlines six principal features of the Soviet-era socialist realist novel:

1. The two-dimensional psychology of its heroes, especially its "positive heroes," in contrast to the psychological complexity of Western counterparts. It might be said, for example, that whereas Western novels

tend to depict a quest for personality, Soviet novels usually depict the hero's quest for impersonality, his struggle to "become one with" his Marxist-Leninist role.

2. Highly formulaic plotting and style. Socialist realist novels often seem to be assembled from interchangeable parts, to be as pre-fabricated as the factories their heroes construct.
3. Themes that seem to Western readers to be singularly unamenable to novelistic treatment. Rather than rivals in love, for example, a socialist realist novel might deal with rival plans for constructing a machine to be used in the centrifugal casting of sewerage pipes (the plot of Vladimir Dudintsev's *Not by Bread Alone*, 1956).
4. The inclusion of political sermons, often in high-flown rhetorical language, even in fiction about apparently apolitical themes.
5. Perhaps most disturbing to Western readers, a lack of irony. In possession of the Marxist-Leninist method for solving all problems, the socialist realist novel eschews the kind of ambiguity and limited or individualized point of view that readers of Western novels value and in terms of which they often define literary art.
6. Strong closure and a mandatory happy or "constructive" ending.[5]

In *The Soviet Novel: History as Ritual,* Katerina Clark notes that Morson's criteria can be subsumed within a single master plot that generally operates along the lines of the three-stage heroic/mythic quest. She describes six major variants of the socialist realist novel:

- Production novel
- Historical novel
- Novel concerning a worthy intellectual or inventor
- Novel of war or revolution
- Spy or villain novel
- Novel about the West

In this sense the socialist realist novel is highly ritualized. The behavior of the hero and the ensuing plot elements are carefully encoded to create Marxist-Leninist parables.

All Night Long contains most of Morson's features, and it falls easily into Clark's categories of the war or the villain novel. Whether Caldwell intended to emulate the socialist realist novel has gone unrecorded, but he certainly could have been influenced by the movement. He and Bourke-White visited many of the "approved" writers and cultural figures of the period during their five months in Moscow. On the other hand, *All Night Long* was never translated into Russian, nor was it written with a Russian audience in mind. It is also unlikely that Caldwell read any contemporary socialist realist novels because, with the exception of Mikhail Sholokov's *And Quiet Flows the Don*, a translation of which had been available since 1934, none had been translated into English.

As Clark notes, in a novel of socialist realism the hero is expected to be "an emblem of Bolshevik virtue, someone the reading public might be inspired to emulate, and his life should be patterned to 'show the forward movement of history' in an allegorical representation of one stage in history's dialectical progress."[6] Sergei and Natasha, the heroic couple of *All Night Long*, meet Morson's and Clark's criteria for the "positive hero."

A Primer on Partisans

Whether or not *All Night Long* can be thought of as an American contribution to this genre, contextualization of the novel requires a consideration of the sociopolitical background of the partisan movement. There were clear differences between actual partisan warfare and the contemporary "spin" the Soviet government applied to it. *All Night Long* reflected the spin.

Guerillas have for centuries helped rebuff foreign incursions into the *rodina*, the Russian motherland. For example, the causes of the French debacle following Napoleon's invasion of 1812 were certainly legion, but the resistance of Russian patriots in the rear of the advancing Grande Armée was effective in slowing its progress. Stalin, discounting the obvious differences in allegiance to Russia of those occupied regions in 1812 as opposed to 1941, often drew on this example as evidence for deeply held Russian valor and patriotism.

In the nineteenth century, Karl Marx and Friedrich Engels studied the idea of partisan resistance and its relevance to a socialist counterinsurgency against the Romanov dynasty. Neither was a theoretician of war, but both recognized the contributions insurgent rebels could provide, though they also favored an organized militia over peasant armies. Nonetheless, their writings on the subject did provide sufficient impetus for the partisan concept to remain a viable alternative for the expansion of a Communist agenda that would be especially germane during the chaotic politics of the first quarter of the twentieth century. Guerilla fighters, whether organized or operating independently, played significant roles in the late nineteenth-century resistance to the tsars, the revolutions of 1905–6 and 1917–18, and especially in the ensuing chaos of the civil war (1917–22), when multihued insurrectionary forces—Red, White,

Green—engaged in a confusing and crippling maelstrom of combat. Vladimir Lenin also saw clearly the value of partisans but at the same time recognized that for the Soviet state to thrive, such irregulars must be harnessed by a central regime. As early as 1918 Lenin established the Central Headquarters of Partisan Detachments within the People's Commissariat for Military and Naval Affairs, thereby establishing a chain of command between party chiefs and field operations.

In the years that followed Lenin's death, the thinking about the value of regularized partisans changed. In the decade following the civil war, central Russian authority was plagued by peasant unrest and armed bands protesting the heavy-handed rural collectivization. Furthermore, in the western Soviet Union, particularly in Ukraine and the Baltic states, well-organized rump nationalist militias added to the incendiary clamor. Because partisans had the odor of rebellion about them, Stalin and other Kremlin leaders saw them as antistate security risks and thus discouraged their further development as Russia modernized its armed forces.

Commencing in the late 1920s Stalin initiated a series of five-year plans designed to drag the Soviet Union from the backwaters of its serf and peasant heritage into the mainstream of the twentieth century. The first Five-Year Plan (1928–32) concentrated on revolutionizing agriculture through the collectivization of farming and husbandry while at the same time promoting investment in industry, energy, and transportation. In 1930 Bourke-White had been welcomed into the country to document with her camera the changes Stalin had wrought. The second Five-Year Plan (1933–37) focused on the expansion of heavy industry along with improving communication and rail systems and maximizing natural-resource extraction, while the third Five-Year Plan, beginning in 1938 and continuing through the period of the Ribbentrop-Molotov truce of 1939, emphasized augmenting military assets, especially light and heavy weaponry, as well as munitions.

In concert with Stalin's efforts during the three five-year plans (1928–41) to make the Soviet Union not just self-reliant and up to date but a world economic leader was a shift in the philosophy of national self-defense: the military would be modernized to the degree that such backward ideas as guerilla warfare would no longer be embraced. The Red Army would be sufficiently strengthened so that it could repulse any foreign attack *at the border*. As part of the 1939 Russo-German nonaggression pact, Hitler and Stalin agreed secretly that neither Russian annexation of portions of eastern Poland and the Baltic states nor German incursions to the west would meet with objection. Despite this national industrial and political overhaul, all evidence suggests a remarkable degree of Russian *unpreparedness* for the onslaught of Barbarossa, Hitler's surprise attack.

Paranoia was deeply ingrained within Stalinism. Joseph Stalin's purges, show trials, secrecy, and bunker mentality are all consonant with state and personal paranoia. The partisan movement that proved to be such a valuable adjunct in the defense of the *rodina* during World War II was problematic from its inception because of the understandable state paranoia that surrounded it. The hallmarks of Stalinism—political discipline, collectivism, obedience, social hierarchy and order, and material stratification—were antithetical to the romantic notions of partisan life (*partizanshchina*): autonomy, isolation, chaos, and freedom, especially freedom from outside totalitarian domination. The state inevitably prevailed, but at the same time, as propaganda, it promoted partisans as free-spirited yet patriotic heroes.

Despite the wholesale overhaul of the military, in 1940–41 there still existed interest in, and even some planning for, limited partisan operations. Lenin's concept that all partisans must remain under central party control was a philosophy Stalin readily adopted. It is not surprising, then, that once the successes of guerilla resistance came to be known and valued, state control inexorably followed closely. To minimize the risk of rogue cadres, the Kremlin encouraged the party to recruit from proven loyalists and then to maintain partisan units under party control.[7] To this end partisan units were organized with dual leadership, as were all units of the Red Army. Every military unit was to be commanded by a regular army officer as well as by a party representative. The military officer would have primary tactical control, while the Communist deputy was to be in charge of political matters and "education."[8]

On July 17 Caldwell broadcast the text of a decree from the Presidium of the Supreme Council of the USSR issued the previous day. It stated that "in all regiments, divisions, headquarters, military high schools and organizations of the Red Army an institute of military commissars and in detachments, units, batteries, squadrons an institute of political leaders" would be introduced. He then went on to quote Stalin: "If the commander of the regiment is the head of the Regiment, the commissar of the regiment has to be the father and soul of the entire regiment."[9] It was one of the remarkable facts of the organization of the Red Army throughout the Great Patriotic War that such a dual hierarchy remained intact.

This policy was not without its detractors. In his 1959 *Victims and Heroes*, Russian novelist and journalist Konstantin Simonov painted a portrait of a fighting force hamstrung by this dual leadership. Theoretically, all operational decisions were to be made through their collaboration. In fact, tactical decisions based on the logistical and real-time military situation were often subverted by the need to consider their political and party ramifications. Simonov surmised an endemic Kremlin paranoia concerning the reliability of individual soldiers, their leaders, and even entire units. In particular, there developed a heightened distrust of those, individually or severally, who had found themselves encircled by Nazi forces. There was about such soldiers an odor of treachery as an explanation for their predicaments. Panic mongers and cowards were believed to be hiding around every corner, behind every tree, or cowering in every abandoned trench. Simonov's thesis was that the fault lay with the leadership structure of the Red Army itself. Because of this dual control of every unit and because of remarkably inept logistical support, military intelligence, and strategic planning throughout the Red Army, which was compounded by the tactical advantages Hitler gained through his surprise attack, encirclement of Russian forces was inevitable across the entire western front, but especially in the central Smolensk salient.[10]

The Nazi blitzkrieg that commenced on June 22, 1941, had all the power of a tsunami sweeping across the western reaches of the Soviet Union, but especially the republics of Ukraine and Belarus. It progressed so rapidly and with such devastation across a vast and relatively unprepared area that, overnight, peasant farmers and villages and towns that were once Russian were now occupied by representatives of the Third Reich. Initially it was a toss-up for residents whether this was a good thing or bad. Much of the land in far western Ukraine and Belarus had been acquired through a hostile takeover several years earlier; this had been Polish land parceled out by the Molotov-Ribbentrop understanding just two years earlier. The ruin of war was complete in many areas. Catastrophe overtook the Red Army as units found themselves completely encircled with the front moving rapidly eastward.

Three months later, Adolf Hitler launched the second phase of Barbarossa, Operation Typhoon, whose aim was the occupation of Moscow before the onset of winter. The German push, begun on September 30, reached its easternmost verge in early December. On December 5 Soviet forces began a series of counteroffensives that finally stemmed the German tide. By the end of 1941, though there was much war still to be fought and other turning points to effect, the myth of Nazi invincibility had been exposed.

Immediately following the German invasion, western Belarusians and Ukrainians, now sundered from direct Soviet control, fell under Nazi authority. German plans had called for these regions to be used as colonial appendages to the Reich. Three possible fates were to befall these residents of future eastern German outposts: (a) captivity followed by exportation to the Fatherland as slave laborers, (b) vassals to be kept where they lived to maintain agriculture and industry for German benefit, or (c) death for the aged, infirm, or wounded. Captive Red Army soldiers could look forward to forced indenture into the German military, repatriation into Russia as spies, or death through malnutrition, inadequate health care, or execution.

Not surprisingly, early recruits into the Soviet partisan movement came from these peoples, driven both by hope and by fear, initially the latter, but as the war's momentum slowly changed, the former. The ethos of German strategy toward occupied regions was brutality of an unprecedented intensity. Reichsminister Hermann Goering's attitude toward the civilian population of the German east in October 1941, as reflected in the papers of Count Galeazzo Ciano, the Italian foreign minister, was instructive: "This year between twenty and thirty million persons will die of hunger in Russia. Perhaps it is well that it should be so, for certain nations to be decimated. But even if it were not, nothing can be done about it."[11]

As much as the Russian propaganda machine worked to create a sense of unfettered patriotism west of the retreating front, the reality was that not all the people in occupied territories were pro-Soviet. This was especially the case in rural areas of Ukraine, where there were still horrific memories of the famine following Stalin's forced agricultural and industrial collectivization that had begun in 1929. Of the six to eight million famine-related deaths in the USSR, two-thirds to three-quarters occurred in Ukraine and Belarus.[12] Understandably, some peasants looked to the Germans as liberators, but, unfortunately, the official policy of the Reich occupiers maintained the principles of Soviet collectivization. This drove even more peasants into the ranks of the partisans.

A similar sensibility was prevalent among encircled members of the Red Army, particularly officers and Communist Party members, all of whom faced even more horrible captivity than would the foot soldiers. But attempted self-repatriation into their own or other front-line Red Army units was fraught, because they were often accused of cowardice or treason to account for their encirclement. Alexander Bek's *Volokolamsk Highway* (1944) follows the harrowing efforts of a loyal Red Army unit to return to respectability after being encircled by Germans and then repatriated.

Most forward units functioned not only under the dual leadership of a party commissar and a Red Army officer but also under the scrutiny of secret service (NKVD) operatives as well. Many Russian troops isolated behind the German lines believed it was safer to remain in the woods than to attempt to recross the front lines. For this reason, in the early months of the war ex- or active-duty

Red Army soldiers (the *okruzhentsky*) comprised the majority of active partisans in rural areas and in nascent urban underground cells.

But patriotism also played a powerful role in the recruitment of partisans, especially after Stalin's November 7 speech in Red Square in Moscow. For the first time he called on the nation to resist the Nazis, not just in the service of communism, but on behalf of the *rodina* as well. Although he did invoke Lenin in this speech, he also declaimed, "Let the manly images of our great ancestors—Aleksandr Nevsky, Dmitrii Donskoi, Kuz'ma Minin, Dmitrii Pzharsky, Aleksandr Suvorov, and Mikhail Kutusov—inspire you in this war!"[13] The emphases of his speech were on encouraging Russian resistance behind German lines and in areas not yet under attack, inspiring governments in exile to continue to resist fascism, while at the same time assuring the Allied nations that Russian nationalism had replaced communism as the dominant ideology.[14]

At no time was the partisan movement simply one of grassroots heroism. Rather, it was the result of a not very carefully worked-out strategy over which the Communist Party and its local representatives, NKVD operatives, and the Red Army fought for nominal control, each with its own agenda for the insurgents. Although the party had taken the first steps to form rural partisan units and urban underground cells in western Ukraine and Belarus as early as June 25, and although Stalin issued statements on June 29 and July 16 in which he encouraged partisan activity, bitter bureaucratic feuding left the movement in limbo. Although the Soviet Information Bureau fed the Western journalists a regular diet of tales of partisan bravado and derring-do, the German occupiers were all the while successfully quelling much of the unconventional warfare. Soviet sources indicate that while there were 87,000 partisans active in September 1941, by the following January there were but 30,000; most of the attrition occurred in the areas farthest from Moscow along the far western front. Only 7 percent of the partisans on the Ukrainian steppes survived, succumbing to inadequate preparation, training, equipment, resupply, and medical support.[15]

As the situation grew more dire in the winter of 1941, the Kremlin reassessed its earlier concern that a strong guerilla movement could devolve into anarchy, emboldening Ukrainian and Belarusian separatist groups. By December plans were afoot for the formation of a Central Staff of the Partisan Movement to be led by the Belarusian first secretary Panteleiman K. Ponomarenko, long a strong advocate for the guerillas and one of the first regional chiefs to respond to Stalin's call on June 29 for the training of local resistance groups. Nonetheless, intense interagency infighting delayed its implementation until

May 30, 1942. Thereafter the partisan movement thrived even as regular Soviet defenses still struggled mightily against the Nazis.

German mismanagement of the occupied regions contributed to a resurgence in patriotic zeal among the occupied. This, in turn, grew the partisan rolls rapidly: to 70,000 in June, 103,000 in December.[16] No longer were the most fit men automatically recruited into the Red Army. The Kremlin came to accept that a powerful insurgency behind enemy lines should be on equal footing with the Red Army itself.

On the other hand, although the bureaucratic duplication, parallelism, and confusion that had previously resulted in field mismanagement, inefficiency, and ineffectiveness waned, it never disappeared. For example, only belatedly did the Kremlin see to it that partisan units were adequately equipped with radios, and this was accomplished as much to guarantee central political control as to improve field operations. At the onset of the blitzkrieg the government had confiscated all radios so that communication in the field was limited mostly to foot courier and the occasional airplane drop. Hence, by 1942 and 1943, the logistical nightmare that had once debilitated field supply operations had been mostly corrected. "When necessary," writes historian Kenneth Slepyan, "[partisans] circumvented, deceived, and used state agencies to achieve their goals. In exploiting interagency competition, the lack of reliable and accurate communications, blurred jurisdictions, and regional rivalries, the partisans often manipulated authorities while appearing to follow instructions."[17]

The effectiveness of partisan units has been questioned. Certainly, the tone of the Soviet Information Bureau's press releases was completely upbeat, reflecting signals from Stalin himself.[18] They were also disingenuous. Western journalists were regaled with tales of partisan and Red Army heroism and given direct access to some of these heroes. Correspondents were led to believe that partisan operational procedures included "extensive use of ruses and deception, skilful camouflage, high mobility, and maximum exploitation of all terrain features,"[19] the goal of which was to disrupt German military, economic, and political activities. By taking advantage of the extensive forests and swamplands of western Russia, and of the limits on military transportation imposed by autumn and winter weather ("General Mud"), soon the guerillas became capable of widespread sabotage of German transport and communication systems as well as mounting attacks on German forces.[20] Nonetheless, as British historian Graham Stephenson writes, "The partisan war behind German lines has been the subject of much romantic and propagandising mythology."[21] This was not reflected in the writings of the Western press nor in *All Night Long*.

In the summer of 1941 partisans were truly a thuggish, ragtag bunch, a fact the Western correspondents might have surmised had they been permitted open access to the ever-retreating front lines.

Representation of the partisans was a contested issue. The Kremlin's goal was twofold: it pressed hard to have the Russian public perceive the partisans as dashing and brave, even heroic, patriots for the defense of the *rodina* and the Soviet cause, yet also as loyalists who accepted the Stalinist precepts of order, hierarchy, and obedience. For Western consumption, pro-Communist idealism was downplayed. Although the following paean to a group of partisans who had been brought to Moscow appeared in a September 1942 issue of *Izvestia*, it is typical of the tributes written in 1941 as well. "In people who have arrived from the partisan detachments, there is something special, distinguishing them from others. A special expression of the face, a special look, their eyes have seen much, things we have not seen. In these people there is a surprising calm, forming from the maximum effort of will and infinite hatred."[22] A year earlier a *Pravda* panegyric to the partisans glorified them as "modest [and] inconspicuous in peacetime" but "on the field of battle legendary folk warriors, winning their renown with wondrous achievements for the Soviet motherland."[23] In *All Night Long*, Caldwell's partisans are certainly cut from this heroic mold.

At the same time, the partisans had to walk a tightrope. *Partizanshchina*, the idea that these fighters were freedom-loving, free-spirited volunteers defending their land, had come to be a pejorative term, interpreted by Bolshevik leaders as "disobedience, lack of political consciousness, possessing an Orthodox or even hostile ideology, and pursuing the interests of one's self or one's group over those of the state."[24] Thus, while many guerillas internalized the mythologized, carefree patriot-terrorist image the propaganda machinery encouraged in order to remain in the good graces of the Stalinist regime, they had to adopt a different stance. Inevitably, tensions developed between Moscow and the partisan field units, but also within detachments themselves whenever traditional ethnonational frictions flared. Nothing of this kind is evident in *All Night Long*.

Additionally, antagonism existed among the three principal types of partisan detachments: (1) the volunteer units worrisomely infected with *partizanshchina* traditions; (2) units, many of which were urban underground cells, established by the Communist Party and dominated by party members and recruits from the Komsomol, the party's youth division;[25] and (3) companies formed from encircled Red Army men, the *okruzhentsky*. At times the rivalry among these groups flared into bitterness. Repeatedly, *okruzhentsky* were assumed simply to be Nazi operatives in disguise or spies.

The position adopted early by the Soviet Information Bureau was to lionize only the partisans of its own mythmaking, while barely acknowledging the important contributions made by both *okruzhentsky* and party-recruited units to the partisan movement in general. As such, the partisans took on the popular and Kremlin-acceptable "dual roles of witnesses to and avengers of enemy atrocities."[26] Caldwell's *All Night Long* depicts only this representation.

In effect, the ideal partisan unit was to be organized as a microcosm of mainland Soviet society, and as such, partisan units were not immune to the dysfunctions of that society. The Stalinist power edifice imagined itself always to be at risk from enemies both within and without, fears that came to be validated on June 22, 1941. Not surprisingly, the resulting top-down nature of the Soviet hierarchy, the paranoia and secrecy of its administrative structure, and the resulting social and police state all were reflected in the partisan movement. The success of any given detachment was often presented as rooted in the effectiveness of its leader as a mini-Stalin father figure; its ability to negotiate the ever-shifting shoals of paranoia and obedience to the Communist Party, the Red Army, and the NKVD; and its aptitude for the careful balancing of partisan ethos (*partizanshchina*) against dutiful allegiance to Stalinist ideals. Again, these internal stresses are absent from *All Night Long*.

In the late summer of 1941, the strength and legitimacy of the Red Army reflected, in large part, the personality cult emanating from Stalin. This Stalin mystique drew upon elements of (hyper)masculinity, ascendant power, and dominance, all expressed most clearly in the representation of Stalin as the charismatic father of the nation. Kenneth Slepyan observes:

> Many elements of Stalin's cult of personality came into play in the relationship between commanders and Partisans, including patriarchy; the family as a metaphor for the unit (and the Soviet Union); the personal ties between the commanding and the commanded, moderated by a certain aloofness; and a down-to-earth, roll-up-your-sleeves-and-get-down-to-it manner that showed little patience for bourgeois niceties. And like Stalin, partisan leaders protected their charges from the encircling enemies in the outside world.[27]

In fact, in a December 1942 article *Pravda* describes a partisan commander come to Moscow in this way: "broad shouldered, stocky, a 35 year old man. The energy, decisiveness, in this person is inexhaustible. He has tremendous physical strength. It seems that this person was born for the partisan struggle. And what was he before the war? A surgeon, a district surgeon."[28] In many ways, this is the figure of Stalin himself.

Another balancing act partisan groups had to achieve was harmonizing the seemingly mutually exclusive demands of Soviet social stratification and *partizanshchina* egalitarianism. Membership in partisan brigades was tightly regulated by one's background. Party-recruited men always were at the top of the social order, formerly encircled Red Army soldiers or escaped prisoners of war (the *okruzhentsky*) always at the bottom of the pecking order. Falling between these extremes were urban recruits, Jews, and women, who until late in the war were generally unwelcome in partisan cadres. A volunteer, especially a peasant volunteer, was acceptable in direct proportion to, first, the proximity of his home to the vicinity in which a partisan group operated (so that he'd presumably be more familiar with the terrain) and, second, the specific skill set he brought to the band, such as training in radio operation or experience with demolition. In addition, just as Stakhanovite overproducers had been rewarded with higher salaries and other perks during the series of five-year plans beginning in 1928, so too especially brave, dashing, and accomplished partisans were rewarded with more prestigious assignments, such as sabotage work, with the resulting national adulation.[29] To a degree, there was the possibility of upward mobility for partisan recruits, though often such promotions were more the result of battlefield casualties and attrition.

In assessing partisan behavior and attitudes during the early months of the war, it is instructive to consider not just the Soviet side of the equation but the Reich's as well. The Wehrmacht's approach to the pacification of its newly occupied territories was based on two reinforcing philosophies: first, the tradition, dating to the Franco-Prussian War of 1870–71, of the complete and forceful extirpation of all examples of real or imagined local or guerrilla resistance; second, the belief that Jews—and to a lesser extent Slavs and Asiatics—were subhuman and valuable only as slave labor, and the concomitant assumption that the Bolsheviks were the embodiment of Satan.[30] While most Reich strategists understood the need for the preservation of agricultural and industrial resources to support German expansion eastward across the Soviet Union, during the initial months of Barbarossa the strategy of extermination was paramount. This was due in some measure to the German Army's fear that Soviet citizens could rapidly coalesce into a massive anti-occupier resistance force, and in part to the rigid hierarchy of authority within the Wehrmacht. Utilizing official reports and letters and diaries of soldiers and officers, Jeff Rutherford has summarized the attitude of a prototypical German infantry division: "As the 121st Infantry Division went to war in June 1941, it carried with it a brutal irregular warfare doctrine resulting from the Nazi radicalisation of the army's already ruthless anti-insurgency policies. This potent mix created the preconditions for the *Wehrmacht*'s savage treatment of any and all resistance, real or imagined."[31] Truman Anderson has performed a similar analysis of the operations of the 62nd Infantry Division active in central Ukraine in late 1941, concluding that the attitudes and behavior of villagers were determined more by "the pragmatic, day-to-day calculus of personal survival" than "either pro-German sentiment (rooted in Ukrainian regional hostility to the Soviet regime) or Soviet patriotism."[32] There are hints of these issues in *All Night Long*, but Caldwell does not highlight them.

Yet there can be problems in overgeneralizing the picture of partisan warfare on the Soviet western front. There necessarily existed a relational triangle among the Germans, the local residents, and the Russian resistance. And since these groups were not static in composition, interactions among them were complex. The German side included the military and the matériel of the Wehrmacht itself as it passed through an area. Most of the soldiers were at the actual front, but some remained behind in such support roles as rearmament and repair, motor pool, construction, medical care, and the quartermaster corps. The rear guard also included Reich personnel involved in the pacification and exploitation of the occupied territory, including not just the armed Schutzstaffel (Waffen-SS), the paramilitary shock troops, but also the German gendarmerie, the police force introduced into occupied territory, which came to assume a major role in antipartisan repression. Caldwell was probably unaware of this domestic German police force, and so it does not factor into *All Night Long*.

The Russian resistance included the Red Army itself, both at the front and in pockets of encircled soldiers occasionally numbering in the tens of thousands and in prisoner-of-war camps. The partisan movement was the principal resistance *behind* German lines. It incorporated nonfrontline Red Army; refugees dispossessed by the German occupation at the front lines; racial groups earmarked for extermination, especially Jews; and peasants and urbanites drawn to the anti-Nazi cause for a variety of reasons, ranging from patriotism for the *rodina*, a desire for revenge, or adventure to simple displacement and homelessness. The relevance of the partisan movement to the general war effort not only evolved as the shape of the conflict changed but also varied based on local geography and topography, regional demographic profiles, the prior attitudes and experiences of the local populations toward the Soviet Union and communism, and the behavior of the occupying German forces.

Finally, the peasants themselves, especially the rural ones, played a central role in the destiny of the partisan movement. They were the ones trapped between the German hammer and the Soviet anvil, a common metaphor for chroniclers of the period. To them fell the responsibility of supplying the fruits of agriculture and husbandry to either the German occupiers or the partisans. They personally faced the decision whether to carry out the edicts of the Kremlin to scorch their own earth or run afoul of the party. In many ways they were trapped in a no-win situation, risking personal harm and death from either faction depending on their perceived collaborations at the moment.

Mining recently made available German and Soviet World War II documents, Eric Haberer writes of the peasant-partisan-occupier ménage à trois in central and western Belarus:

> For when the partisans were gone, the Germans were still there. In other words, occupation did not just mean exploitation, it also meant a modicum of stability and a degree of authority that was obeyed, if not respected, by much of the population in the first year and a half of occupation, and had not completely evaporated even by 1943–44. This was reflected in the willingness, even anxiousness, of locals to report on the whereabouts of partisans. For the most part, this information was not coerced from an uncooperative and frightened population, nor was it just in the nature of denunciations or long-standing vendettas, though these undoubtedly did exist. The bottom line is that the informants were ordinary peasants rather than informers, that is, indigenous agents working for the Germans. All this needs to be kept in mind when dealing with the Gendarmerie's onerous task of defending their turf and its inhabitants against the partisans.[33]

The discourse of 1941 and 1942 within which Caldwell was writing *All Night Long* was dominated by the propaganda needs of the Soviet war effort. It was necessary that the Russians put forth a unified face to the Western world, an image of universal and deeply held patriotism. It was important to present the Nazi war strategy as one of genocidal hatred and atrocity, generalized carnage, and violent affronts to all human dignity. There was no room for any description or analysis of the mundane housekeeping chores of the occupying forces. The peasants had to be represented as an innocent population subject to every imaginable horror that the German war machine was capable of, as a helpless populace incapable of resistance, and as a people pining for the liberating intervention of Mother Russia and its Communist regime. The partisans were to be depicted as heroic patriots, hardened to danger and excited by adventure, inspired by nationalist loyalty and the ideals of the Communist Party, who worked in concert with the frightened yet loyal peasant masses. Socialist realism was the perfect literary vehicle for this portrayal. And Caldwell's novel met all these goals.

On the other hand, Haberer's studies of the German gendarmerie have documented the actual situation: "Both [Germans and partisans] were invasive forces and predatory in their demand of goods and recruits. Yet the partisans were more disruptive, unpredictable and intrusive—and thus, a more immediate threat to life and village. To protect themselves, peasants were inclined to call upon the imposed authority, however foreign, which appeared to represent 'law and order,' as they understood it, to reign in the 'banditry' that engulfed their world."[34] As the partisans' need for food and supplies escalated, the balance shifted toward the occupiers, but later in the war when German demands became both greater and more desperate, the pendulum moved in the opposite direction.

For Americans in 1942 and 1943 these insider details were not available, and if they had been, they surely would have been suppressed. With this caveat, *All Night Long* is a remarkably well-crafted depiction of partisan warfare, as the Kremlin would have the West believe it to be. The Russian propaganda machine designed to win the hearts, souls, and pocketbooks of the West for the defense of the Soviet Union began to operate simultaneously with the escalation of actual physical hostilities along the USSR's western frontier following the onset of Operation Barbarossa. A central element in that propaganda war was the effort to disabuse the American public of its notion that the USSR was synonymous with communism. The most worrisome long-term fear for many in the West in 1941 was not so much Hitler's advance, frightening as this was, but rather the threat of Communist expansion, sentiments the Popular Front movement tried hard to tamp down.

To this end, the romanticism of a particularly Russian brand of guerilla insurgency—partisan warfare—became a staple of Kremlin-approved Western journalism. The spokesmen for the Sovinformburo supplied the Western correspondents in Moscow that summer of 1941 with a steady stream of seemingly newsworthy nuggets, and when after several months this became old hat, provided chaperoned access to partisan fighters. Caldwell was not immune to the storytelling promise such material offered. Nor was Bourke-White blind to its pictorial presentation. They lauded partisan warfare in radio broadcasts and, as did their fellow correspondents, in newspaper and magazine articles. Later Caldwell celebrated partisan warfare in his travel memoir, *All-Out on the Road to Smolensk*, as did Bourke-White in *Shooting the Russian War*. But in the couple's collaborative *Russia at War*, Caldwell includes just a brief mention of the partisans, in which he ascribes a kind of perversity to the Kremlin, attributing more agency to it than in reality it had: "And again, by keeping its people in its villages when the Germans occupy new territory, they [the Germans] have the justly celebrated guerilla activities to combat."[35] Finally, *All Night Long* was his primary fictional contribution to this vision.

In November 1941 Caldwell's Boston publisher, C. R. "Cap" Everitt, had written him asking if "[he knew] any technique whereby we could get a first-rate war experience book out of Russia? As you know, they are piling in from England, and I'm sure there would be a big demand if we hit the right one from Russia."[36] Dashed off in just a few months, *All Night Long* met Everitt's and many readers' expectations, though not those of most critics, excepting those from the leftist press.

CHAPTER 11

All Night Long ★ The Novel

Sergei Mikhailovich Korokov and his beautiful young wife, Natasha Mikhailovna, are the principal protagonists of Caldwell's novel *All Night Long*. Sergei is thirty-six, Natasha just out of her teens, and they have been married two years when, in the early winter or late fall of 1941, the Germans arrive in their village of Ivanovka, located along the Dnieper River in eastern Belarus. Caldwell sets the novel in the same area where the correspondents had traveled the previous autumn, so that his description of the landscape, as is usual for his writing, is rich in the detail of an experienced and observant traveler:

> The front was twenty miles away. It zigzagged through the forests, following streams and hills with alternating layers of barbed wire, minefields, and six-pronged tank hurdles. During the day artillery rumbled constantly, its deep-throated booming sounding like a prolonged thunderstorm. At night the guns blinked through the trees, and on the horizon there were flashes that looked as though hundreds of electric-light bulbs were being turned on and off at random. Every once in a while a dazzling white glow appeared over the front when a parachute flare opened and floated down so slowly it looked as if it were suspended in the air.[1]

He delays the novel's time frame several months to coincide with the Red Army's successful defense of Moscow. This temporal shift supports the novel's political agenda and the tenets of socialist realism, as it shows that the Soviet Union, Stalin, and the Red Army are worthy allies in the Western world's struggle against Hitler. *All Night Long* thus takes place just before Hirohito's attack on Pearl Harbor, at a time when Hitler had turned his attention from bombing London to a wholesale assault on the USSR and Moscow, its capital and heart.

By the time of the novel's publication on November 27, 1942, Hitler had been turned back from Moscow itself, and even the Wehrmacht's position in Stalingrad was about to be reversed, but it was not at all clear that the Russians could continue to withstand the Nazis without outside help. The delay of *All Night Long*'s publication was serendipitous because the United States was by then fully committed to its war effort. This tale of unadulterated heroism on the part of Soviet citizens, villagers, and farmers was powerful propaganda, and Caldwell tells their story well, if formulaically.

Natasha describes Sergei, who in the novel gradually becomes the embodiment of an idealized Stalin: "She could see the quick flickering movement of the muscle under the skin of his cheek. His whole face was tense and when she looked up into his deep blue eyes she could read the flood of thoughts racing through his mind. Sergei was tall and agile with dark wind-tanned skin and large work-hardened hands. She knew that no matter what happened she would never be afraid of anything as long as they were together" (*ANL* 6). She, on the other hand, is Stalin's model female counterpart, a vulnerable product of the male gaze, in need of a strong patriarch's protection: "Natasha's light unbound hair was cascading over her face like a waterfall. She looked more like a child than a woman as she sat almost submerged in the deep fluffy goose-feather mattress. Her skin was flushed and rosy as it always was when she woke up in the morning. Even though she was past twenty, she looked younger than she had when she and Sergei were married two years before. With a sweep of her hand she pushed her hair from her face" (*ANL* 4). Beyond her seductiveness, she has a childlike "will of her own, and it was a determined one when she wanted it to be, but she had uncommon good sense as well" (*ANL* 10). Initially, to be sure, she is appropriately naïve:

> "Are they going to stay here, Sergei?"
> He nodded.
> "How long will they stay?"
> "I don't know," he said. "They'll be here until we drive them away." (*ANL* 5)

But this simple innocence is not to last long.

The plot is predictably straightforward. Sergei, a brigade leader among the partisans, has standing orders once the Germans arrive in Ivanovka to rendezvous with his senior brigadier compatriot, who is holed up somewhere in the backcountry with a force of several dozen volunteers. He leaves Natasha, who is to provide cover for several hours; she is then to follow. When she fails to show up, Sergei soldiers on because he is a Russian partisan first and a young husband only second. After killing a sentry and then a pair of young German soldiers who are stranded because their truck has broken down,[2] he hides in a derelict mill.[3] Nikolai Sorokin is also holed up there. Sorokin is a "political instructor" from a nearby collective farm who teams up with Sergei to reach the partisan brigade headquarters.

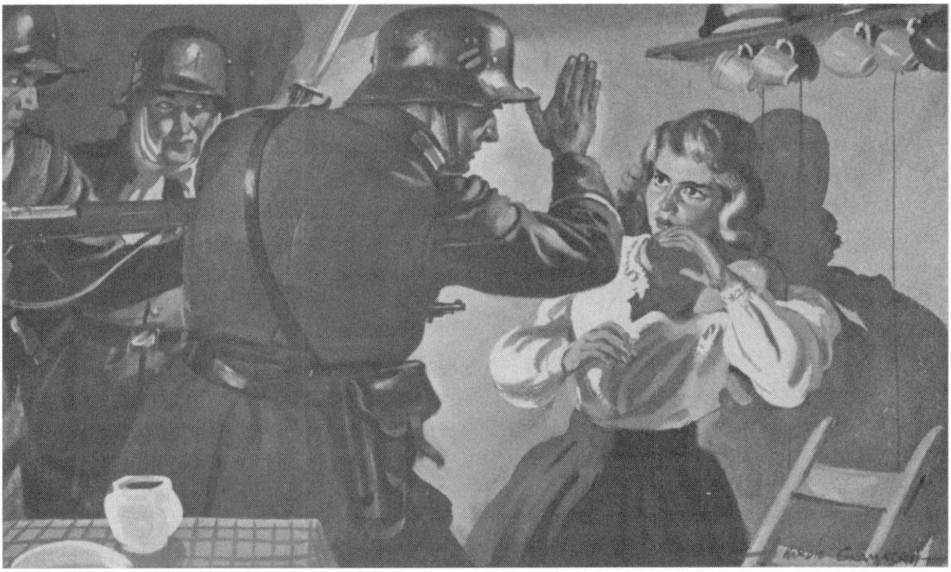

FIGURE 44. *All Night Long* artwork by Hardy Gramatky (from *Redbook* magazine; copyright Hardie Gramatky archives, Beinecke Library, Yale University)

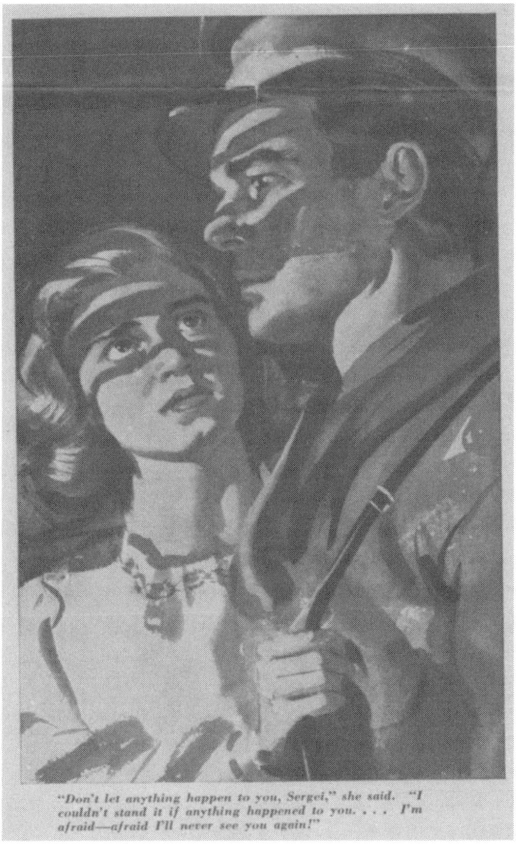

FIGURE 45. *All Night Long* artwork by Hardy Gramatky (from *Redbook* magazine; copyright Hardie Gramatky archives, Beinecke Library, Yale University)

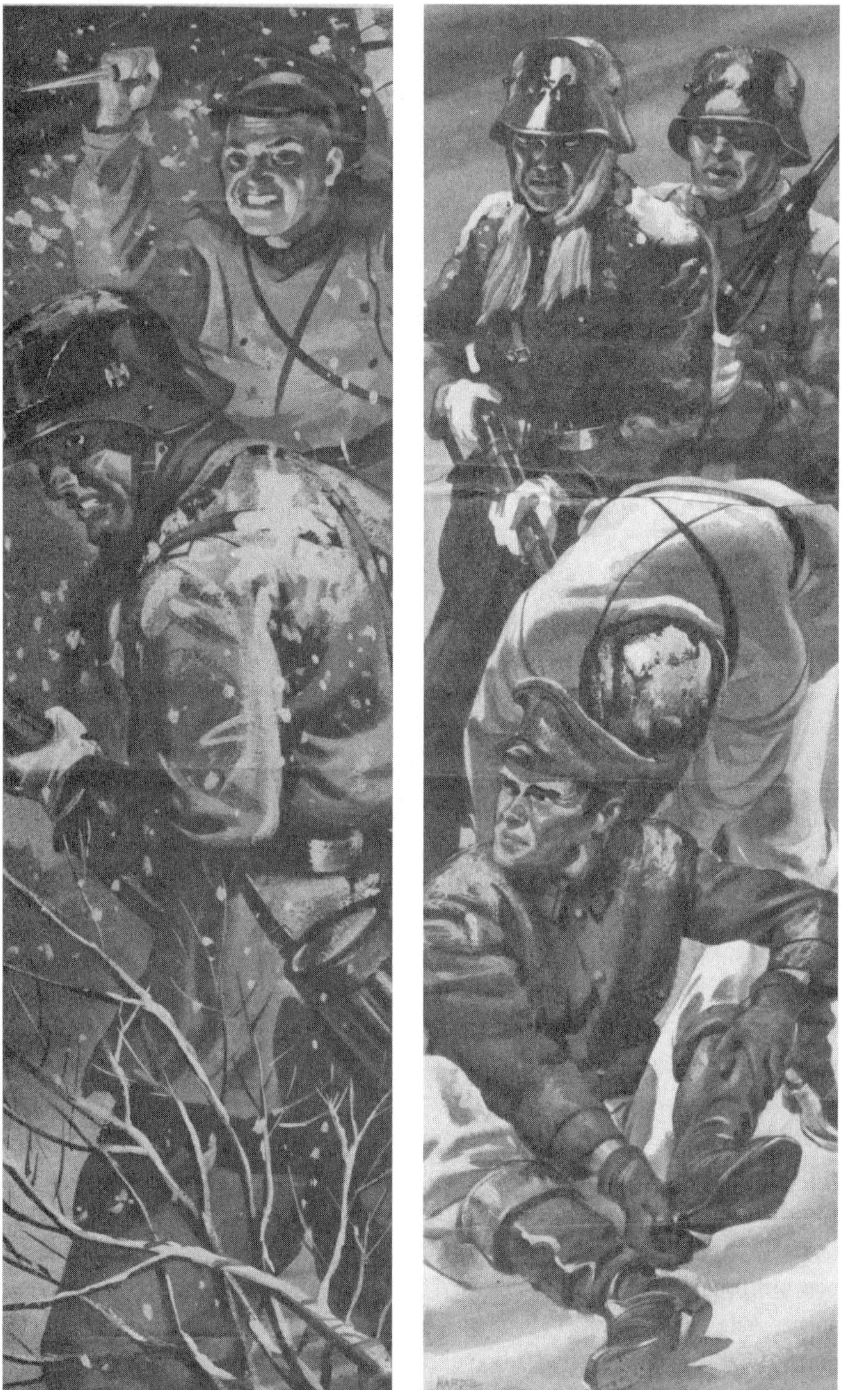

FIGURE 46. *All Night Long* artwork by Hardy Gramatky (from *Redbook* magazine; copyright Hardie Gramatky archives, Beinecke Library, Yale University)

Although Caldwell is silent on the point, a political instructor was a core member of every partisan unit as well as of every Red Army unit. Political instructors were almost always either Communist Party or Comintern members, and it was their job to make sure that partisans remained solid and faithful Soviet citizens, and that the party's line—Stalin's line—was followed. Most partisan units also had a secret police representative, an NKVD man, to ferret out any Nazi moles who might have infiltrated the unit. Caldwell makes no mention of this unsavory element of the partisan movement.[4]

In *All Night Long,* Commissar Sorokin is given the role of providing some of the backstory of the Russian (and the Western) cause: "The political instructor at the collective farm painted a terrifying picture of what could be expected if the Germans succeeded in conquering them. He had told them what the Germans have done to the people of other countries. The Czechs, Poles, and Greeks had been systematically tortured and killed. They had been executed family by family, village by village. Their homes were burned and their fields taken away from them" (*ANL* 51–52). Earlier, we had learned just how well Sergei is already indoctrinated: "He was angry because these men had come to enslave them; if they had come as friends, they would not be at that very moment walking up and down through the darkness ready to kill him on sight. He knew what they were doing then was only the beginning, and that they would steal and plunder, murder and torture, and that finally in the end they would set up a rule of cruelty and enslavement against which there would be no appeal" (*ANL* 43). Caldwell inculcates his characters with simplistic sentiments such as these throughout the novel.

In any event, after Sorokin and Sergei arrive at the main partisan camp, they are assigned the task—perhaps as a test of both their loyalty and worthiness—of taking out a German communications center in the nearby village of Budnya. At the camp Sergei meets another stock character, the fearless and risk-taking partisan, Fyodor Smirnovich, whose entire family has been destroyed in horrendous fashion. Caldwell's narrative, which earlier titillated readers with a scene of a German officer ripping open Natasha's bodice (*ANL* 27),[5] luxuriously details the beating, torturing, and killing of Fyodor's family, in particular the raping of his twelve-year-old daughter before her father's eyes (*ANL* 82–83). This account is a topos of the Nazi occupation of Russia, which Caldwell repeats later when the partisan unit comes across the body of another raped adolescent (*ANL* 188).

Sergei recruits a seven-man commando unit for the raid, but before they set out, Caldwell has the political instructor deliver a pep talk: "'We'll have to fight hard, tovarish,' Nikolai said after a while. 'The Hitlerites are strong, very strong.

It's not going to be easy to beat them. But we will follow them over every inch of ground, killing them one by one if that's the only way, until there's not a single Hitlerite left. For every life they take, we'll take two of theirs'" (*ANL* 58–59). The raid is completely successful. Sergei's commandos dispatch dozens of Nazis via gunfire and grenades. Though Sorokin dies a hero's death, the radio station is destroyed by fire and the Nazis are left in disarray, another trope of the socialist realist novel and of Russian propaganda in general: Russians are united, poised, and effective, whereas Germans are bickering, frightened, and confused. Nonetheless, the partisans lose three of their own, including Commissar Sorokin. A political instructor to his bitter end, Sorokin is not allowed to die without reiterating the Communist agenda: "'I have to die sometime, tovarish,' he said. 'All of us have to die sooner or later.' His voice became more firm and clear. 'I won't live much longer, Sergei. I want you to think of me every time you raid the Nemetskis [Nazis]. Each time I want you to kill a share for me. You'll know that I'm watching you. It will be just the same as if I were there with you. I don't mind dying when I know that you will be doing that for us'" (*ANL* 119). Such attitudes as these reflect core values of socialist realism.

After their return to the partisan stronghold, the senior brigade leader, Ivan Pavlenko, assigns Sergei and Fyodor an even more dangerous mission. Pavlenko, we have learned, is a recent bilateral amputee. When the Nazi blitzkrieg hit his collective farm, the Germans lined up all the village men to shoot them, but instead sadistically ran them over with tanks. Pavlenko escaped with his life, but his legs were crushed. Now he manages with the help of Vladimir, a twelve-year-old whose entire family, like Fyodor's, had been wiped out in front of him by the Nazis. He now serves as Pavlenko's legs; he also serves as the stock character of the lovable but tragically doomed youngster. The message is clear: no one shirks her or his patriotic duty to the *rodina*, regardless of their disability.

Pavlenko sends Sergei and Fyodor to the rail center of Vyndomsk, a town not dissimilar to Vyazma, where Caldwell and the press corps had spent their first evening and witnessed its bombing the following morning. "Vyndomsk is closer to the front than Budnya, and much more important to the enemy. All of their supplies and replacements for the central front pass through Vyndomsk, either on the railroad or the highway" (*ANL* 150). Their first encounter is with a "diversionist." She is a vivacious German, Fräulein Almendinger—a plaything providing sexual favors to German officers—disguised as an old peasant crone who entices the partisan pair into her house for some potatoes but who has much more in store for them. By the time Sergei and Fyodor make their escape, they have killed her and three Germans, all by a silent knife across the throat.

Sergei, the heroic protagonist, hesitates to kill a woman, no matter how heinous her role:

> "This is something I don't like," Sergei said. "I don't like to kill a woman, even if she is a Nemetski. I wish we could turn her over to an execution squad."
>
> [Fyodor:] "We are our own execution squad, tovarish. And, besides, she's a diversionist. All diversionists have to be executed in wartime. It makes no difference if they are male or female." (*ANL* 199)

Fyodor, his bitterness showing no bounds, slits Fräulein Almendinger's throat and mops up her blood with a rug.

Before they leave her cottage they are greeted by a mysterious comrade, Josef Boronov, known as "The Snowbird" because he wears a white rain slicker. Boronov has been expecting them because Pavlenko had gotten word to him, a detail to show that connections among partisan units are well developed and effective, and a counterpoint to the damage they had just done to Nazi communications in Budnya. Caldwell now draws the novel to its cinematic climax. The twenty partisans derail a troop train and wipe out more than half the soldiers aboard, explode an ammunition convoy, and dynamite a key bridge across the Dnieper. Typical of Caldwell's overwrought prose at this point is this passage: "Many of the Germans broke the windows and leaped out, but their bodies, bored with steel-tipped bullets from automatic rifles, fluttered to the ground like insects dropping from the flame of a candle" (*ANL* 233–34). Descriptions such as this appear throughout the book and are consonant with Caldwell's hopes for a cinematic adaptation.

In the middle of this havoc Vladimir reappears. He brings the news that Natasha is alive but captive in a German military brothel in Vyndomsk. Vladimir disappears in the ensuing mayhem, and Boronov introduces Sergei to a Maria Makarova, whose teenage daughter is also enslaved in the brothel. Sergei, Fyodor, Boronov, and a few other guerillas attack the brothel, but not before the Nazis march thousands of the townspeople to the central *platz*, where they hang five captured partisans in reprisal for that evening's raid. Not surprisingly, one of them is Vladimir. The partisan ethos is that if you get caught and are threatened with hanging, you "take one for the team" without identifying any of your comrades. This Vladimir does. Soon, the partisans regroup and slaughter the Nazis at the brothel and rescue Natasha and Tanya Makarova.

Fyodor also dies. With pathos and an appeal to party ideology, he expires with these words on his lips: "'I understand,' Fyodor said. 'He [Vladimir] was killed by the Nemetskis. They will kill me, too, someday. But another Fyodor will take my place. They can't kill all the Fyodors in Russia. That's why they can never defeat us. There will always be a Fyodor to destroy them'" (*ANL* 266). Sergei finally breaks down. Clearly, not everyone has been equally steeled in Fyodor's cauldron of loathing: "'Fyodor!' he said, lifting the heavy body and holding Fyodor's head in his arms. 'You can't die, Fyodor! You can't! You can't leave me now. We've done everything together, tovarish. I can't do it all alone now. I'd be lost without you, Fyodor'" (*ANL* 276). The Korokovs are joyously reunited: "He forgot everything else when he felt her warm body in his arms and her clinging lips against his mouth" (*ANL* 272–73). Sergei spirits Natasha off to a manger in the woods where they truly reunite, but since both remain partisans at heart and a traitor-spy remains on the loose in Vyndomsk, the resistance must continue:

> "We are together now, Sergei," she whispered. "I thought it would never happen again."
>
> He stroked her hair gently, kissing her cheeks, her lips, and her shoulders. They clung to each other desperately for a long time.
>
> When he looked out again, the snow was still falling.
>
> "Natasha," he whispered.
>
> "What is it, Sergei?" she said, waking with a start.
>
> "I'll have to go away for a little while," he said.
>
> Natasha hugged him desperately. (*ANL* 281)

All Night Long clearly is melodrama, the kind Caldwell and his publishers hoped the nondiscriminating reading public would enjoy. Caldwell had the credibility and the celebrity to try to pull it off. Discounting its value as a profit-making vehicle, it was not written with a view toward enduring literary significance but rather as propaganda in a fictional package that was distinct from his earlier newspaper and magazine reporting. And to make money.

All Night Long in Context

Although Caldwell's experience with guerilla warfare had been limited to his supervised meetings in Moscow with politically cleansed veterans and partisan activists and to whatever he gleaned on his own during the correspondents' chaperoned trip toward the Smolensk front, in America he was billed as an expert. As it began its four-part serialization of *All Night Long* in November 1942, *Redbook* magazine crowed: "One of the few foreign correspondents permitted to visit the eastern front, Mr. Caldwell made the acquaintance of the guerrillas while in Russia. His novel is more than a work of fiction; it is a powerful account of the most gigantic struggle ever witnessed by the world."[6] It added: "This grimly realistic novel by the brilliant author of 'Tobacco Road' tells you more about the gigantic struggle in Russia and better succeeds in giving the atmosphere of the total war than all the news dispatches."[7] Caldwell was capable of atmospherics, but he had several agendas over and above accuracy and education. Furthermore, no one in the West, or outside the Kremlin for that matter, actually knew what was transpiring in partisan-impacted regions.

To some degree, however, *All Night Long was* educational, although its message was clearly not an isolationist one. In the first of his two autobiographies, *Call It Experience* (1951), Caldwell writes: "The purpose of the novel was to explain, in fictional form, the part taken in the Soviet Union, during a time of war, by civilians. It seemed to me that partisan warfare, as it was called, was to become an important part of international conflict in the future and that an explanation of it would be of interest to Americans."[8] In the novel Russians are unambiguously writ as heroes. For instance, just before Sergei kills them, two young German truck drivers commiserate about their plight but disagree about which side has the upper hand:

> "What makes you think it [the war] will be over soon?" the other one asked.
>
> "We are moving forward twenty miles a day, aren't we? Moscow can't be much farther away by now."
>
> "I'm afraid of that Moscow," the German on the ground said. "I don't like the looks of things. Did you ever notice how these Russian peasants look at us? Everyone I've ever seen acts as though all he thinks about is how many bullets it's going to take to kill you. Even the children that are no taller than your thumb have that same kind of strange look in their faces." (*ANL* 48–49)

Later, in the fräulein's cottage, one of the German officers complains about his own untenable situation in Vyndomsk:

> Russians are not fools! Guerrillas are wrecking our trains and blowing up bridges every night! They steal the rails and sink them in these god-damn marshes as fast as we can lay them on the road-bed. If those wise men of Berlin know how to combat guerrillas, they ought to be made to come here themselves and have their own throats slit these dark nights. Why don't they send us troops to fight the guerrillas! While we are trying to destroy the Red Army at the front, the guerrillas are annihilating us in the rear! (*ANL* 203)

Germans are stereotypically depicted as subhuman swine. Fyodor, who has had experience with them, is succinct: "They are barbarians—thieves—murderers—nemchura! There's nothing too fiendish for them!" (*ANL* 79). When Sergei kills his first German, Caldwell describes his feelings: "As he felt the blade sink downward easily through the soft flesh, Sergei had no feeling that he was taking a human life; the German was an inanimate object that had to be destroyed before it destroyed him" (*ANL* 44). Germans are inevitably unshaven and filthy, and their faces speak of cruelty: "The sergeant, however, was short in build with a small pinched face studded with round black eyes set deep in his egg-shaped head. His straw-colored hair was close-cropped and bristly. A woman's bright red scarf was wound around his neck, above which were two enormous frost-nipped ears" (*ANL* 20). Mention of the woman's scarf encourages the reader to wonder from whom, and how he had gotten it. Indeed, a clichéd sense of Teutonic anxiety is stressed regularly. One of the favorite refrains of the *All Night Long* partisans is that the Germans are forever "shooting at snowflakes." They are quick to turn on each other, as when Fräulein Almendinger yells at the men who are supposed to be guarding her. Germans are cowards, stupid, and lazy (*ANL* 238, 190, 192, 209, 158, 156).

These are all traditional wartime images—not unique to Russian propaganda or the socialist realist novel—as are the images of atrocity, especially those imbued with sexual overtones:

> Our men are tortured and killed, but our women suffer even more. The fashisti make a sport of degenerate acts. Almost every day there are reports of them indulging in one of their inhuman orgies. Last week a truckload of them caught a girl and abused her for four hours. After they had finished with her, they threw her into the street. She died the next day. Three days ago in another village they drove all the men into the forest and made all the women strip off their clothes and parade in the square. Then the women were forced to indulge in every degenerate act the rotten-minded fashisti could think of. (*ANL* 72–73)

Fyodor's story, of course, is particularly repugnant. After the Germans had tied him up, they forced him to watch them kill his pregnant wife in grotesquely sexualized terms: "She didn't die fast enough to please them. They stuck their bayonets into her while she lay screaming helplessly on the floor. Then they stood and watched her suffer. They didn't want her to die then. They want her to lie there and scream and squirm in agony. They wouldn't even fire a pistol into her head and get it over with. They slashed open her body, cutting the unborn baby in half" (*ANL* 82). The rape of his twelve-year-old daughter immediately follows.

Reading *All Night Long* with seventy years' hindsight is perhaps unfair to its contemporary readers, who were being actively courted with the pro-activist, anti-Fascist, and pro-Soviet messaging of the Popular Front. In 1942 Caldwell portrayed the partisans in a fashion beneficial to the war effort. By the time *All Night Long* was in the hands of readers, the United States had been at war for almost a year, during which time the Russians had been successful in halting and even repelling the Axis powers on several fronts. More importantly, the outcome of the war was then still unclear, particularly when it came to post-war international borders and spheres of political influence. Caldwell's fictional account of the partisan movement was carefully designed to stir American enthusiasm for this remote eastern war and in that regard was successful.

The official Soviet stance was that the war was not being fought against Germans per se, but against Hitlerites specifically: "If Hitler had not inflamed their minds with fascism, they would have been attending classes in a University or working in a shop or factory, and their parents would not someday receive brief notices saying they had died somewhere in Russia" (*ANL* 51). Hitlerites were as subhuman in this view as they themselves considered the Russians to be. As a corollary to this, partisans were reputed to take no prisoners. Counter to the popular distinction between decent and evil Germans, partisans seem to identify every German soldier as a probable Hitlerite. At one point a young German soldier attempts to surrender, but Commissar Sorokin insists: "They'll have to learn to go to the front and give themselves up to the Red Army if they want to surrender. Partisans don't take prisoners. Back here our task is to exterminate Hitlerites, not to prolong their existence" (*ANL* 103).

Caldwell generally depicts partisans as uniformly patriotic volunteers. Brigade leader Pavlenko tells Sergei before his second mission to a town of over five thousand: "All citizens are partisans, no matter where they are, and the people in Vyndomsk are ready to help regardless of the danger. The Nemetskies have been very ruthless there, and so we must be ruthless towards them" (*ANL* 149). Elitism and social stratification based on political connections were not to be part of the partisans' public persona. But Caldwell offers a mixed portrait: "They had volunteered when they became guerrillas, and to be selected to take part in a raid, was an honor" (*ANL* 89). In fact, sometimes the selection was based on past performance and skills, at other times on political preferment.

Although food procurement was problematic, Soviet propaganda took pains to describe the local villagers and peasants as feeding the partisans out of gratitude for the work they were doing and out of dedication to the *rodina*. Caldwell follows suit in this exchange when Sergei and Alexei sneak into Budnya:

> They stepped into the room and the woman closed the door and bolted it securely. There was a warm fire in her stove and they went to the corner and warmed their hands.
>
> "Are you hungry, Alexei Ivanovich?" she asked.
>
> "I'm always hungry. And so is my friend. We are always ready to eat."

> She took a dish of gingerbread from her cupboard and gave it to them.[9]
>
> "I wish I could give you some milk," she said, "but the thieving Nemetskies drove my cow away." (*ANL* 98–99)

It is clear now in hindsight that such heartfelt altruism made for fine reading but was quite unlikely.

One method for preventing the Germans from making off with local foodstuffs was to destroy everything. But in *All Night Long* Caldwell describes a more benign policy: "The wheat and rye had been harvested in late June and early July, several weeks before the Germans had been able to reach the region, and all the grain had been shipped away. Farther north, however, where the standing grain was still green in July, the Germans had been able to harvest the crops for themselves" (*ANL* 96–97). On this subject and on the partisans in general, Caldwell, in his CBS radio broadcast of August 2, 1941, had highlighted the remarks of Simon Lozovsky, the assistant people's commissar of foreign affairs, who gave the correspondent pool nightly briefings on the progress of the war:

> Lozovsky said that Germany's troubles are mounting day by day, and that the problems facing the German command are accute [*sic*]. He said that they had expected to get food supplies in occupied territory, but that Stalin's scorched earth policy had deprived them, not only of food but of drinking water as well. He said the Germans were unable to live off the country they had seized, and that all their supplies had to be transported from Germany.
>
> In addition to finding no food, he said that they were constantly being attacked by partizans [*sic*] in the occupied territories. This unlooked for circumstance, Lozovsky stated, had forced the German command to scrap all their plans and to devote a large part of their energy and equipment to the hopeless task of trying to keep the partizans [*sic*] from destroying their communications.[10]

Later in the war, when the partisans found themselves behind now-retreating German lines, following edicts from the Kremlin they adopted a viciously hard-line policy, which did not sit well with peasants and villagers who found the means for their own survival heartlessly and dispassionately destroyed.

Another policy issue facing the Kremlin was the prioritization of partisan objectives: tactical military ones vs. the protection of the populace. In *All Night Long,* Caldwell describes only the more palatable civil goal. Partisan leader Pavlenko explains that although the demolishment of the Budnya radio station is their principal task, "don't forget that it is equally important that the lives of our people be saved. No man must die if it's possible to save him and at the same time accomplish the task. The lives of our people are dear to us. No matter what you are doing, Korokov, always remember that" (*ANL* 93). Nonetheless, documents that have recently become available are clear that early on, when the Soviet war enterprise was focused on saving Moscow at all costs, the partisans' military role had been primary.[11]

Caldwell portrays the Russian partisan as a member of a small patriotic band of loners, reminiscent of an American cowboy (*partizanshchina*), but one functioning under a stern yet kind and dedicated leader. This perhaps accurately describes the makeup of some partisan units in the very early stages of the war, but within several months the Soviet central establishment had already regained control of this behind-the-lines chain of command and reestablished order, hierarchy, and, most importantly, the cult of Stalin. For Caldwell, Ivan Pavlenko, the partisan chief brigade leader, is just such a figure, his crippling wounds even ennobling him. Just before he sends Sergei out on his mission to Budnya, Pavlenko asks after Natasha and offers his hope for her safe return. "Sergei said nothing, but he squeezed the hand that was gripping his with fatherly devotion" (*ANL* 94). But the flip side of Stalin as kindly patriarch is the stern and uncompromising father commanding obedience, and Sergei, as hero-protagonist of *All Night Long*, exemplifies both types:

> "Tovarish, you are disobeying my order," he [Sergei] said calmly.
>
> Fyodor stopped struggling. He lay still for a long time looking up at Sergei.
>
> "I want to be a good Russian," he said slowly. "I'm sorry, tovarish!"
>
> Sergei reached down and helped him to his feet. Neither said anything right away.
>
> "I disobeyed your order," Fyodor said finally. "It is your duty to report me to Pavlenko." . . .
>
> "But I disobeyed, tovarish."
>
> "All of us are tired. Now that our work for tonight is finished, there's nothing else that matters."
>
> "Then you are not going to keep me from going on the next raid?"
>
> Sergei put his arm around his shoulder, hugging him tightly.
>
> "No, tovarish, not that. I'll order you to go. We will work together from now on." (*ANL* 135–36)

Caldwell is insightful here in terms of partisan structure, in that he makes the command and control protocols clear. When Sergei first encounters the political commissar Sorokin in the old mill, he is grilled by him:

> "Were you ordered to come into the Nemetski rear?"
>
> "Yes," Sergei replied.
>
> "What are your instructions?" Nikolai asked quickly.

> "I am a brigade leader. I was ordered to select a new commander for my brigade and to leave my men in Ivanovka. My instructions are to report to the senior brigadier of the partisans in the Deshva Marsh." (*ANL* 58)

Sergei presumably has received his instructions via coded radio broadcasts. Caldwell employs the perquisites of the novelist to telescope and otherwise manipulate time. While Caldwell's particular partisans are fighting in 1941, they are actually equipped to a level in effect only a year or so later. Before Sorokin appears, Sergei uses a radio set that had been hidden in the spring before the war to receive instructions through coded radio broadcasts: "The reader gave detailed instructions to a certain guerrilla brigade near Smolensk to raid and destroy a field headquarters that had been established by the Germans in a school the day before. The code told how many staff officers were in the village, the number of troops in the garrison, and the location of outposts" (*ANL* 55). Caldwell's partisans are always well supplied with radios. But in reality, the partisan movement almost collapsed from the lack of reliable communication.

This matter of hidden radios was part of a more general effort on the part of the Soviet central command to present itself to the West as well prepared for the German blitzkrieg. This of course had not really been the case. It is also doubtful that weapons had been concealed as Caldwell describes them: "The three rifles were buried in a heavy coffin-like box under the floor of the room. They had been put there, as had the powder and oil in the potato field behind the house and the grenades under the loose bricks in the base of the chimney, when they were distributed early that spring among all the members of the collective farm" (*ANL* 12–13). Not only is Sergei dubiously furnished with weaponry, ammunition, and radios, but Caldwell even has him "studying German in the language school at the kolkhoz [collective farm] that spring" (*ANL* 47), an unlikely enterprise.

Such highly improbable preparations, however, are highlighted as fact in a *New York Post* review of *All Night Long:* "The book opens with the coming of the Nazis. All is prepared for just this arrival. Sergei has been trained intensively for guerrilla warfare. His guns are hidden in the grease beneath the floor. There are secret caches of grenades behind one stone of the fireplace. The attic of the cabin is fixed for a hideaway."[12] In a *Saturday Review* appraisal, Ann Wolfe writes that Sergei is a member "of a partisan group that has been painstakingly and efficiently trained in guerrilla tactics."[13] All this was quite doubtful, but no one in the United States knew that at the time. For the Kremlin, it was a public relations coup.

At the same time, the Germans are painted not so much as strong and steadfast soldiers but as a marauding horde of vicious rapists and murderers. And then, of course, Nazis are cowering cowards, too. One sixteen-year-old German soldier whimpers, "I don't want to fight anymore. All my friends have been killed at the front. I want to go home" (*ANL* 124). Caldwell uses this encounter to establish his own political leanings for the American public. After the boy volunteers some apparently sensitive information about German positions and armament, Sergei tells Fyodor: "The political instructor at my collective farm said Italian boys of sixteen and seventeen did the same thing when they surrendered in Spain during the Civil War" (*ANL* 124). In a single sentence Caldwell supports Stalin's collectivization program as well as the then-hapless Republican cause in Spain, thereby placing himself clearly in the anti-Fascist Popular Front camp.

Most poignant, however, is Caldwell's appeal to pathos, as memories of the motherland, the *rodina*, are rendered with great emotional force. Soon after Sergei's initial dash from Ivanovka, he confronts a young German truck driver. Because, as usual, Sergei is compassionate, he cannot shoot without thinking it over:

> He had a lot to live for. He had his home and his work, holidays on the river in summer, hunting trips in the forest in the autumn, the long winter nights with Natasha, and in the spring the lonely walks over the rain-drenched fields when the willows began to bud and the grass lay like a velvet carpet over the earth. Anger blazed in his heart.
>
> He pressed his finger against the trigger. (*ANL* 50)

Although touting the Soviet way of life would later prove to be contentious, if not dangerous, as Caldwell's later experience working on a Hollywood screenplay for *Mission to Moscow* demonstrated, in 1942 socialism still had many avid supporters in America who were calling attention to the racist policies of the Reich.

Recalling that one of the characteristic features of the socialist realist novel noted by Gary Morson is the embedded "political sermon," it is clear how Caldwell is again true to the genre. Some of the most unnerving and disappointing passages in *All Night Long* occur when Caldwell traffics in hackneyed and saccharine socialist cant. Perhaps because Sorokin is a political commissar, Caldwell has him deliver this absurd speech to Sergei in a dark room where there are only the two of them: "Always remember why they must be killed. We are not killing them because they are men, but because they are Hitlerites. All men are brothers, until some of them try to enslave the others. Some day we will all be brothers again and no man will try to make a slave of another. But until then every human being who is a Hitlerite and a fascist must be destroyed. That's why we must kill without pity. We are fighting for our lives and homes, and for our freedom" (*ANL* 59). Sorokin continues with a family homily after Sergei announces he has bread in his pack: "And I have some sausage. It's a sign of good fortune to meet up with someone who has bread. Now, both of us will have bread and sausage. If we had not met, you would have eaten the bread without sausage, and I would have eaten sausage without bread. That proves how wise my grandfather was, even in his old age. He always said if you share with your neighbor, and your neighbor shares with you, both of you will have more than either had to begin with" (*ANL* 60). Perhaps feeling guilty because he admits to not having killed a single Nazi so far, Sorokin concludes: "The Hitlerites are losing thousands of men. Our Red Army and guerrillas are forcing them to pay more than they can afford for every inch of ground they take. But Hitler pushes them on and on, no matter what the cost. We must fight harder all the time, around the clock day and night, because the only way to stop them is to destroy them" (*ANL* 61).

On the other hand, balancing such ideologically stilted moments are Caldwell's descriptive passages, long his forte. He is adept at placing the reader in physical spaces, whether on the Russian steppe or on a Ukrainian battleground: "A star shell went up from the German trenches, casting a dazzling light over the snowy fields. As it descended slowly, revealing the crouching white figures at the fringe of the silver birches, the Germans began firing automatic rifles and machine guns at them. As soon as the star shell sank to the ground, the Russians changed their position, and the German fire fell harmlessly in the birches" (*ANL* 35–36). Now and then Caldwell seems to recall his own encounters near the front, when he describes the awesome, raw power of war: "Now that the sky had cleared they could see faint red glows on the horizon. There were frequent flashes of intense white light, followed by the faraway sound of cannonading. There was never a pause in the fighting on the front. The relentless pounding of the artillery continued hour after hour from both sides, and even during the middle of the night the thunder and rumble of the big guns shook the earth" (*ANL* 63). At one point Caldwell's experience merges with that of Sergei:

> The sky was clearing when he emerged, and stars were twinkling through the foliage of the trees. He stopped and looked up at the heavens for several moments before going up the path. Halfway to the cave where the men were waiting for him, he stopped again, this time to listen to the rumble of artillery. The big guns always seemed closer when the air was clear, and this time they sounded as though they

were no farther away than the edge of the marsh. Sheets of white flashes flared on the horizon, and occasionally a lingering glow of orange-colored light from the slowly descending flare hung low in the sky. He looked overhead once more at the twinkling stars, wondering how they could appear so calm and peaceful above a world ruled by fire and the sword. (*ANL* 94–95)

All Night Long seemed to meet Caldwell's own goals, and in none of his autobiographical material nor in his letters does he express any doubts about the work's quality. His agent and his publishers saw it as a sure moneymaker.

Publication and After

By the end of June, Caldwell had submitted *All Night Long* to Duell, Sloan and Pearce, and he was ready for a break from writing.[14] But he had a book to sell and possible movie rights to consider, so he couldn't withdraw altogether. Maxim Lieber, his literary agent,[15] was the first to comment, since he had had the advantage of seeing the manuscript before Caldwell turned it in. On July 2 Lieber wrote Caldwell: "This morning I feel I have been put through a ringer. What's more, I'm convinced that almost any reader of VENGEANCE OF THE EARTH [this was an alternative title that ultimately became the film title] will come away from the book with a somewhat similar experience. In my opinion, the script is a little monument to the indomitable courage of an amazing people fighting to the last drop of blood for life, liberty and the pursuit of happiness. (Duell, Sloan & Pearce, please copy for full page ads.)"[16] Lieber took the liberty to be an editor rather than merely giving kudos to his author: his opening compliment was followed by three extensive paragraphs detailing precise changes he thought Caldwell should make, including "a few *tak taks* or a few *da das* may lend some flavor."

On the other hand, the heads of DS&P lined up to champion the novel with unbridled enthusiasm. Sam Sloan apparently loved it and probably saw great commercial potential in it. Writing on July 7 he effused:

> I saved it like a kid saving dessert to read over the weekend when I wouldn't be interrupted. It's wonderful. It reads like a house afire. And how it illumines the news in the papers. "Guerrilla activity" didn't have a hell of a lot of meaning before. No concrete, specific meaning, that is. Now I see it in terms of Sergei and Vladimir and Fyodor (that wonderful guy) and the rest.
>
> I've already started the movie campaign and you've given me plenty so I can put spin on the pitch.
>
> Hooray![17]

Charlie Duell added his compliments the next day: "I have been in a terrific tailspin with snipers after me from all points of cover. I did finish ALL NIGHT LONG on Sunday, and it is magnificent. Many congratulations."[18]

By this time Caldwell had moved his typewriter to Hollywood, where he was endeavoring to put together a screenplay for *Mission to Moscow*. Warner Brothers had obtained the rights to this unwieldy memoir of Joseph E. Davies, the former U.S. ambassador to the USSR, and was now engaged in trying to adapt it for the screen. Constantly multitasking, Caldwell also was still deeply involved in the many facets of bringing *All Night Long* to print. In July he wrote his old friend from Maine and Santa Fe, painter Alfred Morang, that he'd taken Lieber off the Hollywood scent because he thought Al Manuel, his California agent, could do a better job. "I believed Al Manuel could sell it outright. And he did. He sold it yesterday [July 14 to MGM] for $50,000 cash, plus $20,000 additional, making it a total of $70,000, if the published book sells 200,000 copies within one year after publication. I don't believe it will sell that many copies, so I'm going to be perfectly content having fifty thousand."[19]

Two months later, on September 9, in one of his last letters to Bourke-White, Caldwell provides her a far more detailed accounting than she was probably interested in at that point. But he also turns personal, trying to bring her back into a solar system of their own: "I think you ought to take a lot of credit for the novel, because this time was nothing like the other time [*All-Out on the Road to Smolensk*], and I have the feeling you will be even better about it the next time. In other words, you helped me while I was doing it more than you realized. I only wished you had had the time to see it through to the last page. You could have added a great deal to it. Please try next time to see it through from beginning to end. Promise?"

He concludes this two-page, single-spaced, typed letter with one final appeal: "I guess you know I love you. But do you really realize how much I love you? It's more than you think. The reason is that you are the only person. There'll never be anyone else but you. Unless it is the second Kit, and I think I would love both of you enough to go around." He signed the letter, as usual, "Skinny."[20]

All Night Long followed schedule. The reviews, as usual with a Caldwell novel, were mixed, in this case the politics of the reviewer being a significant factor.[21] An anonymous short review in the November *Kirkus Reviews* was encomiastic:

> This stirred me more than anything Erskine Caldwell has written. Here—in a brief and poignant story behind the scenes in Russia's guerilla warfare, his gift of blending realism with tensely emotional values is at its best. Here he is the journalist using his gifts as a story teller, but not merging them in a bitter social

document. . . . Vigorous, dramatic, a revitalizing of one segment of this war behind and within a war. For me it carried more conviction than his news reports.

Sterling North, at the time a literary editor and later a children's book writer, was equally effusive in the *New York Post*.[22] After comparing Hemingway's sympathetic use of guerillas in his Spanish Civil War novel of 1940, *For Whom the Bell Tolls*, he continues: "Not even the lens of Mrs. Caldwell (Margaret Bourke-White) can focus with keener insight than Erskine Caldwell's prose. It has the fierce, biting penetration of wind across the steppes." He concludes with a prediction: "Action has cleared Caldwell's mind of the morbid shadows which have festooned his tales of the South. He has found a better subject than the sex-mad religious fanatics in 'Journeyman' or even the half-witted Jeeters of 'Tobacco Road.' 'All Night Long' will certainly stand with 'God's Little Acre' as a major Caldwell creation." Howard Fast, too, in *The Nation* was effulgent in his praise, even recommending that "a million copies of Caldwell's book, paper bound, would cost less than a battery of anti-aircraft guns, and stowed, each in a soldier's knapsack, would do more good than a new cruiser."[23]

In the December 26 issue of *The Nation*, Margaret Marshall's review is titled "Caldwell Comes a Cropper." It went downhill soon thereafter. After first praising Caldwell as "one of our most talented writers of fiction," she avers, "He came up as a 'natural' storyteller, wrote with a seemingly instinctive, strict, and essentially poetic economy of expression wonderfully suited to his material—which he obviously knew to the point of saturation." She adds that *Tobacco Road* and *Trouble in July* were remarkably good and remarks on how much growth Caldwell had shown as an author. She presumes that he "was on the way to becoming an important novelist, who knew what he was doing." But since, "he has turned journalist and world traveler; he has been caught up, for understandable reasons, in the currents of a world at war."

All Night Long, she insists, is not only poorly written ("It is, I regret to say, one of the worst novels I have ever read"), it is disingenuous, forsaking the heartfelt verisimilitude of his southern novels.

> One may assume that Mr. Caldwell has never been behind the German lines in Soviet Russia and that his book is based on reports of what goes on there. The fact that he was dealing with unfamiliar material might be cited as the reason for the utter unreality of "All Night Long" as a picture not so much of Russian life as of any life whatever. It does not explain the failure of artistic intelligence which led Mr. Caldwell to believe that he could write, on the basis of a few months' observation, a convincing novel about Soviet Russia, let alone a novel about guerrilla warfare based on second-hand reports. It does not explain the far more shocking

> failure in taste and feeling that has led him to write a book which is not only a travesty of his own earlier work but which makes a travesty of the Russian struggle as well.

Finally, after noting that the novel had already been purchased by the film business, she accuses him of selling out to Hollywood. And if that weren't sufficient, she labels him a sensationalist hack: "he has concocted a novel which might have been turned out by any one of a half-dozen 'slick' writers bent only on exploiting the atrocities of war, particularly rape."

Anne Wolfe, writing in the December 19, 1942, *Saturday Review of Literature,* delivers a more nuanced message. She recognizes that because Caldwell, "a master reporter," is a southerner at heart, he cannot write this soul into the partisan psyche: "The partisans (guerrillas) of 'All Night Long' are not spiritually Russians." She concludes: "But for the most part the Caldwell thriller is a saga of hate. Pure adventure fans will be able to take the thrills and let the hatred go. They will have a good time, but they will miss the point of the story."

Others saw *All Night Long* for what it was: second-rate Caldwell without heart. In the *New York Times Book Review,* William Pène du Bois picked up where Wolfe let off. "Those readers who remember Mr. Caldwell as a superb novelist of the South," he opines, "will be vastly disappointed by 'All Night Long,' for it scarcely scratches the surface of the Russian earth and misses the Russian soul entirely. Those who enjoy two-fisted action for its own sake may get their money's worth." He continued:

> Mr. Caldwell has wasted a rare talent on material he feels but cannot encompass. He will always be a Georgia boy, no matter how hard he struggles; his homeland is in the pine-barrens, not in the frozen birch-groves before Moscow; even if his Russian improves, he will wander forever among the moujiks a novelist without a compass.

Du Bois saw the plot as mere undigested melodrama and "as simple as a series of recruiting posters."

> His marauders are supermen, no less; their Nazi opponents mere Keystone cops. After the first score of sentries have been left gutted in the snow, after the last powder magazine has been detonated with a hand grenade, one begins to feel that the market is oversold.

He concluded, "Certainly, if thrillers like 'All Night Long' must be written, they should be left to the carpenters who know the tricks. Wood-pulp fiction is not Mr. Caldwell's trade." But Caldwell perhaps was less interested in the novel's gravitas than in its Hollywood potential.

While the novel enjoyed a short period of heady success, that was not true of the film. As Caldwell had written Morang, Metro-Goldwyn-Mayer had purchased the film rights for $50,000 based only on the evidence of a couple of chapter prospectuses. Originally MGM slated it for a male audience, retitled as *Vengeance of the Earth*. The studio initially signed Spencer Tracy and Wallace Beery as leads, but the MGM moguls soon strategized that they needed a leading lady in it. They hired Elizabeth Reinhardt to rewrite the screenplay and engaged Hedy Lamarr and Jean-Pierre Aumont as Natasha and Sergei. Plans fell apart, however, the following July when Aumont deserted Hollywood to enlist in the Free French Forces in Tunisia.[24]

Despite *All Night Long*'s failure to reach the screen, Russian partisans were well represented on film at the time. In the fall of 1943 RKO filmed *Days of Glory* in the woodlands near Cedar City, Utah, simulating the forests near Tula, about 120 miles south of Moscow, where the guerilla action takes place just before the Russian reversal of fortunes in late autumn 1941. Gregory Peck, as the partisan hero-leader, and Tamara Toumanova, as a beautiful ballerina who is an inept and naïve recruit, took the lead roles. *The North Star*, starring Anne Baxter and Dana Andrews, was released in 1943 and portrays the partisans in their witness-avenger roles.[25] Although both films are clearly oriented toward portraying the Soviet Union as a worthy wartime ally, *The North Star* ran into intense criticism after the war because of its portrayal of the collective farm system as a blissful utopia. Robert Conquest, in *Harvest of Sorrow: Soviet Collectivization and the Terror-Famine*, writes: "One scandalous piece of active, rather than merely conniving, falsification coming as late as in the 1940s, [was] the production in Hollywood of the film *North Star*, which represented a Soviet collective farm as a hygienic, well-fed village of happy peasants—a travesty greater than could have been shown on Soviet screens to audiences used to lies, but experienced in this particular matter to a degree requiring at least a minimum of restraint."[26] The studio rereleased it in 1957 as *Armored Attack*, from which all references to the Russian nationality of the combatants had been scrubbed.

MGM, as things turned out, was not without a float in the pro-Soviet movie parade. In February 1944 it released a Robert Taylor–Susan Peters vehicle, *Song of Russia*. Its story begins before Barbarossa and features the predictable plot of an American conductor falling in love with a Russian musician. Against all odds, their love culminates in marriage, and, improbably, he is able to take her with him to the West. Much of the footage of Russia was official Soviet propaganda film, which so angered the House Committee on Un-American Activities that *Song* was named one of the three strongest pieces of evidence—along with *Mission to Moscow* and *North Star*—"proving" communism's influence in Hollywood.

All Night Long is a fascinating example of the convergence of craft, social activism, and cunning business acumen in a time of war. It reflects a strange deflection of purpose on the part of a popular and successful pre–World War II novelist, and it illustrates the ill-fortune that fame and renown can sometimes redound to a serious writer of fiction. It similarly reflects the lack of sophistication and critical judgment that the exigencies of war and the priorities of patriotism can induce in even an experienced journalist. *All Night Long* is a reminder of how easy it is for the ethics of journalism, with its presumably sacred search for the truth, to be subverted by political purpose or personal expediency, whether the genre be reportage or fiction.

Nevertheless, *All Night Long* sold well, kept Caldwell's name before the public, and in 1942 supported the Kremlin's position that it should be considered an important ally of the West against the Axis. But *All Night Long* was soon forgotten. As Caldwell biographer Dan Miller concludes: "He would not acknowledge that the marketplace was an unreliable barometer of literary worth. . . . In the next few years such self-delusion and greed contributed to an increasingly mediocre literary output."[27] It is hard to know whether Caldwell recognized this in 1942, because at the time the marketplace *was* of central importance to him, as evidenced by his pleasure about the $50,000 sale of the novel Lieber had negotiated.

In *All Night Long*—at best a brief chapter, or at least a footnote in the library of war fiction—Caldwell did still manage to cast a ray of light on the complex, dark, and blind path of war.

EPILOGUE

Wrapping It Up in Hollywood ★ *Mission to Moscow*

Upon the conclusion of their eight-month round-the-world journey with a long summer stopover in Moscow, Caldwell's and Bourke-White's paths diverged, both professionally and emotionally.[1] By the end of spring 1942 she was off to photograph the war, first in North Africa, then Italy, and finally in Germany. Her career was soaring, and with *Life*'s backing her name was gold. Caldwell's fortunes were not so sanguine. *Tobacco Road* had closed on Broadway May 31, 1941, after a record 3,180-performance run, negatively impacting his pocketbook.[2] *All-Out on the Road to Smolensk* had not sold well. The two books he had turned over to his London publisher, *Russia at War* and *Moscow Under Fire*, were busts. But in Hollywood his name was still marketable, and *All Night Long*'s short-term success seemed assured.

Caldwell had been writing nearly nonstop for a year. He had hoped to lease his and Bourke-White's Connecticut house, move to Tucson for the summer, then recommence his writing as he saw fit. But before he left he had a meeting in New York with Jake Wilk, the East Coast head of Warner Brothers' story department. Wilk told him that Joseph Davies, the former ambassador to the Soviet Union, whose memoir *Mission to Moscow* had been published in December—the film rights to which had been acquired by Warner—had asked specifically that Caldwell be hired as the screenwriter. Although Davies did not know Caldwell personally, he thought his Russian experience, his reputation as a writer manifestly sympathetic to the Soviet cause, and his previous familiarity with Hollywood were ideal credentials for his employment as the screenwriter of record.[3] Caldwell's Hollywood agent, Alvin G. Manuel, added to the clamor, hoping to milk the studio for a large stipend.

Davies's memoir presented a challenge. As the subtitle of the book suggests—*A record of confidential dispatches to the State Department, official and personal correspondence, current diary and journal entries, including notes and comments up to October, 1941*—it is a 638-page plotless compendium of documents, compiled and presented to give the impression that they are important, valid, and accurate official materials. Furthermore, despite its being ghostwritten, the prose was turgid. In July 1941 Davies had either been talked into doing the book by President Roosevelt himself, who at the time desperately wanted to upgrade the tenuously pro-Soviet attitude of the nation's intelligentsia, or else Roosevelt strongly endorsed the idea when Davies presented it to him.

In *Better World: Stalinism and the American Intellectuals,* William O'Neill writes that Davies, rather than demonstrating any intellectual gravitas, was actually "naïve beyond the Kremlin's wildest dreams." Nonetheless, "This foolish book [*Mission to Moscow*] was a great success on account of timing. It came out just when Americans, reeling from early defeats, were particularly grateful to Russia for holding on."[4] In any case, when the book was published in December 1941, reviewers quickly saw through this propaganda ploy, and once factual errors were pointed out, *Mission to Moscow* began to shed some of its patina of integrity. Nonetheless, as is sometimes the case, the negative publicity increased its sales to over 700,000 copies, remarkable for such a dry and hefty tome.[5] And for Caldwell, it must have been particularly galling that it outsold his own pro-Soviet memoir, *All-Out on the Road to Smolensk,* which he had based on a more current experience.

Caldwell at first resisted more writing. He was still hoping to rekindle his fading marriage. He had begun to romanticize the Southwest and arranged to stop in Santa Fe to visit his friend, the artist and would-be poet Alfred Morang, whom he had known since their days in Maine in the 1920s. Caldwell had wanted to clear his head, but he couldn't escape Wilk's and Manuel's dunning. Manuel had hinted that he might even be able to swing a deal with a studio for Bourke-White, and he did: $10,000 per year for five years for two months of work each year, mostly shooting promotional stills. But by this time Bourke-White was headed in the opposite direction. In *Portrait of Myself,* she sums up their marital difficulties from a two-decade perspective:

> It took the war actually to separate us. The attack on Pearl Harbor took place and our country was in the war. For me, there was no other choice than to offer my special skills wherever they might be useful. I wanted to go overseas. Erskine wanted to accept a Hollywood offer. He saw to it that I had a very profitable offer, too. He bought a house in a lovely part of Arizona as a present for me. I wouldn't accept the Hollywood offer; I couldn't accept the house, which I felt was another set of golden chains.
>
> I believe by this time both of us began to realize we were leading two separate lives that no longer fitted together. We had had five good, productive years—with occasional tempests, it's true, but with some real happiness. I was relieved when

> it was all over and glad we parted with a mutual affection and respect which still endures.[6]

Bourke-White may have thought they both recognized that their marriage was terminally incompatible, but Caldwell's summer correspondence suggests that he had not yet acknowledged it.

By the first week of July, Caldwell had surrendered to the magnetic pull of ready money and relocated to Southern California, staying at the Knickerbocker Hotel, ready for work. Wherever he was—Moscow, Connecticut, Hollywood—Caldwell generally retained a full-time secretary for business and personal correspondence and for help in juggling his many ventures. He had hired a Los Angeles woman, a Ms. Callahan, but the arrangement did not work out well. In fact, Caldwell telegraphed Bourke-White, who was still in New York on July 7, that Callahan had "WALKED OUT WITHOUT NOTICE FOR NO GOOD REASON."[7] At the time, not only was he involved with his new and lucrative screenwriting project, he was also guiding the multiple vectors of his *All Night Long* property—and all the while still personally involved with his ongoing American Folkways project, of which he was editor in chief. By 1955, this would become a twenty-four-volume celebration of American cultural and geographical diversity, and *his* role was to entice and select writers for the project. To replace Callahan, he asked Mildred Zinn, the young woman he had recruited during a brief layover in Miami in late 1939, to join him. She had been with him since February 1940, and he wrote later of her in *With All My Might*, "she was pleasant company in my loneliness."[8] One can perhaps read between these lines.

The *Mission to Moscow* screenplay was to prove to be the last literary product of his and Bourke-White's Russian adventure, although this one he had to undertake solo. It was a project that was fraught from the beginning with controversy and unsavory political ramifications for almost everyone involved. Nonetheless, each Saturday for the following nine weeks he picked up a $1,250 paycheck from the Warner payroll office.[9]

From Santa Fe, the day before he started work, he had cabled Bourke-White at New York's Barbizon Plaza Hotel.

> AL [Manuel] WANTS YOU APPROVE DEAL PHOTOGRAPHIC SERVICES FIVE YEAR CONTRACT WORK TWO MONTHS YEARLY TEN THOUSAND YEAR. HAS TWO STUDIOS INTERESTED. LOOKS GOOD TO ME. IF YOU INTERESTED WILL YOU LET ME KNOW APPROXIMATE MONTH AND YEAR YOU COULD START. WHY NOT WRITE ME A LETTER A DAY. AIRMAIL ONLY SIX CENTS. YOU DON'T KNOW ANYWHERE NEAR HOW MUCH EYE LOVE YOU = SKINNY

Missing her desperately that first week in Los Angeles, he even tried to talk her into flying out for the weekend, an unusual extravagance for the time. But after a while, as his work intensified and it was evident that she was headed east, not west, he seemed to buckle down, though for the first several weeks he still wrote her almost daily, receiving little in return. His letters frequently contained wistful commentary on the ongoing furnishing of "their" Tucson house, coupled with a sadness about her absence: "I wish you were here. When are you going to begin staying instead of going? I think it's about time to begin staying. Life isn't much without you around. Maybe you can't understand that, but that's exactly the way it is. I have the feeling that you want the same thing." A week or so later, Caldwell wrote in exasperation: "I suppose there will be no way of knowing when you leave until after you'fe [*sic*] left. It's been more than three weeks now since I left New York, and if you had known you would be so long in getting away, you could have come out with me for a couple of weeks."

Another theme of his correspondence was an effort to describe himself to her as an important and vital cog in the film industry. He insisted he was excited about the writing job, and he concluded this letter about his Christmas plans: "I've got a rough draft for the MtoM picture idea down on paper. Now I'll start work on 100 page 'treatment.' That will take two or three weeks. After that, if I'm not wrung out like a dishrag, or if I'm not taken off the story and given a 'wild west' to write, I'll go into the screen play. All in all, it will take at least three months to do the job. It's no easy life, any way you look at it." He wasn't above snarky comments. "Sweetest Kit," he wrote on July 9, "I've just finished my second day at the studio, and it will be a couple more before I can finish reading all of Joe Davies' memos about his early boyhood and whatnot. The guy is certainly crazy about himself. I'd call him Ego #1." This was not an unfounded or uncommon opinion about Davies, for as the work on the film progressed over the summer, Davies annoyed almost everyone associated with the project.

Rarely did Davies let it go unnoticed that his wife was the heiress of the C. W. Post fortune and that she was the founder of General Foods. At the time, she was considered the wealthiest woman in America.[10] While in Moscow, Mr. and Mrs. Davies had invested a great deal of effort amassing what became one of the world's great collections of pre-Revolution Russian art, purchasing objects that had been confiscated from the Romanovs and other royalists by the Communists, items that Stalin then sold off at a relative pittance to favored foreigners in order to raise hard currency for the Soviet state. In any case, Ambassador Davies never let truth stand in the way of his vigorous pro-Stalin political position. Assuming an apologist's stance toward Stalin's show trials of the late 1930s, he excused them as a kind of winnowing of unsavory and unpatriotic elements from the country and the military. In Davies's view, many of these victims were traitors.

But more important than these savors of political opportunism was Davies's difficult personality. When it came to the production of the film, he pointedly exercised one of the contractual obligations for which he had negotiated. Warner's, to get the *Mission* property, had agreed to give Davies absolute control over the script, a highly unusual perquisite then and now. Ultimately this became contentious. Davies objected, after shooting had commenced, that while other actors were reasonable facsimiles of the real people whom they were portraying, Walter Huston did not look like him. The compromise that was finally worked out with Jack Warner was that Davies himself would provide an on-screen introduction, a sort of prologue to augment *Mission to Moscow*'s diplomatic bona fides. Screenwriter Howard Koch, producer Robert Buckner, and director Michael Curtiz were appalled, but there was little they could do.

On July 10 Caldwell wrote Morang, excited about the project. In the meanwhile, other offers kept popping up, and as usual, Caldwell had his eye on his ledger book. Almost a month passed, and by this time Bourke-White was at the Athenaeum Hotel in London. On August 15, after clearing up some domestic issues ("I need to know . . . whether you wish sterling or life-time plated silver for the dining room"), Caldwell summarized his progress to her:

> I'm still working on Mission. I've completed about 2/3 of the 1st draft treatment (adaptation), which means that it will take me another two, three, or four weeks to finish. As you well know there is no picture story in the book itself, and I've had to write what abouts [*sic*] to an original story. The characters are the same, but in my adaptation there is no other resemblance to Davies' little squib. I put everybody in it from Roosevelt to Stalin, and that includes Hitler, Hess, Goebbels, Trotsky, Molotov, Voroshilov, Tukhachevsky, von Ribbentrop, Shigemitsu, Matsoaka, Timoshenko, Rykov, Bukharin, Yagoda, Vyshinsky, and Henry Shapiro. Don't you think a picture with all that in it ought to hold the movie-going public at least through the first half of a double-feature for $.27 before 1 p.m.?

What Caldwell didn't seem to know was that ill winds had begun to blow through the *Mission to Moscow* offices. Although in both his memoirs Caldwell insisted that he wrote the script in collaboration with producer Bob Buckner, Buckner was in fact undercutting him. On August 4 Caldwell filed a 125-page preliminary treatment and on August 21 submitted a revised 122-page version, both of which he believed to have been well received. In an August 20 letter to Bourke-White he claimed: "I've finished ¾ of my adaptation of 'Mission,' but the studio evidently liked what I've done to the story enough not to wait for the remaining ¼. In other words, they have decided to start the picture right away. Another writer is putting my adaptation into screen-play form (shooting script), and casting began this morning. . . . Of course, Davies hasn't seen or approved of it, but Jack Warner isn't worrying, and so I'm not either." But apparently such optimism, or such bluster, was not to be rewarded, although he was correct about another writer doing the screenplay.

Screenwriter Howard Koch recalled years later that although Davies had wanted Caldwell on the project, Caldwell just wasn't experienced enough for the very daunting task of preparing *Mission to Moscow* for the screen. "Caldwell did his best, [but] Davies' book was a ponderous mass of ungraphic details which would have stumped almost any writer."[11] In the end, "It soon proved to be a mistake and a waste of time and money. I liked Caldwell personally but his work and analysis of the problems was quite unacceptable. He was well-paid and excused, and his work on the screenplay was unusable, even by Davies' admission."[12]

In his memoir, *As Time Goes By*, Koch implies that the entire script was his own doing. Recalling the events thirty-seven years later, he recollects a conversation with a Warner's executive who told him: "[Warner's] had bought a book, an important book they were eager to film. There was trouble, the chronic trouble; they had a script they couldn't use, a cast waiting in the wings, and an early shooting date. Would I postpone my vacation long enough to write the screenplay for *Mission to Moscow*?"[13] Koch was either forgetful or suffused with Hollywood self-grandiosity.

Even so, Koch took the assignment, he claims, and a few days later aboard Santa Fe's Super Chief to Chicago, "it happened that between five and six that evening, as we passed through Needles on the California border, the opening sequence to *Mission to Moscow* emerged full-blown."[14] Culbert, on the other hand, having examined all the available treatments and scripts, notes: "In the end the release print followed almost exactly the order and content of the first seventy-seven scenes as Caldwell had prepared them."[15] Yet almost none of Caldwell's dialogue survived, and that may have been fortunate, as it was apparently as ham-handed as much of *All Night Long*'s had been.

Meanwhile, on August 29 Caldwell typed out another letter to Bourke-White, and after pouring out his self-doubts onto a sheet of Warner's Inter-Office Communication stationery with the subject line of "You," he doubled down on his role in the *Mission* project:

> I've got two more weeks to go on my ten-week contract, but judging by the way things are going I'll have to stay here an additional five or six weeks in order to

> complete the picture. It is scheduled to begin shooting October 6th, but even though casting began several days ago, there is still no completed script. In another week or two I'll begin working with another screen writer who'll help polish it off, and so maybe, by degrees, we'll have a shooting script, or at least the first fifty pages of one, by October 6th. The trouble is that Jack Warner wants the story left just as I've done it, but Mike Curtiz wants less personal story and more newsreely inserts. If they'll ever get together and make up their minds what it's going to be, I could finish up and get out of town and start working on the book I want to do. As it's going now I'll be lucky if I get away by November 1st.

He clearly was aware of a rift, but equally clearly, there were issues with inter-office communication.

On August 31 Davies wrote to Jack Warner, "I am very much concerned with the script . . . It is difficult for me to understand the delay."[16] Then, Culbert writes, "To mollify Davies, Buckner and Koch went to the Davies camp in the Adirondacks for a long conference on September 7–8."[17] Caldwell appears to have been carefully removed from the loop without his realizing it, though kept on the payroll. On September 2 he wrote Bourke-White:

> As I wrote you last time, I don't know how much longer I'll be here. My contract is up Sept 15th, but I've been told that I'll have to stay and see this story through, and possibly remain through the shooting, which will take about sixty days. It is now scheduled to begin October 6th. I've got to get to Tucson not later than the middle of November, however, to work on a book. I don't know how I'll be able to talk myself out of this job—I've never argued with anyone about letting me stop cashing a four-figure salary check weekly.

He had expressed similar confidence that he was the master of his own fate in a letter to Alfred Morang on August 22. Moreover, although he doesn't mention *Mission to Moscow* to Bourke-White in a letter on September 9, he expresses no real concern about his status: "I am finishing up here on September 15th. I haven't decided whether I'll do another short picture job or not." His last pay stub is dated September 15, 1942.

Although in July the *New York Times* had reported that Warner's was hoping to have *Mission to Moscow* in theaters by the first of October,[18] shooting didn't begin until November 10, with the final scenes shot in March 1943. It was released on April 30 to robust, even boisterous critical and popular response. Many in the know, like philosopher John Dewey, who had headed an American Association of University Professors' inquiry into the Moscow show trials of the late 1930s, objected vehemently to the film's (and Davies's book's) distortions and outright errors. Nonetheless, if the film's purpose had been to sway public opinion toward the Soviet Union during World War II, its effectiveness was dubious. *Variety* listed it as the eighty-fourth of the ninety-five top-grossing films at the box office that year, and by 1952 it had lost about $600,000.[19]

Several years later *Mission to Moscow* was at the center of what was to become more than another brouhaha. In 1947, by which time Franklin Delano Roosevelt had been dead for two years, the winds of suasion had shifted, as had political alignments. The Cold War was in its infancy, and fears about communism's worldwide penetration into the free world were spreading like wildfire. Friend turned on friend as the House Un-American Activities Committee (HUAC), fearing an internal Communist cabal, began subpoenaing witnesses and fueling a nationwide "Red Scare." From the vantage of 1947, those left leaners who had pushed for, created, and then stumped for the pro-Soviet *Mission to Moscow* were now seen as potential enemies of the American state. Howard Koch was among them. Having been a vocal member of a variety of "leftist" organizations, such as the Hollywood Writers Mobilization, he was served one of the first nineteen subpoenas. That he was not among the infamous Hollywood Ten was only because he had never been an actual member of the Communist Party. Koch recalls the HUAC in action:

> The "friendly witnesses" such as Jack Warner, John Wayne, and Adolphe Menjou were cataloguing our "political sins" in great detail and getting full coverage by the press. Warner testified that in his opinion I was a "Communist"; the studio had had to get rid of me because I was "slipping Communist propaganda into their films." This had a special irony since it was at his urgent request that I wrote the screenplay for *Mission to Moscow*, which had brought him kudos at the time but was now obviously an embarrassment.[20]

Ultimately Koch's name was added to the so-called Gray List and then to the expanded Red Channels List in 1950, both rolls of suspected subversives. All this must have eased whatever residual enmity Caldwell might have harbored about the manner in which he had been dismissed by Warner's. In *Call It Experience* (1951), during the HUAC Red-baiting period, he summed up his experience succinctly and without bitterness:

> I went to work at Warner Brothers' studio in Burbank the following week [after leaving New York]. First I wrote an outline of the story with Robert Buckner, who was producing the picture, and then I wrote a preliminary screenplay. I felt I had done my share of the writing and was willing to let someone else put the screenplay into final form so that I could leave for my delayed vacation in Arizona. The screenwriters who followed me insisted, for political reasons or otherwise, that I should not receive screen credit for the work I had done, and went so far as to

force Warner Brothers, with the approval of The Screenwriters' Guild, to remove my name from the film. Screenwriting, like journalism and the writing of travel books, had always been subordinate to my principal interest in life and the controversy was of minor importance to me. In fact, I was pleased, considering the contribution I had made to the picture, to know that someone believed that *Mission to Moscow* film credits would be helpful to a Hollywood screenwriting career.[21]

But a third of a century later—elaborating on his earlier text and freed from fears about political controversy—he was willing to name names, even as he steadfastly maintained his own innocence while misstating the Mildred Zinn matter:

> I went to work at the Warner Brothers studio in Burbank a few days after arriving in Hollywood with Mildred Zinn [his secretary from Connecticut].
>
> First I wrote a detailed outline for the film version of *Mission to Moscow* in collaboration with Robert Buckner, an earnest young producer, and next I wrote a complete screen treatment of the story. With all that work completed, I felt I had done my share on the film and was willing to let the screenwriters who followed me put the screenplay into final form for the director and his camera crew.
>
> It was at this point I found myself unwittingly involved in a heated political controversy. Considering myself to be an innocent bystander in the conflict between two opposing factions, who were card-carrying members of the Communist Party of the United States and dissident Communist fellow travelers, I'd disclaimed any political motives involving the Soviet Union and *Mission to Moscow*.
>
> In outspoken moments, I had let it be known that, based on what I had heard unofficially in Moscow, I did not consider Joseph Stalin to be an admirable, benevolent, humane leader of his people. It was plainly evident that the film was being made to serve as a propaganda vehicle to gain the approval of the American people to accept in wartime the close alliance of American democracy and Soviet Communism. I was aware that propaganda was an essential factor in modern warfare and decided it was my duty as an American to strive to help win the war and bring about the defeat of Adolf Hitler.[22]

In fact, propaganda had been Caldwell's and Bourke-White's primary agenda in Moscow in 1941.

He concludes, "Supremacy attained by one of the two Communist factions, the two screenwriters who followed me—and with the aid of the Screenwriters Guild—succeeded in having my name removed from the screen credits of *Mission to Moscow*." In fact, he insisted it was really a blessing: "the results of the contention among the political activists was of little interest to me by that time inasmuch as I had completed my thirteen weeks [actually ten] of service for Warner Brothers and was free to leave for Arizona and my new home."[23]

However it had come to pass, Caldwell made it to Tucson six weeks early, in the first part of October. His marriage was in tatters and his literary career, while still filling his bank account, was receiving less and less critical acclaim with each new book, although at first *All Night Long* appeared promising. As a result, he turned his attention to one last property, a series of poignant and humorous sketches, semi-autobiographical in nature, that he had commenced in Connecticut before leaving for Russia in March 1941, worked on in his hotel room in Moscow before the war broke out (much to Bourke-White's derisive and dismissive consternation), and could now wrap up and publish. When it *was* published in 1943, it would be the last of his works to receive favorable reviews for over two decades: *Georgia Boy*.

Caldwell must have looked back at his *Mission to Moscow* experience ambivalently. On one hand, while his Moscow summer had provided insight into what the film was all about, he hadn't been able to translate his time there into anything that would add to his oeuvre. While his film treatment outlines did provide a scaffold onto which Howard Koch could build the shooting script, Caldwell had gotten no recognition. On the other hand, he left freighted with none of the political baggage that would burden those who stayed, and he left with a nicely padded bank account. His marriage would soon be defunct, his future was uncertain, but he left Hollywood in sufficiently good shape that he could return four months later with a 40 percent raise, a new wife, and a new novel that was receiving fairly good reviews. On balance it had been a productive summer for Erskine Caldwell in 1942.

APPENDIX

Shifting Sands ★ The Critical Response to *You Have Seen Their Faces*

While Margaret Bourke-White's professional reputation was established in the pages of *Fortune* and *Life* magazines, and Caldwell's from his 1930s novels of social justice, particularly *Tobacco Road, God's Little Acre,* and *Journeyman,* their joint work, except for *You Have Seen Their Faces,* has received little critical attention. Critical examination did not really begin until the 1960s, a quarter-century after the publication of *You Have Seen Their Faces.* The evolution of that criticism is worth considering in detail because the reputation of both authors, to some degree, is tied to *You Have Seen Their Faces.*

Caldwell and Bourke-White's *You Have Seen Their Faces* seemed to be the ideal book for its moment, yet *Life*'s coverage of it ("The South of Erskine Caldwell Is Photographed by Margaret Bourke-White") paradoxically laid the seed for its later eclipse in the eyes of critics. In its November 27, 1937, issue,[1] *Life* used nine of Bourke-White's sixty-nine *Faces* photographs, selecting four taken at a single white-fundamentalist church service in Examiner, South Carolina, rearranging them, and also adding its own captions, thus removing most of Caldwell's contribution. In its introduction to the article, *Life* wags a stern finger: "Critics at once remarked two motifs in the volume: the ugly economic tragedy of the sharecroppers, already tiresomely familiar to the U.S. public; and the strange sardonic humor that rings through all of Mr. Caldwell's work. Herewith LIFE reproduces a few of the pictures that set forth most poignantly the sharecroppers' peculiar fatalism and the bitter laughter that even hunger cannot silence on their lips." In a 2006 paper published in *American Periodicals,* Chris Vials compares *You Have Seen Their Faces,* the book itself, with *Life*'s presentation of it. He concludes that "[t]aken together, the captioned images" of *Faces* do not portray the southern poor as sentimentalized or brutalized, as many have insisted, but rather "suggest to the reader that if one wants Southern stereotypes when 'looking at' the South, one can find them." But more importantly, through the variety and sensitivity of the images, the book "reveals idleness or comic fatalism to be mere moments within the much larger, more complex reality of suffering, grueling labor, and exploitation."[2]

By contrast, the *Life* display, Vials writes, "is a series of photos and captions representing the southern poor as comic or irrational simpletons," hardly Bourke-White's and Caldwell's intention. In effect, by eliminating Caldwell's and Bourke-White's textual apparatus, Vials argues, *Life* presents the social conflicts in the South as "mere entertainment for a middle class readership." In his impassioned text, Caldwell concluded that such religious fervor as they found in South Carolina was a reasonable reaction to the church's failure to combat economic exploitation by white landlords. The *Life* spread, in contrast, Vials writes—echoing Beaumont Newhall's thesis from 1935 that photographs should be evaluated within their own print milieu,[3] especially if the photographer is not responsible for the print's final display—displays "a set of subjects fundamentally othered, whose 'hysteria' marks them not only as comical, but as potentially susceptible to totalitarian ideologies."[4]

Bourke-White and Caldwell collaborated on captions that, in the form of direct quotation, gave the appearance of being verbatim words or thoughts of the person in the photo. But in fact, *Faces* opens with a disclaimer that reads, in part, "The legends under the pictures are intended to express the authors' own conceptions of the sentiments of the individuals portrayed; they do not pretend to reproduce the actual sentiments of these persons."[5] Many reviewers and readers, however, must have overlooked this page. Captions provide the viewer with a readily graspable handle with which to begin consideration of a photograph. *Faces'* captions, which some considered disingenuous, later became flashpoints in the critical reaction to the book.

Bourke-White's photography—commercial, industrial, social, documentary—was unequivocally popular and successful, and remains so to this day. It is certainly easily identifiable. But it has never been without its detractors. *Faces* stirred these embers of disapproval, and Bourke-White was never able to fully shed that early censure. One of the most vocal of these adversaries was the photographer Walker Evans, whose critique came to define Bourke-White's craft and to damage her artistic legacy.

Walker Evans versus Margaret Bourke-White

A month before Bourke-White and Caldwell headed south in July 1936, *Fortune*'s then editor, Ralph Ingersoll, assigned staff writer James Agee to travel to Alabama and attempt to cultivate a close relationship with a rural family in order to fashion a focused and in-depth study of squalor in the American

South. In essence, Agee was to embed himself in the home of a tenant farmer, which he did finally out of necessity after running his car into a muddy ditch during a rainstorm. He lived with Floyd and Allie Mae Burroughs, the Gudgers of *Let Us Now Praise Famous Men*, for three weeks.[6]

In 1934 Agee had written the text for an October *Fortune* article about the Dust Bowl, "The Drought," only to discover to his dismay that it was intended to accompany the photo-essay of the magazine's star, Margaret Bourke-White. *Fortune* published it with no acknowledgment of Agee's contribution. The entire piece appeared beneath the byline only of Bourke-White, a slight that infuriated Agee. Furthermore, he strongly objected to Bourke-White's style (Bergreen 145) and to the Dust Bowl images in particular,[7] which he believed were "hackneyed Depression propaganda, all windblown fields and starving livestock and concerned looking farm folk."[8]

For the Alabama project, Agee asked Ingersoll to hire Walker Evans, then in the employ of the Resettlement Administration's photo department under Roy Stryker. In return for lending Evans to *Fortune*, Stryker got Ingersoll to allow the RA to retain the ownership of all of Evans's work produced during the assignment, though *Fortune* would have the right of first publication.[9] Evans accomplished most of his work during a series of visits to the homes of three tenant families near Sprott, Alabama, over a period of two weeks, at which point he and Agee separated and Agee went off by auto on a voyage of desperate self-reappraisal, finally ending up in a roadside ditch near the Burroughs's home.[10]

Upon returning to New York two months later, Agee had great difficulty trimming and molding his experiences into sufficiently few words to fit the needs and style of *Fortune*. *Fortune* ultimately agreed to release him from his contract so that he could pursue a book-length presentation of the material. But in December 1937 Charles Pearce, a Harcourt, Brace editor, wrote Agee, "Viking have done such a handsome job of the Bourke-White and Caldwell opus that competition would be ruinous."[11] Agee later proved to be so demanding for several other sets of editors that *Let Us Now Praise Famous Men* was not published until late 1941, by which time concern for tenant farmers in the South had waned and was now on a cool backburner as the threat of U.S. involvement in World War II heated up. The book sold only six hundred copies, and contemporary critics universally panned Agee's self-indulgent prose, which at one point backhandedly excoriates Caldwell's contributions to *Faces:* "George Gudger is a human being, a man, not like any other human being so much as he is like himself. I could invent incidents, appearances, additions to his character, background, surroundings, future, which might well point up and indicate and clinch things relevant to him which in fact I am sure are true, and important, and which George Gudger unchanged and undecorated would not indicate and perhaps could not even suggest. The result, if I was lucky, could be a work of art."[12] Most critics until recently, however, have considered Evans's photography to be eloquent and moving and at quite some remove from Bourke-White's.[13]

When the publication of *Famous Men* was delayed, Evans turned his attention to his own book project, *American Photographs* (1937), and to the exhibition at the Museum of Modern Art that would celebrate it. At this time Evans was still chafing from slights dating back several years. In 1933 Walter Goodwin, J. B. Lippincott's art director, had pushed for Evans to take photographs to illustrate Carleton Beals's book about the Cuban Civil War, *The Crime of Cuba*. Recalling Bourke-White's *Eyes on Russia*, Goodwin had written Beals, "I feel perfectly sure that Evans has the possibilities for [being] another Margaret Bourke-White."[14] Evans had also divulged to Lincoln Kirstein, one of the founders of the American Ballet and a longtime supporter of Evans, his fear that Bourke-White would steal some of his photographic secrets for her own profit.[15] He thus was not in a receptive mood when *Faces* was published to resounding international acclaim *and* commercial success.

In promoting his show, Evans was not averse to having his art framed in contradistinction to Bourke-White's. In September 1938 Kirstein had the MoMA's executive director, Thomas Mabry, work up a press release to praise Evans's images for their honest modernity: "The word modern, in its truest sense, aptly characterizes Mr. Evans' work as it is 'straight' photography, so factual that it may almost be called functional. Its insistence is upon the utmost clarity and detail of the image."[16] In a subsequent release Mabry wrote: "It is the power to create an austere drama from America *as it is* that gives to Evans' work its unique character. There is no trick about his photographs. He never exaggerates by angle shot or unusual perspective. He never sentimentalizes the 'beauty' of the industrial machine, and he respects the industrial worker too much to exploit his pathos. He abhors such easy camera melodrama."[17] Mabry and Kirstein never mention Margaret Bourke-White by name, but in 1938 everyone would have known whom they were shaming. In his afterword to *American Photographs,* Kirstein adds more kindling to the fire: "There has been no need for Evans to dramatize his material with photographic tricks, because the material is already, in itself, intensely dramatic." He also criticizes not just Bourke-White's effects but, indirectly, her technique: "It is 'straight' photography not only in technique but in the rigorous directness of its way of looking. . . . Every object is regarded head-on with the unsparing frankness of a Russian ikon or a Flemish portrait. The facts pile up with the prints."[18] Agee later included in the appendix to *Famous Men* a tongue-in-cheek broadside review of *Faces* written for the *New York Post* by May Cameron, the tone of which is clear from its headline: "Margaret Bourke-White Finds Plenty of Time to Enjoy Life Along with Her Camera Work."[19]

William Stott and the Revival of *Let Us Now Praise Famous Men*

The matter would have languished but for Evans's reissue of *Let Us Now Praise Famous Men* in 1960, in which he subtly resizes and repositions some of his photographs and doubles the number of them to sixty-two.[20] *American Photographs* still had been Evans's only other book, but he had assured his economic and professional security in 1945 when he accepted the position as *Fortune*'s only staff photographer, formerly Bourke-White's sinecure, which he held for the next twenty years.[21] But by this time James Agee, though he had died in May 1955, had won posthumous prominence and a Pulitzer Prize for *A Death in the Family* (1957) and was in general being adulated by a literary establishment that was attempting to suppress his left-leaning political sentiments in favor of promoting him as a modernist and romantic iconoclast.[22]

But the tenor of documentary photography had also changed. Though Bourke-White remained a beacon for feminists, her 1930s celebrity, lifestyle, and lucrative career as *the* American photographer had become a drag on both her reputation and on the reception and interpretation of her photography. To a great degree, Mabry's and Kirstein's public relations hatchet jobs had been successful. For many, her "tricks" were now embarrassing to her legacy and had to be explained. In 1973, two years after Bourke-White's death from Parkinson's disease, William Stott published *Documentary Expression and Thirties America*, using a considerable portion of the book to criticize *You Have Seen Their Faces* and offer kudos to *Let Us Now Praise Famous Men*. Stott, composing an extended and near-hagiographic paean for both Agee and Evans, dismisses Bourke-White for her "gigantism and bathos."[23] When he does discuss her work directly, he foregrounds and adopts the Mabry-Kirstein formalist analysis to explain what he saw as the moral failure of her photography. Stott mentions Beaumont Newhall only in passing and gives little weight to the argument that *Faces* accomplished exactly what its authors set out for it to do: benefit those who appear within its pages. Nor does he acknowledge that *Famous Men* accomplished nothing for the tenant farmer and sharecropper, though after its reissue twenty years later it won fame and respect, if not fortune, for Agee and Evans, its authors. *Famous Men* has thus become important as a work of art on its own merits, while *Faces* spent its life as a relevant and successful social commentary and catalyst for reform.

Moreover, Stott's sympathetic special pleading is weakened by such assertions as, "There can be no doubt that *Let Us Now Praise Famous Men* is a classic of the thirties' documentary genre."[24] This is quite some hyperbole for a book that was remaindered within months of its publication and had no impact whatsoever on the social conditions of the 1930s it purports to document and deplore. Stott himself provided the all-important imprimatur to elevate *Famous Men* to the canonical position he claims it now to have. The most influential examples of the 1930s documentary genre include Herman Clarence Nixon's *Forty Acres and Steel Mules* (1938), Archibald MacLeish's *Land of the Free* (1938), Dorothea Lange and Paul Taylor's *American Exodus* (1939), and perhaps Sherwood Anderson's *Home Town* (1940) and Richard Wright's *12 Million Black Voices* (1941). All contain accessible text (even MacLeish's poetry) and use photographs from the Resettlement Administration's or the Farm Security Administration's federally funded archive, and address specific social concerns: racism, unemployment, poverty, and the westward migration from the eroded Midwest.

Stott's work has become doctrinaire in photojournalism studies, and as such its editorial position has carried significant weight in discussions of documentary photography and its morality. For example, in a 1980 comparison of *You Have Seen Their Faces* with *American Exodus,* Art Hanson reduces Stott's argument to simple mudslinging: "Bourke-White and Caldwell destroyed their credibility by making the sharecroppers seem excessively pathetic and wretched. . . . Bourke-White and Caldwell wanted readers to pity the sharecroppers and see how wretched they were, while Lange and Taylor wanted readers to respect and understand their subjects."[25] Hanson concludes categorically: "The purpose of [*You Have Seen Their Faces*] would be to show the pathetic faces and the deplorable conditions of the southern sharecroppers."[26] In a 1991 dissertation focusing on Bourke-White's 1930s career as a commercial photographer, Melissa McEuen concludes simply: "Bourke-White used her camera as an instrument of manipulation, skewing the image of a face or a scene to fit her purposes."[27]

But Stott's position has not gone uncontested. One of the most regular criticisms of Bourke-White was of her habit of repositioning people and objects in her photos. Caldwell himself had even objected to this once when (by her own account) she had reordered the top of a tenant farmer's wife's dresser: "I rearranged everything. After we left Erskine spoke to me about it. How neat her bureau had been. How she must have valued all her little possessions and how she had them tidily arranged *her* way, which was not my way. This was a new point of view to me. I felt I had done violence."[28] Years later Caldwell recalled, "She was in charge of everything, manipulating people and telling them where to sit and where to look and what not. She was very adept at being able to direct people. She was almost like a motion picture director. Very astute in that respect. That's how she achieved such a good effect, I think, with her settings, and her people."[29]

Walker Evans was especially critical of Bourke-White's modus operandi, insisting on the need for purity of scene. Yet in a careful analysis of Evans's *Famous Men* photographs and his methods, James A. Curtis and Sheila Grannen write:

> Evans's definition of documentary method is misleading and ultimately self-defeating. It perpetuates the notion that photographs are inherently objective artifacts rather than subjective, artistic creations. But in pursuit of an artful composition, Evans often arranged subject matter in ways that directly contradicted his self-proclaimed documentary creed. To achieve a desired effect, he frequently posed his subjects. During his photographic sessions in the sharecroppers' homes in Alabama, he occasionally moved their belongings or arranged to have them moved. When a scene was too cluttered to suit his intent, he removed objects; when necessary he added others to achieve a certain balance.[30]

Stott interviewed Evans in 1974, a year before his death, and asked him about his willingness to move people or things in a composition to improve the harmony of the photo. In the afterword to the second edition of *Documentary Expression,* Stott quotes Evans's adamant response: "I find a howling error in composition, because something is in the wrong place, and I leave it there. God arranged that. I wouldn't touch it."[31]

Further evidence that by 1974 Evans's memory had become selectively eroded can be seen in William Ferris's recent study of storytelling in the American South, *The Storied South: Voices of Writers and Arts.* In a 1974 interview with Ferris, Evans's reminiscences are off the mark.[32] Nonetheless, Evans's and Agee's book now carries such cachet that Ferris writes unabashedly of *Let Us Now Praise Famous Men* as "a classic study of the American South, and Evans's portraits of sharecroppers are forever etched in our memory. His comments about injustice resonate as strongly today as when the work was originally done."[33] In fact, when the work was originally done in 1936–41, Evans was silent on matters of social injustice. Not until the 1960 reissue of *Famous Men* did he make his views known. Evans's uncaptioned photographs are strong stuff, but only the two individual portraits of Floyd and Allie Mae are reproduced regularly.

In a 1998 study, James Goodwin looks at the Wright–Rosskam, Taylor–Lange, Caldwell–Bourke-White, and Agee–Evans collaborations. After noting that the first two were superbly constructed works of cooperative journalism, Goodwin finds *Faces* lacking because "it disavows *both* fictional content *and* a documentary style of objective reportage."[34] He criticizes the authors for failure to "provid[e] at least some composite of fact with fiction" and writes off Bourke-White's photography for all the familiar reasons: "Unmistakably, the book is a generalized, fabricated work and the guiding purpose of its prose is really to provide a picturesque impression of living conditions in the deep South. Its photographs employ blatant stereotypes and enforce the color line in composing genre scenes of black Southern life."[35] In *Famous Men*, however, Goodwin is able to find worth in the very absence of a black presence, which "remain[s] at a considerable physical and social distance, one that excludes the possibility of verbal communication."[36] By presenting blacks only in his prose, "Agee thus identifies with the black social sphere a set of 'painterly' values richer than the photographic tonality of the documentary style appropriate to white tenant life."[37] This strangely implies that blacks are not sufficiently worthy to justify their photographs being taken but should be presented only through the abstraction of words and paintings of others. Finally, he praises Evans for his "independence from the reform discourse"[38] found in *Faces*, which of course was *Faces'* precise purpose.

The Swing of the Pendulum

By the 1980s the critical attitude toward Bourke-White's early work had begun to change. As cultural studies gained a firmer foothold in the academy, so too were scholars open to seeing Bourke-White's and Caldwell's contributions in a more culturally relevant light, and they undertook contextual analyses of her photographs within their contemporary sociopolitical framework.

In *Image and Word* (1987), a study of how photographs and their captions interact, Jefferson Hunter argues that *You Have Seen Their Faces* represents a near perfect marriage of text and photograph, each complementing and, where necessary, explaining.[39] This is not the case with any of their subsequent collaborations, on which, he surmises, they seem to have worked independently. Bourke-White's own recollections of how they together carefully incubated *Faces* in New York over a nine-month period are consonant with Hunter's conclusion: "We wanted a result in which the pictures and words truly supplemented one another, merging into a unified whole."[40] Hunter notes that much of the criticism of *Faces*, other than from predictably offended southern whites, "had perhaps as much to do with the book's success and the celebrity of its authors as with its substance."[41] By a careful analysis of *Faces'* photographic *and* textual structure and content, he contests Stott's and Evans's claims about its moral impurity and Bourke-White's insensitive role in its construction, thereby beginning the rehabilitation of its (and her) reputation.

In his foreword to the 1995 reissue of *You Have Seen Their Faces*, Alan Trachtenberg, employing Beaumont Newhall's argument for context analysis, places *Faces* within the journalistic context of its times:

> Reading *You Have Seen Their Faces* today, one cannot help feeling in Erskine Caldwell's taut, angry prose and in the visual drama of Margaret Bourke-White's images a long-lost moment of artistic protest against economic injustice and suffering. Both a synthesis of concerns and of documentary methods already tried out earlier in the decade, and a signal of a new direction in social journalism, *You Have Seen Their Faces* had helped shape a public discourse, a consensus in the 1930s regarding rural poverty, race relations in the South, and how artists should speak publicly of these issues in words and images.[42]

As for Bourke-White's specific contribution, "Her pictures in this book—among the strongest, most memorable of her career—display her own need to see as close and as rapturously as she can, to make pictures that bring her viewers directly into the scene instead of leaving them outside, untouched."[43]

Hence, both Trachtenberg and Hunter argue that for Evans and Stott to hold Caldwell and Bourke-White accountable to journalistic standards that evolved a generation or two later is disingenuous. Furthermore, Evans and Stott criticize Caldwell and Bourke-White for their commercial success. This, Trachtenberg and Hunter write, misses the point that a book with wide circulation and commercial acceptance may advance, rather than injure, the cause of those represented within it. "*Let Us Now Praise Famous Men*," Hunter concludes, "stands by itself, admirable and infuriating, un-influential now, unsuccessful in 1941, 'experimenting' with the idea of collaboration by spurning it."[44]

In a 2000 dissertation, Paul Hansom, while acknowledging that *Documentary Expression* "has effectively become the starting point for any serious consideration of the genre, and is important in its details and functional classifications,"[45] rejects Stott's Marxist criticism, proposing instead that Caldwell's and Bourke-White's commodification of their project led to an achievable political goal:

> *You Have Seen Their Faces* is both an expression of reformist sentiment and an unconscious articulation of mass cultural relations, and presents the visualization

> of the "Southern Question" as a best seller. The intersection of the documentary format and mass culture promotes a "digest" of people and region, turning lived relations into non-participatory spectacle. This commodification of politics not only handles relevant social-issue information, but provides a psychological politics that attempts to shape reader-response into guided channels.[46]

Guiding their readers into specific channels of psychological and political response had been Caldwell's and Bourke-White's primary goal.

Combining elements of cultural studies and Marxist analysis, Hansom concludes that *You Have Seen Their Faces* "is primarily modernist, urban, and undoubtedly corporatist, predicated as it is on the presentation of an agrarian world that has no say in its own representation. . . . The collection, as it stands, must be seen as a form of functional consumption in that it must be consumed in its entirety, and understood entirely in this process of consumption. Yet *Faces* is more than an extension of a city/country polarity, it is an urban product mediating the idea of the rural for an urban audience."[47] As for *Famous Men*, he criticizes Agee's "neurotic and narcissistic tendencies" but asserts that "Evans' images transform the documentary photograph into 'art,' and Agee's prose becomes self-exploration or self-documentary. This aestheticization of politics turns the social relations under corporate liberalism into consumable art."[48]

Again, arguing against Stott, Hansom rejects the thesis that the documentary should be "purely mimetic." While Stott describes the documentary as "set[ting] out to represent the actual lives of others through the deployment of observable fact,"[49] Hansom prescribes a more holistic and contextual role for it: "the photo-essay form associates itself with factual epistemes and fictional techniques, while relying heavily on visualist counterparts."[50]

In her 2007 dissertation, Kelly Klingensmith assigns the responsibility for the pointedness of the criticism of *Faces* to Agee rather than Stott, overlooking Evans's earlier attacks:

> Many of the book's critics have decried the writer and photographer's method of interaction with and representation of their rural southern subjects. Among the first was James Agee in *Let Us Now Praise Famous Men*, an almost universally respected example of the genre that seems, in part, to be composed in direct rebuttal to Caldwell and Bourke-White. The animus Agee directs at *You Have Seen Their Faces* and Bourke-White in particular is echoed by later critics like William Stott who, in his influential *Documentary Expression [and] Thirties America*, seems to have cemented the valorization of one photographic essay and the damnation of the other.[51]

Klingensmith's principal and nuanced argument is that "despite the differing photographic, rhetorical and production styles of these two books, and despite widely divergent critical appraisals," both fail because they "distance readers from their subjects; they interfere with the reader's access to an understanding of the rural southerners each depicts."[52] She believes that *American Exodus* is the text that gets it right, because "Lange's photographs position readers 'with' her subjects, closing the distance that *You Have Seen Their Faces* and *Let Us Now Praise Famous Men* preserved."[53]

Such critical polarization need not be the fate of documentary photography, however, a sense that Susan Sontag describes in *Regarding the Pain of Others:* "The dual powers of photography—to generate documents and to create works of visual art—have produced some remarkable exaggerations about what photographers ought or ought not to do. Lately, the most common exaggeration is one that regards these powers as opposites."[54] Nonetheless, Sontag seems to take direct aim at the Evans–Agee camp when she observes, "photography that bears witness to the calamitous and the reprehensible is much criticized if it seems 'aesthetic': that is, too much like art."[55]

John Stomberg, in "A Genealogy of Orthodox Documentary," after summarizing some of the above studies, locates *Famous Men* as "a comment on, and not an active participant in, the American tradition of documentary photography in the 1930s," whereas *Faces* is "the key photo-textual document of the 1930s."[56]

While many, such as Klingensmith, valorize the presumed honesty and information-only orientation of *Famous Men*'s photographs, to the discredit of *Faces*, one must accept that while Lange's (and Evans's and MacLeish's and Anderson's) subjects were white, Bourke-White's were white *and* black, and therein lies all the difference. The problems the "Okies" faced on their way westward were of a different magnitude than those faced by the blacks Bourke-White pictured and Caldwell wrote about. The Okies may have been victimized by classism but were not tarred with the added sediment of racism. By contrast, the impoverished whites of *Faces* were incapable of mounting an exodus out of the South. Caldwell's and Bourke-White's tenant-farmers were several rungs below on the social ladder inhabited by Lange and Taylor's dispossessed travelers, and southern blacks were not even on the ladder.

Since Bourke-White was one of only a few photographers richly remunerated at the time in the United States,[57] professional jealousy rested at the heart of attempts to marginalize her, especially since she was a female succeeding in a male sphere. Compounding this were her perceived sense of entitlement (at

Life she had her own darkroom tech as well as her own secretary, *and* she was the only photographer at the magazine who demanded and received a byline), her often prickly personality, and her propensity to aggressively use her alluring sexuality to achieve her goals.

Finally, it should be borne in mind that unlike the tens of thousands of photographs readily available without cost through the Resettlement Administration / Farm Security Administration projects, Margaret Bourke-White's prints long have been held under the tight copyright control of Time-Life and/or her estate, and remain so to this day. Thus, her work has not received the wide distribution within the public sphere that the FSA material has. Among the hundreds of photos printed in the other photo-texts that were published between 1938 and 1941 following *You Have Seen Their Faces*, a Bourke-White image can be found only in *Land of the Free*, in which Archibald MacLeish, who knew Bourke-White at *Fortune* where he worked from 1930 to 1938, included two nondescript landscapes of hers. While this careful control of distribution benefited her and her estate, it has not helped improve her reputation.

NOTES

Prologue. *North of the Danube*

1. Cole, "Bourke-White," 2.

2. Goldberg, *Margaret Bourke-White*, 211.

3. Caldwell, *With All My Might*, 159. See also 159–64 for further detail.

4. Dollars from 1937–42 can be readily converted into inflation-adjusted 2015 currency using the U.S. Bureau of Labor Statistics' CPI (Consumer Price Index) inflation calculator (www.bls.gov/data/inflation_calculator.htm). But for simplicity, applying a factor of fifteen provides an excellent rough estimate. Thus, Caldwell's and Bourke-White's $5,000 investment in *Journeyman* in 1937 translates to $81,220 in today's money.

5. In *With All My Might*, Caldwell states that he was not served with divorce papers until September, after he and Bourke-White had returned from Europe, but this clearly is in error, based on the divorce decree itself. It is, moreover, a reminder that Caldwell's autobiographical material must be warily interpreted.

6. Phillips's short profile at the National Portrait Gallery (www.npg.org.uk) reads: "grandgodfather of photojournalism, a master of lenses and multiple languages; elegant, exuberant and chrome-steel effectual, who has recorded in his own peripatetic way some of the freshest footprints of history."

7. Quoted from McDonald, *Erskine Caldwell*, 188n257.

8. Both quotes from Bourke-White, *Portrait of Myself*, 170.

9. Bourke-White, *Portrait of Myself*, 170.

10. Klevar, *Erskine Caldwell*, 209.

11. Page 75 concludes with the line "'My wife was going to have a baby very soon,' he said. 'They may have . . .'" Page 76 picks up with ". . . streets. Every once in a while we met a group of refugees." The error, created during typesetting, was never corrected. It appears in the Google edition of the book, as it does in the half-dozen library copies of the book I have examined.

12. *Life* featured her photos of this factory in its issue of June 13.

13. See Caldwell and Bourke-White, *North of the Danube*, 61–64. Future references to this work are abbreviated *ND* and provided parenthetically in the text.

14. This letter can be found in Box 1 (Correspondence 1920–1943), Folder 13, in the Mr. and Mrs. I. S. Caldwell Papers at the University of Georgia.

15. *Danube*, 123, 125.

16. Ibid, 128.

17. Bourke-White, *Portrait of Myself*, 170.

18. "Bread in Uzok" in *Town and Country* 94 (Feb. 1939): 58–59, 75; "The Train Through Tatras" in *New Republic* 98 (8 March 1939): 119–21; "The Peasants of Dreharovice" in *Vogue* (1 March 1939): 72–73, 131; "The Dogs of Ceske Budejovice" in *Direction* 2 (March 1939): 4–6; "Agent in Praha" in *New Masses* 30 (28 February 1939): 5–7, as "A Nazi Agent at Work." *When You Think of Me* (1959) reprinted "Bread in Uzok," "The Dogs of Ceske Budejovice," and "Wine of Surany" (MacDonald, *Critical Essays*, 350).

19. See Gale, "Before Munich," 25, 26.

20. See Hindus, "Land That Is No More," 284.

21. See Wolfe, "Hitler Looks Eastward."

22. See Wolfe, "Memorial to Czechoslovakia," 10.

23. See Marshall, rev. of *North of the Danube*, 405.

24. See Cook, "Erskine Caldwell's Nonfiction," 385.

25. Ibid, 383.

26. See MacDonald, "Enough Good Reasons for Reading," 11.

27. See "Bourke-White and Caldwell Merely Co-Tourists, Not Wed."

Chapter 1. Context

1. Just a month before they left Connecticut, on February 20, 1941, Caldwell took part in an NBC "Town Hall Meeting of the Air" broadcast from Birmingham, Alabama, in which he was asked to talk about not just the racial and socioeconomic conditions in the South but also the ramifications for the United States of the looming war in Europe. He shared the stage with Mark F. Ethridge, a liberal newspaperman from the *Louisville Courier-Journal* and the *Louisville Times*, and John Temple Graves II of the *Birmingham Age-Herald*, the conservative defender of segregation and an apologist for lynching. Although much of the town hall was about social issues, occasionally the discussants touched on world affairs. At one point Caldwell and Graves engaged in a brief colloquy during which Caldwell commented, "I don't believe [the European] war is any of our concern. . . . I mean by that, we have in America a problem much greater than we have in Europe. . . . I think that here in America we have something we should work on before we tackle something outside of America" (see Ethridge, Caldwell, and Graves, "Are We a United People?" 21).

2. See Leuchtenburg, *Franklin D. Roosevelt*, 282.

3. See Burns, *Roosevelt*, and U.S. Department of State Office of the Historian, "U.S.-Soviet Alliance, 1941–1945."

4. Levering, *American Opinion*, 41–53.

5. Culbert, *News for Everyman*, 195–96.

6. Culbert, *News for Everyman*, 27–28.

7. Although no formal collections of Bourke-White's works exist other than the "cold storage" holdings of her negatives at the Syracuse University Special Collections Library and those prints available commercially from the *Life* Picture Collection managed by Getty Images (www.gettyimages.com), all of her published photo books may be obtained from general libraries and from secondary markets for used books.

8. Newhall, "Documentary Approach to Photography," 2.

9. See Snyder, "Margaret Bourke-White" and "Spying on Southerners."

10. For many years Bourke-White maintained a subscription to the *Daily Worker*, and she provided photomurals for the Soviet consulate in Washington (Goldberg, *Margaret Bourke-White*, 158). In the 1950s Westbrook Pegler's jeremiad against her concluded that her alliances with organizations such as the Artists' Union, the American Youth Congress, the Film and Photo League, and the League of Women Shoppers were sufficient evidence to indict her as a Communist, let alone her several trips to the Soviet Union in the 1930s (Snyder, "Margaret Bourke-White," 10–11).

11. Throughout the 1930s Caldwell had been clearly aligned with the leftist agenda. Many of his early short stories were published in *The New Masses*, the voice of the American Communist Party under Mike Gold, with whom Caldwell long maintained a personal and professional friendship (Miller, *Erskine Caldwell*, 153–59). In 1932 he was prominently identified with the Communist League of Professional Groups for Foster and Ford, the presidential candidates of the American Communist Party (Dilling, *Red Network*, 140–41; Miller, *Erskine Caldwell*, 158). In 1934 the *Daily Worker* commissioned him to write a series of articles about labor issues in Detroit, which led to his first published work of travel writing, *Some American People*. In 1935 he attended the Congress of American Writers' Union organized by Gold. He provided the rights to several short stories to the Workers' Laboratory Theater and was on the executive board of the New Theater of Action, both leftist organizations (Miller, *Erskine Caldwell*, 222–23).

Chapter 2. Connecticut to Moscow

1. Burns, *Roosevelt*, 94–95.

2. Caldwell, *All-Out on the Road*, 3.

3. Bourke-White, *Shooting the Russian War*, 3. Future references to this work in this chapter are abbreviated *SRW* and included parenthetically in the text.

4. That Bourke-White considers the photos to be central to *Shooting the Russian War* is evident in that she provides a three-page list of illustrations (with page numbers) following the table of contents. There is also a six-page appendix in which she supplies camera and film details for most of these pictures.

5. Caldwell, *Call It Experience*, 192.

6. Goldberg, *Margaret Bourke-White*, 236.

7. Caldwell, *With All My Might*, 177.

8. Klevar, *Erskine Caldwell*, 232–36, and Goldberg, *Margaret Bourke-White*, 235.

9. Caldwell, *With All My Might*, 177–78.

10. Bourke-White, *Portrait of Myself*, 174 (for both quotes).

11. Almost all the Caldwell correspondence, both personal and professional, for the period 1936–1942 can be found in the Erskine Caldwell Papers within the Margaret Bourke-White Archive at the Special Collections Research Center of Syracuse University's E. S. Bird Library.

12. Bourke-White, Letter to Constantin Oumansky, 25 July 1939.

13. Rokotov, Letter to Erskine Caldwell, 28 March 1939.

14. Caldwell, Letter to Timofei Rokotov, 25 July 1939.

15. Lieber, Letters to Erskine Caldwell, Aug. 1939.

16. Roosevelt, Letter to Erskine Caldwell, 23 Aug. 1939.

17. Luce, "American Century," 62.

18. Ibid, 61.

19. Hicks, Cable to Margaret Bourke-White, 21 Feb. 1941.

20. Busch, Letter to Whom It May Concern, 14 Mar. 1941.

21. Hicks, Letter to Margaret Bourke-White, 24 Mar 1941.

22. See note 11 above.

23. All newspaper articles quoted during the Los Angeles–Hong Kong portion of the trip can be found in Scrapbook Vol. XIII of the Erskine Caldwell Papers at Dartmouth University.

24. To convert 1941 monetary values into current money, the U.S. Bureau of Labor CPI inflation calculator is invaluable (www.bls.gov/data/inflation_calculator.htm). For simplicity in calculation, a 1:15 ratio for the 1941–2015 conversion is satisfactory. The cost of each of the Caldwell's one-way first-class tickets would be $2,386.10 in 2015 dollars. See also endnote 4 of the prologue.

25. The travel receipts referenced in this chapter can be found in Box 54 of the Papers of Erskine Caldwell at Dartmouth University, while Bourke-White's shopping and shipping receipts are in Box 15 of the Erskine Caldwell Papers at Syracuse University.

26. Caldwell, Letter to Rhoda Lynn, 2 Apr. 1941.

27. I have used the current Hanyu Pinyin system of romanization of Chinese names, except for the occasional very well-known name, e.g., Chiang Kai-shek (see Mitter xiii). In quotations from the period, however, I have retained the original spelling.

28. Bourke-White, Note to Rhoda Lynn, Apr. 1941.

29. See Caldwell, "Erskine Caldwell at UCLA," 19:00–25:43 of the recording.

30. Bourke-White, Note (on business card) to Rhoda Lynn, Apr. 1941.

31. Bourke-White, Letter to Rhoda Lynn, [Apr. 1941].

32. Chai, Letter to Rhoda Lynn, 15 Sept. 1941. TS. Papers of Erskine Caldwell, Rauner Special Collections Library, Dartmouth University, Hanover, N.H.

33. See note 31 above.

34. Caldwell, "Transit China," 1941.

35. Caldwell, Letter to Rev. & Mrs. I. S. Caldwell, 19 Apr. 1941.

36. Caldwell, "Transit China," 3–4.

37. Ibid, 4; Caldwell, *All-Out on the Road to Smolensk*, 4. Future references to *All-Out on the Road to Smolensk* in this chapter are abbreviated as *Smolensk* and provided parenthetically in the text.

38. Moats, *Blind Date with Mars*, 4. Future references to this work are abbreviated "Moats" and provide parenthetically in this chapter.

39. Caldwell, "Transit China," 29.

40. Caldwell, Letter to Rev. & Mrs. I. S. Caldwell, 19 May 1941.

41. Caldwell, Letter to Rhoda Lynn, 19 May 1941.

42. Caldwell, Letter to Rhoda Lynn, 3 June 1941.

43. Also see Jay Caldwell, "Erskine Caldwell," 510–27.

44. Steinhardt, Telegram to U.S. Sec. of State, 5 June 1941.

45. Eugene Petrov was Yevgeny Petrovich Katayev's pen name.

46. Ilf succumbed to tuberculosis in 1937, and thereafter Petrov was fortunate to survive Stalin's purges of the country's literati. Nonetheless, the two Bender novels remained out of print in the Soviet Union from 1940 until after Stalin's death.

47. Dunkel, "Last Years of Evgenij Petrov," 83.

Chapter 3. Margaret Bourke-White

1. Bourke-White, *Portrait of Myself*, 20.

2. Ibid, 29.

3. Ibid, 29.

4. Hughes, *Shock of the New*, 10–11.

5. See ibid, 215–221.

6. Goldberg, *Margaret Bourke-White*, 82.

7. Bazin, "Ontology of the Photographic Image," 7.

8. Ibid, 9.

9. Ibid, 8.

10. Quoted in Goldberg, *Margaret Bourke-White*, 26.

11. Bergreen, *James Agee*, 118.

12. Bourke-White, *Portrait of Myself*, 78–79.

13. Goldberg, *Margaret Bourke-White*, 130.

14. Ibid, 139.

15. Quoted in ibid, 206.

16. Goldberg, *Margaret Bourke-White*, 206.

17. Snyder, "Erskine Caldwell and Margaret Bourke-White," 394–95.

18. Newhall, "Documentary Approach to Photography," 4.

19. Ibid, 5.

20. Ibid, 6.

21. On April 9, 1941, J. Edgar Hoover, director of the FBI, signed a memorandum to Lawrence M. C. Smith, chief of the Special Defense Unit, recommending that Margaret Bourke-White "be considered for custodial detention in the event of a national

emergency." A subsequent "confidential" letter, however, from Hoover on January 29, 1942, to the special agent in charge at New York City states that Smith's investigation into Bourke-White's "dangerousness" found that the evidence used to place her on the Custodial Detention Index was "not satisfactory to substantiate charges." Whether or not she was subsequently actually placed on the CDI, on July 16, 1943, Attorney General Francis Biddle wrote Hoover, upending his CDI program: "[T]he evidence used for the purpose of making the classifications was inadequate; the standards applied to the evidence for the purpose of making the classifications were defective; and finally, the notion that it is possible to make a valid determination as to how dangerous a person is in the abstract and without reference to time, environment, and other relevant circumstances, is impractical, unwise, and dangerous. . . . For the foregoing reasons I'm satisfied that the adoption of this classification system was a mistake that should be rectified for the future. Accordingly, I direct that the classifications heretofore made should not be regarded as classifications of dangerousness or as a determination of fact in any sense" (FBI Bureau File 100-3518). He added that the program is "hereby canceled." In response, Hoover established a covert Security Index, allowing the FBI to keep Bourke-White under active surveillance for another twenty years; the last document entered into her file is dated June 11, 1965. (See also Snyder, "Margaret Bourke-White.")

22. In an August 20, 1941, letter to Smith, Hoover placed Caldwell in Group A of the Custodial Detention Index, defined as "Individuals believed to be the most dangerous and who in all probability should be interned in event of war." He remained on that list at least to July 1943, but he was then in Group C: "Individuals believed to be the least dangerous and who need not be restricted in absence of additional information, but should be subjected to general surveillance." On June 5, 1943, Hoover wrote the New Haven office: "It is apparent that the activities of Caldwell have not been followed close enough to be at all accurate. It is necessary that all of Caldwell's activities and movements be reported promptly." The last document entered into his file is dated Sept. 22, 1959 (see note 1 above, FBI Bureau File 100–427589, and Snyder, "Spying on Southerners").

23. Bourke-White, *Shooting the Russian War*, 57.

24. Ibid, 293–94.

25. Vials, "The Popular Front," 74.

26. Elson, *Time Inc.*, 1:343. *Collier's* readership during this period was an astonishing 15.9 million at a time when the U.S. population was about 132 million (*1940 Census Records*, www.archives.gov/research/census/1940). *PM's* circulation was never more than several hundred thousand (Goldberg, *Margaret Bourke-White*, 229, 232).

27. Vials, *American Periodicals*, 76.

28. Webb, "Consumer-Citizen," 26.

29. Doss, *Looking at* Life *Magazine*, 48.

30. Vials, *American Periodicals*, 75.

31. Stomberg, *Power and Paper*, 10.

32. Goldberg, *Margaret Bourke-White*, 158.

33. At the sacrifice of some verisimilitude, I have edited the cables to improve their readability. I have substituted punctuation (periods) for "STOP" and silently corrected spelling, but only when necessary for clarity. Otherwise the cables read as they do in the Margaret Bourke-White Papers at Syracuse and in the Erskine Caldwell Papers at Syracuse and Dartmouth.

34. The piece inside on China ("China to the Mountains") was written by *Life*'s editor, Henry R. Luce, with eighteen photos by his wife, Clare Boothe Luce, besides Bourke-White's. The pair had followed the route across the Pacific taken by Caldwell and Bourke-White six weeks earlier.

35. All Bourke-White's *Life* photo-essays are available online through Google Books. See *Life,* 11 August 1941, 17–27.

36. Clarke, *Photograph,* 150.

37. In *Shooting the Russian War,* Bourke-White published a photo of this Stalin statue from the front, one shot from a very low angle near pavement level, emphasizing the premier's heroic stature.

38. Kaplan, "Psychoanalysis," 306, 307.

39. Stone, "Dickens and Leitmotif," 218.

40. See *Life,* 1 Sept. 1941, 15–21.

41. See *Life,* 8 Sept. 1941, 25–29.

42. She used this same image cropped at the tips of his collar in her autobiography (184).

43. Bourke-White, *Shooting the Russian War,* 208.

44. Ibid, 217.

45. Ibid, *Portrait of Myself,* 183–84.

46. Ibid, *Shooting the Russian War,* 218, 219.

47. See *Life,* 13 Oct. 1941, 110–21.

48. See *Life,* 27 Oct. 1941, 27–33.

49. See *Life,* 17 Nov. 1941, 33–39.

50. Ibid, 37.

51. From the point of view of the Allies, Operation Barbarossa took place on the eastern front, but because this study examines the work of Caldwell and Bourke-White from Moscow, I refer to that locus of confrontation from the Russian point of view, that is, the western front.

52. For details, see Bourke-White, *Shooting the Russian War,* 225–38.

53. Bourke-White, *Shooting the Russian War,* 230.

54. See *Life,* 1 Dec. 1941, 118–21.

55. Small, "How We Learned," 459–60.

56. Lord Beaverbrook and his trade delegation had arrived just as the Caldwells were escaping by rail to the north. The Hotel National assigned Beaverbrook to their now-empty but still luxurious suite. Perhaps as payback, the Caldwells were invited to Lord Beaverbrook's 370-acre estate at Cherkley Court, southeast of London, on their way home.

57. Bourke-White, *Shooting the Russian War*, 145.
58. Ibid, 179–80.
59. See Small, "How We Learned," 466–78.

Chapter 4. A Motley Crew

1. Cassidy, *Moscow Dateline*, 61. All Cassidy references are to the American edition unless stated otherwise.
2. "Diplomatic Battle Rages in Rumania," *Canberra Times*, 26 March 1940, 1.
3. Moats, *Blind Date with Mars*, 255–56.
4. See Taylor, "Life, Work, and Times."
5. Ibid, 285.
6. Duranty, "Russians Hungry, but Not Starving," 13.
7. Moats, *Blind Date with Mars*, 5.
8. Ibid, 4, 3.
9. Cassidy, *Moscow Dateline* (London ed.).
10. Ibid, 77–78.
11. Moats, *Blind Date with Mars*, 234.
12. Cassidy, *Moscow Dateline*, 62.
13. "Third Scoop from First Front," *Time*.
14. Cassidy, *Moscow Dateline*, 184, 186–87.
15. Haldane, *Russian Newsreel*, 49.
16. Cassidy, *Moscow Dateline*, 7.
17. Ibid, 37.
18. Bourke-White, *Shooting the Russian War*, 53.
19. All Moats quotes from *Blind Date*, 252.
20. Werth, *Moscow War Diary*, 3, 15.
21. Ibid, 24.
22. Jordan, *Russian Glory*, 2.
23. Ibid, 25–28.
24. Ibid, 106.
25. Ibid, 122.
26. Ibid, 119–20.
27. Ibid, 149–50.
28. Ibid, 149.
29. Sulzberger, "Stalin at Bay," 183.
30. All Sulzberger quotes from "Stalin at Bay," 155–57.
31. Cassidy, *Moscow Dateline*, 44.
32. Ingersoll, *Action on All Fronts*, 81.
33. Ibid, 44.
34. Caldwell, *All-Out*, 185–86.
35. Ingersoll, *Actions on All Fronts*, 87.

36. Ibid, 91.

37. Ibid, 120.

38. Ibid, 93.

39. Ibid, 133–34.

40. Sulzberger, "Stalin at Bay," 161.

41. Typescripts of most of Caldwell's CBS shortwave radio broadcasts can be found in Box 8 of the Erskine Caldwell Papers within the Margaret Bourke-White Archive at Syracuse University's E. S. Bird Library. In general these represent the postcensor version of each broadcast's text.

42. Ingersoll, *Action on All Fronts*, 149.

43. Ibid, 175–76.

44. All quotes, ibid, 176–77.

45. Attwood, "Alf Stringersoll's Report on Brooklyn," 46–49.

46. Miall, "Bartlett, (Charles) Vernon Oldfeld."

47. Bartlett, *Tomorrow Always Comes*, 23–24.

48. Ibid, 28, 29.

49. Review of *Tomorrow Always Comes*, by Vernon Bartlett, *Kirkus Reviews*, 14 February 1944, www.kirkusreviews.com/book-reviews/vernon-bartlett/tomorrow-always-comes/#review.

50. All quotes from Bartlett, *And Now, Tomorrow*, 73–78.

51. Bartlett, *Tomorrow Always Comes*, 84.

52. Although Russia is technically just one of the multitude of ethnic groups and geopolitical polities of which the Soviet Union is constituted, it is frequently used as a synonym for the USSR as a whole. No disrespect was intended. On the other hand, because the Soviet Union was very proud of its army as being composed of many nationalities all fighting for a common cause (i.e., communism), the synonym "Red" was substituted for Russian when referring to it.

53. Carroll, *We're in This with Russia*, 3.

54. Ibid, 7.

55. Ibid, 11.

56. Carroll, *Inside Wartime Russia*.

57. Adamson, *Charlotte Haldane*, 24.

58. Ibid, 17.

59. Charlotte Haldane, *Truth Will Out*, 9.

60. The theme of the novel is the possibility, through science, of predetermining the gender of one's children, a concept that would lead to a plot in which "a scientific autocracy, centralized in the metropolitan cities of 'Nucleus' and 'Centrosome,' obtains control of the political fortunes of the whole white race" (Ernest Bates, "A New Utopia").

61. Adamson, *Charlotte Haldane*, 40.

62. Ibid, 48.

63. Haldane, *Truth Will Out*, 190.

64. See www.spartacus.schoolnet.co.uk/Jsketch.htm for a discussion of the *Sketch*'s fate.

65. Haldane, *Truth Will Out*, 192.

66. Ibid, 193–94.

67. Quoted in Adamson, *Charlotte Haldane*, 139.

68. Haldane, *Truth Will Out*, 261.

69. Ibid, 194.

70. Bartlett, *And Now, Tomorrow*, 73.

71. Ibid, 70.

72. Haldane, *Truth Will Out*, 262.

73. Ibid, 232–33.

74. Ibid, 242.

75. Ibid, 240.

76. Ibid, *Russian Newsreel*, 198.

77. Ibid, *Truth Will Out*, 237.

78. Ibid, *Russian Newsreel*, 163.

79. Ibid, 123–24.

80. Ibid, 207.

81. Topolski, *Fourteen Letters*, unpaginated.

82. Ibid.

83. No periods in the original.

84. Over the ensuing years Topolski traveled the world, sketching world leaders, important figures in arts and letters, as well as the man and woman on the street. In 1975 he began work on what was to become a fifteen-foot-high, six-hundred-foot-long mural that winds across three railway arches under the Hungerford Bridge near the Royal Festival Hall. Known as the *Topolski Century*, it features Topolski's renderings of important twentieth-century events and prominent figures. Rehabilitated between 2006 and 2009 owing to a privately subscribed £3 million trust, it remains open to the public without charge. A remarkable interactive website allows a virtual 360° panoramic tour: www.z360.com/topolski.

85. Haldane, *Truth Will Out*, 207–8.

86. Haynes and Klehr, *Venona*, 236; and Klehr, Haynes, and Firsov, *Secret World of American Communism*, 286–87.

87. Werth, *Moscow War Diary*, 36–37.

88. Smith, *Black Man in Red Russia*, 1.

89. Ibid, 96.

90. Ibid, 112.

91. See Fischer, *Studies in Intelligence*.

92. Lovell, *Soviet Way of Life*, 169–70.

93. Haldane, *Russian Newsreel*, 50.

94. Cassidy, *Moscow Dateline*, 79.

95. Danchev, "Face, or, Senseless Kindness," 42–47.

96. Ehrenburg, *Tempering of Russia*, 100–102.

Chapter 5. Summer 1941

1. This represents about $4,700 in 2015 dollars.

2. See Hagen, "Struggle of Sound Archives," 41–42, for the complete background to this story.

3. This portal at the National Archives provides access to the collection: www.archives.gov/research/arc. A printed listing of this material can be found in Ryan, *History of Sound*.

4. One of the recordings is the broadcast of "The World Today" for July 22, the first night of the air raids. Clearly this was recorded the following evening, because Caldwell describes the effects of the previous night's bombing in detail. Unfortunately, there is no recording or typescript of the previous night's broadcast. In *All-Out on the Road to Smolensk*, however, Caldwell lavishes great detail on his efforts to get to the radio station that night. It is possible that the facility was not functional that evening.

5. Thompson, *Travel Writing*, 173.

6. From "The Solitude of Andrew Selkirk," by William Cowper (1731–1800): "I am monarch of all I survey, / My right there is none to dispute; / From the centre all round to the sea, / I am lord of the fowl and the brute."

7. Pratt, *Imperial Eyes*, 204.

8. Caldwell, *All-Out on the Road to Smolensk*, 28. Future references to this work in this chapter are abbreviated *Smolensk* and provided parenthetically in the text.

9. Because *Georgia Boy*, partially written in Moscow, was much on his mind in 1941 and 1942, some of this cornpone humor may have bled over from that text.

10. Typescripts of most of Caldwell's CBS shortwave radio broadcasts can be found in Box 8 of the Erskine Caldwell papers within the Margaret Bourke-White Archive at Syracuse University's E. S. Bird Library. In general these represent the Soviet-censored version of each broadcast's text.

11. Bourke-White, *Shooting the Russian War*, 95. Future references to this work in this chapter are abbreviated *SRW* and provided parenthetically in the text.

12. Konstantin Simonov (1915–79) had become a national treasure following the publication of his patriotic poem "Wait for Me," in which a soldier asks his wife to wait for him while he goes off to fight the Nazis. Later he became one of the most important Russian writers during the ascendancy of the Soviet realist movement. Evgeniy Iosifovich Gabrilovich (1899–1993) was best known as a postwar film scriptwriter. During World War II, Lev Isaevich Slavin (1896–1984) was a correspondent for both *Krasnaya Zvezda* and *Izvestia* as well as a well-received novelist and playwright whose works, not surprisingly, carefully hewed the Communist Party–socialist realist lines.

13. "British Help."

14. Dating various events, especially air raids, is problematic. When trying to correlate what is clearly the same event, the evidence from the memoirs of the various journalists in Moscow at the time not infrequently conflicts. Caldwell records this evening's activity involving General Mason-MacFarlane in his August 9 diary entry.

15. Caldwell, *Moscow Under Fire*, 52.

16. Caldwell and Bourke-White, *Russia at War*, 19.

17. Ibid, 19.

18. Ehrenburg, *Tempering of Russia*, 9.

19. A coast-to-coast string of discount drugstores begun in the 1930s.

20. Caldwell, *Moscow Under Fire*, 66–67.

21. Carroll, *We're in This with Russia*, 84.

22. See Werth, *Russia at War*, 131–43, for a contemporary view and Mawdsley, *Thunder in the East*, 32–43, for a more recent study.

Chapter 6. Smolensk I

1. In addition to Caldwell's and Bourke-White's five post-Russian publications, within a couple of years many of the other correspondents in Moscow that summer published their recollections of the Smolensk press tour: Wallace Carroll, *Inside Wartime Russia* (1942); Wallace Carroll, *We're in This with Russia* (1942); Henry C. Cassidy, *Moscow Dateline: 1941–1943* (1943); Charlotte Haldane, *Russian Newsreel* (1942); Philip Jordan, *Russian Glory* (1942); Alice-Leone Moats, *Blind Date with Mars* (1943); Alexander Werth, *Moscow War Diary* [US] / *Moscow '41* [UK] (1942). Beyond this, several correspondents revisited the trip in their memoirs published three to thirty years later: Vernon Bartlett, *Tomorrow Always Comes* (1944) and *And Now, Tomorrow* (1960); Charlotte Haldane, *Truth Will Out* (1950); Cyrus Sulzberger, *A Long Row of Candles* (1969); Alexander Werth, *Russia at War, 1941–1945* (1964). Only Cholerton and Steele did not write memoirs, but they filed lengthy dispatches with their newspapers immediately upon their return from the trip.

2. See Stahel, *Operation Barbarossa*, 306–60.

3. See Fritz, *Ostkrieg*, 140–45.

4. See Stahel, *Operation Barbarossa*, 411–12.

5. Jordan, *Russian Glory*, 120–21.

6. Werth, *Moscow War Diary*, 194.

7. Moats, *Blind Date with Mars*, 381.

8. Bourke-White, *Shooting the Russian War*, 221.

9. Caldwell, *Smolensk*, 173.

10. All quotes from Caldwell, *Smolensk*, 174.

11. Caldwell, *Smolensk*, 172.

12. Margaret Bourke-White Papers, Syracuse, Box 5, File: "Molotov, Vyacheslav Mikhaylovich."

13. His cable read: "Within ten days of winding up work in Soviet Union and both feel serious gap needs to be filled by trip to front for material and photographs STOP in view of our work as a whole could you communicate to quarters here importance our combined work frontwards regards—Erskine Caldwell" (Erskine Caldwell Papers, Syracuse, Box 6, File: "Oumansky").

14. Caldwell, *Smolensk*, 175.

15. Ibid, 175.

16. Werth, *Moscow War Diary*, 197.

17. Cassidy, *Moscow Dateline*, 109–10. All references are to the American edition.

18. A bloody battleground in east-central Spain during the Spanish Civil War, which ultimately fell to the Franco forces in early 1938.

19. Haldane, *Russian Newsreel*, 70–71.

20. Ibid, 70.

21. Haldane, *Truth Will Out*, 215.

22. Carroll, *We're in This with Russia*, 94.

23. Ibid, 95–96.

24. Bourke-White, *Shooting the Russian War*, 222.

25. Ibid, 222, 223.

26. Bartlett, *And Now, Tomorrow*, 79.

27. Ibid, 80.

28. Sulzberger, "Stalin at Bay," 164. The reference to "Soviet" here means "a council."

29. Moats, *Blind Date with Mars*, 382.

30. Haldane, *Russian Newsreel*, 71.

31. Bourke-White, *Shooting the Russian War*, 222.

32. This detail is remembered differently by the memoirists: Werth, *Moscow War Diary*, 4 or 5; Bourke-White, *SRW*, 5; Carroll, *We're in This with Russia*, 6; Haldane, *Russian Newsreel*, 8.

33. Bourke-White, *Shooting the Russian Front*, 225, 227.

34. Carroll, *We're in This with Russia*, 96–97.

35. Haldane, *Russian Newsreel*, 71.

36. Werth, *Moscow War Diary*, 201.

37. Haldane, *Russian Newsreel*, 73.

38. Carroll, *We're in This with Russia*, 97.

39. Ibid, 98.

40. Caldwell, *Smolensk*, 176.

41. Jordan, *Russian Glory*, 29.

42. Werth, *Moscow War Diary*, 204. Stalin's Hawks also referred to the planes the pilots flew.

43. Haldane, *Truth Will Out*, 215.

44. Jordan, *Russian Glory*, 29.

45. These were the multiple-rocket launchers related to the devastatingly effective truck-loaded *katyushas*, which were nicknamed after a popular and patriotic 1938 song by Matvei Blanter that became a marching anthem for soldiers at the front ("Into battle for the country, into battle for Stalin" [Werth, *Russia at War*, 185]).

46. Jordan, *Russian Glory*, 31.

47. Cassidy, *Moscow Dateline*, 116.

48. Werth, *Moscow War Diary*, 209.

49. Ibid, 209.

50. Ibid, 209.

51. Cassidy, *Moscow Dateline*, 117.

52. Moats, *Blind Date with Mars*, 384.

53. Carroll, *We're in This with Russia*, 106.

54. Sulzberger, *New York Times*, 25 Sept. 1941, 4.

55. Haldane, *Russian Newsreel*, 76.

56. Ibid, 77.

57. Ibid, 77.

58. Ibid, 77.

59. Caldwell, *Smolensk*, 177.

60. Ibid, 178.

61. *Life* published a seven-page, nine-photo portfolio of her Smolensk pictures in its November 20, 1941, issue, including one from Vyazma.

62. Bourke-White, *Shooting the Russian War*, 231.

63. Ibid, 231.

64. Ibid, 231.

65. In Scrapbook XVIII, Papers of Erskine Caldwell, Dartmouth.

66. He also positioned it as the September 27 diary entry in his hastily compiled *Moscow Under Fire*, published in early 1942 in London.

67. Caldwell, *Smolensk*, 178.

68. Ibid, 178.

69. Haldane, *Russian Newsreel*, 78.

70. Bourke-White, *Shooting the Russian War*, 233.

71. To be found at Bourke-White, *Shooting the Russian War*, 233.

72. Werth, *Moscow War Diary*, 210.

73. Ibid, 211.

74. Ibid, 212.

75. Cassidy, *Moscow Dateline*, 119.

76. Ibid, 118.

77. Haldane, *Russian Newsreel*, 79.

78. Bourke-White, *Shooting the Russian War*, 254.

79. Haldane, *Russian Newsreel*, 79.

80. Ibid, 80.

81. Bourke-White, *Shooting the Russian War*, 259.

82. Ibid, 254.

83. Werth, *Moscow War Diary*, 212.

84. Carroll, *We're in This with Russia*, 110.

85. Haldane, *Russian Newsreel*, 81.

86. Werth, *Moscow War Diary*, 214–15.

87. Carroll, *We're in This with Russia*, 110. Haldane describes Heine as a German Jewish poet "whose works the Nazis had burned and banned when they conquered their own unfortunate country" (Haldane, *Russian Newsreel*, 80).

88. Werth, *Moscow War Diary*, 216.

89. Bourke-White, *Shooting the Russian War*, 234.

90. Ibid, 234.

91. Werth, *Moscow War Diary*, 218.

92. Ibid, 219.

93. Bourke-White, *Shooting the Russian War*, 237.

94. Werth, *Moscow War Diary*, 219.

95. Bourke-White, *Shooting the Russian War*, 239.

96. Haldane, *Russian Newsreel*, 83.

97. Ibid, 86.

98. Bourke-White, *Shooting the Russian War*, 235.

99. Caldwell, *Smolensk*, 180.

Chapter 7. Smolensk II

1. Haldane, *Russian Newsreel*, 86–87.

2. Ibid, 87–88.

3. Caldwell, *All-Out on the Road*, 181–82.

4. Werth, *Moscow War Diary*, 220.

5. Bourke-White, *Shooting the Russian War*, 241–43.

6. Haldane, *Truth Will Out*, 217.

7. Moats, *Blind Date with Mars*, 384.

8. Ibid, 384–85.

9. Bourke-White, *Shooting the Russian War*, 245.

10. Werth, *Moscow War Diary*, 221.

11. Bourke-White, *Shooting the Russian War*, 247.

12. Werth, *Moscow War Diary*, 221. The FW 189 Uhu ("Eagle Owl"), in operation from 1938 to 1944, had a twin fuselage looking like two rungs of a ladder. Caldwell (*Smolensk* 183) refers to the plane as "a twin-ruddered German Dornier," but as that was generally nicknamed the Flying Pencil because of its narrow fuselage, he must be incorrect.

13. Caldwell, *All-Out on the Road*, 183.

14. Bourke-White, *Shooting the Russian War*, 250.

15. Ibid, 250.

16. Ibid, 248.

17. Jordan, *Russian Glory*, 36.

18. Bourke-White, *Shooting the Russian War*, 247.

19. Ibid, 250.

20. Sulzberger, "Stalin at Bay," 163–64.

21. Haldane, *Russian Newsreel*, 90.

22. Caldwell, *All-Out on the Road*, 209.

23. Jordan, *Russian Glory*, 36.

24. Caldwell, *All-Out on the Road*, 210.

25. Haldane, *Russian Newsreel*, 91.

26. Moats, *Blind Date with Mars*, 386.

27. Bourke-White, *Shooting the Russian War*, 255.

28. Werth, *Moscow War Diary*, 227–28.

29. Caldwell, *All-Out on the Road*, 204–6.

30. Werth, *Moscow War Diary*, 228.

31. Ibid, 228–29.

32. Ibid, 229.

33. Carroll, *We're in This with Russia*, 122.

34. Ibid, 126.

35. Werth, *Moscow War Diary*, 231.

36. Ibid, 232.

37. Bourke-White, *Shooting the Russian War*, 263. Somehow that helmet ended up in her ex-husband's possession after their divorce, and for years he displayed it proudly atop one of the bookcases in his study. This helmet, along with a Red Army helmet, can be found in Carton 1 of Series 11 in the Erskine Caldwell Papers (MS-1152) at the University of Georgia Library in Athens. See photo in preface.

38. Werth, *Moscow War Diary*, 232. Carroll offered a different translation: "Brotherly graves of those who died like heroes in the struggle against German fascism, July 29 to September 5, 1941" (Carroll, *We're in This with Russia*, 124).

39. Carroll, *We're in This with Russia*, 126.

40. Werth, *Moscow War Diary*, 233.

41. Bourke-White, *Shooting the Russian War*, 261.

42. Haldane, *Russian Newsreel*, 99.

43. Bourke-White, *Shooting the Russian War*, 270.

44. Werth, *Moscow War Diary*, 233–34.

45. Carroll, *We're in This with Russia*, 126.

46. Jordan, *Russian Glory*, 34.

47. Cassidy, *Moscow Dateline*, 123.

48. Caldwell, *All-Out on the Road*, 211.

49. Ibid, 211–13.

50. Ibid, 214.

51. Werth, *Moscow War Diary*, 236.

52. Carroll, *We're in This with Russia*, 135.

53. Haldane, *Truth Will Out*, 220.

54. Haldane, *Russian Newsreel*, 100.

55. Cassidy, *Moscow Dateline*, 123.

56. Haldane, *Truth Will Out*, 220–21.

57. Ibid, 221.

58. Bartlett, *Tomorrow Always Comes*, 28–29.

59. Curzio Malaparte (1898–1957), the nom de plume of Kurt Erich Suckert, was an Italian journalist who covered the Ukrainian front for *Sera* (*Evening Courier*) during Operation Barbarossa. Prior to the war, Malaparte had been a well-known, if off-message, journalist during the early 1930s, but his brash anti-Mussolini and anti-Hitler tirades in the literary journals of which he was editor and contributor, and in his most famous book, *Coup d'état: The Technique of Revolution*, landed him in internal exile on the isle of Lipari from 1933 to 1938, a full year of it in solitary confinement, and again periodically for the next several years. Having been stripped of his membership in the Partito Nazionale Fascista (PNF), Malaparte was ineligible to work as a credentialed war correspondent, but as a member of the Italian diplomatic corps, and as a former World War I captain in the Alpini, Italy's elite mountain warfare brigade, he could be ordered to do so. Thus, in early February 1941 he and his driver, Lino Pellegrini, a reporter for the Fascist Party's official *Popolo d'Italia*, and later a renowned submarine archaeologist-ethnographer-journalist, found themselves on the eastern front in their Ford coupe, as embedded journalists. Although his dispatches home were written in an environment in which German victory seemed inevitable, they still met disfavor with the Mussolini government, and many were suppressed. But there was no doubt about their authenticity.

60. Malaparte, *Volga Rises in Europe*, 10–11.

61. Ibid, 11.

62. A sense of just how much purchase the events of this Moscow summer had on the American literary consciousness is evident from their echoes in a popular historical romance novel of World War II published thirty years later: Herman Wouk's *The Winds of War*. It is evident that Wouk researched *Winds of War* diligently. When I asked Wouk recently (via e-mail) if he consciously based several of his characters on Caldwell and Bourke-White, he replied that he recalled having on his bookshelf and reading *Shooting the Russian War* and *All-Out on the Road to Smolensk*, along with memoirs by Carroll, Cassidy, and Werth, as he was writing the novel. Wouk's Moscow detail is strikingly accurate, right down to a faithful description of the Caldwells' hotel suite on Red Square.

Wouk insightfully portrays the professional problems of the journalists in Moscow, describing their work as attempting "to make bricks without straw": "The Russians keep the reporters in Moscow, and every other day or so just call them in and give them some phony handout. Most of them think the war's going very badly, but they don't have much to go on besides Moscow rumors and Berlin shortwave broadcasts" (714). Captain Victor "Pug" Henry, President Roosevelt's personal envoy to Stalin, is Wouk's principal protagonist. Soon after he arrives in Moscow with the goal of reaching the front to assess firsthand the situation for Roosevelt, Henry's interpreter tries to explain to him why such a trip seems unlikely: "You won't really get to the front, you know. They've just given some correspondents a tour. They kept them far behind the lines, feeding them caviar, quails, and champagne. Still, the Luftwaffe pulled an air raid on a village and almost nailed them" (738). Henry is persistent, though, and so finally a private tour for three is set up to include Henry, "Talkie" (a British radio broadcaster) Tudsbury, and his daughter Pamela. In early October Lozovsky advises them: "Well, Captain, will tomorrow at dawn suit you? Kindly come here to the Narkomindel, wear warm clothing, a raincoat, and good boots, and be prepared to be out three or four days" (743). They head south toward Leo Tolstoy's birthplace, Yasnaya Polyana, but otherwise the trip is culled from the pages of the correspondents' books, especially Caldwell's and Bourke-White's.

In one of the more strikingly parallel passages, Pamela—the Margaret Bourke-White figure, whom Wouk has converted into an attractive American girl rather than an intrepid photographer—is asked by a general to dance on a makeshift dance floor in a piano-equipped bunker, recalling Bourke-White's dance with one of the "Meat Choppers" at the Siberian regiment's camp to the tune of an accordion (748).

63. Hohenberg, *Foreign Correspondence*, 189.

64. Ibid, 208.

65. Bourke-White, *Portrait of Myself*, 186.

Chapter 8. Getting Out

1. Caldwell, *All-Out on the Road to Smolensk*, 229.

2. Ibid, 230.

3. See Caldwell, *Moscow Under Fire*, 107–12.

4. Bourke-White, *Shooting the Russian War*, 275.

5. Ibid, 271.

6. Moats, *Blind Date with Mars*, 382.

7. I have edited the cables in this chapter to improve their readability. I have substituted punctuation (periods) for "STOP" and silently corrected spelling, but only when necessary for clarity. Otherwise I have left the cables as they exist in the Margaret Bourke-White Papers at Syracuse and in the Erskine Caldwell Papers at Syracuse and Dartmouth. The cables that appear in all caps are transcriptions of the actual telegrams as their copies appear in the archives, while those in standard type are transcriptions of draft copies composed by Caldwell or Bourke-White. Likewise, the letters quoted in this chapter are from the same archives.

Chapter 9. *All-Out on the Road to Smolensk*

1. Klevar, *Erskine Caldwell*, 239.

2. Bourke-White, *Portrait of Myself*, 188.

3. Lieber, Letter to Erskine Caldwell, 6 Nov. 1941.

4. Most of the reviews quoted in this section can be located in Scrapbook Vol. XX of the Papers of Erskine Caldwell at Dartmouth University. Those not located there are cited individually in the bibliography.

5. Koppes and Black, *Hollywood Goes to War*, 190.

6. All sales data can be found in "Books of Erskine Caldwell" in Box 48, Papers of Erskine Caldwell, Dartmouth.

7. Review of *All-Out on the Road to Smolensk*, by Erskine Caldwell, *Kirkus Reviews*, 1942.

8. Sillen, "Caldwell Returns from Smolensk," 23.

9. Ibid, 23.

10. "Reader's List," 406.

11. Thompson, "Book of the Times."

12. Chamberlin, "Reports on the Epic Clash," BR2.

13. Vagts, "Book Reviews," 46.

14. Ibid, 46–47.

15. Ibid, 47.

16. Fischer, "Russia at War," 316.

17. See FBI, Surveillance File on Erskine Caldwell.

Chapter 10. *All Night Long*: Caldwell's Flirtation with Socialist Realism

1. Miller, *Erskine Caldwell*, 313.

2. Bourke-White, *Portrait of Myself*, 171–72.

3. Caldwell, *With All My Might*, 167.

4. Data on book sales can be found in carefully maintained ledgers in the Erskine Caldwell Archives at Dartmouth College.

5. Morson, "Socialist Realism and Literary Theory," 121–22.

6. Katerina Clark, *Soviet Novel*, 46.

7. In the early months of the war, partisan vetting of new recruits was understandably lax, which allowed for infiltration by German agents or sympathizers. This was such an endemic problem that by autumn 1941 the partisan movement was severely crippled and became fully operational again only after the Red Army successfully turned the tide at Moscow in early December (see Truman Anderson, "Incident at Baranivka," 619–23).

8. See Slepyan, *Stalin's Guerillas*, 26.

9. An extensive archive of Caldwell's (and Bourke-White's) CBS radio broadcasts from June to September 1941 can be found in Box 8 of the Erskine Caldwell Papers in the Syracuse Special Collections Library.

10. Simonov, *Victims and Heroes*, 1963.

11. Quoted in Grenkevich, *Soviet Partisan Movement*, 113.

12. "Ukraine," *Encyclopædia Britannica*, 25.

13. Alexander Nevsky (1220–63), prince of Novgorod and grand prince of Vladimir,

preserved early Russian sovereignty against German, Swedish, and Mongol forces; Dmitry Donskoy (1350–89), Dmitry I, prince of Moscow, defeated the Tatars at the Battle of Kulikovo (1380); Kuzma Minin (d. 1616) along with Dmitry Pozharsky (1577–1642) expelled Polish-Lithuanian invaders from the Kremlin in 1612; Alexander Suvorov (1730–1800) never lost a battle against the Ottoman Empire, the Poles, or the Italians; Mikhail Kutuzov (1745–1813), as field marshal of the Russian Empire, fought Napoleon at Borodino in September 1812 and at Smolensk in November 1812.

14. See Grenkevich, *Soviet Partisan Movement*, 81.

15. Slepyan, *Stalin's Guerillas*, 28.

16. Ibid, 51.

17. Ibid, 134.

18. See Alexander Werth's description of the meetings in late July between Stalin and Franklin Roosevelt's emissary, Harry Hopkins—the meetings during which Margaret Bourke-White was granted a photo session. Werth, a Russian-born member of the Western press corps that summer, quotes extensively from Hopkins's White House papers: "He [Stalin] made much of 'insurgent troops' [i.e., partisans] fighting behind the enemy lines, and claimed that there had been no mass surrenders of troops on either side." Stalin also assured Hopkins that Kiev would not fall, which, in fact, it did six weeks later with the loss of millions of troops (*Russia at War* 282, 283).

19. Grenkevich, *Soviet Partisan Movement*, 78.

20. Ibid, 162.

21. Stephenson, *Russia from 1812 to 1945*, 436.

22. Quoted in Slepyan, *Stalin's Guerillas*, 152.

23. Quoted in ibid, 163.

24. Ibid, 136.

25. Members of the All-Union Leninist Young Communist League.

26. Slepyan, *Stalin's Guerillas*, 149.

27. Ibid, 239.

28. Quoted in ibid, 230.

29. For a discussion of the composition and stratification of partisan cadres, see Slepyan, *Stalin's Guerillas*, 253–58.

30. For the historical perspective of the German approach to antiguerilla warfare, see Grenkevich, *Soviet Partisan Movement*, 41–42, and Rutherford, *War in a Twilight World*, 60–62.

31. Rutherford, *War in a Twilight World*, 62.

32. Truman Anderson, "Incident at Baranivka," 623.

33. Haberer, *War in a Twilight World*, 112. These documents are housed in state archives in Lithuania, Belarus, and Ukraine.

34. Haberer, *War in a Twilight World*, 117.

35. Caldwell and Bourke-White, *Russia at War*, 29.

36. Letter dated 7 Nov. 1941, located in Box 22 of the Erskine Caldwell Archives at Dartmouth College.

Chapter 11. *All Night Long*: The Novel

1. Caldwell, *All Night Long*, 76. Future references to this work in this chapter are abbreviated *ANL* and included parenthetically in the text.

2. German trucks were forever breaking down and were ill-designed and ill-prepared for the rigors of the Russian countryside. Both Alan Clark, *Barbarossa*, 55 *et seq*. and 157 *et seq*., and Fritz, *Ostkrieg*, 56–57 and 158–60, argue that this breakdown in the motorized components of the blitzkrieg seriously slowed the Germans' eastward momentum.

3. Part of the Russian strategy was to leave no means of agricultural production intact or serviceable behind advancing German lines. For an extended discussion of the impact the Soviet scorched-earth policy had on German troop support and morale, see Fritz, *Ostkrieg*, 359–403; the major impact of this Russian strategy was not felt until after 1941, but Caldwell shifts it forward to the time frame of *All Night Long.* On the other hand, the Russians blew up their prized Dnepropetrovsk Dam on the Dnieper in September 1941, just before Kiev was encircled, to prevent the Germans from gaining any benefit from it (Alan Clark, *Barbarossa*, 136). Although the Soviets delayed releasing news of this for several days, Caldwell and the other correspondents did become aware of it through the international shortwave radio grapevine (Werth, *Russia at War*, 180).

4. In his in-depth study of guerilla warfare, Kenneth Slepyan writes: "Though there might have been doubts about the reality of internal enemies and foreign spies portrayed by the regime in the 1930s, the partisans' experiences in the occupied territories provided powerful evidence that such types actually existed. The appearance of real collaborators in league with a real foreign enemy gave credibility to earlier Stalinist repressions of enemies and infiltrators and gave new meaning to the Stalinist motifs of internal vigilance and the unmasking of spies" (*Stalin's Guerillas* 252).

5. A similar moment famously appears in *God's Little Acre* and was one of the scenes that led some to deem it pornographic.

6. Erskine Caldwell, "All Night Long: Part I," 4.

7. Ibid, 56.

8. Erskine Caldwell, *Call It Experience*, 209.

9. Gingerbread was a local specialty in Vyazma, the first town Caldwell and the correspondents visited on their junket to the front in September.

10. Transcripts of Caldwell's CBS radio broadcasts from June to September 1941 can be found in Box 8 of the Erskine Caldwell Papers in the Syracuse Special Collections Library.

11. For a discussion of the shifting, conflicted, and ambiguous priorities of the partisans, see Kenneth Slepyan, *Stalin's Guerillas*, 157–62.

12. North, "Caldwell's Strongest Novel."

13. Ann Wolfe, "Mr. Caldwell's Russian Landscape," 8.

14. In *Call It Experience,* he dates the submission to April (210), but letters from his publishers clearly establish a late June date.

15. Lieber was an avowed Communist closely aligned with Whittaker Chambers, who fled the country to Mexico and then to Poland, when he came under the scrutiny of the HUAC in 1950. Upon his death in 1993, his son destroyed all his papers.

16. Lieber, Letter to Erskine Caldwell, 2 July 1942.

17. Sloan, Letter to Erskine Caldwell, 7 July 1942.

18. Duell, Letter to Erskine Caldwell, 8 July 1942.

19. Erskine Caldwell, Letters to Alfred Morang, July–Aug. 1942.

20. Telegrams and letters from Caldwell to Bourke-White during the summer of 1942 are in the Erskine Caldwell Papers at Syracuse University.

21. Most of the reviews quoted in this section can be located in Scrapbook Vol. XX of the Papers of Erskine Caldwell at Dartmouth University. Those not located there are cited individually in the bibliography.

22. In 1935 the *Post* had published a series of articles Caldwell had written on special assignment about the poverty of southern sharecroppers.

23. Quoted in Miller, *Erskine Caldwell,* 297.

24. Shearer, *Beautiful,* 411n25, 167.

25. In February 1943, after returning from the war for a lecture tour, Samuel Goldwyn commissioned Bourke-White to shoot promotional stills for the film (see Saretzky, "Margaret Bourke-White in Print," "F").

26. Conquest, *The Harvest of Sorrow,* 321.

27. Miller, *Erskine Caldwell,* 336.

Epilogue. Wrapping It Up in Hollywood

1. Thorough discussions of the personal and professional intersections of Caldwell's and Bourke-White's lives can be found in their autobiographies, in which each remains respectful of the other, and in their formal biographies: Miller, *Erskine Caldwell,* 226–317; Goldberg, *Margaret Bourke-White,* 161–256; and especially Klevar, *Erskine Caldwell,* 169–252.

2. "'Tobacco Road' Retires Tonight Undefeated," 13.

3. Caldwell had been employed as a Hollywood screenwriter in 1930 and again over the winter of 1934–35.

4. O'Neill, *Better World,* 75.

5. Culbert, *Mission to Moscow,* 13–15.

6. Bourke-White, *Portrait of Myself,* 196–97.

7. Telegrams and letters from Caldwell to Bourke-White and Alfred Morang during the summer of 1942 are in the Erskine Caldwell Papers at Syracuse University.

8. Caldwell, *With All My Might,* 173.

9. Equivalent to about $17,900 in current dollars (U.S. Bureau of Labor Statistics, "CPI Inflation Calculator," www.bls.gov/data/inflation_calculator.htm.

10. In his Hollywood memoir, *As Time Goes By,* screenwriter Howard Koch, who

took over the scriptwriting after Warner's dismissed Caldwell, described Mrs. Davies cautiously yet luminously: "a beautiful woman with a kind of smooth, marble perfection of features and ease of manner often found in those born to wealth" (110).

11. Culbert, *Mission to Moscow*, 254.

12. Ibid, 252.

13. Koch, *As Time Goes By*, 98.

14. Ibid, 106.

15. Culbert, *Mission to Moscow*, 18–19.

16. Quoted in ibid, 20.

17. Ibid, 20.

18. Brady, "Welles versus Hollywood Again," x3.

19. See Culbert, *Mission to Moscow*, for the production details of the film and Caldwell's involvement in it.

20. Koch, *As Time Goes By*, 169.

21. Caldwell, *Call It Experience*, 215.

22. Caldwell, *With All My Might*, 198–99.

23. Ibid, 199.

Appendix. Shifting Sands

1. See Bourke-White, "The South," *Life*, 22 Nov. 1937, *48–52*.

2. Vials, "The Popular Front," 96.

3. See Newhall, "Documentary Approach to Photography," 2–6.

4. Vials, "The Popular Front," 96–97, 97, 98.

5. Caldwell and Bourke-White, *You Have Seen Their Faces*.

6. Bergreen, *James Agee*, 162–77.

7. Ibid, 145.

8. Rathbone, *Walker Evans*, 120.

9. The long-term effect of this arrangement has been that, as with all images captured by the Resettlement Administration photographers, Evans's photos are available to the public without charge and are copyright restriction free.

10. Bergreen, *James Agee*, 166–68.

11. Quoted in Rathbone, *Walker Evans*, 154.

12. Agee and Evans, *Let Us Now Praise Famous Men*, 205.

13. Stomberg, "Genealogy of Orthodox Documentary," 47–51.

14. Quoted in Rathbone, *Walker Evans*, 78–79.

15. Ibid, 84.

16. [Kirstein and Mabry], Museum of Modern Art.

17. Quoted in Stomberg, "Genealogy of Orthodox Documentary," 48.

18. Evans, *American Photographs*, 97.

19. Agee and Evans, *Let Us Now Praise Famous Men*, 398.

20. In *The Making of James Agee,* Hugh Davis writes that "in 1953, just twelve years after its publication, the printing plates for *Now Let Us Praise Famous Men . . .* were melted down as scrap metal during the Korean War" (xii).

21. Rathbone, *Walker Evans,* 197.

22. See Davis, *The Making of James Agee,* for a thorough exploration of this matter.

23. Stott, *Documentary Expression and Thirties America,* 267.

24. Ibid, 266.

25. Hanson, "Comparison of Documentary Approaches," abstract.

26. Ibid, 6.

27. McEuen, "Changing Eyes," 187.

28. Bourke-White, *Portrait of Myself,* 126–27.

29. This 1982 interview quoted in Goldberg, *Margaret Bourke-White,* 168–69.

30. Curtis and Grannen, "Let Us Now Appraise," 2.

31. Stott, *Documentary Expression and Thirties America,* 320.

32. Ferris, *Storied South,* 180.

33. Ibid, 176.

34. Goodwin, "Depression Era," 291.

35. Ibid, 292.

36. Ibid, 302–3.

37. Ibid, 303.

38. Ibid, 295.

39. Hunter, *Image and Word,* 74.

40. Bourke-White, *Portrait of Myself,* 137.

41. Hunter, *Image and Word,* 70.

42. Trachtenberg, *You Have Seen Their Faces,* vi.

43. Ibid, vii.

44. Hunter, *Image and Word,* 79.

45. Hansom, "All Consuming Modernism," 4.

46. Ibid, 14.

47. Ibid, 82.

48. Ibid, 15.

49. Stott, *Documentary Expression and Thirties America,* 5.

50. Hansom, "All Consuming Modernism," 6.

51. Klingensmith, "Translations of Visual Reality," 9–10.

52. Ibid, 10.

53. Ibid, 11.

54. Sontag, *Regarding the Pain of Others,* 76.

55. Ibid, 76.

56. Stomberg, "Genealogy of Orthodox Documentary," 56.

57. For example, in 1937 she received a commission of $4,600 ($74,700 in 2015 dollars), plus expenses, from International Paper Co. for a photo shoot of its logging and paper production operations in the Pacific Northwest (Stomberg, *Power and Paper,* 33n5).

BIBLIOGRAPHY

Archives Consulted

Archives and Special Collections, Arizona State University Library (A. T. Steele)
Hargrett Rare Book and Manuscript Library, University of Georgia (Caldwell, MS-1152; Ira S. and Caroline Bell Caldwell, MS-1557)
Houghton Library, Harvard University (Alfred Morang)
National Archives, Phonoarchive Division, Washington, D.C. (Caldwell and Bourke-White)
Rauner Special Collections Library, Dartmouth College (Caldwell, MS-1046)
Albert and Shirley Small Special Collections Library, University of Virginia (Caldwell)
Special Collections Research Center, Syracuse University E. S. Bird Library (Bourke-White and Caldwell)

Newspapers and Magazines Reviewed

Life (1936–1942)
Fortune (1929–1936)
PM (1941)
Daily Mail (1941)
Collier's (1941)

Memoirs with dates of publication in parentheses

(contemporary with Caldwell and Bourke-White in Moscow, 1941)*

*Vernon Bartlett (1944, 1960)
James E. Brown (1943)
*Wallace Carroll (1942)
*Henry C. Cassidy (1943)
Eve Curie (1944)
Joseph E. Davies (1941)
*Ilya Ehrenburg (1943)

Markoosha Fischer (1944)
*Eddy Gilmore (1954)
*Tamara Gilmore (1968)
Walter Graebner (1943)
*Vasily Grossman (1945)
*Charlotte Haldane (1942, 1950)
Maurice Hindus (1943)
*Ralph Ingersoll (1941)
*Philip Jordan (1942)
Larry Lesueur (1943)
*Maurice H. Lovell (1948)
*Robert Magidoff (1949)
Curzio Malaparte (1943)
*Alice-Leone Moats (1943)
Ralph Parker (1942)
Alexander Poliakov (1942)
Quentin Reynolds (1943)
*Homer Smith (1964)
Edmund Stevens (1945)
*Cyrus L. Sulzberger (1969)
*Feliks Topolski (1942, 1988)
*Alexander Werth (1942, 1964)

Works Cited

Adamson, Judith. *Charlotte Haldane: Woman Writer in a Man's World.* London: Macmillan, 1998. Print.

Agee, James, and Walker Evans. *Let Us Now Praise Famous Men: Three Tenant Families.* 1941. Boston: Mariner–Houghton Mifflin, 2001. Print.

Rev. of *All Night Long,* by Erskine Caldwell. *Kirkus Reviews* 27 (Nov. 1942). Web.

Rev. of *All-Out on the Road to Smolensk,* by Erskine Caldwell. *Kirkus Reviews.* 1942. Web.

Anderson, Sherwood. *Hometown.* Photographs by Farm Security Photographers. The Face of America. Ed. Edwin Rosskam. New York: Alliance, 1940. Print.

Anderson, Truman. "Incident at Baranivka: German Reprisals and the Soviet Partisan Movement in Ukraine, October–December 1941." *Journal of Modern History* 71 (Sept. 1999): 585–623. Print.

Attwood, William. "Alf Stringersoll's Report on Brooklyn." *New Yorker* 22 Nov. 1941: 46–49. Web.

Balina, Marina. "Konstantin (Kirill) Mikhailovich Simonov." In *Russian Prose Writers After World War II.* Ed. Christine Rydel. Dictionary of Literary Biography. Vol. 302. Detroit: Gale, 2005. Web.

Barthes, Roland. *Camera Lucida: Reflections on Photography.* 1980. Trans. Richard Howard. New York: Hill and Wang, 2010. Print.

Bartlett, Vernon. *And Now, Tomorrow.* London: Chatto & Windus, 1960. Print.

———. *Tomorrow Always Comes.* New York: Knopf, 1944. Print.

Bassow, Whitman. *The Moscow Correspondents: Reporting on Russia from the Revolution to Glasnost.* New York: Paragon House, 1988. Print.

Bates, Ernest Sutherland. "A New Utopia." Rev. of *Man's World,* by Charlotte Haldane (1926). *Saturday Review of Literature* 111.31 (26 Feb. 1927): 612. Web.

Bazin, André. "The Ontology of the Photographic Image." Trans. Hugh Gray. *Film Quarterly* 13.4. (Summer 1960): 4–9. Print.

Beck, Alexander. *On the Forward Fringe, a Novel of General Panfilov's Division.* London: Hutchinson, 1945. Print.

Beck, Alexander, and Baurdzhan Momysh-Uly. *Volokolamsk Highway.* 1944. Moscow: Foreign Languages Publishing House, 1945. Print.

Beevor, Antony, and Luba Vinogradova, ed. and trans. *A Writer at War: Vasily Grossman with the Red Army, 1941–1945.* New York: Knopf, 2006. Web.

Bergreen, Laurence. *James Agee: A Life.* New York: Dutton, 1984. Print.

Berkhoff, Karel C. *Motherland in Danger: Soviet Propaganda During World War II.* Cambridge, Mass.: Harvard University Press, 2012. Print.

Bernstein, Lester. "Crusading Editor Dies Rich." Rev. of *Ralph Ingersoll,* by Roy Hoopes. *New York Times* 17 Nov. 1985. Web.

Blackstock, Paul W. "The Tukhachevsky Affair." *Russian Review* 28.2 (Apr. 1969): 171–90. Web.

Boone, Joseph A., and Nancy J. Vickers, coordinators. *Special Topic: Celebrity, Fame, Notoriety.* Spec. issue of *PMLA* 126.4 (Oct. 2011): 897–1188. Print.

"Bourke-White and Caldwell Merely Co-Tourists, Not Wed." *New York World-Telegram* 30 Aug. 1938: 2. Print.

Bourke-White, Margaret. "Children in Chungking Use Symbols of War in Learning How to Count." Clipping in scrapbook. Margaret Bourke-White Papers. Special Collections Research Ctr., Bird Library, Syracuse University, Syracuse, N.Y.

———. *Eyes on Russia.* New York: Simon & Schuster, 1931. Print.

———. "The Drought." Text by James Agee. *Fortune* 10 (Oct. 1934): 76–83. Print.

———. "How I Photographed Stalin and Hopkins Inside the Kremlin." *Life* 11.10 (8 Sept. 1941): 26–27. Web.

———. Letter to Constantin Oumansky. 25 July 1939. TS. Margaret Bourke-White Papers. Special Collections Research Ctr., Bird Library, Syracuse University, Syracuse, N.Y.

———. Letter to Rhoda Lynn. [Apr. 1941]. MS. Papers of Erskine Caldwell. Rauner Special Collections Libr., Dartmouth University, Hanover, N.H.

———. Note to Rhoda Lynn. Apr. 1941. MS. Papers of Erskine Caldwell. Rauner Special Collections Libr., Dartmouth University, Hanover, N.H.

———. Note (on business card) to Rhoda Lynn. Apr. 1941. MS. Papers of Erskine Caldwell. Rauner Special Collections Libr., Dartmouth University, Hanover, N.H.

———. "On the Russian Front: September 1941: Death and Life on the Battlefields." *American Journalism 1938–1944*. Part 1 of *Reporting World War II*. New York: Library of America, 1995. 196–210. Print.

———. *Portrait of Myself*. New York: Simon & Schuster, 1963. Print.

———. *Shooting the Russian War*. Inner Sanctum Books for Victory. New York: Simon & Schuster, 1942. Print.

———. "Trip to the Front: Correspondents Get Plenty of Mud and Vodka." *Life* 11.20 (17 Nov. 1941): 37. Web.

Bourke-White, Margaret, Photographer. "China Relief: U.S. Opens Its Purse." *Life* 10.25 (23 June 1941): 59–67. Web.

———. "Life Goes to a Party: Life Calls on a Russian Movie Star." *Life* 11.22 (1 Dec. 1941): 118–21. Web.

———. "A LIFE Photographer Looks at Moscow a Week Before the Nazi Invasion Began." *Life* 11.6 (11 Aug. 1941): 17–27. Web.

———. "Moscow Fights Off the Nazi Bombers and Prepares for a Long War." *Life* 11.9 (1 Sept. 1941): 15–21. Web.

———. "Muscovites Take Up Their Guns as Nazi Horde Approaches Russian Capital." *Life* 11.17 (27 Oct. 1941): 27–33. Web.

———. "Religion in Russia: Red Godlessness Fails to Empty Churches." *Life* 11.15 (13 Oct. 1941): 110–22. Web.

———. "Roosevelt's Man Hopkins Meets Josef Stalin and Pledges U.S. Supplies." *Life* 11.10 (8 Sept. 1941): 25–29. Web.

———. "Russian Mud and Blood Stall German Army." *Life* 11.20 (17 Nov. 1941): 33–36, 38–39. Web.

———. "The South of Erskine Caldwell Is Photographed by Margaret Bourke-White." *Life* 3.21 (22 Nov. 1936): 48–52. Web.

———. "Special Issue: USSR" *Life* 14.13 (29 March 1943). Cover. Web.

Brady, Thomas F. "Welles Versus Hollywood Again: RKO and the Actor Part Ways—Warners Ready 'Mission to Moscow.'" *New York Times* 12 July 1942, X3. Print.

"British Help: Mission Reaches Moscow." *The West Australian* (Perth) 30 June 1941: 5. Web.

Brown, James E. *Russia Fights*. New York: Charles Scribner's Sons, 1943. Print.

Burns, James MacGregor. *Roosevelt: The Soldier of Freedom*. New York: Harcourt, 1970. Print.

Busch, Noel F. Letter to Whom It May Concern. 14 March 1941. TS. Erskine Caldwell Papers. Special Collections Research Ctr., Bird Libr., Syracuse University, Syracuse, N.Y.

Caldwell, Erskine. *All Night Long*. New York: Duell, Sloan and Pearce, 1942. Print.

———. "All Night Long: Part I." Illus. Hardy Gramatky. *Redbook* 80.1 (Nov. 1942): 56+. Print.

———. "All Night Long: Part Two." Illus. Hardy Gramatky. *Redbook* 80.2 (Dec. 1942): 36+. Print.

———. "All Night Long: Part Three." Illus. Hardy Gramatky. *Redbook* 80.3 (Jan. 1943): 34+. Print.

———. "All Night Long: Conclusion." Illus. Hardy Gramatky. *Redbook* 80.4 (Feb. 1943): 52+. Print.

———. *All-Out on the Road to Smolensk*. New York: Duell, Sloan and Pearce, 1942. Print.

———. "Behind Russian Lines." *Life* 11.4 (28 July 1941): 21. Web.

———. *Call It Experience: The Years of Learning How to Write*. 1951. Athens and London: University of Georgia Press—Brown Thrasher Books, 1996. Print.

———. "Erskine Caldwell at UCLA 3/1/67." UCLA Communications Studies Archive. 8 Apr. 2014. Web.

———. *Georgia Boy*. New York: Duell, Sloan and Pearce, 1943. Print.

———. Letter to Rev. & Mrs. I. S. Caldwell. 19 Apr. 1941. MS. Mr. and Mrs. I. S. Caldwell Papers. Hargrett Rare Book & Manuscript Libr., University of Georgia, Athens.

———. Letter to Rev. & Mrs. I. S. Caldwell. 19 May 1941. TS. Mr. and Mrs. I. S. Caldwell Papers. Hargrett Rare Book & Manuscript Libr., University of Georgia, Athens.

———. Letter to Rev. & Mrs. I. S. Caldwell. 17 July 1941. MS. Mr. and Mrs. I. S. Caldwell Papers. Hargrett Rare Book & Manuscript Libr., University of Georgia, Athens.

———. Letter to Rhoda Lynn. 2 Apr. 1941. TS. Papers of Erskine Caldwell. Rauner Special Collections Libr., Dartmouth University, Hanover, N.H.

———. Letter to Rhoda Lynn. 19 May 1941. TS. Papers of Erskine Caldwell. Rauner Special Collections Libr., Dartmouth University, Hanover, N.H.

———. Letter to Rhoda Lynn. 3 June 1941. TS. Papers of Erskine Caldwell. Rauner Special Collections Libr., Dartmouth University, Hanover, N.H.

———. Letter to Timofei Rokotov. 25 July 1939. TS. Erskine Caldwell Papers. Special Collections Research Ctr., Bird Libr., Syracuse University, Syracuse, N.Y.

———. Letters to Alfred Morang. July–Aug. 1942. MS Am 1638 (96–99), Houghton Library, Harvard University.

———. "Life's Reports: Russia in Wartime." *Life* 11.10 (8 Sept. 1941): 14, 16, 19–20. Web.

———. *Moscow Under Fire*. London: Hutchinson, 1942. Print.

———. Scrapbooks. Papers of Erskine Caldwell. Rauner Special Collections Libr., Dartmouth University, Hanover, N.H.

———. *Some American People*. New York: R. M. MacBride, 1935. Print.

———. "Transit China." 1941. TS. Erskine Caldwell Papers. Special Collections Research Ctr., Bird Library, Syracuse University, Syracuse, N.Y.

———. *With All My Might*. Atlanta: Peachtree Press, 1987. Print.

Caldwell, Erskine, and Margaret Bourke-White. *North of the Danube*. New York: Viking, 1939. Print.

———. *Russia at War*. London and New York: Hutchinson, 1942. Print.

———. *Say, is this the U.S.A.* New York: Duell, Sloan and Pearce, 1941. Print.

———. *You Have Seen Their Faces*. New York: Viking, 1937. Print.

Caldwell, Jay E. "Erskine Caldwell, Margaret Bourke-White, and the Popular Front (Moscow 1941)." PhD diss., University of Arizona, 2014. Web.

Carroll, Wallace. *Inside Wartime Russia; An Eye-Witness Report on the Soviet Union's Battle—Compiled from Dispatches, Censored and Uncensored.* New York: United Press, 1942. Print.

———. *We're in This with Russia.* Boston: Houghton Mifflin, 1942. Print.

Cassidy, Henry C. *Moscow Dateline: 1941–1943.* Boston: Houghton Mifflin, 1943. Print.

———. *Moscow Dateline: 1941–1943.* London: Cassell, 1943. Print.

Chai, Philip. Letter to Rhoda Lynn. 15 Sept. 1941. TS. Papers of Erskine Caldwell. Rauner Special Collections Libr., Dartmouth University, Hanover, N.H.

Chamberlin, W. H. "Reports on the Epic Clash Along the Russian Frontier." Rev. of *All-Out on the Road to Smolensk,* by Erskine Caldwell. *New York Times* 1 March 1942: BR3. Web.

Cholerton, A. T. "Moscow Prepares to Meet Air Raids." *Daily Telegraph and Morning Post* 23 June 1941: 1 + 6. Print.

Clark, Alan. *Barbarossa: The Russian-German Conflict, 1941–45.* 1965. New York: Quill, 1985. Print.

Clark, Katerina. *Moscow, the Fourth Rome: Stalinism, Cosmopolitanism, and the Evolution of Soviet Culture, 1931–1941.* Cambridge: Harvard University Press, 2011. Print.

———. *The Soviet Novel: History as Ritual.* 3rd ed. Bloomington: Indiana University Press, 2000. Print.

Clarke, Graham. *The Photograph.* Oxford History of Art. Oxford: Oxford University Press, 1997. Print.

Cole, Rosamund. "Bourke-White, Caldwell Arrive to Do Work on Central Europe." *New York Herald Tribune* (Paris edition) 10 Apr. 1938: 2. Print.

Conquest, Robert. *The Harvest of Sorrow: Soviet Collectivization and the Terror-Famine.* New York: Oxford University Press, 1986. Print.

Cook, Sylvia. *Erskine Caldwell and the Fiction of Poverty: The Flesh and the Spirit.* Southern Literary Studies. Baton Rouge: LSU Press, 1991. Print.

———. "Erskine Caldwell's Nonfiction." In *Critical Essays on Erskine Caldwell.* Ed. Scott MacDonald. Boston: G. K. Hall, 1981. 375–92. Print.

Culbert, David. *Mission to Moscow.* Wisconsin/Warner Bros. Screenplay Series. Madison: University of Wisconsin Press, 1980. Print.

———. *News for Everyman: Radio and Foreign Affairs in Thirties America.* Westport, Conn.: Greenwood, 1976. Print.

———. "Our Awkward Ally: *Mission to Moscow* (1943)." In *American History / American Film: Interpreting the Hollywood Image.* New expanded ed. Ed. John E. O'Connor and Martin A. Jackson. New York: Continuum, 1988. 147–66. Print.

Curie, Eve. *Journey Among Warriors.* Garden City: Halcyon House, 1944. Print.

Curtis, James C., and Sheila Grannen. "Let Us Now Appraise Famous Photographs: Walker Evans and Documentary Photography." *Winterthur Portfolio* 15.1 (Spring 1980): 1–23. Print.

Danchev, Alex. "The Face, or, Senseless Kindness: War Photography and the Ethics of Responsibility." In *On Art and War and Terror*. Edinburgh: Edinburgh University Press, 2009. 33–57. Web.

David-Fox, Michael. *Showcasing the Great Experiment: Cultural Diplomacy and Western Visitors to the Soviet Union, 1921–1941*. Oxford: Oxford University Press, 2012. Print.

Davidson, Donald. "Erskine Caldwell's Picture Book." *Southern Review* 4 (1 Jan. 1938): 15–25. Print.

Davies, Joseph E. *Mission to Moscow: A Record of Confidential Dispatches to the State Department, Official and Personal Correspondence, Current Diary and Journal Entries, Including Notes and Comment up to October, 1941*. New York: Simon & Schuster, 1941. Print.

Davis, Hugh. *The Making of James Agee*. Knoxville: University of Tennessee Press, 2008. Print.

Days of Glory. Dir. Jacques Tourneur. Screenplay by Melchior Lengyel. RKO, 1944. DVD.

Deuel, Wallace R. "With the People of Russia as They Fight the War." Rev. of *Shooting the Russian War*, by Margaret Bourke-White. *New York Times* 19 July 1942: Book Rev. 3. Print.

Dilling, Elizabeth. *The Red Network: A "Who's Who" and Handbook of Radicalism for Patriots*. Chicago: [self-published], 1934. Print.

"Diplomatic Battle Rages in Rumania." *Canberra Times* 26 March 1940: 1. Web.

Doss, Erika, ed. *Looking at* Life *Magazine*. Washington: Smithsonian Institution Press, 2001. Print.

Du Bois, William Pène. Rev. of *All Night Long*, by Erskine Caldwell. *New York Times Book Review* 6 Dec. 1942: 6. Print.

Duell, Charles H. Letter to Erskine Caldwell. 8 Jul. 1942. TS. Papers of Erskine Caldwell. Rauner Special Collections Libr., Dartmouth University, Hanover, N.H.

Dunkel, Alexander. "The Last Years of Evgenij Petrov (1937–1942)." PhD diss., New York University, 1972. Print.

Duranty, Walter. "Russians Hungry, But Not Starving." *New York Times* 31 March 1933: 13. Print.

Ehrenburg, Ilya. *Russia at War*. 1942. Trans. Alexander Kaun. London: Hamish Hamilton, 1943. Print.

———. *The Tempering of Russia*. 1942. Trans. Gerard Shelley. New York: Knopf, 1944. Print.

Ehrenburg, Ilya, and Vasily Grossman. *The Complete Black Book of Russian Jewry*. 1945. Trans. and ed. David Patterson. New Brunswick, N.J.: Transaction, 2002. Print.

Elson, Robert T. *Time Inc.: The Intimate History of a Publishing Enterprise, 1923–1941*. 4 vols. New York: Atheneum, 1968. Print.

Ethridge, Mark, Erskine Caldwell, and John Temple Graves II. "Are We a United People?" *Town Meeting: Bulletin of America's Town Meeting of the Air* 6.15 (24 Feb. 1941). New York: Columbia University Press, 1941. Print.

Evans, Walker. *American Photographs*. 1938. 50th anniversary ed. Essay by Lincoln Kirstein. New York: Museum of Modern Art, 1988. Print.

Federal Bureau of Investigation. Surveillance File on Margaret Bourke-White. TS. Bufile 100-3518. Washington, D.C.: National Archives, 2012.

———. Surveillance File on Erskine Caldwell. TS. Bufile 100–427589. Record Group 65. Washington, D.C.: National Archives, 2012.

Ferris, William. *The Storied South: Voices of Writers and Artists*. Chapel Hill: University of North Carolina Press, 2013. Print.

Figes, Orlando. *The Whisperers: Private Life in Stalin's Russia*. New York: Metropolitan, 2007. Print.

Fischer, Benjamin A. "The Katyn Controversy: Stalin's Killing Field." Central Intelligence Agency. *Studies in Intelligence* (Winter 1999–2000). Web.

Fischer, Markoosha. *My Lives in Russia*. New York: Harper, 1944. Print.

———. "Russia at War." Rev. of *All-Out on the Road to Smolensk,* by Erskine Caldwell. *The Nation* 154.11 (14 March 1942): 315–16. Print.

Fitzpatrick, Sheila. "Foreigners Observed: Moscow Visitors in the 1930s Under the Gaze of Their Soviet Guides." *Russian History* 35.1–2 (2008): 215–34. Print.

Fleischhauer, Carl, and Beverly W. Brannan, eds. *Documenting America, 1935–1943*. Essays by Lawrence W. Levine and Alan Trachtenberg. Berkeley: University of California Press, 1988. Print.

Fritz, Stephen G. *Ostkrieg: Hitler's War of Extermination in the East*. Lexington: University of Kentucky Press, 2011. Print.

Gale, Bertram. "Before Munich." Rev. of *North of the Danube,* by Erskine Caldwell and Margaret Bourke-White. *New Masses* 25 Apr. 1930: 25–26. Print.

Gayn, Mark. "History-in-the-Making: Russian Round-Up." Rev. of *All-Out on the Road to Smolensk,* by Erskine Caldwell. *Saturday Review* 23 May 1942: 13–16. Web.

———. "With Notebook and Camera in Russia." Rev. of *Shooting the Russian War,* by Margaret Bourke-White. *Saturday Review* 22 Aug. 1942: 10. Print.

Gilmore, Eddy. *Me and My Russian Wife*. Garden City, N.Y.: Doubleday, 1954. Print.

Gilmore, Tamara. *Me and My American Husband*. Garden City, N.Y.: Doubleday, 1968. Print.

Goldberg, Vicki. *Margaret Bourke-White: A Biography*. Radcliffe Biography Series. Reading, Mass.: Addison-Wesley, 1987. Print.

Goodwin, James. "The Depression Era in Black and White: Four American Photo-Texts." *Criticism* 40.2 (Spring 1998): 273–307. Print.

Gorodetsky, Gabriel, ed. *Stafford Cripps in Moscow, 1940–1942: Diaries and Papers*. London: Vallentine Mitchell, 2007. Print.

Graebner, Walter. *Round Trip to Russia*. Philadelphia: J. B. Lippincott, 1943. Print.

Grayson, Benson L., ed. *The American Image of Russia: 1917–1977*. New York: Ungar, 1978. Print.

Grenkevich, Leonid D. *The Soviet Partisan Movement, 1941–1944: A Critical Historiographical Analysis*. Ed. David M. Glantz. London: Frank Cass, 1999. Print.

Grossman, Vasily. *Life and Fate*. 1960. Trans. Robert Chandler. 1985. New York: New York Review Books, 2006.

———. *Writer at War: Vasily Grossman with the Red Army, 1941–1945*. New York: Knopf, 2006. Web.

Haberer, Erich. "The German Gendarmerie and Partisans in Belorussia, 1941–4." In *War in a Twilight World: Partisan and Anti-Partisan Warfare in Eastern Europe, 1939–45*. Ed. Ben Shepherd and Juliette Pattinson. New York: Palgrave, 2010. 102–25. Print.

Hagen, Carlos B. "Struggle of Sound Archives in the United States." *Library Trends* 21.1 (July 1972): 29–52. Print.

Haldane, Charlotte. *Russian Newsreel: An Eye-Witness Account of the Soviet Union at War*. London: Secker and Warburg, 1942. Print.

———. *Truth Will Out*. New York: Vanguard, 1950. Print.

Hansom, Paul. "All Consuming Modernism: The Photo-Essay and American Historical Consciousness." PhD diss., University of Southern California, 2000. Web.

———, ed. *Literary Modernism and Photography*. Westport, Conn., and London: Praeger, 2002. Print.

Hanson, Art. "A Comparison of Documentary Approaches: Margaret Bourke-White and Erskine Caldwell, Authors of *You Have Seen Their Faces*, and Dorothea Lange and Paul S. Taylor, Authors of *An American Exodus*." Paper read at 63rd Annual Meeting of the Association for Education in Journalism, Boston, Aug. 9–13, 1980. Print.

Harris, Donal. "Finding Work: James Agee in the Office." *PMLA* 127.4 (Oct. 2012): 766–81. Print.

Haynes, John Earl, and Harvey Klehr. *Venona: Decoding Soviet Espionage in America*. New Haven: Yale University Press, 1999. Print.

Heckler, Cheryl. *An Accidental Journalist: The Adventures of Edmund Stevens, 1934–1945*. Columbia: University of Missouri Press, 2007. Print.

Hicks, Wilson. Cable to Margaret Bourke-White. 21 Feb. 1941. TS. Margaret Bourke-White Papers. Special Collections Research Ctr., Bird Library, Syracuse University, Syracuse, N.Y.

———. Letter to Margaret Bourke-White. 24 March 1941. TS. Margaret Bourke-White Papers. Special Collections Research Ctr., Bird Library, Syracuse University, Syracuse, N.Y.

———. *Words and Pictures*. 1952. New York: Arno, 1973. Print.

Hindus, Maurice. "The Land That Is No More." Rev. of *North of the Danube*, by Erskine Caldwell and Margaret Bourke-White. *New Republic* 98.1271 (12 Apr. 1939): 284. Print.

———. *Mother Russia*. Garden City, N.Y.: Doubleday, Doran, 1943. Print.

Hohenberg, John. *Foreign Correspondence: The Great Reporters and Their Times*. 2nd ed. Syracuse: Syracuse University Press, 1995. Print.

Homer, William Innes. *Alfred Stieglitz and the American Avant-Garde*. Boston: New York Graphic Society, 1977. Print.

Hoopes, Roy. *Ralph Ingersoll: A Biography*. New York, Athenaeum, 1985. Print.

Hughes, Robert. *The Shock of the New: The Hundred-Year History of Modern Art—Its Rise, Its Dazzling Achievement, Its Fall.* New York: Knopf, 2009. Print.

Hunter, Jefferson. *Image and Word: The Interaction of Twentieth-Century Photographs and Texts.* Cambridge: Harvard University Press, 1987. Print.

Hüppauf, Bernd. "Modernism and the Photographic Representation of War and Destruction." In *Fields of Vision: Essays in Film Studies, Visual Anthropology, and Photography.* Berkeley: University of California Press, 1995. 94–124. Print.

Ingersoll, Ralph. *Action on All Fronts: A Personal Account of This War.* New York: Harper & Brothers, 1941. Print.

Jackson, Bruce. "The Deceptive Anarchy of *Let Us Now Praise Famous Men.*" *Antioch Review* 57.1 (Winter 1999): 38–49. Print.

"Jean Aumont Marries Actress Maria Montez." *Los Angeles Times* 14 July 1943, A1. Print.

Jordan, Philip. "Life's Reports: Moscow Holds On." *Life* 11.24 (15 Dec. 1941): 18, 20–22. Web.

———. *Russian Glory.* London: Cresset, 1942. Print.

Kaplan, E. Ann. "Psychoanalysis and Ideology as Signified in the Staircase: Nancy Meckler's *Sister, My Sister* and Tracey Moffatt's *Laudanum.*" *Communication Review* 6.4 (2003): 301–12. Print.

Kaun, Alexander. Rev. of *Shooting the Russian War,* by Margaret Bourke-White. *Books Abroad* 17.3 (Summer 1943): 274. Print.

Kershaw, Angela. "French and British Female Intellectuals and the Soviet Union: The Journey to the USSR, 1929–1942." *E-rea: Revue électronique d'études sur le monde Anglophone.* 4.2 (2006): Revolving Commitments in France and Britain, 1929–1955. Web.

[Kirstein, Lincoln, and Thomas Mabry] Museum of Modern Art. "American Photographs of Walker Evans." Press Release. 24–25 Sept. 1938. New York. Web.

Klehr, Harvey, John Earl Haynes, and Fridrikh Igorevich Firsov. *The Secret World of American Communism.* Annals of Communism. New Haven: Yale University Press, 1995. Print.

Klevar, Harvey. *Erskine Caldwell: A Biography.* Knoxville: University of Tennessee Press, 1993. Print.

Klingensmith, Kelly Elizabeth. "Translations of Visual Reality: Image, Language, and Ethics in the Photographic Essay." PhD diss., University of Wisconsin, 2007. Web.

Knightley, Phillip. "The Struggle for Mother Russia, 1941–45." In *The First Casualty: The War Correspondent as Hero and Myth-Maker from the Crimea to Iraq.* 1975. 3rd ed. Baltimore: Johns Hopkins University Press, 2004. Web.

Koch, Howard. *As Time Goes By.* New York: Harcourt Brace Jovanovich, 1979. Print.

Koppes, Clayton R., and Gregory D. Black. *Hollywood Goes to War: How Politics, Profits and Propaganda Shaped World War II Movies.* Berkeley: University of California Press, 1987. Print.

Langer, John Daniel. "The Harriman-Beaverbrook Mission and the Debate over Unconditional Aid for the Soviet Union, 1941." *Journal of Contemporary History* 14.3 (July 1979): 463–82. Print.

Lend-Lease Bill, January 10, 1941. Records of the U.S. House of Representatives, HR 77A-D13, Record Group 233, National Archives. Web.

Lesueur, Larry. *Twelve Months That Changed the World.* New York: Knopf, 1943. Print.

"A Letter to Cassidy." *Time* 40.15 (12 Oct. 1942). Web.

Leuchtenburg, William E. *Franklin D. Roosevelt and the New Deal, 1932–1940.* New American Nation Series. New York: Harper & Row, 1963. Print.

Levering, Ralph B. *American Opinion and the Russian Alliance, 1939–1945.* Chapel Hill: University of North Carolina Press, 1976. Print.

Levine, Lawrence W., and Alan Trachtenberg. *Documenting America, 1935–1943.* Ed. Carl Fleischhauer and Beverly W. Brannan. Berkeley: University of California Press, 1988. Print.

Lieber, Maxim. Letters to Erskine Caldwell. Aug. 1939. TS. Erskine Caldwell Papers. Special Collections Research Ctr., Bird Library, Syracuse University, Syracuse, N.Y.

———. Letter to Erskine Caldwell. 6 Nov. 1941. TS. Papers of Erskine Caldwell. Rauner Special Collections Libr., Dartmouth University, Hanover, N.H.

———. Letter to Erskine Caldwell. 2 Jul. 1942. TS. Papers of Erskine Caldwell. Rauner Special Collections Libr., Dartmouth University, Hanover, N.H.

Lovell, Maurice H. *The Soviet Way of Life: An Examination.* Home Study Books. London: Methuen, 1948. Print.

Luce, Henry R. "The American Century." *Life* 17 Feb. 1941: 61–65. Print.

Lyons, Eugene. *Assignment in Utopia.* New York: Harcourt, Brace, 1937.

MacDonald, Scott. *Critical Essays on Erskine Caldwell.* Boston: G. K. Hall, 1981. Print.

———. "Enough Good Reasons for Reading, Studying and Teaching Erskine Caldwell." *Pembroke Magazine* 11 (1979): 7–18. Print.

Magidoff, Robert. *In Anger and Pity: A Report on Russia.* Garden City, N.Y.: Doubleday, 1949. Print.

Malaparte, Curzio. *Kaputt.* 1943. Trans. Cesare Foligno. New York: New York Review Books, 2005. Print.

———. *The Volga Rises in Europe.* 1943. Trans. David Moore. London: Redman, 1957. Print.

Margulies, Sylvia. *The Pilgrimage to Russia: The Soviet Union and the Treatment of Foreigners, 1924–1937.* Madison: University of Wisconsin Press, 1968.

Marshall, Margaret. "Notes by the Way: Caldwell Comes a Cropper." Rev. of *All Night Long,* by Erskine Caldwell. *The Nation* 155:26 (26 Dec. 1942): 720. Print.

———. "Notes by the Way." Rev. of *North of the Danube,* by Erskine Caldwell and Margaret Bourke-White. *Nation* 148:15 (8 Apr. 1939): 405. Print.

Mawdsley, Evan. *Thunder in the East: The Nazi-Soviet War, 1941–1945.* London: Hodder Arnold, 2005. Print.

McDonald, Robert L., ed. *The Critical Response to Erskine Caldwell.* Critical Responses in Arts and Letters, No. 38. Westport, Conn.: Greenwood, 1997. Print.

———. *Erskine Caldwell: Selected Letters, 1929–1955.* Jefferson, N.C., and London: McFarland, 1999. Print.

———. *Reading Erskine Caldwell: New Essays*. Jefferson, N.C., and London: McFarland, 2006. Print.

McEuen, Melissa A. "Changing Eyes: American Culture and the Photographic Image, 1918–1941." PhD diss., Louisiana State University, 1991. Print.

Miall, Leonard. "Bartlett, (Charles) Vernon Oldfeld (1894–1983)." In *Oxford Dictionary of National Biography*. Oxford: Oxford University Press, 2004. Web.

Miller, Dan B. *Erskine Caldwell: The Journey from Tobacco Road*. New York: Knopf, 1995. Print.

Minear, Richard H. "Dr. Seuss Went to War." *Dr. Seuss Collection*. Mandeville Special Collections Library. University of California, San Diego, 2012. Web.

Mission to Moscow. Dir. Michael Curtiz. Warner Bros., 1942. DVD.

Mitter, Rana. *Forgotten Ally: China's World War II, 1937–1945*. Boston: Houghton Mifflin Harcourt, 2013. Print.

Moats, Alice-Leone. *Blind Date with Mars*. Garden City, N.Y.: Doubleday, Doran, 1943. Print.

Morson, Gary Saul. Rev. of *The Bones of Berdichev: The Life and Fate of Vasily Grossman*, by John and Carol Garrard. *Commentary* 102.3 (1996): 80+. Web.

———. "Socialist Realism and Literary Theory." *Journal of Aesthetics and Art Criticism* 38.2 (Winter 1979): 121–33. Print.

"Mr. Roosevelt's Popular Front." *Chicago Daily Tribune (1923–1963)* 12 (26 Oct. 1936). Web.

Nel, Philip. "About the Newspaper *PM*." *Crockett Johnson Homepage*. Kansas State University. 3 Aug. 2005. Web.

Nerhood, Harry W., comp. *To Russia and Return: An Annotated Bibliography of Travelers' English-language Accounts of Russia from the Ninth Century to the Present*. Columbus: Ohio State University Press, 1968. Print.

Newhall, Beaumont. "Documentary Approach to Photography." *Parnassus* 10.3 (Mar. 1938): 2–6. Print.

———. *Photography: Essays and Images: Illustrated Readings in the History of Photography*. New York: Museum of Modern Art, 1980. Print.

"News of the Screen: Hedy Lamarr, Pierre Aumont Slated for Leads in 'Vengeance of the Earth.'" *New York Times* 3 Nov. 1942: 19. Print.

North, Sterling. "Caldwell's Strongest Novel." Rev. of *All Night Long*, by Erskine Caldwell. *New York Post* 2 Dec. 1942: Christmas Books 2. Print.

The North Star. Dir. Lewis Milestone. Screenplay by Lillian Hellman. Goldwyn, 1943. DVD.

O'Neill, William L. *A Better World: Stalinism and the American Intellectuals*. 1982. New Brunswick, N.J.: Transaction, 1990. Print.

Panter-Downes, Mollie. "Profiles [Sir Stafford Cripps]: No. 11 Downing Street." *New Yorker* 8 Aug. 1942: 19–29. Web.

Parker, Ralph. *Moscow Correspondent*. London: Frederick Muller, 1942. Print.

Pearce, Charles A. Letter to Erskine Caldwell. 13 Jul. 1942. TS. Papers of Erskine Caldwell. Rauner Special Collections Libr. Dartmouth University, Hanover, N.H.

Poliakov, Alexander. *Russians Don't Surrender*. Trans. Norbert Guterman. New York: Dutton, 1942.

Poliakov, Alexandr F. *With a Soviet Unit Through the Nazi Lines*. London and Melbourne: Hutchinson, 1941. Print.

Pratt, Mary Louise. *Imperial Eyes: Travel Writing and Transculturation*. London: Routledge, 1992. Print.

Rathbone, Belinda. *Walker Evans: A Biography*. Boston: Houghton Mifflin, 1995. Print.

"A Reader's List." Rev. of *All-Out on the Road to Smolensk*, by Erskine Caldwell. *New Republic* 106.12 (23 March 1942): 406. Print.

Reinhardt, Mark, Holly Edwards, and Erina Duganne, eds. *Beautiful Suffering: Photography and the Traffic in Pain*. Chicago: University of Chicago Press–Williams College Museum of Art, 2007. Print.

Reynolds, Quentin. *Only the Stars Are Neutral*. Garden City, N.Y.: Blue Ribbon Books, 1943. Print.

Rokotov, Timofei. Letter to Erskine Caldwell. 28 March 1939. TS. Erskine Caldwell Papers. Special Collections Research Ctr., Bird Library, Syracuse University, Syracuse, N.Y.

Roosevelt, Theodore [Jr.]. Letter to Erskine Caldwell. 23 Aug. 1939. TS. Erskine Caldwell Papers. Special Collections Research Ctr., Bird Library, Syracuse University, Syracuse, N.Y.

Rutherford, Jeff. "'One senses danger from all sides, especially from fanatical civilians': The 121st Infantry Division and Partisan War, June 1941–April 1942." In *War in a Twilight World: Partisan and Anti-Partisan Warfare in Eastern Europe, 1939–45*. Ed. Ben Shepherd and Juliette Pattinson. New York: Palgrave, 2010. 58–79. Print.

Ryan, Milo. *History in Sound: A Descriptive Listing of the* KIRO-CBS *Collection of Broadcasts of the World War II Years and After, in the Phonoarchives of the University of Washington*. Seattle: University of Washington Press, 1963. Print.

Saretzky, Gary D., curator. *Margaret Bourke-White in Print: An Exhibition*. Archibald S. Alexander Library, Rutgers University, New Brunswick, N.J. Jan.–June 2006. Web.

Schallert, Edwin. "Aumont, Lamarr Will Co-Star as Guerillas." *Los Angeles Times* 3 Nov. 1942: 15. Print.

Shearer, Stephen Michael. *Beautiful: The Life of Hedy Lamarr*. New York: Thomas Dunne–St. Martin's, 2010. Print.

Shepherd, Ben, and Juliette Pattinson, eds. *War in a Twilight World: Partisan and Anti-Partisan Warfare in Eastern Europe, 1939–45*. New York: Palgrave, 2010. Print.

Shiffman, Dan. "Ethnographic Pilgrimages in Depression-era America." *Mosaic: A Journal for the Interdisciplinary Study of Literature* 36.4 (Dec. 2003): 156–69. Print.

Sillen, Samuel. "Caldwell Returns from Smolensk." Rev. of *All-Out on the Road to Smolensk*, by Erskine Caldwell. *New Masses* 10 March 1942: 23–24. Web.

Simkin, John. “The Daily Sketch.” Spartacus Educational. www.spartacus-educational.com/Jsketch.htm. Aug. 2014. Web.

Simonov, Konstantin. *Victims and Heroes* (*The Living and the Dead*). 1959. Trans. R. Ainsztein. London: Hutchinson, 1963. Print.

Slepyan, Kenneth. *Stalin's Guerillas: Soviet Partisans in World War II.* Modern War Studies. Lawrence: University Press of Kansas, 2006. Print.

Sloan, Sam. Letter to Erskine Caldwell. 7 Jul. 1942. TS. Papers of Erskine Caldwell. Rauner Special Collections Libr., Dartmouth University, Hanover, N.H.

Small, Melvin. “Buffoons and Brave Hearts: Hollywood Portrays the Russians, 1939–1944.” *California Historical Quarterly* 52.4 (Winter 1973): 326–37. Print.

———. “How We Learned to Love the Russians: American Media and the Soviet Union During World War II.” *Historian* 36.3 (May 1974): 455–78. Print.

Smelser, Ronald, and Edward J. Davies II. *The Myth of the Eastern Front: The Nazi-Soviet War in American Popular Culture.* Cambridge: Cambridge University Press, 2008. Print.

Smith, Homer. *Black Man in Red Russia: A Memoir.* Intro. Harrison Salisbury. Chicago: Johnson, 1964. Print.

Snow, Edgar. *People on Our Side.* New York: Random House, 1944. Print.

Snyder, Robert E. “Erskine Caldwell and Margaret Bourke-White: You Have Seen Their Faces.” *Prospects* 11 (1986): 393–405. Print.

———. “Margaret Bourke-White and the Communist Witch Hunt.” *Journal of American Studies* 19.1 (Apr. 1985): 5–25. Print.

———. “Spying on Southerners: The FBI and Erskine Caldwell.” *Georgia Historical Quarterly* 72.2 (Summer 1988): 248–81. Print.

Snyder, Timothy. *Bloodlands: Europe Between Hitler and Stalin.* New York: Basic Books, 2010. Print.

“Socialist Realism Proclaimed.” *Russian Life* 52.4 (July–Aug. 2009): 21–23. Print.

Song of Russia. Dir. Lewis Milestone. Screenplay by Paul Jarrico. MGM, 1944. DVD.

Sontag, Susan. *On Photography.* New York: Picador–Farrar, Straus and Giroux, 1977. Print.

———. “A Photograph Is Not an Opinion. Or Is It?” In *Women,* by Annie Leibovitz. New York: Random House, 1999. 18–36. Print.

———. *Regarding the Pain of Others.* New York: Picador–Farrar, Straus and Giroux, 2003. Print.

“Soviets Cheer Their Heroes.” *Life* 11.3 (21 July 1941): 26–27. Print.

Stahel, David. *Operation Barbarossa and Germany's Defeat in the East.* Cambridge Military Histories. Cambridge: Cambridge University Press, 2009. Print.

Starr, Roger. “*PM:* New York's Highbrow Tabloid.” *City Journal.* Summer 1993. Web.

Steinhardt, Laurence A. Telegram to U.S. Sec. of State. 5 June 1941. TS. Record item T124.61/175. File unit 124.61/173–215. Central Decimal Files, 1940–44. Records of the Department of State, Record Group 59. National Archives and Records Administration, College Park, Md.

Stephenson, Graham. *Russia from 1812 to 1945: A History*. 1969. New York: Praeger, 1970. Print.

Stevens, Edmund. *Russia Is No Riddle*. New York: Greenberg, 1945. Print.

Stieglitz, Alfred. "Modern Pictorial Photography." *Century Illustrated Monthly Magazine* 64 (May–Oct. 1902): 322–25. Web.

Stomberg, John. "A Genealogy of Orthodox Documentary." In *Beautiful Suffering: Photography and the Traffic in Pain*. Ed. Mark Reinhardt, Holly Edwards, and Erina Duganne. Chicago: University of Chicago Press–Williams College Museum of Art, 2007. 37–56. Print.

———. *Power and Paper: Margaret Bourke-White, Modernity, and the Documentary Mode*. Intro. Kim Sichel. Exhibition Catalog. Boston University Art Gallery. March 6–Apr. 12, 1998. Seattle: University of Washington Press, 1998. Print.

Stone, Harry. "Dickens and Leitmotif: Music-Staircase Imagery in *Dombey and Son*." *College English* 25.3 (Dec. 1963): 217–20. Web.

Stott, William. *Documentary Expression and Thirties America*. Chicago: University of Chicago Press, 1986. Print.

Strada, Michael J., and Harold R. Troper. *Friend or Foe? Russians in American Film and Foreign Policy, 1933–1991*. Lanham, Md.: Scarecrow, 1997. Print.

Sulzberger, Cyrus L. "Air War Is Waged Night and Day Over the Central Front in Russia." *New York Times* 25 Sept. 1941: 4. Print.

———. "Stalin at Bay." In *A Long Row of Candles: Memoirs and Diaries, [1934–1954]*. Toronto: Macmillan, 1969. 153–86. Print.

Taylor, Sally. "A Blanket of Silence: The Response of the Western Press Corps in Moscow to the Ukraine Famine of 1932–33." In *Holodomor: The Ukrainian Famine-Genocide, 1932–33*. Ukrainian Canadian Congress, 2008. Web.

———. "The Life, Work, and Times of Walter Duranty, Moscow Correspondent for the *New York Times*, 1921–1941." PhD diss., Southern Illinois University, 1980. Print.

"Third Scoop from First Front." *Time* 41.1 (4 Jan. 1943). Print.

Thompson, Carl. *Travel Writing*. The New Critical Idiom. London: Routledge, 2011. Print.

Thompson, Ralph. "Books of the Times." Rev. of *All-Out on the Road to Smolensk*, by Erskine Caldwell. *New York Times* 18 Feb. 1942. Web.

"'Tobacco Road' Retires Tonight Undefeated; Champ of All Plays Beat Critics 3,180 Rounds." *New York Times* 31 May 1941: 13. Print.

Topolski, Feliks. *Fourteen Letters*. London: Faber & Faber, 1988. n.p. Print.

———. *Russia in War: London, Summer 1941; Russia-Bound Convoy; A British Cruiser; Iceland*. London: Methuen, 1942. Print.

Trachtenberg, Alan. Foreword to *You Have Seen Their Faces*. 1937. Athens, Ga., and London: University of Georgia Press–Brown Thrasher Books, 1995. v–viii. Print.

Tzouliadis, Tim. *The Forsaken: An American Tragedy in Stalin's Russia*. New York: Penguin, 2009. Print.

"Ukraine." *Encyclopædia Britannica Online*. Encyclopædia Britannica Inc., 2012. Web.

United States Dept. of State. Office of the Historian. "U.S.-Soviet Alliance, 1941–1945." In *Milestones 1937–1945*. Web.

Vagts, Alfred. "Book Reviews." Rev. of *All-Out on the Road to Smolensk,* by Erskine Caldwell. *Military Affairs* 7.1 (Spring 1943): 46–48. Print.

Vials, Chris. "The Popular Front in the American Century: *Life* Magazine, Margaret Bourke-White, and Consumer Realism, 1936–1941." *American Periodicals* 16.1 (2006): 74–102. Web.

———. *Realism for the Masses: Aesthetics, Popular Front Pluralism, and U.S. Culture, 1935–1947*. Jackson: University Press of Mississippi, 2009. Print.

Webb, Sheila. "The Consumer-Citizen: *Life Magazine*'s Construction of a Middle-Class Lifestyle Through Consumption Scenarios." *Studies in Popular Culture* 34.2 (Spring 2012): 23–47. Print.

Weil, Edmund. "Portrait of the USSR." Rev. of *Shooting the Russian War,* by Margaret Bourke-White. *New Masses* 18 Aug. 1942: 24–25. Print.

Werth, Alexander. *Moscow '41*. London: Hamish Hamilton, 1942. Print.

———. *Moscow War Diary*. New York: Knopf, 1942. Print.

———. *Russia at War, 1941–1945*. New York: Dutton, 1964. Print.

Wolfe, Ann F. "Mr. Caldwell's Russian Landscape." Rev. of *All Night Long,* by Erskine Caldwell. *Saturday Review of Literature* 19 Dec. 1942: 8. Print.

Wolfe, Henry C. "Hitler Looks Eastward." *Atlantic* 159 (4 Feb. 1937). Web.

———. "A Memorial to Czechoslovakia." Rev. of *North of the Danube,* by Erskine Caldwell and Margaret Bourke-White. *Saturday Review* 1 Apr. 1939: 10. Web.

Wolfe, Thomas K. "The League of American Writers: Communist Organizational Activity Among American Writers, 1929–1942." PhD diss., Yale University, 1956. Web.

Woolbert, Robert Gale. "Recent Books on International Relations." Revs. of *All-Out on the Road to Smolensk* and *Shooting the Russian War*. *Foreign Affairs* 21.1 (Oct. 1942): 174–89. Print.

Wouk, Herman. *The Winds of War*. Boston: Little, Brown, 1971. Print.

Zacharoff, Lucien, ed. *The Voice of Fighting Russia*. New York: Alliance Book Co., 1942. Print.

INDEX